God of Our Soil

Towards Subaltern Trinitarian Theology

God of Our Soil

Towards Subaltern Trinitarian Theology

Francis Gonsalves, S.J.

Tercentenary Publication
ISPCK / VIEWS
2010

God of Our Soil: Towards Subaltern Trinitarian Theology - Published by the Rev. Dr. Ashish Amos of the Indian Society for Promoting Christian Knowledge (ISPCK), Post Box 1585, 1654, Madarsa Road, Kashmere Gate, Delhi-110006, for Vidyajyoti Educational Welfare Society (VIEWS), 4-A, Rajniwas Marg, Delhi - 110054.

© Francis Gonsalves, S.J. 2010

Imprimi Potest: Fr. Edward Mudavassery, S.J.
Jesuit Provincial of South Asia,
New Delhi 110003.

ISBN: 978-81-8465-077-8

Laser typeset at **ISPCK,** Post Box 1585, 1654, Madarsa Road, Kashmere Gate, Delhi-110006
Tel: 23866323, 23866322
e-mail–ashish@ispck.org.in • ella@ispck.org.in
website-www.ispck.org.in

Dedicated to ...

My family members

in my janmabhoomi,

Mumbai, who taught me to pray to

The Triune God through music...

And to my Adivasi Parivar and my

Friends in my karmabhoomi, Gujarat,

who made me aware of God's power and presence

In the delightful, divine Naachnu (Dance) of Life.

Jai Prabhu ! Jai Adivasi !

Contents

**CHAPTER ONE: THEOLOGY FROM OUR SOIL:
CONTEXTUAL AND COMMUNITARIAN
CONCERNS**

CHAPTER FOUR: GOD IS TRIBE: TRAJECTORIES OF SUBALTERN TRINITARIAN THEOLOGY

Foreword

The Trinity is a mystery. I do not think that anyone really understands how God is one nature in three persons. The terms 'nature' and 'person' are not used in the sense in which we use them today. The term 'person' used when talking about the Trinity and Jesus Christ do not seem to have the same meaning. While the doctrinal formulation of the Trinity was not controverted, that of Jesus Christ never concluded the discussion. Theologians say that Chalcedon was a compromise that did not satisfy either party to the dispute. And yet, one is surprised to read theologians speculate about the inner life of the Trinity as if they were eye witnesses. A respectful silence would be much better and more meaningful.

While what the Trinity is in itself is an unknowable mystery, how it relates to us is experienced and narrated, for example, in the Creed. It speaks of the Father as the Creator, the Son as the Redeemer and the Spirit as the Sanctifier. The theologians would hurry to warn us that what God does outside Godself is common to all three, though it is attributed to the different Persons. But there is no doubt that this is how we experience God. After all, our experience of God as One and Three starts with our experience of Jesus as divine and of the Spirit poured into our hearts, encouraging and empowering us. This experience is available to us even today. The speculations of St. Augustine that spoke of the Trinity as similar to the human person with his/her memory, intellect and will or the suggestion of the Indians that the Trinity is *Saccidananda* – being, knowledge and bliss – are just that, speculations, when compared with the prayer that we address to the Father through the Son in the Spirit. I would suggest that we should speak of the economic Trinity of our experience and keep silent about the immanent Trinity which is a mystery. While speculations are limited to intellectuals, experience is open to all.

This is demonstrated by Francis Gonsalves in this book *God of Our Soil: Towards Subaltern Trinitarian Theology.* He is making himself the spokesperson of the Tribal peoples of India, in Gujarat and elsewhere. They may be scattered across the country, but have a common way of experiencing God. Though they may be socially Subalterns there is nothing subaltern about their God-experience or their theology which may find expression in prayer, song and dance. This may happen even without their being fully aware of it.

It is redundant to call Francis' theology 'contextual' because all theology is contextual, even if some pretend to be universal. What is special about it is that it is experiential and not merely rational. It is not abstract and impoverished, but living and dynamic. It highlights theological pluralism. Even the 'dogmas' are not revelations of God, but theological efforts of particular humans in a particular historical and cultural situation to make sense of their experience of faith in the context of contesting interpretations and expressions. Such expressions too may change in the course of history and in different cultures.

I appreciate particularly the image of the dance. I do not particularly like the usual attempts to present the Trinity as a model of community. I think that it somehow destroys the unity of the Godhead, which I think is more important than the diversity of persons, if this diversity is seen in terms of numbers. We have to avoid, not only monism and dualism, but also pluralism at this level. But the dynamism of the dance evokes a plurality of manifestations that merge into one movement. I think that there is something here that needs further exploration.

In promoting Tribal or other contextual theologies, especially when it is done in a university setting, there may be a danger of imposing theoretical frameworks drawn from the social sciences. These seem to take the place that philosophy used to have in Scholastic theology. They come with their own ideological and intellectual underpinnings. They may stifle the spontaneous expressions and reflections of a Tribal group. The Tribals may be happy to express themselves in song and dance. Is it necessary to fit them into a 'theoretical framework'? It is a question worth reflecting upon.

Contextual theologies are not yet in fashion, at least officially. So I appreciate and congratulate Francis for his pioneering effort. Hopefully it will inspire the Tribals themselves – and others too, why not – to pick up the challenge. They would need the encouragement and protection of well-wishers. It is time that they started. Maybe they have started already and we have not yet recognized them, because of our own presuppositions and expectations. They are living their faith, even suffering for it. Let us leave them free and encourage them to sing and dance their lives in the Trinity. We are grateful to Francis for being among the pioneers. May their tribe increase!

Prof. Michael Amaladoss, S.J.
Director,
Institute for Dialogue with Cultures and Religions,
Chennai, Tamil Nadu, India

Preface

Truly, the soil for *God of Our Soil* has been carefully laid, loved and laboured upon for close to fifty years now. Fanciful though this claim might be, when I trace the origins of my faith, I realize that the soil for religious belief, the seeds of religious practice and the sprouts of religious life sprung up from parental nursing and familial nurturing. Yes, it's through my family that I've received touching and treasured experiences of both, God and community, the two foci of this book. My affectionate, caring and faith-full family planted *vestigia trinitatis* – traces of Trinity – into my infantile imagination and taught me to invoke the Triune God in times of joy and sorrow, success and failure. My late dad, Julius, imaged *Abba* by his artistic creativity, faith and fidelity. My mum, Teresa, though aged, continues to symbolize spirited *Shakti* – courageous and caring to the core. It was always a joy and challenge to relate to mum and dad as son. Over the years, my three siblings Margaret, Goretti and John also gave me rich experiences of community-in-love. Likewise, the other members of my family – Joseph, Carlette, Ruth, Rachel, Jamie, Prerna and Varun – have kept the experience of God and community ever alive and awe-inspiring for me. Words fail to express the world of gratitude I owe to each of them.

Transcending the cozy nursery of my family and friends in my *janmabhoomi*, Mumbai, to be transported and transplanted into the initially strange soil of my *karmabhoomi*, Gujarat, was another step in preparing the ground for godly harvests. In Gujarat, during the early stages of my Jesuit formation in the 1980s, the experience of being part of a larger community filled me with great joy; yet, I could sense that all was not well in Gujarat. The weeds of communalism were being surreptitiously sowed by groups with vested interests. Nonetheless, my 1988-1989 *INNED* (Innovative Education Programme) daily involvement with the *Saragara Marwadi* community at *Mahanjanno-Vando*, Ahmedabad, gave me valuable firsthand experience of a poor, urban community.

From the years 1992 to 1994, daily visits to the adivasi (tribal) villages around Zhankhvav and Dadwada in Surat District, south Gujarat, made me aware of the deep bonds that united adivasi communities. Though an outsider, I felt accepted and adopted as *motabhai* (elder brother) among the adivasis. I can never forget the affection and hospitality of adivasi *agewaans* (leaders), *balwadi* teachers, *yuvak-mandali* (youth groups) and *mahila-mandal* (women's groups) members of numerous villages. Their vivacity, joys, pains, struggles, songs, *naach* (dances), dreams, faith and fortitude form the fabric of this book. I am deeply grateful to exemplary Jesuit mentors and missioners in Gujarat, Arana and Galdos, in particular; as well as many 'religious' friends – Bishop Godfrey Rosario, Carmen Borges, Albert Delgado, Stanny Pinto, Venita, Ishwan, Corral, Vally, Thomas Pereira, Jeevanlata, Saby, Kishore, Annette, Hemant, Stanny Jebamalai and Xavier Manjooran – who inspire me by their commitment to the adivasi cause.

Equipped with heartwarming memories of family and community in Mumbai and Gujarat, during my Licentiate studies at the Gregorian University, Rome, I was almost magnetically drawn towards the 'Jesuit trinity' of Profs. Gerald O'Collins, Philip Rosato and Frans Jozef van Beeck who enthusiastically encouraged me to embark upon the path of 'trinitarian dialogue'. These three, together with Archbishop Luis F. Ladaria – currently Secretary of the Congregation for the Doctrine of Faith (CDF) – instilled in me a passion and thirst for God: Father-Son-Spirit. Gerry O'Collins, in particular, was ever eager to patiently listen to my insights, challenge my theories, hone my writings and plant new dreams in my mind and heart. Returning home from Rome in 1997, the idea of entering a *Thirdspace* of Trinity held me captive. I decided to delve deeper into the fascinating and faith-fortifying mystery of the Trinity.

The period from 1997 onwards saw sweeping changes in the socio-political-cultural landscape of Gujarat. My incorporation into the staff of Vidyajyoti College, Delhi, and my renewed involvement with the struggles of Gujarat's adivasi communities and Delhi's 'Sanjay Amar Colony' slum made me acutely aware of the many problems these subaltern communities faced vis-à-vis the inadequacy of my religious studies to respond to the challenges they posed. During this period, Archbishop Vincent Concessao, Dr. John Dayal, and Jesuit colleagues like the late 'Paddy' and Prof. T.K. John were models of compassion, as well as deep commitment to social causes involving the poor.

In 1998-1999, south Gujarat's Christian adivasis suffered severe persecutions, which I recorded in some random writings.[1] Disturbed with all that was happening in Gujarat, in particular, and in India, at large, I began doctoral studies at the University of Madras in April 2001 wishing to wed two seemingly irreconcilable 'fields':[2] the religio-theological with the socio-political. On the one hand, I felt that all that was happening in the socio-political arena was moulding my way of thinking and teaching theology, while, on the other, the theology I was 'doing' – especially in the line of trinitarian theology – promised potential to further inspire and intensify my involvement in the socio-political scenario. Hence, like a befuddled Moses standing sandal-less before the "I AM WHO I AM" (Ex 3:14) of the burning bush, I had the unsettling feeling of embarking upon an uncharted pilgrimage with God, with lots of eagerness and not-so-little apprehension.

God of Our Soil is offspring of my doctoral research. In the interdisciplinary approach that I've adopted for this work of 'contextual theology', I've tried to be 'down-to-earth', meaning, beginning with analyses of the conflicts that subaltern communities faced 'on the ground' – especially in Gujarat, my *karmabhoomi* – I gathered insights from various disciplines so as to provide a theological synthesis with inspiration from Scripture and Tradition. Thus, the initial three chapters might resemble more a work of sociology or political theory than of theology, as such. Apologies to those who feel that the first triad of chapters is too 'political' or 'technical'!

The second triad of chapters is more properly 'theology' as such. However, my theological synthesis is tentative in the sense that it contains preliminary thoughts and insights into what can be termed 'subaltern trinitarian theology'. I make copious use of subaltern religio-cultural resources and symbolisms to think of the Trinity as a Tribal God-in-Communion and a Tribal God-of-Community in whom "we live and move and have our being" (Acts 17:28). While primarily aimed at addressing the Indian Christian community and offering an adivasi symbol of Trinity as 'representation of God', the book also invites people of other religions and ideologies to evolve new representations, myths, symbols, stories, songs and conceptions of God that will inspire all Indians to work in harmony for building up a peaceful and prosperous India for all God's people.

This book would not have been published if not for the valuable contributions of innumerable people who, consciously or unconsciously, chipped in their mite for its thought, texture and text. First and foremost, I am deeply grateful to the supervisor and guide of my doctoral studies, Prof. Felix Wilfred, for his untiring efforts to bring out the best in me. His creative genius, out-of-the-box thinking, astute analyses, breadth of reading and depth of learning were awesome. Special thanks to the Professors of the Department of Christian Studies: old-timers, Profs. Thomas George, Joe Mannath and Sampath Kumar, who were always available for guidance, and newcomers, Drs. Patrick, Roy and Pushpa who added their mite. I remember the kind help of the former Assistant Registrar of the University of Madras, Mr. J. Ignatius, and Secretary Ms. Rexy Joseph who cheerfully negotiated office procedures. The 'Study Circle' – with incisive insights from Patrick, Jose, James, Sebastian, Mike, Lawry, Shalini, Metti, Kulandaisamy, Joe Francis, Mary John, Xavier Arul Raj and Jerome – helped me immensely.

From 2001 to 2005, shuttling between my lecturing at Vidyajyoti, Delhi, and my research in Chennai, many good Samaritans were ever ready to help out along the way. Special thanks to Profs. Gispert-Sauch and Michael Amaladoss who painstakingly went through my work and gave me valuable suggestions to improve it. As always, Prof. Amaladoss said a wholehearted "Yes!" when I requested him to write the 'Foreword' of this book. Friends like Bishop Anil Couto and Lester Coutinho, Jesuit superiors like Frs. Lisbert, Hector and Edward, as well as the staff and students of Vidyajyoti College were a solid support to me. While thanking them, I also treasure the help of Vidyajyoti librarians, Dr. Desiderio Pinto and Masroorji, who helped out by issuing books even at odd hours. The *Satya Nilayam* Jesuit community in Chennai was my assigned 'mother house'. I thank Bro. Thirithuvaraj, Frs. Peter Pappu, Lawry, Vally and Boniface, as well as Nelson D'Silva and the Gujarat-Jesuit philosophers for their kind ministrations. Schol. Vijay Gonsalves deserves thanks for the artwork on the cover pages.

Reading and reflecting upon a topic like Community and Trinity would've been an esoteric exercise if not for my so-called 'Trinity next-door' – a communion of three persons who were the mainstay of the 'Emmaus community' that was 'Home' to me throughout my stay in Chennai. Prof. Tom George was *Abba* to me: gracious father and mentor. James Ponniah provided caring and cheerful companionship – like the *Son*, I mused. And, Andrew Mathai's *Spirit*-animated life was to me a challenge to counter the current. These three at 'Emmaus' epitomized what community is all about. A million thanks to Tom and the Emmaus extended family – Fr. Lawrence Raj, Joe, Anju, Chinnu and Santosh, in particular, and innumerable others who made life in Chennai celestial.

Besides interviews and information from tribals in Gujarat, I record with gratitude the valuable insights given by theologians of the Chotanagpur region especially Drs. Agapit Tirkey, John Mundu, John Lakra, Marianus and Sudhir Kujur. Faithful friend Milianus Beck even posted me material from faraway Leuven, Belgium. Thanks also to those attached to libraries and institutes of learning who helped immensely: Fr. Cedric Prakash and his staff at *Prashant*, Ahmedabad, Dr. Lancy Lobo at the *CCD*, Vadodara, the library staff and friends Dr. Evangeline and Samuel Rajkumar at *UTC*, Bangalore, and Dr. Anant Kumar Giri of *MIDS*, Chennai, went out of their way to provide the materials I needed. Moreover, I sincerely thank Rev. Dr. Ashish Amos, Ms. Ella Sonawane and all the staff of ISPCK, Delhi, who meticulously saw to every detail pertaining to the publishing and printing of this book.

Finally, there is not an iota of doubt that this seminal work on the Trinity would never have seen daylight if not for Three Persons – invisible, yet ever present, every day, at every stage of the studies and the subsequent long gestation period of the publication of this book. All glory and eternal praise be to the Trinitarian God – Father, Son, Holy Spirit – whom I've audaciously attempted to understand and interpret within the cramped confines of this book. Foolhardy though this endeavour seemed to many a colleague and critic at the outset of my theological ramblings, I always inwardly knew that I'd ever remain restless unless and until I articulated, even if most imperfectly, something of SOMEONE who had gripped me so intensely. I end by adapting and adopting the words of the prayer which the great Augustine composed to conclude his *De Trinitate*:

> *"O Lord, the One God, God the Trinity, whatever I have said in these pages that comes from you, may they acknowledge who are yours; but for whatever comes merely from myself, may you and they who are yours forgive me."*

Feast of St. Ignatius of Loyola

July 31, 2010

Francis Gonsalves, S.J.

Vidyajyoti College,
4-A, Rajniwas Marg,
Delhi – 110 054
India.
Email: fragons@gmail.com

ENDNOTES FOR PREFACE

[1] See my articles "Grisly Christmas for Christians in Gujarat," *Communalism Combat* 6/50 (January 1999): 11-4; "Debating Conversions," *Indian Currents* XI/6 (February 8, 1999): 35-6; "Saffron Shrouds YKJ 2000 in Gujarat," *Communalism Combat* 7/55 (January 2000): 15-7, among others.

[2] In this book the word 'field' will be used with the nuance of Pierre Bourdieu, *The Field of Cultural Production: Essays on Art and Literature*, ed. R. Johnson (Cambridge: Polity Press, 1993), 6, in the sense of "a structured space with its own laws of functioning and its own relations of force."

Glossary

akhra	–	dancing-ground where Chotanagpur adivasis celebrate life
bin-adivasi	–	non-adivasis
bhuva	–	a mediator or adivasi priest in the south Gujarat context
dholak	–	big drum used by south Gujarat adivasis to provide rhythm
gharvapasi	–	literally, 'home-coming' used to signify reconversion to Hinduism
lathi	–	wooden stick that can be used as walking stick or a weapon
madrasas	–	schools run by Muslims where the medium of instruction is either Urdu or Hindi
mahajan	–	wealthy trader or moneylender
mandir	–	temple
masjid	–	mosque
naach/nu	–	circular adivasi dance with arms entwined, songs and drumbeat
pahan	–	a mediator or adivasi priest in the Chotanagpur context
patta	–	document of land entitlement
pipudi	–	an adivasi wind instrument for playing melodies during *naach*
savarna	–	a person belonging to a high caste (*varna*)

shuddhikaran	–	purification or ritual, purificatory rite
trishul	–	trident (weapon of Lord Shiva) distributed to youth by RSS, VHP
ujjaliyat	–	literally, *fair* or *bright* used by adivasis for the higher castes.
vanvasi	–	literally, 'forest dwellers' used by Sangh Parivar for adivasis
Varle Dev	–	*literally, 'God above' referring to a personal conception of God by* the south Gujarat adivasis
Ucchaliyo Dev	–	same as *Varle Dev*, above

List of Abbreviations

ABVP	–	*Akhil Bharatiya Vidyarthi Parishad*
ACS	–	African Christian Studies
AG	–	*Ad Gentes* of VC II
AJOT	–	Asian Journal of Theology
ATC	–	Asian Trading Corporation
ATJ	–	African Theological Journal
ATR	–	Anglican Theological Review
BCC	–	British Council of Churches
BCs	–	Backward Castes
BJP	–	*Bharatiya Janata* Party
CBCI	–	Catholic Bishops' Conference of India
CBQ	–	Catholic Biblical Quarterly
CC	–	Cross Currents
CCD	–	Centre for Culture and Development
CICR	–	*Communio* International Catholic Review
CISRS	–	The Christian Institute for the Study of Religion and Society
CLS	–	The Christian Literature Society
CM	–	Clergy Monthly
COUP	–	Columbia University Press
CSS	–	*Christava Sahitya Samithy*
CTJ	–	Calvin Theological Journal
CUP	–	Cambridge University Press

DAA	–	Dialogue and Alliance
DV	–	*Dei Verbum* of VC II
EATWOT	–	Ecumenical Association of Third World Theologians
EPW	–	Economic and Political Weekly
ER	–	Ecumenical Review
GAVP	–	*Gujarat Adijati Vikas Paksh*
GLTCRI	–	Gurukul Lutheran Theological College & Research Institute
GUP	–	Gregorian University Press
GS	–	*Gaudium et Spes* of VC II
GSP	–	Gujarat *Sahitya Prakash*
HCSB	–	Hindu-Christian Studies Bulletin
HIBT	–	Horizons in Biblical Theology
HUP	–	Harvard University Press
HVK	–	Hindu *Vivek Kendra*
IBMR	–	International Bulletin of Missionary Research
IMF	–	International Monetary Fund
IROM	–	International Review of Mission
ISPCK	–	Indian Society for Promoting Christian Knowledge
ITA	–	Indian Theological Association
ITJ	–	Irish Theological Journal
ITS	–	Indian Theological Studies
JBC	–	Jerome Biblical Commentary
JOD	–	Journal of Dharma
JOES	–	Journal of Ecumenical Studies
JOR	–	Journal of Religion
KHAM	–	*Kshatriyas-Harijans-Adivasis-Muslims*
LG	–	*Lumen Gentium* of VC II
MIDS	–	Madras Institute of Development Studies

MNC	–	Multi-National Company
MT	–	Modern Theology
NA	–	*Nostra Aetate* of VC II
NBA	–	Narmada *Bachao Andolan*
NBCLC	–	National Biblical, Catechetical and Liturgical Centre
NBF	–	New Blackfriars
NCR	–	National Catholic Reporter
NDUP	–	Notre Dame University Press
NRI	–	Non-Resident Indian
NT	–	New Testament of the Bible
OBCs	–	Other Backward Castes
OT	–	Old Testament of the Bible
OUP	–	Oxford University Press
PIRS	–	Perspectives in Religious Studies
PO	–	*Pesbyterorum Ordinis* of VC II
PUP	–	Princeton University Press
R&S	–	Religion and Society
RSS	–	*Rashtriya Swayamsevak Sangh*
RTR	–	Reformed Theological Review
SAP	–	Structural Adjustment Programme
SBET	–	Scottish Bulletin of Evangelical Theology
SCs	–	Scheduled Castes
SEBC	–	Socially and Educationally Backward Classes
SID	–	Studies in Interreligious Dialogue
SIR	–	Studies in Religion
SJM	–	*Swadeshi Jagran Manch*
SJOT	–	Scottish Journal of Theology
SNP	–	*Satya Nilayam* Publications
SSP	–	*Sardar Sarovar* Project (Narmada Dam)
STs	–	Scheduled Tribes

SVTQ	–	St. Vladimir's Theological Quarterly
TACR	–	The Australasian Catholic Record
TCC	–	The Christian Century
TD	–	Theology Digest
TDDT	–	The Department of Dalit Theology
TDR	–	The Downside Review
THJ	–	The Heythrop Journal
TITQ	–	The Irish Theological Quarterly
TPI	–	Theological Publications in India
TS	–	Theological Studies
TT	–	Theology Today
T.Th.	–	The Thomist
UCP	–	University of Chicago Press
UCAP	–	University of California Press
UOM	–	University of Madras
UPA	–	United Progressive Alliance
UPOA	–	University Press of America
UR	–	*Unitatis Redintegratio* of VC II
USQR	–	Union Seminary Quarterly Review
UTC	–	United Theological College
UTP	–	University of Toronto Press
VAK	–	*Vikas Adhyayan Kendra*
VC II	–	The Second Vatican Council
VHP	–	*Vishwa Hindu Parishad*
VJTR	–	Vidyajyoti Journal of Theological Reflection
VSS	–	*Vanvasi Seva Sangh*
VVS	–	*Vanvasi Vikas Sangh*
WB	–	World Bank
WCC	–	World Council of Churches

List of Pictures

CHAPTER ONE

Theology from Our Soil:
Contextual and Communitarian Concerns

1.1 The 'Forgotten God' Beyond Sacred Soil and Restorative Rivers

Among the miracles narrated of Prophet Elisha in the Book of Kings, the story of Namaan is interesting, yet intriguing (2 Kings 5:1-19). Namaan can be considered as the 'Gentile enemy' of the Israelites, God's chosen people. This mighty commander of the army of the king of Aram who suffers from leprosy is directed to Elisha, renowned for his healing powers. When Elisha asks Namaan to bathe in the river Jordan, he protests: "Are not Abana and Pharpar, the rivers of Damascus, better than all the waters of Israel? Could I not wash in them and be clean?" (v.12). However, when persuaded by his servants to faithfully follow Elisha's instructions, Namaan dips himself seven times in the Jordan and is healed. The story so far is similar to other healing narratives in the Bible. But, it ends quite differently.

Miraculously healed from his leprosy, an overjoyed Namaan proclaims the sovereignty of the God of Israel and offers presents to Elijah, who refuses to accept anything for he is but God's servant. Namaan then makes a strange request to Elisha: "Please let two mule-loads of earth be given to your servant; for your servant will no longer offer burnt offering or sacrifice to any god except the Lord" (v.17). Odd as this request may sound to us, today, Namaan's plea would've probably seemed reasonable to the people, and consonant with the thinking, of his time and place. Namaan echoes the religious belief of the ancient world that linked and limited a deity to a specific place. Believing that shrines and sacrifices to Yahweh could only flourish upon Israelite soil, the healed and converted Namaan wanted to carry Israelite soil to Syrian territory – where Rimmon is otherwise worshipped – to build an altar for worship to Yahweh there. Centuries later, the Babylonian exiles would express a similar sentiment: "How can we sing the Lord's song in a foreign land?" (Ps 137:4). Prayers and psalms, they too believed, could only be effectively offered from Israelite soil.

Three points are noteworthy from Namaan's narrative: first, it would be surprising that a Gentile enemy, a so-called defiled 'pagan', should receive God's gift of healing. Many unquestioningly believed that God granted such favours only to God's 'chosen people'. Second, it was believed that certain rivers flowing through Israelite territory, or certain lands inhabited by the tribes of Israel, were sacred since God had gifted these to the covenanted people. Consequently, Yahweh could exclusively and effectively be encountered and worshipped only in and upon these rivers and lands. Third, there was a widespread belief that God was preferentially partial to the 'chosen ones' by virtue of their birth and belonging to a particular people. Thus, it would be hard to hold that God was universally loving and providentially caring of all the earth's peoples.

Much water has flowed down the river Jordan since Namaan was healed. Times have changed. So has religious consciousness. And with this change, there is a growing awareness that, in the words of the psalmist, "The earth is the Lord's and all that is in it, the world, and those who live in it" (Ps 24:1). Today, no Indian Christian is likely to labour like Namaan to transport mule-loads, perhaps planeloads, of soil from the Holy Land upon which to build a shrine for Jesus in India. So also, much as river Jordan is seen as sacred to the Jews, Indian Christians respect the sacredness attached to the river Ganga by their Hindu neighbours. Likewise, the Indian Christian community, too, attributes healing power to springs and rivers near Marian shrines, or, for instance, in places formerly inhabited by saints like Thomas, the 'apostle of the Gentiles', or Francis Xavier, 'patron of the missions'. Indeed, apart from holy rivers, the sacred soil and shrines of Mecca and Medina, Bethlehem and Rome, Rishikesh and Tirupati remind us that, while God can be locally and specifically encountered in places and at rivers considered holy by some communities, God's Spirit also universally "blows where it wills" (Jn 3:8), inspiring all peoples, inhering in every river and inhabiting all places.

In its effort to decipher God's plans and the Spirit's power in all peoples, places and times, the task of theology today is to situate itself in specific contexts, otherwise it runs the risk of ending 'up in the clouds'. While we accept that, due to certain historical and spatiotemporal exigencies, some places, times and people have been chosen sites, sources or seers of divine *darshan* and thus deemed 'sacred', we must also encounter God 'on our own soil', so to say. To interpret and invoke this 'God of our soil' in indigenous idiom and images is the contemporary challenge facing all religions and religionists in India. Moreover, being a so-called 'minority religion' of India, Indian Christians have a great responsibility to speak about God in ways that will capture not only Christian interest and imagination, but that of our neighbours – Indians of diverse creeds, castes, classes and cultures – who relentlessly seek and serve God, albeit under various names and forms. Thus, theology must truly be contextual, while being true to the Great Catholic Tradition that speaks of God as 'Trinity': Father, Son and Holy Spirit.

Recently, much ink has flowed to talk about the Trinity in intelligible terms not only in the West, but also in the East. This is perhaps due to the fact that, for long, Christians – and Catholics, in particular – have tended to either overlook or downplay the centrality of the Trinity. Thus, Catholic theologian Karl Rahner rightly opines that, "Christians are, in their life, almost mere 'monotheists',"[1] meaning, most Christians find it difficult to reconcile and relate to the *tri-unity* of God. This is surprising since we routinely begin and end every prayer, every Eucharist and every blessing in the name of the Holy Trinity. It is not without reason that the British Council of Churches' document on the Trinity is titled "The Forgotten Trinity."[2] To compensate for this amnesia of the Trinity, today, there is need to 'remember the Forgotten Trinity', so to say, and to reinterpret it for our times and in terms that are intelligible to Indian peoples. By so doing, we seek to reinstate the Trinity at the centre not only of Christian belief, but also of Christian prayer and of human life, at large. However, before entering into any reflection on the Trinity, it is fitting to highlight why our theology ought to be contextual and to stress the concerns that we, in India, must concretely address.

1.2 Current Concerns of Our Contextual Theology

The most common and classical definition of theology is perhaps that of Anselm of Canterbury (1033-1109) who defined it as *"fides quaerens intellectum"* or "faith seeking understanding."[3] This definition is sometimes used by theologians even today;[4] and, though it rightly maintains that faith is a prerequisite for understanding divine mysteries, it suffers from some lacunae: first, it privileges human understanding (cognition) over other dimensions of human life; second, it implicitly limits the task of theology to seeking and finding divine truths as if they were unrelated to human contexts that are subjective and invested with different meanings as a result of their specific location, history, traditions, experiences and so on; third, faith itself seems to comprise in 'right thinking' rather than in 'right deciding' and 'right doing'. Aware of these shortcomings, we must broaden our understanding, and, subsequently, the scope of theology.

We can expand our understanding of theology by first seeing it as a systematic study of revelation and an interpretation of faith in tune with the 'signs of the times'[5] and 'signs of the place'.[6] The terms of these two assertions, i.e., (a) signs, and (b) time-place, are important. Indeed, theology must constantly listen to, look at, learn from, and reinterpret signs – or, more aptly, 'symbols'. Moreover, although these signs and symbols give meaning to a Transcendental Being, they are always bound to human conceptions of time-place. Second, the fact that theology presupposes faith does not dispense theologians from the demand to be scientific or scholarly, since "absolute commitment can perfectly well coexist with a critical attitude that does not *a priori* exclude anything from the ambit of its critical investigation."[7] Third, we will take theology as "part and parcel of the process of study and reflection on the problems and questions facing the people and as a search for ways and means to meet the challenges of life."[8]

In sum, the ultimate aim of theology "is *not* [merely] faith seeking understanding, but *faith transforming life*."[9] This entails being faithful to the 'God of Life'[10] and to the God-given Life that must be shared fully and equally by all God's peoples. Specifically, our contextual theology will strive: (i) to be critical and constructive; (ii) to reflect upon socio-political issues, and (iii) to dialogue with other disciplines and religions while seeking to build community. A word about these functions will clarify our concerns.

1.2.1 *The Critical and Constructive Function of our Contextual Theology*

Since theology is an interpretative science that employs symbols and language that bear the marks of our finite humanity, it can have – and has had – ideological biases. Indeed, theology has been used to defend monarchy, capitalism, imperialism, colonialism, the Crusades and the Inquisition. Thus, it is necessary to perform a critical function by being aware of the historicity of error,[11] attempting to divest theology of its ideological bias and false consciousness, and demolishing myths that distort the truth about God and Life.

As a human enterprise theology is socially determined and there is a correlation between social structures and theology, the latter being product of the former.[12] Recognizing this, the critical function will be complemented by theological 'construction' of a God-image that will be meaningful in context.[13] This construction or *re-presentation* will tap indigenous resources, more specifically, the religio-cultural resources and spirituality of subaltern communities in India. In Kaufman's words:[14]

> .... Christian theology is completely free – indeed, theology is under the imperative – *to become fully indigenous in every respect* in each culture in which the Christian believes, lives and works, so long as the Principle of God's absoluteness and the Principle of God's humanness are maintained. The central task of theologians in every culture is *to work out, to construct, an image/concept of God appropriate to contemporary life.*

Such attempts at critical and constructive contextual theology in order to construct meaningful images of God have been made in many contexts and in some continents,[15] with a large measure of success. This work is an effort in that direction.

1.2.2 *The Socio-Political and Public Function of our Contextual Theology*

Formerly, especially in the West, there was a dichotomy between the 'sacred' and the 'secular', with theology dealing with the former. Religion too was, by and large, relegated to the 'private' realm and was believed to have nothing to contribute to the public life of peoples. However, the theology enshrined in the documents of VC II – especially *GS, AG* and *NA* – was truly an *aggiornamento* that encouraged theologians to break walls and build bridges in the public realm to engage with everything 'human' and to be affected by it. Later, with the birth of liberation theology, liberation theologians like Johann Baptist Metz and others argued that orthopraxis was more important than orthodoxy; and, theology's vital function was to critically articulate the faith of the community in the light of the Gospel lived out in concrete socio-political contexts.

Theology, we note, can also never be apolitical; for, God is pained when human beings are in pain due to victimization and dehumanization,[16] and God acts in response to human struggles.

Unfortunately in India, Christianity has been closely connected with colonialisation and is, on the one hand, still considered a 'foreign religion' of the elites, while, on the other, a majority of Indian Christians belong to the unprivileged and dispossessed groups who are struggling to secure their basic rights to food, land and just living. These communities are also often marginalized in the Church. Thus, theology has a dual responsibility of: (a) divesting itself of its foreign trappings and elitist agenda, and (b) committing itself to addressing 'political' issues like affirmative action (reservations) for Dalit Christians, land alienation and mass migration of adivasis, the rights and responsibilities of minority communities, etc.

Indian theologians today are endorsing a 'public theology' not as reaction to the growing secularization as is largely the case in the West, but as response to the awareness that religions – especially in a deeply religious country like India – have a positive role to play in the public and political life of peoples. Indian theologian Felix Wilfred, for instance, has advocated the doing of 'public theology' which must blend into the secular space, be founded on sound ethical principles, be organic, dialogical, interdisciplinary, and must affect 'political society' so that the poor and underprivileged are enabled and empowered to rally for their rights, form movements of resistance and protest, and ensure that God's Reign becomes a reality, today.[17] Such a theology "provides the justification and motivation for the Christian community to engage itself with the affairs of the world."[18] Undoubtedly, such a theology will be inclusive and will address not merely the miniscule Indian Christian community, but the Indian peoples, at large.

1.2.3 *The Dialogical and Communitarian Function of our Contextual Theology*

Given its function to be 'public' and inclusive, Indian contextual theology cannot but be dialogical in character. This follows from the fact that India is deeply 'religious' in character, being animated by Indic religions like Hinduism, Buddhism, Jainism, Sikhism and other subaltern, folk and popular religions that have originated here. Moreover, world religions like Islam and Christianity have millions of Indian devotees often outnumbering those of professedly Islamic or Christian nations. Limited in its scope, although we will seek inspiration from other religions, this work will mainly dialogue with the religious worldview of the subaltern groups. In this sense, our contextual theology can be defined as "faith seeking dialogue" (*fides quaerens dialogum*).[19]

While taking cognizance of India's dazzling diversity, we note that dialogue is not an 'end' in itself but is a 'means' to foster relationship at various levels. The question of relationship is central to our reflections since, ultimately, we are interested in reflecting upon the relationship between Father-Son-Spirit, the 'Tribal God of Community and Communion', who, it is hoped, will empower us to engage in the concerted task of community building and the resolution of conflict that, sadly, has been masquerading as 'religious conflict' and creating tension among religious communities in India.

Although this work's immediate focus for community-building is the subaltern groups and Indian Christian communities, in particular, its basic arguments will apply to all other communities, worldwide, for, community building is not the prerogative of any one particular religious group. The aforementioned theological task of "faith seeking dialogue" thus intends to lead to "faith seeking relationship" (*fides quaerens relationem*); and, finally, to "faith seeking community" (*fides quaerens communitatem*). In the Biblical vision of origins and ends, much as we see God musing that "it is not good that the man should be alone" (Gen 2:18) and creates woman, so do we all strive, with God, to be co-creators of a new humanity – a "new heaven and a new earth" (Rev 21:1). From the confusion and conflicts that we often experience in and around us, the task of contextual theology will be to provide paradigms of community and pathways of peace till we achieve our end when "God will be all in all" (1 Cor 15:28). Since community is a prime concern of our theologizing, a quick look at what community refers to, what conflicts imply, and how community is constructed, will assist us in sharpening our reflections.

1.3 The Contours and Concerns of Community

The word 'community' is normally used for a group of persons who live together and are bound together by some commonality that can be conceptualized at various levels or on the basis of many dimensions. For our purposes, we could think of at least four levels or dimensions of community, as follows.

1.3.1 The Geographical Confines of Community

The commonest way of perceiving community is to see it as a shared territory or a well-defined geographical area inhabited by a particular group of people. A group's location upon a particular land affects its way of life, or, as Maciver maintains, "Whenever people live together they develop in some kind and degree distinctive common characteristics – manners, traditions, modes of speech, and so on. These are the signs and consequences of an effective common life." [20] The question of 'land' is of prime importance here. Land is particularly important for Indian tribals, the *adivasis*, for whom "the land and its inhabitants are two aspects of one reality" since "it is a foundation of their history, existence and identity." [21]

Many thinkers have attempted to study what is it that makes individuals come together and cohere in communities. Among these, the structuralist thinkers like Emile Durkheim asserted that individuals are subjected to fixed social processes and functioned within webs of relationships that are structured in a kind of mechanical unity. In other words, the structuralists saw human communities as structured 'social facts' that could be studied objectively since, according to them, social structure determined behaviour, or, to quote Durkheim, there is a "society living and acting within us." [22]

While one can accept the structuralist view as partially true, it does not recognize the truth that human beings are not wholly determined by what society bequeaths to them as 'given', but that they are also free to take new decisions, to chart out their own course of action and to determine their future. In trying to show that communities have not collapsed into anomie due to the presence of supportive societal structures, structuralist thinkers did not adequately account for the question of 'meaning', and did not explain how individuals within a group can subjectively evolve meaning that is generative of new forms of societal relationships and changing patterns of power. By contrast, focusing their attention on questions of meaning among the members of a group, the proponents of 'symbolic interactionism' [23] sought to fill the lacuna of the structuralist line of thinking by positing another level of conceptualizing community, namely, the symbolic.

1.3.2 *The Symbolic Conception of Community*

At a second – perhaps, not-so-conspicuous – level of conceptualizing community, we can speak of a 'symbolic dimension'. This symbolic level embraces a commonality of ideas, myths, symbols, stories and narratives that can also bind individuals into community. Here, the members of a community may live in very different and distant geographical locations (external), and yet, the dynamism of the symbolic component (internal) may induce in them a sense of community. Cohen, among others, argues that it is not helpful to think of community only in territorial terms since community is basically a symbolic construct, its boundary and defining element being constituted through symbols.[24]

As distinct from the aforementioned purely land-bound or structural perspective that sees community either as 'geographical' or as 'given', respectively, the symbolic conception focuses on community as something which is continuously constructed by virtue of what people imagine, think and conceptualize. In other words, rather than seeing community as 'out there' (as in the structuralist view), the community is a cultural field 'within us' with complex symbols whose meanings mould and motivate its members in differing degree. Thus, it is important to decipher the complex relationship between symbolisms, culture and meaning. In the words of Cohen:[25]

> Culture – the community as experienced by its members – does not consist in social structure or in 'the doing' of social behaviour. It inheres, rather, in 'the thinking' about it. It is in this sense that *we can speak of the community as a symbolic, rather than a structural, construct*. In seeking to understand the phenomenon of community we have to regard its constituent social relations as repositories of meaning for its members, not as a set of mechanical linkages. … *Community exists in the minds of its members* and should not be confused with geographic or sociographic assertions of 'fact'. By extension, the distinctiveness of communities and, thus, the reality of their boundaries, similarly lies in the mind, in the meanings which people attach to them, not in their structural forms… [t]his reality of *community is expressed and embellished symbolically*.

Conceiving of community along symbolic lines is a central point of this book. The question of 'symbolic construction of community' is important for the following reasons: [a] studies on society have largely stressed the eco-socio-historical factors that construct or destroy community, but not much importance has been given to the cultural elements of community (comprising of complex symbolic systems); [b] communities in India are increasingly being defined – or are struggling to be identified and defined – on the basis of extra-territorial considerations like ethnicity, culture, religion and language that are complex symbolic fields of human activity; [c] globalisation, today, has either blurred or broken traditional geographical boundaries of continents, nations and states[26] and replaced these with a new logic of spatiality that needs new ways of conceptualizing and critiquing community.

1.3.3 *The Community of Common Characteristics*

A third way of viewing community is on the basis of common characteristics, which can either be inherent (race or tribe), or imputed (caste) or imbibed (class). In the case of inherent common characteristics like those of race or tribe, communitarian bonding is deep and durable. This is so even in cases where racial and tribal sensibilities and affinities are publicly professed to be weak or insignificant.[27] While the internal bonds of race and tribe are usually strong, the imbibed common characteristics of class seem to be more fluid; and, the question of caste cohesion is uniquely characteristic of India. Caste is an example of an 'imputed' common characteristic since, although the institution of caste is made out to be of divine ordination and eternal origin, from the viewpoint of sociologists, it is but one way of conceptualizing Indian society.

In the area of common characteristics – especially when it comes to issues of caste and clan – India has always faced seemingly insurmountable difficulties. For example, today, the issue of caste is being hotly debated with regard to whether the census of 2011 should include a citizen's caste as an identity-marker, or not. In villages of north India, too, conflicts on the basis of caste arise in matters of marriage – can two youth belonging to the same '*gotra*' marry?[28] Although these issues are so complex that it is not easy to come up with adequate answers to the many questions that arise in the negotiation of caste, clan, tribe or class identities and loyalties, we shall nonetheless later examine how these common characteristics play a positive role in building community, or, negatively, how they fuel conflict.[29] For the present, it suffices to state that caste, tribe and class are important factors for building or breaking community.

1.3.4 *The Community of Common Interests*

At a fourth level, commonality can also be one of 'interests'. People form communities on the basis of their common interests. These common interests could be in the realms of religion and culture, the arts and the sciences, the hobbies and professions of human beings. For instance, in the Catholic Church we have so-called 'religious' communities or congregations of the Carmelites, Salesians, Jesuits and so on, bound together by a common charism or vision of the founder(s). Likewise, social workers, artisans or professionals may cohere for the promotion of common tasks and the furtherance of common interests.

Within the commonality of interests, we could think of the subdivision of 'association'. An association is a group of human beings organized and established for the pursuit of a common interest that may be permanent or transient. Associations may be political, cultural, religious, educational, scientific, artistic, etc. Examples of associations are 'Friends of the Earth' (ecological), the 'All India Trade Union Congress' (labourers) or *Sangh Parivar* that comprises of associates like the BJP (political), the RSS (cultural), the VHP (religious), the ABVP (educational), the SJM (economic) and the like.[30]

1.3.5 *Community, Collectivity and Society*

Having mentioned four commonalities – namely, geographical location, symbolic interactions, characteristics and interests – that constitute community, we distinguish community from (a) collectivity and (b) society that also deal with some form of commonality. A 'collectivity' is a crowd or a mass of people who come together without any long-term goals uniting them. It is a loose and ephemeral group with calculable and conditional relations between individuals.[31] Examples of a collectivity are football fans watching the World Cup matches where all that is required for achieving the interests of the collectivity is that each one does not disturb the other and allows the other to view proceedings peacefully. A collectivity could also be a group of citizens, for example, who sit on *dharna* to protest and press for their demands like pure drinking water, cheap fuel, free education for their children, etc. Once their demands are met, the group breaks up.

The word 'society' is often used as synonym for 'community'. Though the two are used interchangeably, they are distinct. Tönnies's distinction between *Gemeinschaft* (community) and *Gesellschaft* (society) is noteworthy:[32]

> ... *Gesellschaft* deals with the artificial construction of an aggregate of human beings which superficially resembles the *Gemeinschaft* in so far as individuals peacefully live and dwell together. However, in the *Gemeinschaft* they remain essentially united in spite of all separating factors, whereas in the *Gesellschaft* they are essentially separated in spite of all uniting factors.

This distinction was drawn in the context of the growth of modernity from traditionalism, whereby the traditional forms of family, village, tribe and community were giving way to modern cities and urban societies. Modern and urban settlements were different in that industrialization and production patterns were determining the forms of organization of peoples. In other words, there was a difference between the 'naturalness' of community living in the clan and village and the 'unnaturalness' of being organized as a workforce in the cities and factories. Thus, one of the basic insights from Tönnies is important, namely, that *as* community, the group has a 'natural life' of its own that is superior to that of its individual members. We saw earlier that this natural, communitarian life is fostered by shared territory, symbolic coherence, common characteristics and interests.

Society is different from community, since, *as* 'society' the group of human beings is merely a means to achieve an end. Society functions on the basis of laws, doctrines, contractual solidarity, structural and organizational interests, private property and individual will. What constitutes community, and is often lacking in society, is a 'we-feeling' that, at the micro level, can unite a nuclear family of at least three members,[33] or, in macro terms, can comprise of the 'human community' embracing all of humankind.

The sense of 'belonging' to communities is not exclusive. In other words, one can belong to many communities at the same time with differing loyalties and intensities of community feeling. For example, one can simultaneously belong to a joint-family community, neighbourhood community, religious community, linguistic community and the like. But, in times of conflict, it is natural that members rally around those interests that are most valuable and vulnerable to attack. For instance, although people may live peaceably in a neighbourhood community, if, due to circumstances, their religion is threatened, the 'we-feeling' with co-religionists from elsewhere may colour and control their behaviour and attitudes towards their immediate neighbours with whom, in normal circumstances, they live amicably.[34] In this case, conflict has disturbed boundaries and heightened ideas of distance and difference,[35] creating a situation where the 'we-feeling' of religion grows stronger than the 'we-feeling' of the neighbourliness that is outcome of either living side-by-side or shared interests.

1.3.6 *The Cultural Nation and the Political State*

Two communities or societies that are important for our discussion are 'nation' and 'state'. These two entities must be defined for they can be misunderstood. These two terms create confusion since, in the historicity of modern state formation in Western Europe, 'nation' invariably meant a linguistic collectivity with a territorial base. The general principle 'one-nation, one-state' rendered these two terms coterminous. This confusion can be avoided by insisting on a distinction between state (a political entity) and nation (a cultural entity).[36]

In India, especially over the past two decades or so, the borders of the state are being blurred with questions of nation and nationalism. This has not only generated controversy but also violent confrontations between those who define a particular brand of religio-cultural nationalism (for e.g., *Hindutva*) and those who are excluded from it. The dynamics of this conflict will be discussed later. Political scientist Oommen argues that, besides psychological or natural affinity to some territory, it is vital to assess moral legitimacy in evaluating any claims of nationhood,[37] meaning, any group must have sufficient and convincing reasons when it stakes claims to nationhood. This is no mean task in India marked by great diversity and a burgeoning population on the one hand, and fast-depleting natural resources on the other. While we shall reflect upon the resultant conflicts later, for the present we note that, in keeping with our distinction between community and society, 'nation' is indicative of 'community' while 'state' is a politically constituted 'society'. By this logic, since the Indian state is one, but made up of many cultures, we could consider India as 'a multinational-state',[38] although it is more commonly considered a nation-state.

1.4 The Conflicts that Threaten Community

Although human beings feel the need of living peacefully in community, conflicts often arise thereby threatening community and causing tension among the individuals within a community, and also against other communities that are perceived to be a threat to the existence of one's own community. In popular parlance the word 'conflict' is used both as a noun, to mean a fight, struggle, collision, or clashing (of opposed principles, etc.), and as an intransitive verb: to come into disagreement with, to struggle or clash with.[39] Weber refers to a social relationship as 'conflict' "in so far as action within it is oriented intentionally to carrying out the actor's own will against the resistance of the other party or parties."[40] He stresses that there are contrary wills of two or more parties in a conflict that, when enforced, give rise to resistance. A more comprehensive definition is given by Coser: "A struggle over values and claims to scarce status, power and resources in which the aims of the opponents are to neutralize, injure or eliminate their rivals."[41]

Conflict can be individual or communitarian. In this book, we do not deal with individual, internal conflict,[42] but only with social or community conflicts.[43] These need not always be negative; for example, there can be the conflict of 'competition', entailing a non-violent attempt to control opportunities and advantages.[44] Since conflict need not always be negative, there are 'integrative' and 'disintegrative' aspects of conflict.[45] Conflict, at times, increases cohesion, clarifies issues, defines values, fosters new consensus, keeps a group's interests alive and leads to alliances with other groups as often happens in parliamentary or legislative assemblies in India. These are some 'integrative aspects' of conflict, while the 'disintegrative aspects' are increase in tension, bitterness, destruction, bloodshed, disruption of channels of cooperation and the diversion of attention from other vital, common interests. We are mainly concerned with the latter since they are problematic in today's Indian context.

1.4.1   The Causes of Conflict

Conflict can arise on account of many causes or reasons.[46] In the previous section we saw that community could be conceptualized on the basis of four commonalities. Ironically, much as these four commonalities can create community, they also present possibilities for destroying it, as follows. First, conflicts arise in the realm of geographical location. Struggles related to the ownership of land, entitlement to natural resources like forests and rivers, claims to nationhood and so on, come under this category.

At a second level, we mentioned that symbolic interactions result in the construction of community. Symbols convey multiple meanings and address different individuals and groups in differing degrees of emotional intensity. Hence, there is always the possibility of conflict in the very nature of symbolization. At this stage we shall not go into details of how symbolisms work. Yet, it is helpful to point out even here that symbols are codes of communication that are susceptible to being interpreted and misinterpreted in manifold ways. For instance, Saberwal argues that the root of crisis in Indian society is the dissonance that has arisen between the functioning of traditional Indian society with its whole gamut of symbolic, religious, cultural and social institutions and relationships, and that of modern, postcolonial India influenced by Western institutions and symbolic forms of communication.[47] Thus, the complex structures and dynamics that underlie all forms of symbolic communication are fertile grounds for breeding conflict.[48]

At the level of commonality of characteristics, when communities are bound in structures that are stratified and hierarchical, conflicts arise. Thus, conflicts can arise between the rich and the poor, or between the upper and lower classes. But, in India, besides class conflicts, those that arise on account of caste lead to violent clashes.[49] This is partly due to the fact that, while one can change one's social class – since class is not determined by birth – one can never change one's caste, and even if one's wealth, status or power may increase, one will still be considered of inferior social rank due to one's caste label.[50]

Finally, the commonality of interests can also give rise to a clash of interests. Marx, for instance, saw material or economic interests as the prime factors, if not the only ones, that create conflict.[51] He posited that conflicts arose since there were contradictions in society due to the skewed relations of production that led to unequal and unjust distribution of wealth and the creation of two classes, bourgeois and proletariat.[52] The inevitable result of the clash between these groups would be revolution and a deposing of the bourgeois. Conflicts of interest are often seen in trade unionism, or when associations with similar goals and target-groups disagree over issues affecting their arts, trades, businesses and the like.

Among the many causes of conflict mentioned above, one might question whether it is possible to pinpoint a 'root cause' as, for example, in Marxian analyses that view conflict solely from the economic perspective, or even to highlight 'main causes' as in the case of the Weberian tradition that maintains that wealth, status and power are prime parameters generative of social stratification and conflict.[53] It is clear that economic factors, as well as status and power are crucial components in conflicts. However, I do not pay singular attention to only one set of factors like economics, but hold that conflict can arise from a multiplicity of factors, which I shall attempt to examine.

1.5 The Subaltern as God's Option and Our Option

Every theologian reflects upon reality from a vantage viewpoint or from a particular perspective. Likewise, I do not claim to be 'neutral' in theologizing, but concretely make an option or adopt a 'subaltern perspective'. By 'subaltern' is meant: "those of inferior rank ... [i]n terms of class, caste, age, gender and office or in any other way."[54] Concretely, I shall take 'subaltern' in a very broad sense to include the economically poor, the adivasis,[55] the Dalits,[56] minorities of all types, and women, who live in positions of subordination in Indian society.

A subaltern perspective implies that, throughout this work, the reading of texts, hermeneutics, biblical exegeses and theological reflections will be undertaken from the viewpoint of the aforementioned communities.[57] It is common knowledge that, in times of conflict, subaltern communities are usually the ones that suffer most not only the loss of life and property, but also in terms of the violation of their rights and loss of their land and identity. Browsing through the Bible, one sees that God has special love for the poor. I will first highlight the theological bases for my 'subaltern option', showing that it is in consonance with God's option, and then argue that there are also sound historical and socio-political reasons for adopting this perspective and making this option.

1.5.1   *The Theological Premises for Privileging the Subaltern*

The Bible can be summed up as being the story of the family or community that God intends to create. The Genesis Creation myth basically reveals God's plan of creating human beings to be happy by virtue of their right relationship with God, with all other human beings, and with the cosmos, at large. However, the happiness and harmony of pristine paradise is always frustrated by conflicts arising on account of human selfishness and sin. Consequently, certain individuals and groups are exploited, even killed, by the powerful. Thus, God wields divine power in favour of certain groups – collectively called the *anawim* – comprising widows, orphans and aliens (Ps 68:5, 146:9, Deut 26:12). God providentially protects these groups since they experience a 'lack' due to the absence of spouse, parents or friends, respectively. This 'lack' is a deprivation that requires redress.

Apart from a special protection of weak individuals, Yahweh chooses to protect victims of injustice *as community* because God sees their affliction in slavery, hears their cries, knows their sufferings, and opts to deliver them (Ex 3:7-8). Furthermore, this option is reiterated through Israel's prophets by warning those who exploit the needy (Am 8:4 ff). It is important to note that the defence of the poor and the weak is not merely indicative of the gratuitousness of God, but is, more appropriately, an ethical imperative and "an option for justice"[58] that must be observed for the functioning of a society and world created, and cared for, by God.

In consonance with God's 'option for justice' and in conformity with the prophetic tradition, Jesus specifically brings "good news to the poor" (Lk 4:18). The *anawim* or 'subalterns' for Jesus were those unjustly relegated to the margin due to religious affiliation (Gentiles and Samaritans), social segregation (Publicans and tax-collectors), moral laxity (sinners and harlots) and physiological or psychological infirmity (lepers, the deformed and those possessed by evil spirits). Jesus' attitude to women, too, was revolutionary and posed problems for the patriarchy of his times. Jesus' subaltern preference led to his challenging social, religious and political hierarchies and hegemony.

Cutting across continents, it would not be wrong to say that Jesus' Gospel can only be read from a subaltern perspective since this perspective radically reflects Jesus' own option.[59] Indeed, Jesus preached that one's salvation or damnation would depend upon one's response or lack of response to the poor (Mt 25:31-46). In the Asian context –[60] and particularly in India with massive poverty, injustice and exclusion at various levels – viewing God as 'God of the subalterns' is not only important, but indispensable.

1.5.2   *The Historical Necessity for Subaltern Privileging*

Lest one conclude that, besides theological bases, there is little reason to justify subaltern privileging, we need to establish that the subalterns have been marginalized on many counts. For instance, it was traditionally believed and widely held that human history is linear, scientific, impartial, universal and representative of 'objective truth'. By sharp contrast, critical theory, today, contests all claims of impartiality and objectivity, and demonstrates that all histories are coloured by their own assumptions and tailored for particular addressees. Moreover, the written histories assume hegemony over the oral traditions that remain unrecorded in printed texts that have a power of their own. As an antidote to this universalistic and objectivist thinking, we see the emergence of particularistic and constructionist histories of the borderlands.[61] Today, there is a 'struggle for the past'[62] – a battle for identity and legitimacy – between the dominant and the repressed histories since historiography itself is seen as a site invested with power. In this quest for power, the dominant histories in India – for instance, the colonial, Marxist and national – have been coloured by self-interest, leaving little space for the subalterns on society's borders.[63] These three histories suffer from some limitations.

First, colonial history was coloured by Orientalism, which Said described as "a Western style for dominating, restructuring and having authority over the Orient" that emphasized the nobility of the colonizer and the primitiveness of the native, thereby rationalizing and legitimizing colonialism.[64] Furthermore, Fanon argued that colonizers were not only content to delimit the place of the natives with army, police force and guns, but represented them as a "sort of quintessence of evil," as well as "insensible to ethics," to the point of being "the absolute evil."[65] Colonial historiography failed to recognize the moral agency of native, indigenous groups.[66] Thus, to use the words of Foucault, there is need to revive the "historical knowledge of struggles" and "the memory of hostile encounters which even up to this day have been confined to the margins of knowledge."[67]

Second, Marxist historiography in India highlighted the contradictions in society largely in terms of class struggle. Historians like D.D. Kosambi developed Marxist methodology with new insights into India's past.[68] Marxist methodology provided a novel way of analyzing Indian society. However, while the eco-political factors were given due weight for interpreting peoples' struggles in Indian history, such historiography tended to downplay the import of issues like caste, culture, religion and ideology.[69] Rather than account for the complex dynamics of these issues, they were dismissed as being mere *epi-phenomena*. Thus, conflicts that arose in these realms, and which affected subalterns adversely, were neither fully recognized nor aptly represented in Marxist historiography.

Finally, nationalist historiographies – whether 'Hindu' or 'Indian'[70] – were elitist, homogenizing, and thus underplayed differences between peoples in representing an alternative force to the colonial powers. What characterized these nationalist histories was "a failure to acknowledge, far less interpret, the contribution made by the people *on their own*, that is, *independently of the elite* to the making and development of this nationalism."[71] The contributions of the subalterns in nationalist history were grossly overlooked.[72] Moreover, the cultural and other resources of the subaltern groups have never found expression in discourses on nationalism, whether Hindu or Indian.

We see that three dominant Indian histories have failed to represent the subalterns. Although many tribal, peasant and Dalit movements, as well as minority groups, were vital part of the freedom struggle, their contributions went unrecorded and unrecognized.[73] Thus, it is crucial to record the subalterns' role in the history of the formation of Indian community and to give expression to their religio-cultural resources in the larger public arena. Today, preliminary efforts are being made in this direction.[74]

1.5.3   *The Socio-Political Bases for Privileging the Subaltern*

Besides theological and historical factors that call for privileging of subaltern groups, we can also think of socio-political reasons that necessitate such privileging. The fact that India is a democratic state does not necessarily imply that all its citizens enjoy equal benefits of its democratic processes. Moreover, although civil society is expected to foster the well being of *all* citizens, there is no guarantee that it actually does so.[75] Chandhoke is circumspect about the efficacy of civil society, for, "civil societies are what their inhabitants make of them. Therefore, if inhabitants are inclined towards democracy, they will have to constantly monitor both the monopoly of the state as well as the monopoly of power within their own home ground."[76] This does not happen in a large country like India beset with problems of illiteracy, poverty and overpopulation that result in unequal social agents battling for scarce national resources. In this battle, it is most often the subalterns who bear greater burdens.

As regards relationships among diverse communities, civil society and the state, the post-Independence experience has shown two extremes to be harmful to India's poor: first, India is threatened by what Gramsci termed a *'statolatry'* where the state, wooed by the lure of capital and capitalists, assumes full control of civil society and influences it to subjugate the masses.[77] Since the upper classes and castes control the mechanisms of the Indian state, there is the possibility of the state subserving the interests of these groups resulting in the furtherance of divisive and majoritarian agenda harmful to subaltern groups. Second, the roles and responsibilities of the state and civil society with regard to welfare of the citizens, especially the most needy, are ambiguous. Thus, it is possible that the Indian state could shed its responsibility towards subaltern groups,[78] as it often does. As a consequence, Constitution ideals like equality, justice and democracy could remain mere theoretical ideals unless there is a socio-political commitment towards subaltern groups. Parekh points out that this is an ethical option that cannot be dispensed with:[79]

> Our inescapable moral commitment to help disadvantaged groups remains an impotent rhetoric unless translated into a

collective political commitment. Morality and politics are integrally related Morality lacks power and efficacy unless it finds adequate political articulation. And politics lacks depth and significance unless it becomes a medium for realizing socially relevant values.

Since the state may fail in its obligation to intervene on behalf of the disadvantaged groups and depend solely upon the organs of civil society, it must be reminded to create effective infrastructures and to remedy social imbalances in favour of the subalterns who are most likely to suffer on account of negligence on the part of the state.[80] This is a responsibility that all of us must accept and act upon if we are to be true to the option to the poor and underprivileged.

In view of the preceding theological, historical and socio-political reasons that call for subaltern privileging, I consciously adopt 'subaltern hermeneutics'[81] – i.e., a hermeneutic by the oppressed – to understand community and its underlying conflicts. This is also vital for the Indian Christian community since disadvantaged groups form a major portion of its membership. By adopting subaltern hermeneutics, I hope to creatively tap the religio-cultural resources of the subalterns. A few preliminary notes on the nature of this work and its method will help to understand its scope and relevance.

1.6 The Nature of this Theological Inquiry and its Method

Theology has, over centuries, been synonymous with 'Western' Dogmatic or Systematic Theology,[82] which claimed to be universally relevant until Vatican Council II exhorted theologians worldwide to dialogue with the disciplines and other religions.[83] In response, Indian theologians largely dialogued with the 'big' religious traditions that were elitist and divorced from the concerns of subalterns, sections of whom form a large part of the Indian Christian community. However, current socio-political conditions – compounded by globalisation, fundamentalism and 'religious nationalism'[84] or *Hindutva* – [85] has made theologians rethink their orientation since the Indian Church finds itself doubly alienated: on the one hand, the Church's services to the elite classes and castes – mainly in the fields of education and public health – are now being regarded as redundant, and, on the other, the Church has ignored the wisdom and concerns of the 'little traditions' – mainly the Dalits and adivasis. To counter this lacuna in a small way, the contextual concerns and muted voices of disadvantaged communities will enter into the theology of this book.

My reflections flow from my 'engagement'[86] and experiences[87] with subaltern communities in Gujarat, .especially those of south Gujarat. Using an inductive method, I proceed from the ground realities of subaltern communities to reflect upon the life they are called to live from the viewpoint of faith. The inductive method is recommended by the Congregation for the Clergy in its 'General Directory for Catechesis' (1971):[88]

> It is a method which has many advantages, because it conforms to the economy of Revelation. It corresponds to a profound urge of the human spirit to come to knowledge of unintelligible things by means of visible things. It also conforms to the characteristics of knowledge of the faith, which is knowledge by means of signs.

The inductive method takes the question of 'signs' seriously, which, as mentioned earlier, is central to our theologizing. However, it does not exclude a deductive approach since, as the Directory adds, the inductive method "requires the deductive method which explains and describes facts by proceeding from their causes. The deductive synthesis, however, has full value, only when the inductive process is completed."[89] This inductive-deductive approach raises the question of hermeneutics since the 'signs' (or symbols) of 'time-place' (the context) must not only be read, but also interpreted.

The hermeneutics involves the reality and resources of subaltern communities in Gujarat as 'test case' to draw up a 'subaltern hermeneutic of community', which I shall do in the third chapter. Next, reinterpretation of the symbolic representation of Trinity will be done by incorporating insights of the subaltern religio-cultural universe; finally, this trinitarian reinterpretation will function as a blueprint to renew Indian Christian identity and reorient its mission. As pointed out above, this 'subaltern hermeneutics' is not objective or neutral,[90] but in line with the approach of hermeneutists like Gadamer,[91] Lonergan,[92] and Panikkar,[93] it strives to be critical of its' own premises and prejudices while conversing with hermeneutic positions of others. The theology herein is also 'exploratory' in that it explores the possibility of reinterpreting Trinity not through exclusive use of Christian Scripture and Tradition, but also by using symbolisms, social structures and the worldview of subaltern communities. Furthermore, it also explores how theology and religion can either play a liberating role in society, or become a force to legitimize evil structures.

My reflections on the Trinity have been shaped not only by conversations and unstructured interviews with adivasi *agewaans* (leaders) but also by my 'participation'[94] in the context, being involved as 'theological observer' in 2003-2004 in a comprehensive exercise involving all mission personnel and some adivasi *agewaans* of south Gujarat to evaluate the developmental work and mission interventions among south Gujarat's adivasis.[95] This helped to get an overview of the concerns of the adivasi Christian community vis-à-vis the overall tribal situation.

Two conflicts that have concretely affected my reflections on God and on human community have been: (a) the atrocities against the adivasi Christian community that climaxed with the events of south Gujarat's Dangs district (1998-1999), and (b) the train-burning episode at Godhra and what has come to be called the 'Gujarat Carnage' (2002). The scholarly analyses in scientific journals, as well as reports by NGOs and other study groups have been used to more fully understand the socio-eco-political crises facing the affected subaltern groups. On the theological front, my focus is 'social trinitarianism',[96] studying the theology of the important authors, both Indian and foreign. Very few works are available on 'tribal theology' especially of the Chotanagpur belt.[97] However, through interactions with tribal theologians of the area, I have obtained some insights.

Dialogue with diverse disciplines is indispensable to theology, today. VC II had suggested the interdisciplinary theological method decades ago in the following words:[98]

> Theologians are invited to seek continually for *more suitable ways of communicating doctrine* to people of their times … In pastoral care, appropriate use must be made not only of theological principles, but also of *the findings of the secular sciences, especially of psychology and sociology.* Thus the faithful can be brought *to live the faith* in a more thorough and mature way.

In conformity with this mandate of VC II and the current global context of the 'collapse of borders', I shall draw insights and use analyses not only from the fields of sociology and social psychology,[99] but also from anthropology, political theory, history, philosophy and economics.[100] This interdisciplinary[101] approach will enable me to view the context more critically and understand community more clearly.

Beyond interdisciplinary investigation, a 'transdisciplinarity'[102] will enable me to deal with issues of religion and ethics that affect public life. Transdisciplinarity is vital in the Indian context, since – as authors like Ashis Nandy, André Béteille and T.N. Madan have opined – the religious resources of various Indian communities cannot but inform its collective ethic and public life. This is so because religion is so indispensable and constitutive of the Indian psyche. These religious resources being so important to various Indian communities, it would be incomplete to evaluate community life without studying the underlying socio-religious undercurrents that animate particular communities.

Finally, I hold that particularity or locality concomitant with a contextual approach does not go against 'catholicity', understood as 'universality'. In this age of globalisation, I examine issues synoptically insofar as the global affects the local, while the local must be understood in its relation to the global.[103] Thus, there is an intertwining of the local, national and global. In this way, the study stresses 'relatedness' in all its aspects so as to truly evolve a theology that can be termed, as mentioned earlier, a *fides quaerens relationem et communitatem*: faith seeking relationship and community.

1.7 The Frameworks for Our Theological Reflections

Many thinkers have discussed issues of community. In line with the interdisciplinary and transdisciplinary methodology used, I do not only rely on the theory of any one author, but take insights from various thinkers based on what helps the subaltern perspective. This eclectic approach not only allows for the use of ideas of those who have theorized on community, but it also modifies some insights for the purpose of our own reflections.

1.7.1 *Negotiating Space: Production of Space and the Problems it Poses*

Community has normally been conceptualized in terms of historicity (focus on time) and sociality (focus on relationships). While historical studies have tried to understand society in terms of series of events having a cause-effect relationship over a temporal axis, most sociological studies have dwelt on the dynamics of the diverse relationships that exist, say, between the state and its citizens, or between the organs of civil society and the government, or, between the majority group and the minorities, etc. While conceding that historicity and sociality provide vital perspectives to understanding society, the question of 'space' and 'spatiality' has largely been overlooked. This omission is serious since every community is located in space, and its very location influences, first, the way its members relate to each other and to other communities (active dimension) and, the way other communities relate to it (passive dimension).

Tribal theologians have recognized the importance of space. Bishop Nirmal Minz, a pioneering adivasi thinker and social activist, writes: "Space means the physical-geographical conditions in which communities live. Time and space both change … and change in time and space either make or break the communities according to their beliefs, attitudes and behaviours."[104] Likewise, Longchar stresses, "Among the tribal/indigenous, their history, culture, religion, spirituality and even the Supreme Being cannot be conceived without 'creation/land' or 'space'."[105] Elsewhere, Longchar more emphatically states: "[F]or the tribals, the point of departure is space. Space is the point of reference and the key to understanding selfhood, God, and spirit. ….. 'space' is the foundation for liberation."[106] While endorsing Minz's and Longchar's emphases on the importance of space, they are basically concerned with physical or geographical space. However, critical theory and postmodern thought have come up with fresh and insightful thinking on spatiality.[107] For my trinitarian reflections, I draw upon the insights of the French thinker, Henri Lefebvre, who holds that there are 'three spaces' and argues that space is socially produced.[108] Let us briefly examine his key ideas that will be useful to us.

Lefebvre describes *three spaces* or fields of human life in the following words:[109]

> The fields we are concerned with are, first, the *physical* – nature, the Cosmos; secondly, the *mental*, including logical and formal abstractions; and thirdly, the *social*. In other words, we are concerned with logico-epistemological space, the space of social practice, the space occupied by sensory phenomena, including products of the imagination such as projects and projections, symbols and utopias.

He calls these three spaces: (a) *spatial practice* or 'perceived space', (b) *representations of space* or 'conceived space', and, (c) *representational spaces* or 'lived space'.[110] Commenting on this framework, Soja terms these three spaces as *firstspace* or 'real' space, *secondspace* or 'imagined' space, and *thirdspace* or 'real-and-imagined' or, in a neologism coined by him 'realandimagined' space.[111]

The important insight of Lefebvre is that, rather than describe reality in terms of a dialectic (as in the Hegelian and Marxian tradition), he posits a *'trialectic of spatiality'* or a *'spatial trialectic'* comprising three 'moments' or 'spatialities' that are distinct from each other, yet, closely related:[112]

> ... After all, since two terms are not sufficient, it becomes necessary to introduce a third term ... the third term is the *other*, with all that this term implies (*alterity*, the relation between the present/absent other, *alteration-alienation*) ... Reflexive thought and hence philosophy has for a long time accentuated dyads. Those of the dry and the humid, the large and the small, the finite and the infinite, as in Greek antiquity. Then those that constituted the Western philosophical paradigm: subject-object, continuity-discontinuity, open-closed, etc. Finally, in the modern era there are the binary oppositions between signifier and signified, knowledge and non-knowledge, center and periphery ... [But] is there ever a relation only between two terms? One always has Three. There is always the Other.

I shall elaborate upon this *trialectic spatiality* later. What is important to note here is that Lefebvre argued that these spaces are *sites of power*, since they are 'socially produced'.[113] Let us delve into the dynamics of the three spaces and how they are related.

First, *spatial practice* is the site of production and reproduction. It is the material, sensible and empirical space that is capable of being measured and described. In this sense it is 'perceived'. Second, *representations of space* are the imagined or 'conceived spaces' that deal with signs and symbols, and are also tied to the relations of production, especially to the order or design that they impose. Such order and design is constituted via control over knowledge, signs and codes. For Lefebvre, "This is the dominant space in any society (or mode of production),"[114] a reservoir of epistemological power controlled by the "scientists, planners, technocratic subdividers and social engineers," and, one might add, theologians too. Third, *representational spaces* is space as "directly *lived* through its associated images and symbols, and hence the space of 'inhabitants and 'users' ... This is the dominated – and hence passively experienced – space which the imagination seeks to change and appropriate."[115] This *lived* space combines the real and imagined, things and thoughts, the knowable and the mysterious. It includes the 'counter-spaces' of resistance, the spaces for struggle, liberation and emancipation.[116]

It is important to note that Lefebvre's spatiality can never be dissociated from the dynamics of power. In other words, spatiality is not merely concerned with a 'geography of space' – perceived, conceived or lived – but also with a 'politics of space'.[117] This entails a critical analysis of all the spaces produced, for each space is invested with a peculiar dynamics of power. For instance, since the *representations of space* pertain to ideas and conceptions of some form of production, they are inevitably sources of knowledge that exert great power. This point is forcefully expressed by Foucault who holds that, we do not live in a "homogenous or empty space," but "inside a set of relations that delineates sites which are irreducible to one another."[118] This set of relations is held together in a trialectic of power-knowledge-space,[119] each dependent on and affecting the other two. In sum, there can be no space divorced from some form of knowledge and some dynamics of power, just as there can be no knowledge abstracted from some space and unrelated to power. And so it is with power. We will go into details of this dynamic later in the book.

1.7.2 *Subaltern Communities as 'Political Society'*

We have earlier differentiated between 'community' (*Gemeinschaft*) and 'society' (*Gesellschaft*), the former being result of emotive 'natural' factors, while the latter, on the basis of laws and contracts. In like manner, Partha Chatterjee speaks of 'political society' as a social entity neither identified with the state nor with the associations of civil society.[120] Thus, it refers to political transactions that take place outside the framework of formal institutions. The 'political society' is vital because it organizes itself around issues pertaining to rights, and rallies for the acquisition of its rights within the democratic framework of the Constitution.

While we focus on the religio-cultural resources of subaltern communities, we must simultaneously recognize that these weaker communities are also 'political' entities in need of their legitimate rights. If the political dimensions of these groups are not recognized and their rights not ensured on the political front, they will not be able to stand on an equal footing with other groups in India. While accepting that the political dimension is important for the construction of any community, we will ascertain how the legal and constitutional requirements of 'political society' must coexist with the other natural factors that make up community.

1.7.3 *The State's Responsibility towards Subaltern Communities*

At a time when communities in India – especially subaltern communities – are increasingly being faced with conflict, Neera Chandhoke raises pertinent questions about the role of the state and its responsibilities towards ensuring the welfare of all its constituent communities. Her contention is that the Indian state and the organs of civil society have failed to ensure the welfare of all communities, especially the more vulnerable ones. This contention is backed by theorizing on the need for the state to go beyond the demands of secularism so as to ensure that its communities – in particular, the religious minorities – are given special rights in the political arena.[121] Thus, she argues for equity and egalitarianism in allocating national resources among communities.

Neera Chandhoke's theorizing and reasoning is based on ethical grounds and has a strong communitarian focus. She also argues that unless and until 'recognition' is given to any community's religious, social and cultural resources, it is never likely to feel equal to other communities that may enforce their own majoritarian agenda on all the citizens of the country. The insights borrowed from Chandhoke will be developed later.

1.7.4 *The 'Performance' and 'Function' of Religions in a Global Village*

We live in a 'global village' where boundaries and borders have collapsed.[122] This is not only true with regard to national boundaries and financial markets, but also in the realm of religion. Peter Beyer uses the binary of 'performance' and 'function' to explain the role of religion in global society.[123] 'Function' has to do with the aspects of doctrine, creed, devotion, worship and so on. Beyer holds that "function is the pure, 'sacred' communication involving the transcendent and the aspect that religious institutions claim for themselves."[124] Performance, by contrast, occurs when religion is 'applied' to problems generated in other systems or sub-systems in society.[125] While function has to do with "the holism of religion, its effort to determine the whole of existence through the possibility of communication with the posited transcendence,"[126] performance concerns about how religion relates to other subsystems such as economy, polity, law and the like.

Based on Beyer's understanding of religion in global society, I stress the 'performance' role of religion so as to inspire Christian communities to reflect upon, and respond to, the many problems engendered by societal subsystems that often lead to a disintegration of communities, especially the disadvantaged ones. While stressing the performance role, I shall also reinterpret the functional aspects of religion since the matters that are regarded as 'internal' to a religion are also crucial to shaping its identity and orientation. I shall incorporate insights from Beyer in the final chapter.

1.8. Conclusion: Fixing Foundations for our Faith Reflections

Like the foundations upon which a building is built, this first chapter provides a base upon which our theorizing and theologizing is founded and will be fortified. So far we have clarified the contextual nature of our theologizing, i.e., we aim at reinterpreting the central image of God as Trinity in conformity with the worldview, and by using the religio-cultural resources, of subaltern communities. In other words, we seek to evolve an indigenous image of the 'God of our soil', in tune with Indian indigenous imagination, and simultaneously faithful to the Catholic Tradition and to Scripture. We have stressed that theology is always done from a particular perspective and with a concrete option – in our case an option for the subaltern groups, or, what's commonly called an 'option for the poor' – that will influence our hermeneutics and method.

We are primarily interested in Indian subaltern communities – in particular, the Dalits and adivasis (tribals) – large numbers of which are Christians. And Christians, in general, are only about 2.34% of the total population of India, which is quite clearly a 'minority' or 'little flock'. Consequently, Christian communities, nationwide, suffer on many fronts: social, economic, political, and even religious. The 'religious' realm is of particular interest to us, since, although religion is meant to be a builder of community, it is being manipulated to destroy peace and harmony in India, today. We once again note that community is not necessarily formed by virtue of geographical proximity of its members, but also on the basis of symbolic interactions, common characteristics and interests. Since religion 'produces' signs, symbols, myths, narratives and the like, which are all sites of power, theology has a vital role to play in evolving religious symbols that will catalyze the construction of community in India.

We have highlighted the distinction between *Gemeinschaft* (community) and *Gesellschaft* (society) since, besides feeling at home with the 'naturalness' of being community, every group is situated in the nation and world also as 'political society' with rights, but also with responsibilities. The frameworks we shall employ – namely, Chatterjee's understanding of 'political society' and Chandhoke's insistence of minority rights 'beyond secularism' – will help us in our theorizing at the macro level, while Beyer's insights into religion in a global society will help us to situate our reflections in the landscape of today's borderless world, at large – wherein, the groups of our theological option are rendered marginal, if not victimized and considered unwanted. Finally, we will seriously look at the question of 'space' using Lefebvre's theorizing to develop a God-image since the trialectic space-knowledge-power dynamically interrelate and can be used to advantage for building up community. In the next chapter we will take a look at the Indian context with special focus on the situation in Gujarat.

ENDNOTES FOR CHAPTER ONE

[1] See Karl Rahner, *The Trinity*, trans. J. Donceel (London: Burns and Oates, 1986), 10.

[2] See *The Forgotten Trinity: Report of the BCC Study Commission on Trinitarian Doctrine Today* (London: British Council of Churches, Inter-Church House, 1989).

[3] See *St. Anselm: Basic Writings*, trans. S.N. Deane (Las Salle, Illinois: Open Court, 1968), 7.

[4] See, for instance, *The New Dictionary of Theology*, ed. J. A. Komonchak et al., (Bangalore: TPI, 1993), 1013, s.v. "Theology." Also see, R. Panikkar, "Indian Theology: A Theological Mutation," in *Theologizing in India*, ed. M. Amaladoss et al., (Bangalore: TPI, 1981), 27-9, John W. de Gruchy, "The Nature, Necessity and Task of Theology," in *Doing Theology in Context: South African Perspectives*, ed. idem and C. Villa-Vicencio (New York: Orbis and Johannesburg: David Philip, 1994), 4-9, among others.

[5] See Juan Luis Segundo, *Signs of the Times: Theological Reflections*, ed. A.T. Hennelly, trans. R.R. Barr (New York: Orbis, 1993), esp. ch. 9 "Revelation, Faith, Signs of the Times," 128-48, where a relationship between revelation, faith and 'signs of the times' is drawn, the latter necessitating reading "with an open, sensitive heart" that will "prevent the 'letter' – i.e., revelation bound by human language – from becoming 'lethal' and leading astray." The Documents of VC II – for e.g., UR n.4, GS nn.4,11, PO n.9 – speak of the 'signs of the times' as indispensable for deciphering the presence of God.

[6] Felix Wilfred, *Asian Dreams and Christian Hope: At the Dawn of the Millennium* (Delhi: ISPCK, 2003), 186, adds that, besides the '*chronos*' (time), listening to the '*topos*' (place or context) is vital especially since Christianity must strive to be an active interlocutor in the public realm of civil society.

[7] See Karl Rahner and Herbert Vorgrimler, *Concise Theological Dictionary*, 2nd ed. (London: Burns & Oates, 1983), s.v. "Theology," quote from p. 498.

[8] See Felix Wilfred, *On the Banks of Ganges: Doing Contextual Theology* (Delhi: ISPCK, 2002), xi.

[9] Michael Amaladoss, "A Cycle Opening to Pluralism," in *The Pastoral Circle Revisited: A Critical Quest for Truth and Information,"* ed. F. Wijsen et al., (New York: Orbis, 2005), 179; italics and brackets added.

[10] Gustavo Gutierrez, *The God of Life* (New York: Orbis, 1981), argues that any conception of the Divine that has no bearing on life can only be an idol.

[11] See Gregory Baum, "The Impact of Sociology on Christian Theology," in *Theology and Sociology: A Reader*, ed. R. Gill (London: Geoffrey Chapman & New York: Paulist Press, 1987), 130-44, for details.

[12] This point is well argued by Robin Gill, "Sociology Assessing Theology," in *Theology and Sociology: A Reader*, ed. idem (London: Geoffrey Chapman & New York: Paulist Press, 1987), 145-64.

[13] For critical, constructive and contextual functions of theology, see, Gordon D. Kaufman, *The Theological Imagination: Constructing the Concept of God* (Philadelphia: The Westminster Press, 1981), 263-79.

[14] *Ibid.,* 278-9, italics added.

[15] See, for instance, Gailyn Van Rheenen, *Communicating Christ in Animistic Contexts* (Grand Rapids, Michigan: Baker Book House), 95-125, wherein the contrasting worldviews of Christianity and Animism are explained; see also A. Wati Longchar and Larry E. Davis, eds., *Doing Theology with Tribal Resources* (Jorhat, Assam: Tribal Study Centre, Eastern Theological College, 1999); and, Bénézet Bujo, *African Theology in its Social Context*, trans. J. O'Donohue (Maryknoll, New York: Orbis Books, 1992).

[16] See, for instance, Dorothee Sölle, "God's Pain and Our Pain," in *The Future of Liberation Theology: Essays in Honor of Gustavo Gutiérrez*, ed. M. H. Ellis and O. Maduro, 326-33 (New York: Orbis Books, 1989), who argues that God is concerned about human struggle and pain and committed to addressing it.

[17] See Felix Wilfred, "Towards an Inter-Religious Asian Public Theology" in *VJTR* 74/2 (February 2010): 103-16, for details.

[18] *Ibid.,* 110.

[19] See Wilfred, *Banks of the Ganges*, 9-15, on why and how Indian Theology must always be dialogal.

[20] R.M. Maciver, *Community: A Sociological Study* (London: Macmillan and Co., 1928), 23.

[21] See A. Wati Longchar, "An Assessment of the Tribal Theology: Trends and Challenges for the Future," in *Tribal Theology On The Move*, ed. S. Shimray and L. Longkumer (Jorhat, Assam: Tribal/Women Study Centres, 2006), 9,

who stresses that land sustains and nourishes the tribals and gives them identity.

[22] Emile Durkheim, *The Division of Labour in Society* (New York: The Free Press, 1964), 129.

[23] For details of the contributions of the proponents of 'symbolic interactionism', see, Herbert Blumer, *Symbolic Interactionism: Perspective and Method* (New Jersey: Prentice-Hall, Inc., 1969), 2-21, also George Herbert Mead, *The Social Psychology of George Herbert Mead*, ed. A. Strauss (Chicago: UCP, 1956), 284-94, who shows how relationships are forged through the medium of significant symbols.

[24] See Anthony P. Cohen, *The Symbolic Construction of Community* (Chichester: Ellis Horwood Limited and London & New York: Tavistock Publications, 1985), 11-38.

[25] *Ibid.*, 98; italics added.

[26] See Talal Asad, "Where are the Margins of the State?" in *Anthropology in the Margins of the State*, ed. V. Das and D. Poole (New Delhi: OUP, 2004), 279-88, for an insightful discussion on this point..

[27] In India it is not uncommon to see ministers and politicians pretending to be public servants and interested in the welfare of all citizens, but who only really ensure that their own caste or tribe interests are fostered. Indeed, it is often pointed out that caste and tribe identities are of prime importance in India.

[28] The newspapers have reported a spate of so-called 'honour killings' when members of the families of youth who 'dare' marry within in the same *gotra* (clan) kill the ones who intend to marry. The reasoning behind such killings is that youth in the same *gotra* must live like brothers and sisters and cannot marry.

[29] See M.N. Srinivas, *The Dominant Caste and Other Essays* (Delhi: OUP, 1987); Louis Dumont, *Homo Hierarchicus: The Caste System and its Implications* (Delhi: OUP, 1988); Nicholas Dirks, *Castes of Mind: Colonialism and the Making of Modern India* (Delhi: Permanent Black & New Jersey: PUP, 2002), and Steven M. Parish, *Hierarchy and its Discontents: Culture and the Politics of Consciousness in Caste Society* (Delhi: OUP, 1997), among others, for good analyses of the dynamics of the caste system

[30] Please refer to the 'List of Abbreviations' for the full form of these abbreviations.

[31] Gabriel Marcel distinguishes between collectivity and community and discusses the indispensability of the latter for the proper growth of the individual. See, John E. Smith, "The Individual, the Collective, and the Community," in *The Philosophy of Gabriel Marcel. The Library of Living Philosophers*, vol. 17, ed. P.A. Schilpp and L.E. Hahn (Carbondale: Southern Illinois University, 1984), 337-49.

[32] See Ferdinand Tönnies, *Community and Association*, trans. C. P Loomis (London: Routledge & Kegan Paul, 1974), 37-116, for details; quote taken from p.74.

[33] I hold that a minimum number of 'three' is required for 'community'. Association between 'two' people could be referred to as 'couple'. The dynamics between 2 persons is not as problematic as that among 3. In the case of 'two', one is either attracted or antagonistic to the other and can either decide to relate with or ignore the other. In the case of 'three' persons the relationships are complicated since one does not relate merely at the 'I-thou' level, but as 'I-thou-(s)he'. There could be rich possibilities of relationship as seen in the trinities and the *trimurtis* that are upheld as models of harmony. However, there is also the ever-present possibility of discomfort or hostility when three are put together; see, for e.g., Jean Paul Sartre, *No Exit and Three Other Plays* (New York: Random House, 1955), 1-48.

[34] See Sudhir Kakar, *The Colours of Violence* (New Delhi: Viking & Penguin Books, 1995), 239-53, for socio-psychological insights into this phenomenon.

[35] See Robert Redfield, *The Little Community and Peasant Society and Culture* (Chicago: UCP, 1971), 113, who conceives of "community within communities" where boundaries are drawn on the basis of those who are 'out there' (distance) and 'not like us' (difference).

[36] See T.K. Oommen, *State and Society in India: Studies in Nation-Building* (New Delhi: Sage Publications, 1990), 12. See pp. 31-42 for further clarifications with regard to nation, state and ethnicity.

[37] *Ibid.*, 11.

[38] *Ibid.*, 13. Likewise, Amalendu Guha, "The Indian National Question: A Conceptual Framework," in *Nationalism Question in India* (Pune: Training for Development Scholarship Society, 1987), 26, calls India a 'many-nationality State'.

[39] See N. Jayaram and S. Saberwal, eds., "Introduction," *Social Conflict* (New Delhi: OUP, 1995), 4.

[40] See Max Weber, *The Theory of Social and Economic Organization*, trans. A.M. Henderson and T. Parsons (New York: The Free Press, 1964), 132.

[41] Lewis Coser, *The Functions of Social Conflict* (Glencoe: The Free Press, 1956), 8.

[42] For e.g., someone experiencing psychic unrest and conflict may consult a psychotherapist and get advice.

[43] See Amrita Basu and Atul Kohli, eds., *Community Conflicts and the State in India* (New Delhi: OUP, 1998), for analyses of the issues involved in some cases of conflicts among communities in India.

[44] Weber, *ibid*.

[45] See Horton and Hunt, *Sociology* (New York: McGraw Hill, 1968), 310.

[46] See, for e.g., Randall Collins, *Four Sociological Traditions: Selected Readings* (New York: OUP, 1985), 3-132, for the main theories of "The Conflict Tradition" by Marx, Engels, Weber, Dahrendorf, Lenski, etc.

[47] See Satish Saberwal, *Roots of Crisis: Interpreting Contemporary Indian Society* (New Delhi: Sage Publications, 1996), 30-51.

[48] See Jayaram & Saberwal, "Appendix: Symbols & Conflict," in *Social Conflict*, 527-30, for more details.

[49] One can cite the question of the Mandal Commission's recommendations for reservations on the basis of caste that created communal conflagrations nationwide in the 1990s.

[50] This is, obviously, a rather simplistic way of conceptualizing caste. Sociologists, today, analyze its more complex functioning in India. See, for e.g., M.N. Srinivas, "Mobility in the Caste System," in *Structure and Change in Indian Society*, ed. M. Singer and B.S. Cohn (New Delhi: Rawat Publications, 1996), 189-200.

[51] See, for instance, excerpts from Karl Marx and Friedrich Engels in *Four Sociological Traditions: Selected Readings*, ed. R. Collins (New York: OUP, 1994), 3-35, for details.

[52] See Karl Marx, *Selected Writings in Sociology and Social Philosophy*, ed., T. B. Bottomore and M. Rubel (Harmondsworth: Penguin Books, 1963).

[53] See Weber, "Class, Status, Party," in *From Max Weber: Essays in Sociology*, ed. H.H. Gerth and C. W. Mills (New York: OUP, 1946), reprinted in *Social Stratification*, ed. D. Gupta (Delhi: OUP, 1991), 455-70.

[54] See Ranajit Guha, ed., "Preface," in *Subaltern Studies I: Writings on South Asian History and Society* (Delhi: OUP, 1991), vii. See also his 'note' on p.8.

[55] The appellation *adivasi* (meaning 'original inhabitant') is coterminous with the more common word 'tribal' or 'aboriginal', and is equivalent to the UN's category of 'indigenous people'. G.S. Ghurye, *The Scheduled Tribes*, 2nd ed (Bombay: Popular Press, 1959), 20, describes *adivasis* as 'Backward Hindus'. A.M. Shah, "The Tribes – So-called – of Gujarat: In the Perspective of Time," *EPW* 38 (January 11, 2003): 95-7, views tribes as part of Hindu society through what M.N. Srivinas has termed 'Sanskritization'. The adivasis have been designated with many disparaging terms like *kaliparaj* (black-people), *janglis* (uncivilized, forest-people), *raniparaj* (wild-people) and so on. Politically, the adivasis come under the 'Scheduled Tribes' (ST) category. They are also termed *'vanvasis'* (meaning 'forest dwellers') by the Hindu Right or *Sangh Parivar*.

[56] The term *'Dalit'* literally means 'broken'. See M.E. Prabhakar, "The Search for a Dalit Theology," in *A Reader in Dalit Theology*, ed. A.P. Nirmal (Madras: The Department of Dalit Theology, GLTCRI, n.d.), 41, who writes: "The word 'Dalit' means the oppressed or broken victims and refers both to the people who are deprived and dehumanized and the state of their deprivation/dehumanization. Dalit is thus both a sociological and theological

category." The 'Dalit' community is regarded as so-called 'low caste' or former 'Untouchables' whom Gandhiji called *'Harijans'* – a term that now is rejected as derogatory and paternalistic. Politically, the 'Dalits' are categorized under the 'Scheduled Castes' (SC) group.

[57] Recently, a *One Volume Dalit Bible Commentary* has been published for the *New Testament* by the Centre for Dalit/Subaltern Studies, New Delhi, 2010. This volume is a compilation of commentaries on the NT by various authors from either the Dalit perspective, in particular, or the subaltern one, in general.

[58] See José M. Vigil, "The Option for the Poor is an Option for Justice, and not Preferential: A New Theological-Systematic Framework for the Option for the Poor," *VJTR* 68/7 (July 2004): 509-20, who criticizes the 'softened' stand of Gustavo Gutiérrez and other Latin-American Liberation theologians who now interpret 'option of the poor' to mean mere 'gratuitousness of God'. Vigil argues that this option is God's option for justice in favour of "victims of injustice".

[59] Segundo, "The Option for the Poor," in *Signs of the Times*, 120-2, maintains that this option is not merely a theme of theology but "the epistemological premise for an interpretation of the word of God". For perspectives from other continents and cultures, see, Dennis P. McCann, "Option for the Poor: Rethinking a Catholic Tradition," in *The Preferential Option for the Poor*, ed. R. J. Neuhaus (Grand Rapids, Michigan: William B. Eerdmans, 1988), 35-52, in the North American context; Gustavo Gutiérrez, *The Power of the Poor in History* (New York: Orbis, 1983), 93, and, *The Poor and the Church in Latin America* (London: Catholic Institute, 1987) in the Latin American context; Gregory Baum, *Theology and Society* (New York, Mahwah: Paulist Press, 1987), 170-8, in the Canadian context and James Armstrong, *From The Underside: Evangelism From a Third World Vantage Point* (New York: Orbis, 1981), for an evangelical perspective.

[60] Aloysius Pieris, *An Asian Theology of Liberation* (New York: Orbis, 1988), 120-1, maintains that two biblical axioms, rooted in the word of God, are indispensable to any Asian, Liberation Theology, viz., (1) the irreconcilable antagonism between *God and mammon,* and (2) the irrevocable covenant between *God and the poor* (i.e., a defense pact against their common enemy: mammon).

[61] See, for e.g., Sharmila Rege, "Histories from the Borderlands," *Seminar* 495 (November 2000): 55-61, who discusses the developments in Indian feminist studies in the academy over the past fifty years. See also Saskia Sassen, *Globalization and its Discontents: Essays on the New Mobility of People and Money* (New York: The New Press, 1998), ch. 1, that describes 'borderlands' as spaces of silence and absence, spaces that are constituted in terms of discontinuities rather than clear-cut dividing lines. As a result of economic globalisation, these 'borderlands' become the terrain inhabited by women, children and migrants.

[62] See *The Struggle for the Past: Historiography Today*, ed. F. Wilfred and J.D. Maliekal (Chennai: UOM, 2002), for perspectives on alternative historiographies.

[63] K.N. Panikkar, "Alternative Historiographies: Changing Paradigm of Power," in *ibid.*, 11-20, discusses the weaknesses of these.

[64] See Edward Said, *Orientalism: Western Conceptions of the Orient* (New Delhi: Penguin Books, 2001), 3.

[65] See Frantz Fanon, *The Wretched of the Earth*, trans. C. Farrington (New York: Grove Press, 1963), 41.

[66] See, for instance, Ramachandra Guha, "Savaging the Civilized: Verrier Elwin and the Tribal Question in Late Colonial India," *EPW* 31/35, 36, 37 (September 1996): 2375-89, who asserts that tribals were conspicuously absent from colonial histories. Elwin was the first to bring their concerns to the academy

[67] These are phrases used by Michel Foucault, *Power/Knowledge: Selected Interviews and Other Writings – 1972-1977*, ed. C. Gordon (New York: Pantheon Books, 1980), 83.

[68] See Romila Thapar, "The Contribution of D.D. Kosambi to Indology," in *History and Beyond* (New Delhi: OUP, 2000), 89-113, for Kosambi's contribution to history. See also D.D. Kosambi, *The Culture and Civilization of Ancient India in Historical Outline* (New Delhi: Vikas Publishing House, 1981).

[69] Panikkar, "Alternative Historiographies," 15-7, shows the lacunae of Marxist historiography. Kosambi's definition of history as: "the presentation in chronological order of successive *changes in the means and relations of production*," seems to stress economics much more than other factors. See Kosambi, 10.

[70] John Zavos, "Searching for Hindu Nationalism in Modern Indian History: Analysis of Some Early Ideological Developments," *EPW* 34 (August 7, 1999): 2270-1, makes a distinction between 'Hindu' (communal) nationalism and "Indian' that included all Indians and all communities in British India.

[71] Ranajit Guha, "On Some Aspects of the Historiography of Colonial India," in *Subaltern Studies*, vol. I, 3.

[72] See, for instance, George Oommen, "Historiography of Indian Christianity and Challenges to Subaltern Methodology," *JOD* 28/2 (April–June 2003): 212-31, for problems of historiography of Christians.

[73] Foucault, *Power/Knowledge*, 81-2, speaks of the 'insurrection of subjugated knowledges' of 'popular knowledge' (*le savoir des gens*) that are "buried, disguised and disqualified" due to the dynamics of power.

[74] The work of tribal theologians like Nirmal Minz and others seek to fill this gap. See, for instance, his "Religion and Culture as Power in the Context of Tribal Aspirations in India," in *Pearls of Indigenous Wisdom: Selected Essays from Lifetime Contributions by Bishop Dr. Nirmal Minz, An Adivasi Intellectual*, ed.

J. M. Kujur and S. Minz (New Delhi: ISI and Bangalore: CISRS, 2007): 143-54, wherein he highlights the various tribal movements for India's Independence, as well as stresses that tribal religio-cultural resources were instrumental in ameliorating the eco-socio-political lot of tribals in India.

[75] There is a certain exaggerated optimism regarding 'civil society' among the so-called 'communitarians' of the West. See, for instance, Michael Walzer, "The Concept of Civil Society," in *Towards a Global Civil Society*, ed. idem. (Providence: Berghahn Books, 1998), 16, who claims: "We are by nature social, before we are political or economic beings." The Indian situation does not warrant such optimism.

[76] Neera Chandhoke, *The Conceits of Civil Society* (New Delhi: OUP, 2003), 31.

[77] See Antonio Gramsci, *Selections from the Prison Notebooks*, ed. and trans. Q. Hoare and G.N. Smith (Madras: Orient Longman, 1996), 210-76, especially 268-9, where he explains 'statolatry'.

[78] Neera Chandhoke, "'Seeing' the State in India," *EPW* 40 (March 12, 2005): 1033-9, shows that while the poor expect the State to address their basic needs, the State increasingly delegates its responsibilities to the organizations of civil society with the result that welfare measures are not always effective.

[79] Bhiku Parekh, "A Case for Positive Discrimination," in *Democracy, Difference and Social Justice*, ed. G. Mahajan (New Delhi: OUP, 2000), 383, makes a strong case for positive discrimination on ethical grounds.

[80] For instance, Gurpreet Mahajan, "Civil Society and Its Avtars: What Happened to Freedom and Democracy?" *EPW* 34 (May 15, 1999): 1188-96, stresses that the state is necessary to protect the institutions of civil society and ensure social equality and nondiscrimination along with individual liberty.

[81] See Felix Wilfred, "Towards a Subaltern Hermeneutics: Beyond the Contemporary Polarities in the Interpretation of Religious Traditions," in *Voices from the Third World, Ecumenical Association of the Third World Theologians*, 19/2 (1996), 128-48; also, idem, *The Sling of Utopia* (Delhi: ISPCK, 2005), 33-6, 137-63, for characteristics of subaltern religious experience and 'subaltern hermeneutics'.

[82] The term 'Dogmatic Theology' is more commonly used by the Roman schools of Theology that attempt to coherently defend the dogmas of the Catholic Church drawing upon scripture and tradition as sources of revelation. 'Systematic Theology', on the other hand, is more commonly used by the English-speaking schools that, besides expounding Christian doctrines in a systematic and scholarly fashion, may address moral issues and pay greater attention to methodology, terminology and philosophical principles. See, G. O'Collins and E.G. Farrugia, *A Concise Dictionary of Theology* (London: HarperCollins, 1991), 58, 235.

[83] See for e.g., the following documents of VC II: *AG* 3,9,11,18; *GS* 22,28,92; *LG* 16; *NA* 1,2,3,9,11,18, etc.

[84] Mark Juergensmeyer, *Religious Nationalism Confronts the Secular State* (Delhi: OUP, 1993), 6, uses the term 'religious nationalism' in preference to 'fundamentalism' since the ideologues of 'religious nationalism' deploy religious means to grab political power. Thus, this is a unique form of fundamentalism.

[85] The study distinguishes between '*Hindutva*' and 'Hinduism'. The former refers to the militant brand of Hinduism aggressively propagated by the Hindu Right; the latter, to the normal practice of Hinduism. For further details on *Hindutva*, see Parvathy Appaiah. *Hindutva: Ideology and Politics* (New Delhi: Deep & Deep Publications, 2003); G.S. Hingle, *Hindutva Reawakened* (Delhi: Vikas Publishing, 1999); Debashis Chakrabarti, "Hindutva: The Religious Incongruity," *The Hindu*, 6 February 2001, open page 1, and others.

[86] Hwa Yung, *Mangoes or Bananas? The Quest for an Authentic Asian Christian Theology* (Oxford: Regnum and Paternoster Publishing, 1997), 8-9, sees Western Theology as largely 'unengaged' and holds that Asian Theology must be 'engaged' in the sense of being 'committed' to transforming social reality.

[87] The role of 'experience' is vital in Indian contextual theology: see, for e.g., Sr. Vandana, "Indian Theologizing: The Role of Experience," in *Theologizing in India*, 81-115, Raimundo Panikkar, "The Ultimate Experience," *Theology Digest* 20 (1972): 219-26; and, Michael Amaladoss, "From Experience to Theology: Methodological Explorations," *VJTR* 61/6 (June 1997): 372-85, among others.

[88] See the 1997 revised edition, n. 150.

[89] *Ibid.*

[90] Werner Jeanrond, *Theological Hermeneutics: Development and Significance* (London: SCM Press Ltd, 1994), 5, states that all our interpretations are conditioned by our prior understandings of reality. See also Segundo, 122-5, who dismisses the possibility of a 'neutral approach' to understand the gospel

[91] See Hans-Georg Gadamer, *Truth and Method*, 2nd ed., trans. W. Glen-Doepel (London: Sheed and Ward, 1981), 245-53, who demonstrates how tradition is always tempered by a certain pre-understanding that cannot be dispensed with even in the sciences. He warns about a "prejudice against prejudice."

[92] Bernard Lonergan, *Method in Theology* (London: Darton, Longman & Todd, 1975), 157, cautions about "the principle of the empty head" whereby one must be aware that one cannot theologize in a vacuum.

[93] Raimundo Panikkar, *The Intrareligious Dialogue* (Bangalore: ATC, 1984), 81, critiques the *epoché* – from the Greek, meaning 'bracketing' originally used by Husserl to describe his method of 'detachment from any point of view regarding the objective world' – as being "psychologically impracticable, phenomenologically inappropriate, philosophically defective, theologically weak and religiously barren."

[94] With regard to trinitarian theology, Frans Jozef van Beeck, "Trinitarian Theology as Participation," in *The Trinity*, ed. S. Davis et al., 295-325, stresses the need for the theologian's 'participative knowledge' as a hermeneutical task not merely limited to the human or ethical level, but also in the line of the *theological*.

[95] The outcome of this evaluation-exercise was the publishing of two documents, namely, *Where Do We Stand?* and *Where Do We Go?* (Vadodara: CCD, 2003, 2004). For my 'theological reflections' on the same, see my "Sinking Sands and Shifting Stands: Approaching Adivasi Apostolate Anew," *VJTR* 68/4 (May 2004): 325-37.

[96] 'Social trinitarianism' deals with reinterpreting the Trinity as a model or symbol of human community. This is perhaps best expressed by the 19th century Russian Orthodox theologian Nikolai Fedorov: "The Trinity is our social programme." Contemporary theologians like J. Bracken and C. M. LaCugna (USA), L. Boff (Latin America), J. Moltmann (Europe) and J. Y. Lee (Asia) have contributed to 'social trinitarianism'.

[97] 'Chotanagpur' (literally, 'small Nagpur') refers to the tribal belt of Central India, embracing Jharkhand, Chhattisgarh and parts of Orissa. See M. Banerjee, *An Historical Outline of Pre-British Chotanagpur* (Ranchi: Educational Publications, 1989), 5-8, for details about the appellation.

[98] See VC II's *GS*, n. 62, italics added. See also *LG* 13 and *AG* 22 that echo similar thoughts.

[99] For e.g., Peter L. Berger, *The Social Reality of Religion* (Norwich: Penguin University Books, 1973), 181-90, discusses the possibility of 'conversations' between theology and sociology: "... a theology that proceeds in a step-by-step correlation with what can be said about man empirically is well worth a serious try...such a conversation between sociology and theology is most likely to bear intellectual fruits" (p. 189).

[100] See, "Political Theology in the Indian Context," in *Theologizing in Context: Statements of the Indian Theological Association*, ed. J. Parappally (Bangalore: Dharmaram Publications, 2002), 66, that reads, "The theologian in India has a special task to learn from the findings of the human sciences like sociology and psychology and politics and interpret the political reality in the light of faith."

[101] For the scope of interdisciplinarity see Ananta Kumar Giri, "Disciplinary Boundaries: Rethinking Theories and Methods," in *Frontier Violations*, ed. F. Wilfred and O. Beozzo, *Concilium* 2 (1999): 54-61. Also, *Crossing the Borders*, ed. A. Amaladass and R. Rocha (Chennai: SNP, 2001). While academics are increasingly adopting interdisciplinary approaches, certain apprehensions about the method have also been voiced; see for e.g., Satish Saberwal, "On Crossing Boundaries," *Seminar* 495 (November 2000): 29-32.

[102] See Ananta Kumar Giri, "The Calling of a Creative Transdisciplinarity," *Futures* 34 (2000): 103-15; also, idem, *Spiritual Cultivation for a Secular Society,*

working paper of the MIDS, Chennai, n.d., who discusses the possibilities of transdisciplinarity in the Indian context.

[103] In this regard see Robert J. Schreiter, *Constructing Local Theologies*; also *The New Catholicity: Theology between the Global and the Local* (New York: Orbis, 2000), 127-33, who speaks of a 'New Catholicity' with a new agenda for a globalised world.

[104] See *Pearls of Indigenous Wisdom*, 31.

[105] In Shimray and Longkumer, *ibid.*, 9.

[106] A. Wati Longchar, *An Emerging Asian Theology: Tribal Theology – Issue, Method and Perspective* (Jorhat, Assam: Tribal Study Centre, 2000), 68.

[107] See, for e.g., Mike Crang and Nigel Thrift, eds., *Thinking Space* (London and New York: Routledge, 2000), for an overview of the works of theorists like Bakhtin, Foucault, Bourdieu, Lefebvre and others.

[108] See his *The Production of Space*, trans. D. N-Smith (Oxford UK & Cambridge USA: Blackwell, 1991), which contains the main lines of his theory. This book will hereafter be abbreviated as *Production of Space*.

[109] *Ibid.*, 11-2; italics as in the original text.

[110] *Ibid.*, 33.

[111] Edward W. Soja, *Thirdspace: Journeys to Los Angeles and Other Real-and-Imagined Places* (Oxford, UK & Massachusetts, USA: Blackwell, 1996), 11. This book will hereafter be abbreviated as *Thirdspace*.

[112] In *La Présence et l'absence* (Paris: Casterman, 1980), 225 and 143, as quoted in Soja, *Thirdspace*, 53.

[113] See Andy Merrifield, "Henri Lefebvre: A Socialist in Space," in *Thinking Space*, 167-82, for details.

[114] *Production of Space*, 38-9.

[115] *Ibid.*, 39.

[116] See Soja, *Thirdspace*, 68, who believes that although Lefebvre did not prioritize any space, it is in the *thirdspace* that he sees the potential for resistance to and change of the social order.

[117] In *Production of Space*, 60, Lefebvre talks of a 'politics of space'.

[118] See Michel Foucault, "Of Other Spaces," *Diacritics* 16 (1986): 22-7; quote from p. 23.

[119] See Michel Foucault, "Space, Knowledge, and Power," in *The Foucault Reader*, ed. P. Rainbow (London: Penguin Books, 1984), 239-56.

[120] See Partha Chatterjee, "Beyond the Nation or Within?" *EPW* 32 (January 11, 1997): 30-4; "Community in the East," *EPW* 33 (February 7, 1998): 277-82,

and "On Civil and Political Society in Post-Colonial Democracy," in *Civil Society*, ed. S. Kaviraj and S. Khilnani (Cambridge: CUP, 2001), 165-78.

[121] See Neera Chandhoke, *Beyond Secularism: The Rights of Religious Minorities* (Delhi: OUP, 1999).

[122] Today, a lot of theorizing is being done with the awareness of the collapse of borders in a global era; see for e.g., *Negotiating Borders: Theological Explorations in the Global Era. Essays in Honour of Prof. Felix Wilfred*, ed. G. Patrick and E. Schüssler Fiorenza (Delhi: ISPCK 2008), for some viewpoints in this area.

[123] See Peter Beyer, *Religion and Globalization* (London: Sage Publications, 1997).

[124] *Ibid.*, 80.

[125] *Ibid.*

[126] *Ibid.*, 81.

CHAPTER TWO

The Subaltern Scenario:
Community and Conflicts in Gujarat

2.1 Gazing at 'Gandhi's Gujarat' from Subaltern Perspective

In the past decade or so, Gujarat has been hitting headlines for being a state wherein paradoxes coexist. Earlier, often famously called 'Gandhi's Gujarat' since the *satyagrahi* par excellence Mahatma Gandhi was born and lived here,[1] it is now also infamous among Indian states since the severest forms of violence have occurred in Gujarat in the recent past. Second in India only to the state of Punjab in terms of economic prosperity and per capita income, peace is fragile in Gujarat since violence and bloodshed break out with frightening frequency. In this chapter I take Gujarat as a 'test case' and choose to map the conflicts that subaltern communities face here since Gujarat has been my *karmabhoomi*, the area of my involvement and research with subaltern groups, as mentioned earlier. However, I will also provide parallel examples pertaining to other subaltern groups in India since my observations are not specific only to Gujarat but apply to others as well.

Rather than enumerate and describe the numerous incidents of violence in Gujarat, I look at some of the causes and consequences, and the meanings derived from such conflicts. This will primarily be done from a subaltern perspective and through the prism of 'spatiality', meaning, I will ask: what have been the repercussions of conflict and violence upon the 'space' which subalterns have owned in the past, and are occupying at present? I will basically examine two well-known situations of community conflict, namely: (a) the violence in the tribal Dangs district (1998-9),[2] and (b) the violence connected with the Godhra train burning and subsequent carnage (2002).[3] The subaltern groups that

I focus upon are mainly the adivasis (STs), Dalits (SCs)[4] and minorities (here, the 'religious minorities', especially the Christians and Muslims who were worst affected in the two events, respectively. The members of these three groups very often – though, not always – belong to the 'economically poor' category. A short profile of the socio-cultural-political scenario of Gujarat's subaltern communities will help us understand their context and composition, as well as the causes and the consequences of conflicts they face. Locating these communities in their own geographical and socio-religio-cultural landscapes will perhaps help us to better decipher the influences that have either fostered their growth *as* community, or frustrated it.

2.2 Socio-Politico-Religio-Cultural Profile of Subaltern Communities in Gujarat

According to the 2001 census, out of a total population of 50,671,017, the SCs account for 3,582,715 or 7.1% of the total population while the STs account for 7,481,160 or 14.8%.[5] Nearly one-tenth of the adivasis in India live in Gujarat.[6] Together, the SC and ST communities account for more than one-fifth of the total population of Gujarat. As far as the 'religious minorities' are concerned, Christians number about 0.44% and Muslims 9%,[7] although these groups are not entirely homogenous, just as the label 'Hindu' does not refer to one homogenous group.[8] This is so because, in India, there have been processes of mutation and overlapping of group identities due to several social, economic, religio-cultural and political factors.

Given the fluidity of identities, it is not easy to study the impact of events on any particular community since its borders are porous and rarely clearly defined. However, while we focus on the 'subalterns' as a category, we differentiate among the groups that are included therein. In other words, it is helpful to highlight the commonalities as well as some distinguishing characteristics of groups like Dalits[9] and adivasis, so as to avoid simplistic blurring of differences. Earlier, there were attempts to trace the common ancestral and historical roots of adivasis and Dalits dating back to pre-Aryan times.[10] It is beyond the scope of this book to research the same. Yet, establishing commonality and solidarity among subaltern groups strengthens their efforts at acquiring their rights and asserting their identities.[11] Hence, we now view common features of subaltern groups.

2.2.1 *The Situation of Subordination and the Subaltern Quest for Agency*

The situation of subordination is common to all subaltern groups. The adivasis are exploited by non-adivasis (called *ujjaliyat* in south Gujarat)[12] comprising, initially, the colonizers, and now including traders, moneylenders, landlords and Government officials. For the Dalits, the exploiters are the so-called 'upper castes', collectively called *savarna*. For both, the suppression is structural, and result of centuries of exploitation. As a result, it is difficult to alter the situation of subordination, especially if such change is left to the intervention of outsiders or to the beneficence of the state, since these are often accomplices in the subordinating processes of these weaker communities.[13] Moreover, due to protracted subjugation, the subalterns are usually victims of society. Given the fact of the common 'victimization' of these groups, the difference in the domination arises because adivasis have been outside the pale of caste-structured Hindu society, and hence did not suffer from the cumulative dominance of powerlessness (political), poverty (economic) and debasing 'impure' ritual status (socio-religious) as in the case of Dalits.[14]

Coupled with the aspect of subordination is the contrasting reality of the subalterns' capacity to define their own goals, plan their own strategies and tap their own resources to resist oppression and revolt against their oppressors.[15] This is what Gramsci termed 'contradictory consciousness':[16] a communitarian consciousness that can either challenge the status quo and seek redress, or redefine reality in terms strikingly contrary from the dominant one imposed on them. Thus, although there is an 'imposed social Self' forced upon these communities by the dominant groups, these communities strive for their 'true Self' by asserting their identity and rights in *thirdspace*, i.e., their 'lived space'. These two 'Selfs' exist uneasily with each other,[17] leading to conflict and assertion of subaltern agency. Adivasi assertion, for instance, was evident in the *Devi* movement that united south Gujarat's adivasis cutting across tribes in the 1920s.[18] Of late, there have also been associations to stress the rejuvenation of adivasi culture and self-rule; for example, the *Adivasi Ekta Parishad*,[19] and its offspring the *Gujarat Adijati Vikas Paksh* (GAVP) that was formed on the eve of the 1995 state assembly elections to enhance adivasi representation in the Gujarat Assembly. There is also a *'Jai Adivasi'* movement in south Gujarat that fosters the *'adivasi-ness'* of tribal society, so as to unite all tribals under the *'adivasi'* appellation and to stall the moves of fundamentalist groups keen on breaking up tribal solidarity.

Like the adivasis, the *Vankar* (Dalit)[20] community, too, has been in the forefront of the Dalit struggle in Gujarat.[21]

2.2.2 *The Subaltern Sense of Community, Communion and Solidarity*

The sense of community is strong among subaltern groups not only in Gujarat, but also in many parts of India.[22] Among adivasis, individual identity is not stressed. One attains identity only in relation to one's clan and tribe. Thus, only after the completion of adivasi initiation rites – like the *panchora-vidhi* of Gujarat's Kokanas,[23] the name-giving ceremony of Gujarat's Gamits,[24] the ear-piercing ceremony in Jharkhand or *Cati* among the Mundas – does an infant become member of the tribe. If the infant dies before this, it is not buried in the common burial-ground (grove) for it is considered a stranger.[25] At the initiation rite, the prayer of the *pahan* (priest) too indicates strong community bonding:[26]

> In the shade of the highest god, under the protection of Mother Earth, this child of ours, this offspring of ours, in our brotherhood, in the family of our relatives, s/he will be recognized among them. Till yesterday, s/he was counted outside of us, separate from us. From today onwards, in our group, in the family of relatives, s/he will be included, s/he will be taken into account in hunger, in thirst, in sickness, in misery, the community will be her/his shade, society will be her/his umbrella.

Adivasis understand community neither as a society of many independent individuals nor as a utilitarian association of self-seeking subjects dependent on one another, but as a dynamic *communion* of beings where the internal bonds are seen as vital, indispensable and organic. There is no such thing as absolute independence or absolute primacy of one individual being. The interrelationship is characterized by each being sharing its total self in bringing forth the common good.[27] Indeed, this 'sharing of the self' is characteristic of the tribes of Northeastern India too; for e.g., Mizos have a communitarian, ethical principle termed *Tiawmngaihna*, which literally means, "resistance in being helped by others by helping others who are in need. The emphasis is on a denial of self rather than an effort to be independent."[28] Among Ao Nagas too, a parallel term referring to a social ethic is *Sobaliba*. In Gujarat, there is the *gaav-reet* (literally, 'village way') that is an unwritten ethical code of community life. One must note that, when adivasis refer to 'common good', they are not only referring to the welfare of the human community alone, but also embracing the "organic and egalitarian communion" comprising other visible beings (nature and other creatures, besides human beings) plus invisible beings (ancestors, The Absolute).[29]

Unlike as in tribal society, the Dalit sense of community has, over centuries, been moulded as an antithesis to the dominant castes. Here we have an example of what we have seen as a *politics of space*. Geographically, Dalit settlements in Gujarat – as everywhere in India – are always on the margins of villages, and the borders that demarcate Dalit dwellings are regarded as defiling for the so-called 'upper castes'. Consequently, the 'geo-political' situation of the Dalits living always in close proximity to these so-called 'higher castes' and yet always in subordination to them, renders their identity and sense of dignity weak.[30] Nonetheless, the internal bonds of solidarity among members of particular Dalit groups – that are often the fruit of their subordination – have given rise to a sense of community. Their very socio-cultural discrimination and their eco-political deprivation become sources for establishing solidarity in their struggles for full emancipation.[31]

The subaltern sense of community and concomitant solidarity is not something that is organized, enforced or imposed; it is more instinctive and spontaneous, and to use Tönnies term, a *Gemeinschaft*-type of bonding that animates each and every activity of subaltern communities: birth,[32] marriage,[33] farming,[34] feasting,[35] dancing,[36] fishing and hunting,[37] and death.[38] What is noteworthy in adivasi communitarian activity is that it is always inclusive (among members of the tribe), and special care is taken of the 'weaker ones' like widows, children, women, the handicapped and sick, so that a basic principle of egalitarianism is maintained and the legitimate needs of everyone are adequately met.

2.2.3 Subaltern Religiosity and Communitarian Ethic

On the one hand, it seems inappropriate to discuss subaltern religiosity since, for the subaltern, the 'religious' is not a distinct realm separable from, say, the social, economic, cultural or political realms, but is coterminous with life itself. However, on the other hand, there is a basic substratum of *dharma* not in the sense of doctrine (ideas),[39] but in the sense of a worldview that gives rise to a code of life (ethic) which ensures smooth functioning of subaltern community. This *dharma* – if one might call it that –[40] is fundamentally drawn from the sense of community and the basic relationship and interdependence of all beings.[41] But though there is oneness of everyone and everything, there are three 'levels' of being: first, on the surface, there are visible beings (humans, animals, other created entities), second come the invisible beings (ancestors, benevolent and malevolent spirits) and, thirdly, at the deepest level, is the primordial, as follows:[42]

> For the Mundas, there is a triple world: firstly, our empirical world, secondly, the world beyond perception, and thirdly the primordial world. With our eyes, we see only what is on top: a horizontal picture, the present empirical world. Underneath and coextensive with it, is an invisible one, always in motion, always in action. Further down stands the unchangeable root out of which everything else has grown: this is the primordial.

The three levels or 'triple world' referred to is also seen as 'three dimensions' of communion; for example, the Ho adivasis are bound in: (a) communion with *Singbonga* in terms of grandparent-grandchild, (b) communion with *bongako* [ancestral spirits] and (c) communion with *ote-hasa*, nature.[43] Of these dimensions, two pertain to the invisible world (namely, a and b), and the third pertains to the visible (c). A caution is in order here. When referring to three levels or dimensions, one might conclude that there are degrees of importance ascribed to each level or dimension, for instance, that the primordial is most important and the visible is least important, or communion with *Singbonga* is more important than communion with *ote hasa*. This is quite untrue since adivasis perceive the three levels and dimensions as closely connected; and, actions in each govern the other. Thus, if one considers the 'primordial' to be some supreme deity like *Ucchaliyo-Dev* and *Varle-Dev* (literally, God-above) of Gujarat, or *Dharmes*,[44] *Haram* and *Singbonga* (literally, Sun-Spirit) of Chotanagpur, and asserts: "Nature/human beings (visible) depend on God (primordial)," then, the reverse is also equally true, namely, "God depends on human beings/nature'; for, although *Singbonga* is primordial being, "like a human person he desires, thinks and listens to others; he is perplexed by problems but he succeeds *with the help of others* in solving them in the end."[45]

God or Deity, therefore, is not enthroned in heaven, unconcerned about human life and nature, but is the primordial substratum that supports all, animates all, protects all and is accessible to all in myriad down-to-earth manifestations that can be encountered by adivasis in Gujarat for the following 'life-contexts': in times of sickness, *baliya-dev* (cholera-god), for women's illness during pregnancy, epidemics and untimely death, *mavlima* (mother-goddess); for a good harvest, *kansari-devi* (grain-goddess);

for warding off evil from the village, *dungar-dev* (mountain-god); for protecting the village borders, *simaliya-dev* (boundary-god);[46] for fruitful hunting, *vaag-dev* (tiger-god) and so on.[47]

The myriad manifestations of deity neither require special temples as residence nor fixed formulae from standardized scripture for worship. They can be encountered in groves (*bagaichha*), in forests, amidst waters (e.g., *dev-mogra*, crocodile god), in the fireplace or cattle shed, and even in cremation-grounds. Viewed spatially, the 'sacred geography' of adivasis is not delimited to some temple or shrine, but is coextensive with the village:[48]

> The tribals believe that they are fully surrounded by a number of gods and deities or superpowers residing in all the places where their people are. So the whole tribal village and its vicinity may be treated as the sacred area of the tribal gods and deities. Their gods are not venerated in a particular area of the village but are spread all over the region. Hence the whole tribal village and the hills and forests in its neighbourhood may be taken as one unit as far as the sacred area is concerned.

Due to the interdependency binding (a) the primordial, (b) the ancestral/ spiritual and (c) the natural/human, when one dies, one's soul does not rise to another world or rest in heaven but one remains in communion with the community as spirit. Thus, the *baap-dada* (*bongako*, for Ho adivasis), the ancestral spirits, continue to live on in the community; and, according to the life they led on earth, and the type of death they endured, they are regarded as 'benevolent' and 'malevolent' for the good and evil effects they have on people, respectively. Dalits share a similar worldview, noted by Ilaiah:[49]

> [L]ife after death is not important. If a person lives a socially useful life, it acquires meaning. Death is an end in itself. If someone plays a socially negative role, after death such a person becomes a devil and keeps hanging around troubling others. Thus, the difference between *punyam* and *paapam* is that *punyam* ends life forever, while *paapam* turns a person into a devil. Dalitbahujan castes perform third day and eleventh day ceremonies, but after that the dead people lose their identity. Anniversaries are not celebrated and the identity of the dead person is not retained. All the dead become part of the *peddalu* (elders who have passed away).

The continuity-in-discontinuity aspect of the life-death of subalterns is, once again, consonant with the strong communitarian focus of subaltern communities. Ram Dayal Munda explains, "To act anti-social is to 'sin', to act for the benefit of society is to earn 'merit'. To be social is to enjoy heaven, and to be anti-social is like living in hell."[50] Thus, in Gujarat's Gamit community, sin means breaking the bonds of community; and, in this sense, adivasis consider it sinful to own excess land or to leave their neighbours hungry.[51] Individual offences are not considered as sinful as the ones that affect community: "Getting drunk," for instance, "is no sin since it only affects the drunkard."[52] But, offences against the neighbour – especially those of greed and pride[53] – are deemed grievous. Moreover, since the members of family, clan and tribe are so closely related, the effect of one's sins may fall upon another member of the same family, clan or tribe.

2.2.4 *Subaltern Structures of Governance and Power-Sharing*

Due to the strong bonds of communion of subaltern groups and deep suspicion of outsiders, indigenous administration takes precedence over any superimposed hierarchy of alien politicians, professionals and priests. In Gujarat's subaltern groups – be they adivasi or Dalit – the *panch* acts as administrator of societal structures, animator of community activity and arbitrator of community-conflict. The Gujarati axiom *"Panch, te Parmeshwar,"* meaning, "The *panch* is god!" indicates that *panch* decisions are religiously respected and obeyed. The *panch* comprises of a *sarpanch* (headman) or *karbhari* (administrator), a *patel* (enforcer of law and order),[54] village-elders (*vadils*) and leaders (*agewaans*), and meets in a convenient place where the meeting is open to all, although membership in the *panch* is usually restricted to males. Some villages now have women in the *panch*. There is no hierarchy among members and roles and responsibilities can be changed according to communitarian needs and socio-political circumstances.

The *panch* is powerful, and its jurisdiction is pervasive. Among Gujarat's Gamits and Kokanas, for instance, the *panch* decides the wages of work, the days of work and rest, the areas where community-work must be undertaken, the prices of grain to be sold outside the village, the dates of festivals and marriages, the mode of celebration of all festivals and occasions like birth/marriage/death, the rituals to be performed, the contributions to be collected from families. It also arranges the *sandhalya* (voluntary-work-committee)[55] to offer free service to households that urgently require it but cannot afford to pay wages, and the amounts to be exchanged, should the need for barter of farm produce arise. Besides performing a legislative and executive function, the *panch* also performs a judicial role in settling land-feuds, fixing penalties for dishonouring contracts, settling marriage-disputes, providing compensation for losses and the like.[56]

Deducing from the preceding data and discussion, one might conclude that subaltern groups live in ideal situations of perfect sharing, mutual trust, equality, communion and justice. This is not true; for, although there is strong sense of equality and community, there are also 'inequalities' or 'classes' among Gujarat's adivasis since there are peasants who own large tracts of land, and are likely to further the interests of their own 'class' rather than be concerned about the welfare of poorer adivasis.[57] There is also the issue of the community violating the basic rights of the individual, or, loyalty to community being stressed to such a degree so as to lead to falsehood and hypocrisy.[58]

While communion among members of a clan or tribe is strong, it is also true that such a sense of communion does not always exist among tribes, as, for instance, between the Chaudharis and Vasavis of south Gujarat, where the former implicitly consider themselves superior to the latter, being economically well off. However, we can generally say that, although subaltern groups are animated by noble ideals, there are many factors – both, *intra* and *extra*-communitarian – that disrupt their smooth functioning. The effects of migration and modernity, as well as the evils of caste, have left lethal and lasting wounds in the corporate identity and sense of communion of these communities, as has happened in Gujarat among the communities we are examining.

2.2.5 *The Effect of Migration and Modernity on Subaltern Communities*

Migration and modernity have not been effective processes for furthering the cause of subaltern communities. The *Chhappaniyo* (referring to Vikram Era 1956) or the Great Famine of 1900 still remains a painful remembrance in the collective consciousness of Gujarat.[59] Followed by widespread plague, the *Chhappaniyo* famine led to mass exodus of the rural poor towards the cities. Besides poor rural peasants, many adivasis and Dalits too moved towards the cities in search of employment. At the same time, many Brahmins and Baniyas (traders), as well as Muslims with a trading background – namely, the Bohras, Khojas and Memons – who migrated to cities, began diversifying into modern sectors like commerce, industry and technical education resulting in widespread urbanization. In 1911, less than 20% of the population of Gujarat was concentrated in urban areas. By 1951, 27% of the population was urbanized, of which 36% was concentrated in six cities with population more than 100,000.[60] In 2001, 36% of the Gujarati population was urban, making it one of India's most industrialized states.

Urbanization engendered greater industrialization and created new possibilities in fields like medicine, engineering, agricultural science, pharmacy and banking. The land-owning communities – especially the *Patidars*[61] diversified into these avenues but retained their links with agriculture with the two worlds reinforcing one another. Jain and Vaishnava *Banias* thrived on competition and resolved business conflicts through compromise. While the structure of Gujarati society was feudal, public life and business dealings were governed by the norm: "Conflict is always inauspicious." ("*kajiyanu moh kaalu*").[62] Thus, due to accommodation of mutual business interests in the fields of agriculture and industry, the migrant upper castes and classes were in a position to gain capital out of both, the rural, as well as the urban sectors; but the same cannot be said of the subaltern groups who, largely, could not capitalize from either sector.

Urbanization and industrialization created new wealth and prosperity for some groups in Gujarat's social hierarchy who promoted their own interests amidst stiff competition. Gandhiji warned about the dangers of this capitalist outlook and stressed an ethic based on need, not greed, for promoting the ideal of *sarvodaya* – a reawakening of *all* in society. This didn't happen in Gujarat because of the skewed developmental model adopted at the national level. For example, India's five-year plans – initiated by P.C. Mahalanobis on the behest of Nehru – sought excessive industrialization that, rather than solve economic problems, led to lopsided development, unrest in cities, destruction of village and cottage industries, and massive unemployment. The unemployed flocked to urban centres in search of work, in numbers beyond the industrial and urban capacity to absorb them, heaping misery on the most vulnerable sections of our societies.[63]

In Gujarat, widespread displacement of STs, SCs, and other backward communities led not only to exploitation on the economic front, but also to a fragmentation of subaltern community. It is important to note that the problems of migration were not outcome of industrialization alone, but have also arisen due to depletion of natural resources, deforestation, the construction of big dams, etc., that have always benefited the 'outsider' and never weaker communities *as* community.[64] One cannot naïvely say that modernity was bane to the weak sections of society since many of them benefited on account of education, new social movements, greater awareness, and the possibility to choose from a variety of occupations apart from the trades traditionally forced upon them. Moreover, modernity mitigated the harmful effects of the caste system to some extent due to the anonymity and homogenizing tendencies of the factory system. However, it also had its pitfalls. Indeed, "the path to modernity for the Dalits has been tortuous. Neither the rapid urbanization nor industrialization has made their entry into the modern sector any easier."[65] The Dalit middle class hoped that with economic progress they would enjoy the benefits of modernity and shed their caste labels. This did not occur due to complex caste equations that were influencing Gujarat's political scenario.

2.2.6 *Caste Configurations and Subaltern Mobilisation*

Besides the issues of migration, urbanization and modernity that are important for understanding the tensions existing among diverse communities especially in urban Gujarat, the mobilisation of Gujarati society along caste lines has also created conflict in large areas of Gujarat. Indeed, Gujarat is a highly caste-conscious society, about 35% belonging to the socially, economically and politically powerful upper castes, mainly, the Brahmins, Patels and Banias who, together with the many sub-castes of the Kshatriya group, not only have promoted a *Mahajan* or *Bhadra*[66] culture in big cities like Ahmedabad and Surat,[67] but also own most of the land in the rural areas. These caste groups have zealously safeguarded their own economic interests while also ensuring that no major mobilisation of subaltern groups threatens their power and domination.

There was the mobilisation of Dalits in Gujarat at the dawn of the 20th century due to the influence of the *bhakti* movement, Christian missionaries, and leaders like Ambedkar, Gandhi and Vallabhbhai Patel.[68] However, while Ambedkar sought to strike at the root of the problem, i.e., the inequalities and injustices inherent in the caste (*varna*) system, Gandhi and Patel sought mobilisation of, and help from, the lower castes/classes only for piecemeal projects like protesting oppressive land laws;[69] but, they, in the words of Dhanagare, "did not disturb the traditional social structure. The structural dependence of the lower castes on the superior had not weakened, but on the contrary was reinforced by the Gandhian political ethic."[70] Later, in the 1930s, the Dalit workers were organized under the banner of *Majoor Mahajan*, the first trade union of industrial workers but this mobilisation was not widespread. The post-independence period of Dalit mobilisation centered on issues related to temple, restaurant and public transport entries, land alienation, conversion to Christianity and Buddhism, Dalit literature, reservations, etc. Thus, although successful in earning minor gains within the caste structure, the Dalit movement in Gujarat never succeeded in uniting all the backward castes and classes,[71] for, the upper castes and classes stymied all such attempts at mass mobilisation.

The mobilisation of Gujarat's adivasis too was similar to that of the Dalits. In so-called 'freedom movements' like the Bardoli *satyagraha* and the Dandi March, their help was secured without addressing problems pertaining to their 'true freedom' as regards their socio-economic status.[72] There was also a stream of apparent 'religious mobilisation' in the *Devi* (goddess) movement among south Gujarat's adivasis that provided them with a practical 'political ethic' to fight against their exploitation, especially by the landowners and liquor distillers.[73] Noteworthy in this movement is that the leadership and practices emerged from below. The 'mediums' who went into a trance or became possessed by the *Devi* were ordinary adivasis, both men and women. Moreover, the dictates of the *Devi* (also called *Salahbai*, literally meaning 'advice-woman') during possession related not to values *per se*, but to values *related to power*. In other words, the values that the adivasis endorsed were those of the classes which possessed political power. In acting as they did, the adivasis revealed their understanding of the relationship between values and power.[74] But, this movement too was weakened by Gandhians who, while upholding 'purification' (*shuddikaran*) and adding injunctions like the use of *khadi* and *charkha*-spinning, urged adivasis to continue labouring for their masters.[75] Thus, but for localized tribal struggles that fought for minimum wages, right to forest produce and land occupancy,[76] there was no adivasi struggle in Gujarat mobilizing all the strata of adivasi society.[77]

The first systematic mobilisation of Gujarat's underprivileged groups came in the 1970s with the Congress's *KHAM* (Kshatriya-Harijan-Adivasi-Muslim) combine that, rather than uniting the subalterns along lines that would benefit their cause, forged an alliance along caste-communal lines mainly for political gains.[78] The *KHAM* strategy reaped electoral benefits for the Gujarat Congress in the 1980 Assembly elections, and for the first time the *savarna* (upper) castes sensed a political and economic threat to their domination and felt that their political power was being transferred to the SCs and OBCs. The *savarnas* began blaming their socio-economic and unemployment woes to the 21% reservation for SCs and STs.[79] To offset the apparent gains of the subalterns, the *savarnas* (mainly Brahmins, *Banias* and *Patidars*) agitated against the reservation system in 1981.[80] Another anti-reservation agitation surfaced in 1985;[81] and in both these, the Dalit communities suffered heaviest losses.[82] The *KHAM* combine – disbanded in 1985 – proved not only to be a mirage for socially backward communities, but also became catalyst for forging a *savarna* unity with *Hindutva* as the unifier: "The combined effect of the internal weakness of *KHAM* and the emerging *Hindutva* forces in Gujarat dismantled the *KHAM* that became the victim of both demobilisation and counter-mobilisation."[83]

Hindutva played a vital role in community mobilisation in Gujarat in the late 1980s, and continues to do so till today. On the one hand, the STs, SCs and minorities were becoming increasingly disillusioned with Congress politics, and on the other, the *savarna* Brahmin-*Bania*-*Patidar* combine were seeking a way to consolidate their socio-eco-political hegemony over the masses. It is here that the BJP emerged as a party that could meet the exigencies and expectations of both groups. By appealing to *Hindutva*, the BJP could win over the Dalits and adivasis who were drawn towards *Hindutva* seeing in the ideology a chance to get social acceptance and gain political parity with *savarna* society.[84] *Savarna* society, likewise, saw in the BJP and its politics a ploy for forging a make-believe unity of all castes so as to use SCs, OBCs and adivasis in their campaign against minorities.[85] Shah writes, "The major challenge for the proponents of *Hindutva* is to build unity among all Hindus without disturbing dominance of the upper castes and classes."[86] This has been achieved largely due to mobilisation along religious lines.

The mobilisation of the weaker sections of society was neither the result of deeper political consciousness nor awareness of their rights, but the consequence of a religio-cultural revival – Hindu *Jagruti* (awakening) – through massive deployment of religious symbols: *yatras* (pilgrimages), *karseva* (voluntary service) of carrying bricks from remote Gujarati villages to construct the Ram *janmabhumi* mandir (temple on Lord Ram's birthplace) at Ayodhya,[87] rites involving the use of holy Ganga-*jal* (water from Ganga) and so on. Besides the mobilisation of diverse caste groups into a unity based on *Hindutva*, that was directed against religious minorities, *Hindutva* was also instrumental in dividing the adivasis of south Gujarat where the so-called 'Hindu tribals' were pitted against 'Christian tribals' creating conflicts.[88] *Hindutva* has played a decisive, but divisive, role in reconfiguring Gujarati society along communal lines, which was a root cause in creating the conflicts that we are trying to analyze since these are regarded as 'religious conflicts' and affect the identity and existence of the religious communities – especially the 'religious minorities' like the Muslims and Christians. Let us thus carefully examine the 'fields' wherein conflicts arose and the consequences of such conflicts.

2.3 The Fields of Conflict from Subaltern Perspective

The two conflicts that we are examining – namely, the Dangs events (1998-9) and the 'Gujarat Carnage: 2002' – took place across certain 'fields'[89] that contained their own structures, dynamics, agents and forces that worked together to create conflict. It is not easy to draw clear lines separating the various fields – religio-cultural, socio-political, and economic – in order to map the conflicts. However, aware of overlaps in the fields, we shall examine some of the causes of conflict in the light of the subaltern situation.[90]

2.3.1 *The Debate on Conversions and the Subaltern View of Religion*

The core controversy igniting the Dangs' incidents of violence against Christian tribals was that of conversions. This seems to be the Achilles' heel of all Christian missionary work. It was alleged that, due to the demographic imbalances created on account of 'forced mass conversions' to Christianity, the Hindu majority would soon become a minority.[91] There were also allegations that the adivasis who embraced Christianity were alienated from adivasi culture, despised adivasi religion, divided adivasi community and created tensions leading to the outbreak of violence. The then-PM, A.B. Vajpayee, visited the Dangs in January 1999 and announced a 'national debate on conversions' that evoked opposition. At stake seemed to be an attempt not only to justify the violence, but also to rake up the decades-old controversy traceable to – and apparently resolved by – the Constitutional debates of the Indian Constituent Assembly (1947-9).[92] Much earlier, religious reformers like Swami Vivekananda, Raja Ram Mohan Roy and Gandhiji,[93] had expressed apprehensions about conversions to another religion.

The arguments on either side of the conversions' debate have been widely discussed,[94] and hence, only mentioned here in brief: From the Hindu side, conversions go against the basic religious principles of *dharma* and *karma* and disrupt Hindu society while also feeding the myth that Christianity is superior to Hinduism although it is apparently 'foreign'. The methods used for conversion by missionaries are seen as unfair, coercive, manipulative and even implicitly violent; and, the fact that many 'converts' come from the lower castes and classes implies that such change is more the result of socio-eco-educational benefits arising from conversion rather than true 'internal conversion' or reformation. On the other hand, Christians defend conversions on the basis of 'rights' enshrined in the Constitution, especially the fundamental right to "profess, practise and propagate religion."[95] While maintaining that conversion is a deeply personal, moral, religious choice, Christians also point out that 'propagation' of Christianity belongs to its very essence. Both sides speak of freedom of religion; but, while for the Christians it is the freedom to propagate Christianity and for anyone to accept it, for the Hindus the freedom refers to that of the one receiving propaganda not be converted by unethical means. What is conspicuously absent in these debates is the subalterns' voice itself, and a failure to look at the conversions' issue from the viewpoint of the subaltern communities.

The term 'conversion' itself is contentious in a subaltern context. While subaltern acceptance of Christianity and Islam is termed conversion, the acceptance of Hinduism is termed *gharvapasi* (literally, home-coming) or *shuddhikaran* (ritual purification).[96] Although academics like G.S. Ghurye term adivasis 'Backward Hindus',[97] there are others who consider this categorization faulty since, according to Shah, if Hinduism refers to the *varna-dharma*, Vedic philosophy and ritual (im)purity, then adivasis are certainly not Hindus,[98] but, if it refers merely to a plurality of religious beliefs, worship in different ways to multiple gods and goddesses, nature and spirits, and diverse rituals and beliefs about life and death, then adivasis – especially *Dangis* – could be called Hindu.[99]

From the viewpoint of spatiality, the terms *gharvapasi* and *shuddhikaran* are alien to the subaltern worldview. For an adivasi, every place is sacred. Thus, first, the term home-coming (*ghar-vapasi*) would imply that some members have left the 'home', the adivasi community. This is impossible, since every adivasi always remains a member of her/his tribe no matter what deity s/he worships, and, s/he is always 'at home' in adivasi sacred geography notwithstanding her/his religious affiliation. Second, in subaltern context there is no concept of ritual purity or impurity. Such categories are imposed *from above* – from *varnadharma* – and create nonexistent borders. These are examples of how 'conceived space' produced by ideologues can wield power to cause divisions in the adivasi context and to further fundamentalist and fanatic agenda.

The so-called *gharvapasi* and *shuddhikaran* ceremonies can also be seen as impositions by the way in which they were conducted. In south Gujarat, these rituals were conducted at the *garamkund* (hot-springs) at Unai, in Gujarat's Navsari district with a ritual bathing in the hot-springs, and an investiture ceremony with Hanuman-*chalisa*[100] performed by a Hindu priest. The use of sacred objects, presence of special cultic personnel, performance of purification rites and distribution of religious texts show that what is being undergone is a change of *dharma* (in the sense of organized religion). Thus, from adivasi viewpoint, change of faith to Hinduism,[101] is not different from change of faith to Christianity. Both being equally alien could be called *dharma-parivartan* (change of religion).[102]

Debates on conversion do not take adivasi spatio-temporality seriously, for, there is excessive focus either on a 'before-life' (as in the Hindu claim that conversion disturbs the eternal laws of *karma* and the *rta*: cosmic order) or on 'afterlife' (as in the Christian exclusivist claim of mediating salvation or 'saving souls'). However, there is a marked silence on the importance of the here-and-now, the present space-time for subaltern groups. Here, Ambedkar-inspired movements are vital since their premise for acceptance or rejection of religion is its potentiality to address the questions of 'this-life'. Thus, it is not for the so-called big or classical traditions to judge 'whether' and 'why' a subaltern community 'should' or 'should not' practise a particular religion. The subaltern, evidently, is not just 'victim', but also 'agent'. Gauri Viswanathan expresses this well:[103]

> In believing that conversion to Buddhism would restore to Dalits an agency that untouchability had eroded, Ambedkar brilliantly provided a religious framework for a politics of Dalit renewal. .. Ambedkar's conversion to Buddhism unsettled the complacency of Hindu reformers who believed the initiative for social change lay exclusively with them.

Besides Buddhism, the *bhakti* movements too have revealed subaltern agency in choosing belief-systems and practices that, for instance, are syntheses of Hinduism and Islam. Here too, as Omvedt has shown, the proponents of *Hindutva* "falsify the *bhakti* movement,"[104] and "mask its radicalism" because, "the history, interpretation and institutionalization of the movement has been in upper-caste hands."[105] Shifting the debate to the subaltern terrain is an important step in viewing the dynamics of conversions.

The allegation that the subalterns' choice of a religion is guided not by 'religious' or 'pure' motivations but by eco-socio-political reasons is based on two false premises: first, such thinking represent subalterns as being incapable of rationally and responsibly weighing alternatives regarding their own lives and future; second, it has a dichotomous view of religion itself. As seen earlier, subalterns have *'contradictory consciousness'* and are capable of asserting their agency in matters of choice. It is not for outsiders to judge about how/what they should choose. Moreover, in the subaltern worldview, there is no dichotomy between sacred-secular, this-life and afterlife, and realms like social, economic, political, etc. Such dichotomy is often the outcome of *varna*-ideology that imputes false value to some realms of life and associates certain caste-groups with them; for e.g. Brahmins with the religious realm, *Kshatriyas* with politics, *Banias* with economics and so on. Such dichotomous thinking not only disqualifies the subaltern groups from staking agency and claiming power in the religious, social, economic and political realms, but also disallows the subaltern the freedom of will and autonomy.

Rival interlocutors in the conversion debate do not fully recognize the adivasi sense of community. The Christian argumentation from the point of rights, though acceptable from a legal point of view, is premised on the Enlightenment's stress on individual autonomy. Thus, while the Christianization of some individuals or small groups can be justified on the basis of rights, such Christianization – especially carried out by fundamentalist Christian sects – have fractured the adivasi sense of community. Christianized adivasis, for example, often speak about, and seek, mere otherworld salvation, denounce adivasi culture and adivasi gods as evil, refuse to contribute to and join in adivasi celebrations,[106] condemn the wearing of traditional ornaments and dress, the distilling and drinking of *mahuda*[107] and so on. On the Hindu side too, the building of temples, enforcing of ideas of purity and pollution, establishing of divisions and hierarchy, etc., have also destroyed the sense of equality and communion. Thus, the conflicts and problems arise not because of conversion to another religion (beliefs and rituals) but *conversion to another lifestyle* with an increasing focus on individuals, individualism and denial of community (alien ethic).

In the conversions' debate, subalterns must also seriously contest the distorted picture of religion of the non-subalterns who consider religion as an 'end' and not a 'means' for fostering human life. Thus, attempts to define subalterns as Christians, Hindus, Animists, etc., are all implicitly violent since they are attempts at 'essentialising religion' thereby not recognizing the porous boundaries and the dynamism inherent in *dharma-parivartan*. One of the gains of modernity is the freedom of choice, and it is this freedom that must be guarded by disadvantaged communities for whom religion is coextensive with life itself.[108] Christianity has appealed to certain aspects of tribal life, for e.g., dispelling of fears from malevolent spirits, fostering formal education, health care, group prayer, etc.,[109] and so has been 'added on' to a substratum of primordial adivasi belief. Similarly, Hinduism allows for addition of some gods and goddesses, as well as identification with a power-centre, the *savarnas*. Shedding *adivasiness* in favour of inheriting a so-called *ujjaliyat* identity is one way of attempting to wrest the power that has become increasingly the monopoly of the so-called *ujjaliyats*. Here, Hinduism comes handy. Thus, adivasi ethic can easily accommodate both, Christianity and Hinduism, in varying degrees and can also dispense with them should their adoption prove burdensome.[110] This choice is not one forced upon them by illiteracy, ignorance or poverty, but is freely formed and founded upon the subaltern sense of reason, morality and justice,[111] leading to empowerment,

Based on the preceding reasoning, when assessed from a subaltern perspective of spatiality, the oft-repeated reasons for and against so-called 'conversions' make little sense. The rifts have arisen because of faulty understanding of the adivasi worldview, and misconstrued symbolic boundaries that have created conceptions like *gharvapasi, shuddhikaran* and so on, and divisive spaces like outside/inside and pure/impure. The entire debate must be shifted to the axis of its benefits or losses for subaltern communities *as* community. Beneath and beyond the religious realm, there are more basic factors that we must examine. Indeed, it is often in the area of spatiality that many conflicts arise; since, as we have asserted, the question of 'space' or 'land' is extremely important for the subalterns.

2.3.2 *Jungle-Jal-Jamin and Conflict Between Subalterns and the State*

The adivasi sense of identity and community, we have seen, is inextricably bound to ecology and earth – a relationship with jungle, water (*jal*) and land (*jamin*). Divorced from any one of these, adivasis not only lose their sense of identity but also disintegrate as community. We earlier saw that adivasis understand life as an unbroken communion between three 'levels' or 'dimensions' of being: (a) primordial, (b) ancestral or spiritual, and (c) visible. *Jungle-jal-jamin* belong to the visible world (nature) that are 'means' of life, not ends in themselves. They are regarded as holy and "not the means of production, but the means of livelihood" for adivasis community.[112] Thus, land grabbing, ravaging of forests, building illegal *bunds* (dams) across rivers, privatization of natural resources and ecological exploitation are abominable not merely in monetary or mercantile terms, but are deemed alien in community ethics.[113] A brief note on the allocation and appropriation of these resources in south Gujarat context will help us understand the conflicts involved.

'Dangs' literally means 'forests'. Out of a total area of 1,778 sq. kms., 95% is regarded as forests. Thus, of the total forest area of 1,760 sq. kms. 936 sq. kms. are 'reserved forests' and 824 sq. kms. are 'protected forests'. The tribals are allowed to make use of the 'protected forestlands' for inhabitation and cultivation.[114] For the Dangis, land and forest were shared by all and there was no personal ownership of land till Independence.[115] Shifting cultivation, hunting and collection of forest products were their sources of livelihood. During the 1960s, the Gujarat government carried out a survey of the Dangs with the aim of giving land occupancy deeds to the adivasi cultivators. As a result, 79,913 hectares was classed as 'farmland', which represented 45% of the total area. By 1989-90 'farmland' was further reduced to 61,400 hectares, which is 36% of the area. The 'reserved forests' area is totally under the control of the Government and the Forest Department controls it. Here, the adivasis are not only prohibited from cultivation, but are also not allowed to extract or use any forest products. According to a survey in 1968-9, from 79,409 hectares cultivated by the adivasis, the forest department acquired 21,154 hectares by using all kinds of means for forest plantation.

According to official records, only 30% of adivasi households have been registered as legal cultivators and others live and toil the land without any entitlement. Under the 'protected forests' the Government Forest department carries out plantation work, sometimes on the agricultural land of adivasis by destroying their standing crops.[116] This is being done even by violating a Gujarat High Court order of 1993. Adivasis are frequently harassed and beaten up by Forest Department officials. Thus, instead of owning the land and enjoying the fruit of their labour, adivasis have either become badly paid labourers of the Forest Department or have been forced to migrate to work as sugarcane cutters or casual labourers in the neighbouring Surat and Valsad districts. An incident of injustice was the Inspector General of Forest's (IGF) circular of May 3, 2002, ordering the eviction of all the adivasis who do not have land in their name from the forests. After mass mobilisation of the adivasis by NGOs and many protest rallies, a "Recognition of Forest Rights Bill" was drafted in 2005 for making 1980 the 'cut off' point for transferring forest land to adivasi households for family use.[117] However, till May 2010, except for the drafting of the Bill after many years of protest and struggle, the state has failed in its responsibility to assure south Gujarat adivasis of their legitimate *lived space*. Even worse, not only has it abdicated its duty of protecting the rights of adivasis, but, as the present case indicates, it has assumed the role of victimizer.

In view of the above-mentioned gross violations of the rights of adivasis to land and forests, as well as the atrocities perpetrated by state functionaries, Shah observes:[118]

> The Dangs is in turmoil. During the last three decades the Dangis have been pushed out of their forest-based subsistence economy. ... They are almost debarred from using major and minor forest products. The quantum of forest labour has declined significantly, forcing them to migrate outside to work on low wages and in wretched conditions. ... Various welfare programmes have not taken off the ground. Restlessness among the Dangis has been manifest in various forms, resulting in several agitations. Atrocities against adivasis involving the forest and police departments have increased. Instead of solving their basic issues of survival, the present agitation focusing on Christian missionaries has been fostered from outside, diverting the prevailing tension and dividing the Dangis on religious lines which are a non-issue for the Dangis.

It is clear that while the real problems are socio-economic, as well as a depletion of tribal *lived space*, the religious issue is often raked up and made out to be the most crucial factor in creating conflict. This diffuses attention from real problems faced by the poor.

Besides the problems of jungle and *jamin*, the problem of water resources (*jal*) has never been resolved by the state. The *Sardar Sarovar* Dam has never taken the needs and welfare of the adivasis into consideration.[119] Thus, while the beneficiaries are the business class, both Indian and foreign, the victims are displaced adivasis, struggling close to two decades for their rights. The NBA movement reveals adivasi protest against the state.[120] Chakraborty sees the atrocities against adivasis as a retaliation by the state:[121]

> The movement has enabled the adivasi communities to reinforce their local identities and to rediscover specific histories, languages and regional specifications. The movement has thus rattled the state of Gujarat as well as the Indian state. The elite have now brought out their most lethal weapon – religion. The business classes wanted religious unity between them and the adivasi communities whom they had earlier proselytised. They used the ideology of *Hindutva* to divide the struggling subalterns. The attacks on adivasi communities are an indication of this nexus between the *Hindutva* forces and the business classes.

As if the lessons from the victimization of adivasis have not been learnt, the Gujarat BJP government is keen on building many more dams especially in the Dangs district.

Without entering into further details of the *jungle-jal-jamin* conflicts, we can conclude that conflicts arise due to non-allocation of legitimate space to the adivasis, on the one hand, and, due to unjust appropriation of the same by *ujjaliyats*, on the other. Today, while adivasis suffer due to abuse of the habitat by outsiders, local politicians, Government officials and the state, the socio-economic problems are made out to be a direct result of *dharma-parivartan* or conversions.[122] These allegations are based on a long history of rival groups trying to define nationalism and staking their claims to be the only true, patriotic citizens of the Indian nation. We shall briefly look at this chequered history that has led to much bloodshed in Gujarat, culminating in the 2002 violence that is probably unparalleled in Independent India's history.

2.3.3 *Conflicts Inherent in Nationalism, Communalism and Minorityism*

The train-burning episode at Godhra and the numerous incidents of violence that followed it are well-known and do not require elaboration. The post-Godhra violence has been described not only as a communal riot but variously as a pogrom,[123] holocaust,[124] and genocide.[125] This communal violence has roots in a history spanning over a century. We view this violence from the perspective of the minority Muslim community in Gujarat that suffered most in terms of loss of human lives, crimes against women, damage to property, and what is now considered as *ghettoisation*.[126] For this, we situate the March 2002 violence against the backdrop of communalism and the emerging nationalisms of the past century.

Communalism refers to the ideology that, in Bipan Chandra's words, "assumes that Indian society is divided into religious communities whose interests not only differ but are even opposed to each other. Communalism starts with the belief that in India people can be organized and grouped together for secular, that is, economic and political, as also social and cultural purposes, *only around their religious identities*."[127] Thus, communal ideologues maintain that communal identity and division have always pervaded Indian society, and that by strengthening their 'religious community' over and above other groups, all their eco-socio-political problems will be automatically solved.[128]

The term 'communalism' emerged in the context of the anti-colonial struggle; and thus, 'communal' is inevitably juxtaposed with 'national', and perceived as a threat to 'nationalism';[129] or, as "the Other of nationalism;"[130] for, during the struggle for Independence, "every time the Hindu-Muslim divide surfaced politically it constituted a setback for the national movement and weakened its viable bargaining power."[131] However, there is disagreement about whether communalism and nationalism are radical and moderate tendencies within the same ideology of nationalism, respectively, or whether they differ. Van der Veer perceives them as different in degree within the same spectrum of nationalism, based on pre-colonial notions of religious community,[132] Zavos, however, sees communalism as a simple ideology that regards the non-Self as inimical to the appropriation of political power due to the Self, and, nationalism as a more complex ideology that seeks to construct a community (i.e., a nation) on the basis of a common culture configured by particular notions.[133] Communalism,[134] as well as nationalism,[135] can be of many forms and can well be spoken of in the plural. Nonetheless, we only deal with Hindu-Muslim communalism; and, will take 'Hindu nationalism' to be the complex 'ideology'[136] with roots traceable to the period of the close of the 19th century.

To maintain, as the proponents of *Hindutva* do, that some 'Indian nation' has existed for centuries, is to endorse what Anderson and Kaviraj term *'imagined community'*.[137] Such conceptions have emerged partly due to the fact that colonial historians like James Mill naïvely periodised Indian history in terms of Hindu civilization, Muslim civilization and the British period, which makes it convenient for *Hindutva* ideologues to conclude that the latter two were instrumental in destroying an ancient 'golden Hindu epoch'.[138] Contesting this view, Thapar shows that community configurations and cohesion were determined by location, language, occupation and caste, none of which were necessarily bound together by a common religious identity.[139] However, towards the end of the 19th century, two streams of what might be called 'national consciousness' were slowly emerging in colonial India: first, with the birth and growth of the Indian National Congress in 1885, second, with the Hindu revival movement led by the Arya Samaj and religious reformers like Tilak, Aurobindo and others who began mobilizing people along cultural-religious lines.[140] Common to both these strands of nationalism was the fact that the upper castes and classes governed them and gave them direction while the concerns and contributions of other groups went unrecognized and unrecorded by the mainstream.

The political developments in the late 19th and early 20th century seem to be catalysts for the creation of communal consciousness in the context of nationalism. With the decennial 'All India Census' instituted in 1871, the problem of enumerating the population in calculable categories arose. Attempts to gain a clearer picture of religious affiliation in the 1881 census met with failure, since, in the enumerators' schedules where 'religion' should have been entered, there were entries regarding castes, tribes and sects, but no known religion.[141] This nebulosity led the colonial administration to gradually consider 'Hindus' as that category identifiable with what was 'non-Muslim' and 'non-Christian'.[142] Later, through the 1909 Morley-Minto reforms, by the institution of exclusive Muslim colleges in the electorate for provincial legislative councils, the colonial state explicitly affirmed the recognition of a Muslim community, and in doing so also implicitly affirmed the recognition of a Hindu community.[143]

The 1907 split in the Congress saw rival factions, namely, the moderates (G.K. Gokhale and others) and the extremists (Aurobindo Ghose of Bengal, B.G. Tilak of Maharashtra and others) operating on the same discursive terrain of middle class consciousness, and addressing the same central question of how 'the people' should be represented in relation to the state. While the former represented nationalism in political terms, the latter perceived it in cultural-religious terms, which began to be codified in the 1920s through the Hindu Sabha and the efforts and writings of V.D. Savarkar, Lala Lal Chand, Swami Shraddhanand and Lajpat Rai.[144] This stream of national consciousness criticized the impotency of Congress moderatism and its ideals of composite nationhood and sought to create a Hindu community, an organizational *sangathan* (unity), to safeguard Hindu interests. Thus, it sought to 'organize' itself within the disorganization of what was being considered 'Hindu' by the colonial state, the census and the various strands of religiosity and sacred texts it could accommodate.[145] Movements like the cow protection of the early 1890s and bodies like the Hindu Mahasabha and the RSS facilitated such organization.[146]

The success of mobilisation of the people along communal lines largely depended on the presence of an 'Other',[147] made out to be the Muslim, whose cause, prior to Independence, was taken up by Jinnah and the Muslim League, but with no tangible benefits for the common Muslim.[148] In its Ahmedabad session of 1937, the Hindu Mahasabha endorsed Jinnah's two-nation theory,[149] for, it dovetailed with both, its own communal politics, as well as its programme of representing the presence of Muslims in India as inimical to the welfare of the Hindu nation. The Hindu-Muslim partition riots were so cataclysmic that it was difficult for Muslims to play the same role in politics as they did before partition. They maintained a low-key looking to the Congress to insure their safety and well being.[150] That the Congress, and later, in particular, Indira Gandhi used the Muslims – as well as the SCs and STs – of Gujarat for her own political mileage cannot be denied.[151] The 1969 communal riots in Gujarat sent shock waves throughout India, and this was followed by the *Jan Sangh's*[152] December 1969 resolution in Patna for the 'Indianisation of Muslims'.[153] This lent credence to the critique that Muslim loyalty lay outside India, i.e., in Pakistan; and to heighten conflict, Gujarat's proximity to Pakistan made it easier to propagate and perpetuate such prevarications and prejudices.

We have earlier discussed the failure of the Congress with regard to its *KHAM* mobilisation of the disadvantaged groups. However, while the first three groups were being absorbed into *Hindutva* politics, the Muslims were not only being steadily marginalized from mainline politics, but were being made scapegoats and represented as the cause for all societal problems: the inimical 'other'.[154] As pointed out by P.R. Ram:[155]

> In Gujarat, one can clearly see the social functionality of creating the 'other' (Muslim). Here earlier the ultimate object of hate was the Dalit, by a clever manoeuvre, the Muslim is substituted for that, the Dalit is unleashed upon the 'other', a [sic] atmosphere of terror is created, which helps to maintain a 'status quo' of social hierarchy.

The demonising[156] of Muslims was the underside of a more proactive campaign to induce spatiotemporal specificity into *Hindutva*'s nationalist movement.[157] The symbolisms of the popular TV serials *Mahabharata* and *Ramayana*,[158] fresh in the late 1980s' religious consciousness of people, were manipulated and gave an impetus to a mass movement that cut across divides of urban-rural, castes, sects, languages, etc. L.K. Advani's *rath yatra*, flagged off from Somnath in Gujarat and culminating in Ayodhya,[159] made the Ram *mandir* controversy in Ayodhya serve the *Hindutva* nationalist cause in two ways: first, it historicized Lord Ram and gave to Hindu nationalism geographical location for forging a unity and asserting its pride; second, it also wrecked historical vengeance for a 'Muslim wrong'. Concealing the real socio-politico-economic and educational situation of the Muslims as minority, poor, politically insignificant and unthreatening,[160] the *rath*'s rhetoric projected the Muslims as the progeny of Babar, Akbar and Aurangzeb. In the ensuing violence, Gujarat came second with 26 riots and 99 people dead in just 2 months (after U.P. with 28 riots and 224 dead),[161] and violence against the Muslim minority was already assuming fearful forms like murder, rape, looting and destruction of property.[162]

The demolition of the Babri *masjid* in December 1992 became a symbolic landmark and victory for *Hindutva* pride and the subsequent propagation of its agenda. The success of Hindu nationalism was that it succeeded in mounting a multi-pronged assault by, on the one hand, working within the democratic spaces and political processes of the country as evidenced by the spectacular success of the BJP in Gujarat,[163] and on the other, by redefining the nation and nationhood in representations that hardly left any civil space unaffected. The broad base of organizational capacity of the various associates of the Sangh Parivar – for e.g., the RSS (cultural) and *Rashtrasevika Samiti* (women's wing), the VHP (religious), the ABVP (educational), the SJM (economic), the VVS (for adivasis)[164] and so on –

besides allowing for an infiltration of all sectors of society, also provided space for fluidity in fixing frontiers, mounting offensives, arranging defence, etc. As a result of this majoritarian agenda, the Muslim community was internalizing a 'minority' identity which, when seen in the larger socio-political landscape of Gujarat can be termed *'minorityism'*.[165] *Minorityism* of the religious minorities can largely be blamed on the fundamentalist forces in India who hijacked the nationalist movement to serve their own interests. The consequences were severe for the minorities.

2.4 The Consequences of Conflict on Subaltern Communities

Rather than deal with physical or quantifiable consequences in the form of number of deaths, rapes, property destroyed, etc., we deal with the communitarian, socio-cultural and political consequences of the two events, namely, the Dangs' and post-Godhra violence on subaltern groups. From the 'fields' of conflict above, it seems that weaker communities are being subjected to twin processes of: (a) inclusion-assimilation and (b) exclusion-aggression in the nationalist discourse that, we shall now discuss.

2.4.1 The Politics of Inclusion: Ascribed Assimilation

By creating boundaries – geographical and symbolic – the state, its functionaries and its organizations delimit zones of inclusion and exclusion. The space of inclusion draws a border beyond which is the 'non-included' or excluded. This latter space becomes the area of danger, mistrust, fear, defilement and, sometimes, of violence.[166] Conceptions like *Hindu Rashtra* might seem to be 'inclusive' because 'Hindu' was earlier understood as either the appellation of the peoples beyond the Indus River (geographical),[167] or a culture that was expressive of the many peoples and traditions that embraced what is today 'India' (cultural). Thus, on the basis of this geographical or cultural typology, many Indians would not have objected to being called *Hindu* even two decades ago. However, as the appellation is now identified only with religious overtones, many Indians do not accept the term as being purely 'cultural'.[168] Thus, today, Buddhists, Jains, Sikhs,[169] Muslims and Christians hesitate to use a prefix like 'Hindu-Buddhist' or 'Hindu-Christian'. The problem is more acute when it comes to the adivasis and Dalits.

The inclusion of adivasis into a nationalist framework is problematic. This is clear, for example, in the case of Northeast tribals who belong to a different Mongoloid ethnic stock and do not identify themselves with the so-called 'mainland'.[170] But, in Gujarat, the adivasis growth *as* community depends upon their hold over the *jungle-jamin-jal* – 'lived space' – ownership over which can be established if it can be shown that they occupied the forest and neighbouring land before the arrival of any other group. In this regard, the *adi-vasi* appellation (literally, original inhabitant) protects adivasi right over land and forests.[171] But, in Hindu nationalist discourse there is neither acceptance of the adivasi right to land nor appreciation of the ancient value of adivasi culture. Adivasis are simply identified as *van-vasis* (forest dwellers)[172] and enumerated as 'Hindu' thereby undermining the adivasis' right to choose and practise their own indigenous religion and also to stake their claims to the land they have long inhabited.. Indeed, as Devy argues, "The *adivasi-ness* of the tribals is a serious threat to *Hindutva.*"[173]

The assimilation of subaltern groups into a dominant group could be termed an 'ascribed assimilation' since the latter inevitably defines subaltern communities, demarcates their territory, positions them within hierarchies, and dictates terms upon which their life must be lived. This is the 'conceived space' where power rests with the dominant group. The freedom of self-definition is denied to subordinated groups and they are made to conform to a socio-religio-cultural ethos that is alien to them. Take, for e.g., the term *vanvasi* which, besides meaning forest-dweller is also translated as *jungli*, a derogatory label implying that adivasis are uncivilized and primitive, and thus, on the one hand, are not intelligent enough to choose what is vital for their existence, and, on the other, require to be 'civilized' by outside intervention. Such intervention has been in the form of Christian missionaries too, who might think that they are indispensable for 'civilizing' backward peoples. We note that, the very group that randomly defines others does not define itself, as evident in the writings of *Hindutva* ideologues.[174] This allows for fluidity at the frontiers and facilitates easy absorption of other groups who are defined and relegated to performing secondary roles within a 'dominant-subordinate' framework.

State apparatuses like the census, too, which are supposed to be enumerative tools to facilitate Government policies, have become instruments of oppression since they incite communal passions by arbitrary categorization.[175] The colonial census was responsible for creating communal identity. And, the fundamentalist forces that fostered a communal, nationalist agenda knew the power of the census and warned:[176]

> There is one point on which we have to be specially forewarned. And that is the census .. The Hindus should not remain ignorant of the potency of numbers ... Further, all Hindus, to whatever sect, caste, clan, or tribe they may belong, must put down their community as 'Hindu' only.

In the forthcoming 2011 census, too, it is unfortunate that adivasi indigenous religion is blatantly being blotted out and all adivasis are being enumerated as 'Hindus'. The motive behind assimilation of castes and tribes does not seem to be the welfare of the weaker communities in terms of providing them their legitimate space, fostering equality, solidarity or assuring them of a better life and future, but ultimately to avail of the political benefits that accrue from the 'power of numbers' that, understandably, is vital in any democratic setup. This was also the case of the *KHAM* combine that did not benefit any of the assimilated groups but assured the Congress of electoral gains.

Ascribed assimilation also affects the religious practice of Gujarat's adivasis. In the aftermath of the Dangs' conflict, besides the *shuddhikaran* and *gharvapasi* ceremonies mentioned earlier, the enforcement of Hanuman as the adivasi *ishtadeva* (main deity) with indoctrination ceremonies and Hanuman *mandirs* also seemed to be a case of providing a 'lesser god' to a 'lesser people'.[177] While there is no difficulty in adding Hanuman to the galaxy of tribal gods, the way in which such practices are undertaken harms the adivasi sense of freedom. Nonetheless, there are the 'counter spaces' of resistance; and, the adivasis "do not feel comfortable in calling themselves *vanvasis*. The VSS and BJP have achieved a measure of success in providing the tribals a political agenda of hatred, but they have not succeeded in changing the tribal sense of identity."[178] This is due to the fact that adivasi sense of community is strong and though victimized, they retain their agency and resistance despite the pressures of ascribed assimilation.

2.4.2 *The Politics of Exclusion: Alienation and Aggression*

'Non-inclusion' or exclusion is the other side of the process of assimilation. The failure to assimilate weaker groups into majoritarian agenda,[179] or the expediency to sideline such groups, leads to a 'politics of exclusion'. This was evident in Fascism, Nazism, and earlier in India in the exclusionary tactics adopted against the Sikhs in the mid-1980s. The anti-Muslim campaign in Gujarat since the late 1960s,[180] particularly after the demolition of the Babri *masjid* and 2002 carnage, resembles Fascism,[181] and has led to ghettoisation of the Muslim community. Let us look at the implications of the 2002 violence from the perspective of the spatiality of Gujarat's Muslim community.

The *Hindu Rashtra* denies the Muslim community any share in the nationalist project; since, to be included, one must not only have India as birthplace (*janmabhoomi*), but must also revere India as one's 'holy land' (*punyabhoomi* or *pitrubhoomi*). Hindu nationalists stressed the primacy of territoriality for nationalism and established that this was to be exclusively identified with *Hindutva*.[182] They concentrated on the 'inner border' of community that engendered deep internal feelings of pride, patriotism, and readiness to die for the *pitrubhoomi*; in opposition to these were "internal threats"[183] of "enemies and invaders".[184] The "spirit of national oneness was ingrained in the blood of every Hindu from the womb itself."[185] Thus, those who did fulfill these conditions "fall out of the pale of National Life" and they "deserve no privileges, far less any preferential treatment, not even citizen rights."[186] These discourses fuel hatred against non-Hindus.

Latent in all the nationalist discourses is the need for discipline, organization, *Semitisation* of Hinduism and power, especially political power,[187] for the furtherance of the nationalist cause.[188] These discourses have created what Deshpande has termed as 'hegemonic spatial strategies'.[189] These are strategies built with the awareness that "social space is not merely an arena *in which* power relations 'happen', but also one of the means *with which* power is sought to be exercised."[190] Thus, power is being exercised to take control over the nation-space.

The roots of conflict, then, are already present in the founding texts of *Hindutva* nationalism. Gujarat Muslims are victims of its exclusionary politics. Problems of urbanization, economic progress of Muslims, unemployment among youth, failure of trade unions, manipulation by political parties, dereliction of duty by the state, the declining role of civil society and the middle-classes' new found identity in *Hindutva* are precipitating causes of violence. As a result, cities in Gujarat, especially Ahmedabad, are divided along communal lines, and there are hardly any 'mixed areas' with the two communities living peaceably side-by-side.[191]

The 'perceived space' of Ahmedabad, today, maps a Hindu-Muslim divide. River Sabarmati divides the East of Ahmedabad with its slums, crowds, small-industries, the 'walled city' and Muslim areas – called 'Mini Pakistan' – from the Western part with its big buildings, shopping malls, recreational facilities, etc. Mahadevia observes, "The process of exclusion starts from the segmented city structure, which was earlier segmented on the basis of class but now on the basis of religion."[192]

The process of ghettoisation in Ahmedabad has taken place in two stages: first, at the level of neighbourhood, people of the same community began living together to get a sense of security; second, members of the minority Muslim community were driven out of localities in which they had lived for generations.[193] Spatially this can be construed as a case where the 'Other' is wiped off the landscape and is constructed "as having neither name nor face and becomes demonized as an anti-social, criminal underclass that cannot be accepted as part and parcel of mainstream society." Breman sees this as 'Social Darwinism' and writes, "The end of *Hindutva* politics of exclusion is not yet in sight."[194]

The ghettoisation of Gujarat's Muslims not only pertains to housing, but also to business establishments that were systematically targeted. Pamphlets were distributed calling for a total boycott of Muslim shopkeepers, restaurants, teachers, film actors and so forth. Muslim children too were not spared from segregation: "Parents are being told by school officials to remove their children from these (English medium) schools on the grounds that their safety could not be guaranteed. Such tactics help to ensure that Muslim children are confined to *madrasas*, or Muslim-run schools, where education is in Hindi or Urdu – limiting severely the students' career prospects."[195] The state of the Muslim community is summed up in this Human Rights Watch Report titled "Ghettoization":[196]

> Successive episodes of Hindu-Muslim violence in Gujarat (in 1969, 1985, 1989, 1990, and 1992) have resulted in the increasing ghettoization of the state's Muslim community. The pattern is now reinforcing itself as Muslim residents once again look for safety in numbers and refuse to return to what is left of their residences alongside Hindu neighbors. The reconstruction of homes has largely taken place along communal lines. Muslims cannot work, reside, or send their children to schools in Hindu dominated localities. As the segregation of communities continues, hope for community dialogue or reconciliation has dissipated.

Beyond the geographical ghettoisation of the Muslim minority, there is the symbolic construction of community that defines borders. Social psychologists like Kakar explain the processes of exclusion through the psychological mechanisms of 'introjection' (of what is considered the 'pure We') and demonization (of what is the 'defiling Other').[197] Such processes aid the formation of communities and delineate the clear boundaries of social intercourse. All that is 'good' and 'desirable' is identified with the members of one's own community and whatever is bad within oneself is projected onto the 'Other' who is then represented as bad, dirty, licentious, drunken, etc.[198] In sum, what Jung has called the 'personal shadow' is projected onto the Other. Gandhy claims that, "all nations need 'Shadow Brothers'",[199] and the Muslims were made out to be the 'shadow' of the Hindus.[200] The problem became acute, however, when the 'community feeling' got translated into 'communal feeling' and led to the unleashing of violence.

One final point that requires comment in this politics of exclusion is that the state and its functionaries were not only unable to protect the minorities, but were also named as accomplices in the violence, bloodshed and destruction of property. This was not only the allegation made by victims, but also by members of the majority group, as well as investigators covering the violence.[201] But, we must also note that the interest of political parties and state governments, as well as electoral possibilities and minority-manipulation have always been factors that have influenced riots in post-Independent India, especially in Gujarat. But, the end-result is the same, "the minorities suffer disproportionately."[202]

2.4.3 Subaltern Instrumentalization and Agency

The incidents of violence discussed above were unique in the sense that there was reportedly large-scale involvement of the subaltern groups for the first time in the history of Gujarat, for e.g., in the Dangs' incidents it was assumed that conversions had caused a split in adivasi society with Christianized adivasis attacking Hinduized adivasis, and, in the 2002 events it was alleged that the STs and SCs had finally realized the dangers that Muslims posed to national integration and thus took up arms to attack them.[203] Such claims require verification with finer divisions as to the nature of violence and the actors involved. Shah divides these into four groups:[204] (a) the 'organizers' who meticulously prepare plans and evolve strategies but may not be present at the site of violence, (b) the 'skilled executors' who have mastered the craft of breaking shutters, destroying walls, setting fire with petrol, kerosene, gas-cylinders and so on, (c) the 'provocateurs' who spread rumours, shout slogans, instigate and direct the mobs, and (d) the 'mobs' who in communally charged atmosphere resort to violence depending on whether the state enforces law and order or not.

There has been, to some extent, polarization of adivasi society by Christianization and Hinduization of the Dangi adivasis.[205] This is because, as mentioned earlier, of the failure of fundamentalist Christian groups to respect adivasi culture and traditions, as well as of fanatic Hindu groups' interventions in adivasi society. However, earlier, this religious polarization never led to widespread violence except when there was intervention from 'outsiders'. In the Dangs, part of the violence can be attributed to the adivasi mobs. But, the 'organizers' and 'provocateurs' were outsiders, especially the VHP, SJM and Bajrang Dal. The Christmas Day rally and violence was meticulously planned with distribution of incendiary pamphlets and speeches.[206] Witnesses mentioned that the violence was the "creation of politics" with the rampaging mobs "coming from outside at night."[207] Thus, there was more an 'instrumentalization' of the adivasis by politicians who wanted to shift focus from their failures at the socio-economic level by raising the conversions' bogey.[208]

The violence against the Muslim community in 2002 was more organized and lethal involving all the four above-mentioned groups, and, the stage had been set over the years with anti-Muslim propaganda systematically fed to all sections of society. A majority of the 'organizers' were Brahmins.[209] The 'skilled executors' were hardened *Hindutvavadis* who can be compared "to Muslim terrorists or Christian fundamentalists. For them, their caste or other identity is not important, though it would seem that the majority of them belong to upper and middle castes."[210] The 'provocateurs' were activists of the *Sangh Parivar* accompanied at times by professionals like doctors and advocates, social activists and active members of the *Parivar*.[211] The 'mobs' were disparate groups who belonged to all castes and classes and very often "were encouraged by police for looting at several places."[212] Many of those in the mob did not know where Godhra was and what exactly had happened; and, post-violence, many were shocked that so many Muslims were killed. TV transmitted scenes of well-to-do citizenry of Ahmedabad – many of them upper class and caste women – who came in cars to carry home what was looted from Muslim shops that were broken into.[213] Dipankar Gupta uses the term 'picnic rioting' to describe the manner in which Hindu mobs celebrated the killing of Muslims.[214]

Seen from the perspective of the disprivileged groups, the violence of 2002 has seen a fairly large mobilisation of SCs and STs,[215] certainly not as the 'organizers' or 'skilled executors' of the carnage, and perhaps not even in large numbers as 'provocateurs', but as 'mobs'[216] "fed on a politics of hatred."[217] The 'agency' of subaltern groups seemed absent, and the preceding rituals of distributing *trishuls* by the VHP and Bajrang Dal to the subaltern youth in Gujarat only served the vested interests of these groups and the state. Ilaiah sees this as a ploy to keep subaltern youth away from books, education and knowledge, which will bring them true awareness and empowerment. He considers this as "an attempt to build muscle power around the oppressed communities to use in the cause of Brahmanism," and adds, "Youth belonging to the SCs, STs and OBCs have been brutalised, and their humanity suppressed, by their having been used as muscle power; considered good only for using weapons."[218]

When speaking of 'brutalisation" of subaltern communities, the role of, and effects on, women – both, subaltern and of other classes/castes – need mention. The dehumanisation of many women in Gujarat was revealed when they sympathized with the *Hindutva* cause and identified with majoritarianism[219] rather than empathize with their Muslim sisters who were raped and burned.[220] From subaltern perspective, the violence on women has been unprecedented,[221] and there are deep feelings of shock, outrage and shame, nationwide, about what happened. The incidents of stripping women, raping them, removing and burning of foetuses, etc., besides being indicative of the animality that accompanies mindless communal violence, also suggests 'symbolic violence' on the bodies of minority women. On the one hand, there was shame and speechlessness in the testimonies of victimized women,[222] and, on the other, "it had taken the form of Everywoman's narrative. Women wanted to talk to anyone who was prepared to listen" to them.[223] Despite such gross forms of violence, collapse of social systems and all democratic norms, even now, after many years of investigations and reports, nothing has been done to punish the guilty and restore some sense of confidence among Muslims.[224]

2.5 Making Meaning of Conflict from Subaltern Perspective

Having examined the causes and consequences of conflict, we now ascertain what 'meaning' they carry for subalterns from the viewpoint of community. We shall do this by examining the meaning of conflicts from the prism of 'commonalties' discussed in the first chapter – i.e., those based on (a) geographical location, (b) symbolic interactions, (c) characteristics, and (d) interests – against the larger framework of spatiality.

2.5.1 *Geographical Location and Relocation of Subaltern Communities*

The preceding discussions reveal that social conflicts adversely affect the geographical location or spatiality of Gujarat's weaker communities. By virtue of their *adivasi* identity, adivasis should rightfully stake claims over the *jungle-jal-jamin* that they have lived in communion with over centuries, and have transformed by virtue of their non-acquisitive ethos and natural bonding with the earth. However, either by abrogating adivasi rights to land and forest, or by displacing them from their traditional habitats for the SSP and other developmental projects, they are not only denied their rights as equal citizens of the country, but pushed towards extinction *as* community.

The adivasis of Gujarat, today, still struggle to maintain their rooting in, and relationship with, the land and all its resources. The *vanvasi* (forest-dweller) label imposed upon adivasi community is another dislocation that sounds innocuous but which is employed with insidious intent. First and foremost, even though adivasis are referred to as *vanvasis*, they do not own the forests they live in and the land they work upon. Second, by negating the *adivasiness* of adivasis, there is a distortion of history because, in that case, the 'Aryan invasion' theory gets refuted and the proponents of *Hindutva* can legitimize their claims to being the original residents of the land, and consequently, the privileged ones of the Indian nation.

Assessing the conflicts of 2002, the relocation of the Muslim religious minority in the *Hindutva* spatial schema is unjust. In terms of the *Hindu Rashtra*, the religious minorities are, at best, second grade citizens, and at worst, depicted as being inimical to the nationalist cause, and thus, dispensable for the birth of a new, glorious nation. The ghettoisation of Muslims in Gujarat is a clear sign of this possibility. One can say that the subaltern groups are geographically, quite literally, 'marginal' in the nation-space.

2.5.2 *Symbolic Violence and Symbolic Construction of Community*

We saw earlier how community is constructed by symbolic interactions. Cohen explains how symbol, culture and community are related;[225] and,

Lefebvre shows how the 'conceived space' of scientists, semioticians, planners and ideologues is the 'dominant space' that wields great power. Those who control symbolisms and produce ideas in society, to use Bourdieu's terms, have the "language of power and the power of language,"[226] which can lead to what he terms 'symbolic violence'.[227] In the next chapter, we shall discuss the dynamics of symbolisation and its inherent power. But, the question remains whether, and to what extent, weaker groups have the power to *produce space*.

The conceptualizing of Indian society is almost exclusively done by the upper castes and classes while the others are kept content with paltry economic packages. Ilaiah stresses that what subalterns need instead is, "a philosophical self-image and discourse of their own,"[228] and an awareness of how the culture of the dominant classes and castes creates a "fictitious integration of society as a whole" and a "false consciousness" among subalterns thereby legitimizing the established order.[229] For e.g., the *Hindu Rashtra* is being symbolized as coterminous with the geographical spatiality of India. Likewise, *Ram Rajya* is a mythical construct that has, in the Ayodhya context, been given historicity and made symbol of a glorious nation with an undivided history. This causes problems: first, *Ram Rajya* is not a univocal concept since there are many diverse and often divergent narratives around Rama and the Râmâyana,[230] including what might be called 'subaltern readings' where Rama is the anti-hero judged by subaltern ethos;[231] second, it has engendered symbolisms ranging from the religio-cultural to the violent that can be manipulated by groups with vested interests against weaker communities.[232]

As opposed to the spatial strategy of Hindutva, termed *Hinduization*, there is need for *Dalitization*[233]as 'counter conceived space' that would lead to the empowerment of disprivileged groups. Thus, instead of being assimilated into *Rashtra*-space that is oppressive and exclusionary, subalterns need to stress their 'local space' as an epistemological 'centre' that can provide larger society with communitarian ideals:[234]

> *Dalitization* requires that the whole of Indian society learns form the *Dalitwaadas* ... It requires that we look at the *Dalitwaadas* in order to acquire a new consciousness. It requires that we attend to life in these *waadas*; that we appreciate what is positive, what is human and what can be extended from *Dalitwaadas* to the whole society.

Beyond extreme physical violence, the post-Godhra violence on Muslim women, too, can also be seen as 'symbolic violence' because they were symbolically constructed as "historical bodies" and "alien bodies, out of place" in "our territory". Behind the rapes, burning of foetuses and brutalizing of women's bodies, there was also intent – conscious or unconscious – of punishing the Muslim male-stereotype as being excessively sexually oriented (four wives, many children, easy divorces, etc.).[235] Thus, the 'weaker sex' of the minorities, too, has been subjected to great violence, both physical and symbolic.

2.5.3 *Contestation of Nationalism Based on Characteristics and Interests*

We mentioned that communities are formed on the basis of characteristics – inherent, imputed and imbibed, as for example, the racial divide between STs and other Indians, or the man-made distinctions between castes (SCs and OBCs), or the differences in class, respectively. In forging nationalisms based on inherent/imputed characteristics, or along religio-cultural affiliations, problems are bound to arise, as borne out by world history,[236] because processes of inclusion and exclusion – often accompanied by violence – are the only ways of forming such nations. Gujarat too has shown how the *Parivar* has destroyed national amity by its processes of inclusion, exclusion and ghettoisation:[237]

> [I]n the process of mobilizing Dalits and Adivasis in this manner, the VHP is successfully accomplishing its other, more central agenda, which is to homogenize culture and Hinduise it. Thus obliterating the identity and individuality of the Dalits and Adivasis, situating them firmly in the lowest rung of the Hindu hierarchy. This is compounded by the fact of their illiteracy, poverty and unemployment and their consequent inability to comprehend in any depth the process that they are being co-opted into Hindu fold, and Muslims in this manner are wiped out by their elimination through genocide.

As regards 'interests', there is hardly any attempt to further the interests of the subaltern groups. In the spread of religio-cultural nationalism and political mobilisation like *KHAM*, subaltern groups were co-opted because of their susceptibility to manipulation during elections. Fuelled by communal propaganda of the 2002-carnage, the success of the BJP at the December-2002 state Assembly elections was a reminder that communalism could effectively be used to divide peoples. Moreover, five years later, in the 2007 Gujarat Legislative Assembly elections, the BJP won 117 out of 182 seats, this being the fourth consecutive electoral victory for the BJP in Gujarat. While election promises focus on a strong economy and prosperity for all, the socio-religious conflicts remain unresolved with great detriment to the weaker communities and tangible gains for the parties that engineer the conflicts and divide communities.[238]

2.6 Conclusion: Broken and Bleeding, but not Crushed

To decipher the dynamics of conflict enmeshing subaltern communities, we have examined two conflicts that have arisen in Gujarat. This has been undertaken in subaltern perspective, i.e., keeping in mind the causes and consequences of these conflicts on groups like the adivasis (STs), Dalits (SCs) and minorities, and within the theoretical framework of spatiality. To better understand the conflict-in-context, we mapped the socio-religio-cultural-political world of Gujarat's subalterns, focusing on the subaltern religio-cultural ethos, their sense of solidarity and communion, and the structures governing community life. Next, we discussed factors that have displaced subaltern communities from their traditional habitat, especially migration, modernity and the mobilizations based on caste and other factors.

We have discussed the fields within which conflicts arose, for e.g., the conversions' issue that allegedly caused the Dangs' disturbances. Here, we addressed the related issue of adivasi relationship with *jungle-jal-jamin*, and saw how the state has often failed to insure basic rights of land-ownership for adivasis, and how its role in the Gujarat carnage was dubious. While the Dangs' issue was discussed against the larger backdrop of the situation of south Gujarat's adivasis, the 2002-violence on the minority Muslim community was placed in the context of the emerging ideologies of 19th century communalism and nationalism that influenced the shaping of independent India and also provided space for the growth of *Hindutva* nationalist ideology that has succeeded to some extent in marginalizing minorities and manipulating other disadvantaged groups.

We have also examined the consequences of conflict for the subalterns from the viewpoint of spatiality – the twin processes of inclusion and exclusion that are inimical to the formation of subaltern communities – and seen how the instrumentality of the weaker sections takes place to foster the agenda of the elite and powerful groups. Finally, we moved to the level of 'meaning' where we critically examined what meaning the situations of conflict held for subaltern communities in terms of their geographical location and relocation, their symbolic fields, and the characteristics and interests that affect their everyday life.

What emerges from our discussions in this chapter are the following:

a)   that subalterns communities are faced with conflicts which threaten their very existence *as* community;

b)   that these conflicts are often caused by dominant groups who benefit from the conflicts while the subalterns are the ones who suffer the most;

c)   that the 'roots of conflict' can be traced within a spatial framework largely to the ownership of land (*jungle-jal-jamin*) and entitlement to the nation-space, and though these fields are characterized by complex social, economic, historical and political factors, they are often represented in religious-cultural terms on account of the possibility of greater mobilisation in this latter realm;

d)   that the state, as well as 'outsiders' who intervene, are either unfamiliar with the deeper substratum of subaltern religio-cultural and socio-eco-political contexts or they consciously or unconsciously undermine these for their own vested interests;

e)   that, unless the 'counter spaces' that restore agency to subaltern communities are retrieved by struggle, protest or the deployment of 'counter-symbols', these communities are unlikely to recapture lost space in the nation.

In view of the above, the next chapter will try to establish certain principles and proposals which will enable subaltern communities to, negatively expressed, resist conflict, and, positively, ensure the building of community.

ENDNOTES FOR CHAPTER TWO

[1] Although Gujarat is called the 'land of Gandhi', his influence upon present day Gujarat is minimal since: (i) On March 12, 1930, Gandhi started his Dandi march never to return to Gujarat, (ii) his movements were 'experiments in truth' suited to persons of high moral caliber with a 'dialogal' bent of mind. His followers, unfortunately, have torn Gandhism apart and appropriated him piecemeal with little or no success. Thus, Gandhi is long forgotten in Gujarat except for the twice-yearly (Jan 30th, Oct 2nd) garlands his statue gets from people of every ideology, including the Sangh Parivar whose associate Nathuram Godse shot him.

[2] See Kamal Mitra Chenoy, ed., *Citizen's Commission's Report on the Incidents in Dangs District* (NAWO, 1999); Ghanshyam Shah, "Conversion, Reconversion and the State: Recent Events in the Dangs," *EPW* 34 (February 6, 1999): 312-8; Somen Chakraborty, "Gujarat: Attacks on Christians – Looking Beyond Communalism," *EPW* 34 (April 17, 1999): 949-52; Satyakam Joshi, "Tribals, Missionaries and Sadhus: Understanding Violence in the Dangs," *EPW* 34 (September 11, 1999): 2667-75. See also endnote no. 1 of the 'Preface' for my own reporting on the events in the Dangs District of Gujarat.

[3] The 2002-violence has been covered extensively in the media and academy. For the buildup, chronology of events, names of victims, etc., see 'Gujarat Genocide' 2002, *Communalism Combat* (March – April, 2002) and "Society Under Siege," *Seminar* 513 (May 2002). These are 'special issues' dealing exclusively with the violence and analyses by scholars. See also 'reports' by fact-finding commissions and human rights' groups. Also see Siddharth Varadarajan, ed., *Gujarat: The Making of a Tragedy* (New Delhi: Penguin, 2002); "Crime Against Humanity" 2-part report on the Gujarat Carnage carried out by the "Concerned Citizens Tribunal", 2002; Rafiq Zakaria, *Communal Rage in Secular India* (Mumbai: Popular Prakashan, 2002); Ashutosh Varshney, *Ethnic Conflict and Civic Life: Hindus and Muslims in India* (New Delhi: OUP, 2002); M.L. Sondhi and Apratim Mukarji, eds., *The Black Book of Gujarat* (New Delhi: Manak Publications, 2002); Chandan Sengupta, Anil Kumar, and Katy Y. Gandevia. *Communal Riots in Gujarat, 2002: A Study of Contextual Factors* (Mumbai: Tata Institute of Social Sciences, 2003); Radhika. Desai "Hindutva's Gujarat: The Image of India's Future?" in *Slouching Towards Ayodhya* (New Delhi: Three Essays Collective, 2003), 111-47, and Upendra Baxi, "The Second Gujarat Catastrophe," *EPW* 37 (August 24, 2002): 3519-31, among others.

[4] The category OBC (Other Backward Classes) could also be included. But, there are castes in the OBC category – for e.g., the *Koli-Patels* of Gujarat – that have not really suffered discrimination and are still being granted reservations for political purposes. The inclusion of such OBCs under a 'Dalit' label will defeat the purpose of seeing 'Dalit' as 'broken' people. Hence, I consider such groups as non-Dalit.

[5] Unless otherwise indicated, the census figures will be taken from the "Primary Census Abstract" from the *Census of India Data, 2001* (New Delhi: Office of the Registrar General of India). At the time of writing, the spadework for the 2011 census is being done although there are many controversies with regard to the inclusion of caste as an index of identity, as well as the inclusion of certain religions like 'tribal religion'.

[6] See Ghanshyam Shah, "Unrest among the Adivasis and their Struggles," in *The Other Gujarat: Social Transformations among Weaker Sections*, ed. T. Shinoda (Mumbai: Popular Prakashan, 2002), 98.

[7] According to the 1991 *Census of India*.

[8] Romila Thapar, "The Tyranny of Labels," in *The Concerned Indian's Guide to Communalism*, ed. K.N. Panikkar (New Delhi: Viking, 1999), 1-31, warns against naively viewing religious communities, specially Hindus and Muslims,

as two distinct religious communities separated on the basis of religious affiliation.

[9] Within the 'Dalit' group in Gujarat itself, there are so many differences. See A.M. Shah, "The 'Dalit' Category and its Differentiation," *EPW* 37 (April 6, 2002): 1317-8, who writes: "These lists (for SCs) should make one pause before making general statements. Even a comparatively small state like Gujarat has a schedule of around 30 castes. There is sub-regional distribution of these castes, such that any one local area includes only about half-a-dozen of them, and any one village includes hardly two or three, sometimes even one, of them." Quote from p. 1317.

[10] See, for instance, James Massey, *Roots: A Concise History of Dalits*, 2nd ed., (Delhi: ISPCK, 1994), 52, who mentions scholars who have linked the roots of the Dalits with a large number of adivasi groups

[11] Nirmal Minz, "Dalit-Tribal: A Search for Common Ideology," in *Towards a Common Dalit Ideology*, ed. A.P. Nirmal (Madras: GLTCRI & TDDT, n.d.), 97-107; and, Albert Minz, "Dalits and Tribals: A Search For Solidarity," in *Frontiers of Dalit Theology*, ed. V. Devasahayam (Delhi: ISPCK & Madras: GLTCRI, 1997), 130-58, discuss the repercussions of Dalit-tribal solidarity at an ideological-theological plane.

[12] *Ujjaliyat* literally means 'fair-skinned' or 'bright ones' and refers to non-adivasis, usually the *savarnas*.

[13] An example of the state subordinating the subalterns is that of the SSP on the River Narmada. See, for instance, Meena Menon, "Narmada: They Have Little to Cheer About," *The Hindu*, 29 November 2005, 15.

[14] T.K. Oommen, *Protest and Change: Studies in Social Movements* (New Delhi: Sage Publications, 1990), 254-7, studies the domination of the Dalits using these three as parameters.

[15] See, for instance, Gail Omvedt, *Dalits and the Democratic Revolution: Dr. Ambedkar and the Dalit Movement in Colonial India* (New Delhi: Sage Publications, 1994), for understanding the effect and spread of the Dalit movement, and Oommen, *Protest and Change*, 74-85 and 254-71, for the salient features of 'tribal movements' & the 'sources of deprivation and styles of protest' of the Dalit movement, respectively.

[16] Gramsci, *ibid*.

[17] See, for e.g., Parish, *Hierarchy and its Discontents*, for an example of resistance by the lower castes.

[18] See David Hardiman, *The Coming of the Devi: Adivasi Assertion in Western India* (Delhi: OUP, 1987).

[19] See, for e.g., Lancy Lobo, "We belong to Bharat, not Hindustan," *Communalism Combat* 8/75-6 (January - February 2002): 40-2, for adivasi assertion of their distinct religio-cultural identity in south Gujarat.

[20] One must be cautious when referring to 'Dalit' as a general category. The *Vankar* community is the group of weavers in Gujarat considered as one of the OBCs.

[21] See Ghanshyam Shah, *Social Movements in India: A Review of the Literature* (New Delhi: Sage Publications, 1990), 107-20, for 'Dalit Movements'. Mention of the Gujarati *Vankar*-contribution on p.116.

[22] Besides my own personal experiences, this fact has been repeatedly mentioned by those working with adivasis interviewed in Gujarat, as well as the tribal thinkers consulted in the Jharkhand area.

[23] Details of the *panchora-vidhi* were obtained from an interview with Gamanbhai Kalubhai Kokani of Bardipada village (*Uplu Faliyu*), Vyara taluk, Surat district, Gujarat.

[24] See J.A. Corral, *The Gamit World of Meaning: Adivasi Religion and Culture. Tribal Sources – II* (Anand: GSP, 2001), 120-2, for details of the Gamit name-giving ceremony.

[25] See A. Van Exem, *The Religious System of the Munda Tribe: An Essay in Religious Anthropology* (St. Augustin: Haus Völker und Kulturen, and Ranchi: Catholic Press, 1982), 76.

[26] Ram Dayal Munda, *Adi-Dharam: Religious Beliefs of the Adivasis of India* (Coimbatore: Sarini & Jharkhand: BIRSA, n.d.), 31.

[27] See John B. Mundu, *The Ho Christian Community: Towards a New Self-Understanding as Communion* (Delhi: Media House, 2003), 34.

[28] See K. Thanzauva, *Theology of Community: Tribal Theology in the Making* (Aizawl: Mizo Theological Conference, 1997), 120-33, for further details.

[29] Mundu, 270.

[30] See N. Minz, 99-102, for what he calls 'geo-political' situation and its effects on Dalits. 'Geo-political' refers to the geographical context (spatial) and the political situation (social).

[31] See *Towards a Common Dalit Ideology*, ed. A.P Nirmal, 'Seminar Statement', 128.

[32] As seen, for instance, in the spirit of sharing and cooperation in the '*panchora-vidhi*' (initiation rite of the Kokanas), see also Munda, 30-2.

[33] Marriages involve the whole village to make the *mandavo* (marriage-bower) among adivasis in south Gujarat. In Jharkhand, *marwa* is a marriage bower made with *sal* branches and leaves, under which the marriage ceremony takes place. The village community gives a helping hand in getting wood, branches and leaves for preparing *mandavo* and *marwa* and is fed by the marriage-party with a simple meal. I am grateful to John Lakra for this information. See also Corral, *ibid.*, 123-30, for details about the Gamit South Gujrat adivasi context.

[34] Since the land is considered as common to all adivasis, there is a sense of 'cooperative farming'. In Jharkhand, *pancha* is a cooperative system by which a family is able to get the required help of the whole village for a nominal fee of a rupee or two for accomplishing a big task – e.g., fixing a broken *bandh* (dam), transplantation of paddy, etc. – that would otherwise require plenty of money. To render such helps, individuals have to sacrifice their own interests. I am grateful to John Lakra for this information.

[35] Hosting a village-meal for important occasions is integral to adivasi culture.

[36] The adivasis of south Gujarat dance together in a circle called '*naachnu*' or '*ubhu bhajan*' with a drummer in the centre. Likewise, in Jharkhand, the '*akhra*' is a round, public dancing place where dancers hold hands and move around in a circle.

[37] Among south Gujarat's adivasis, fishing is done in rivers and involves mostly women. Hunting is exclusively for men although women partake of the ritual-activity prior to the hunting. In Jharkhand, '*sendra*' is a ceremonial annual hunt in the lunar month of *Phagun*. Menfolk go into the jungle to hunt. The dividing of the game even among those who did not participate in the hunt is an expression of their community feeling and solidarity. This information was given by John Lakra.

[38] When an adivasi dies in south Gujarat, the neighbours gather at the deceased's hut to condole the family, provide food for them, prepare the body for burial, and do '*ujaagro*' (night-watch). At the cremation, every male brings a piece of wood for the funeral-pyre and makes a contribution for the funeral expenses and the expenses of feeding the village later. The deceased is believed to still be a member of the tribal community.

[39] J.A. Corral, who has worked with Vasavi and Gamit adivasis in south Gujarat for over three decades, stressed, "Adivasis are not at home with concepts and ideas but with examples from nature and real life-experiences." Also Van Exem, 15-21, explains the logic behind adivasi thinking, symbols and myths.

[40] I use the word '*dharma*' – loosely translated as 'religion' but more implying 'one's duty – for want of a better term. Ghanshyam Shah, "Conversion, Reconversion and the State," 314, points out that unless an adivasi specifically states that s/he is Christian or Muslim, s/he will be categorized as 'Hindu'. This problem arises in the collection of census data whereby all adivasis are enumerated as 'Hindu'. The same malicious intent is present in the Census 2011 that is now being conducted by the Government of India.

[41] Corral, *ibid.*, 142, writes: "life in all its forms is interconnected in meaning."

[42] Van Exem, 20.

[43] See Mundu, 98-9.

[44] *Dharmes* is the Supreme Being of the Oraon tribe. For details, see Varghese Palatty Koonathan, *The Religion of the Oraons: A Comparative Study*

of the Concept of God in the Sarna Religion of the Oraons and the Christian Conception of God (Shillong: Don Bosco Centre For Indigenous Cultures, 1999), 170-1.

[45] Mundu, 31; italics added.

[46] There are parallels in other subaltern traditions; e.g., the goddess *Ellaiamma* of rural Tamil Nadu is known to protect the village boundaries from outside intrusion of the higher castes and classes.

[47] See Satyakam Joshi, 2668-9, for details of these Dangi village gods/ goddesses. Also Corral, 153-231.

[48] See L.P. Vidyarthi and Binay Kumar Rai, *The Tribal Culture of India*, 2nd ed., (New Delhi: Concept Publishing Company, 1985), 254.

[49] Kancha Ilaiah, *Why I Am Not a Hindu: A Sudra Critique of Hindutva Philosophy, Culture and Political Economy* (Calcutta: Samya, 1996), 111. Instead of *Dalit*, Ilaiah uses the more inclusive word *Dalitbahujan* to mean, "people and castes who form the exploited and suppressed majority." See p. ix.

[50] *Ibid.*, 8.

[51] Narrated by J.A. Corral in an interview.

[52] Van Exem, 142; see 141-5 for details about the Munda communitarian ethic.

[53] See George Soares-Prabhu, "Anti-greed and Anti-pride," *Jeevadhara* 24/ 140 (1994): 130-50. See also Paulus Kullu, "Tribal Religion and Culture," *Jeevadhara* 24/140 (1994): 92-3, for the same idea.

[54] The *'patel'* is sometimes called *'police patel'* and is not the same as the caste-label, 'Patel'.

[55] The *'sandhalya'* – also called *'handolia'* – refers to field-labour given free or exchanged among adivasis.

[56] Information received from Bhagubhai Thagiabhai Gamit of Raniamba village, Vyara taluk, Surat district.

[57] See Pradip Kumar Bose, "Stratification among Tribals in Gujarat," in *Social Inequality in India: Profiles of Caste, Class, Power and Social Mobility*, ed. K.L. Sharma (Jaipur & New Delhi: Rawat Publications, 1995), 411-26, who holds that changes in adivasi society are best studied by viewing the dynamics of class.

[58] Informant I. Galdos, who has lived with adivasis for close to four decades, narrated an incident when a buffalo was killed in village Jamkui and the suspected culprit was murdered as an act of vengeance. Later, although the killers were known to members of the *Panch*, they refused to take action on the simple principle: "what is over, is over!" It was felt that the dead man could not be resuscitated and thus there was no need for bringing justice. Galdos observed, "Tribal loyalty and solidarity also has a negative side."

[59] See Achyut Yagnik, "The Pathology of Gujarat," *Seminar* 513 (May 2002): 19-25, for details.

[60] *Ibid.*, 20.

[61] The term 'Patidar' generally refers to the landowning caste within the generic group called 'Patel' who are economically and socially dominant. They are known by different names in different regions; e.g., in Central Gujarat they are known as 'Leuva Patel', in Saurashtra and Kutch as 'Kanbi Patel', in North Gujarat as 'Chaudhari' and South Gujarat as 'Koli Patel'.

[62] Yagnik, "The Pathology of Gujarat," 20.

[63] See L.C. Jain, "Securing their Future," *Seminar* 523 (March 2003): 63-7.

[64] Adivasi displacement has taken place on a large scale in Gujarat due to the building of huge dams at Ukai, Karzan and Madhuban. For issues and problems related to the *SSP* (Narmada Dam), see Jean Dreze, Meera Samson, and Satyajit Singh, eds., *The Dam and the Nation: Displacement and Resettlement in the Narmada Valley* (New Delhi: OUP, 1997).

[65] See Achyut Yagnik, "Search for Dalit Self-Identity in Gujarat," in *The Other Gujarat*, 23.

[66] 'Bhadra' refers to the elite culture as opposed to the 'Aam' or 'common' peoples' culture. See Achyut Yagnik and Suchitra Sheth, "Whither Gujarat? Violence and After," *EPW* 37 (March 16, 2002): 1009-11.

[67] Ashutosh Varshney has identified 8 of the most riot-prone cities in India, and Ahmedabad and Surat are among them, besides Mumbai, Aligarh, Hyderabad, Meerut, Kolkata and Delhi. These 8 cities account for 49% of all urban riot deaths but represent a mere 18% of India's urban population.

[68] For details on the mobilisation of subaltern communities, see Sengupta et al., 59-91.

[69] Gandhian politics was weak because, besides not being critical of the caste-system, Gandhi did not consider 'social boycott' to be an effective tool for his 'Civil Disobedience Movement' and hence, his nationalist movement almost always dissolved mobilisation in the subaltern domain and allowed the dominant classes/castes "to pilot the political activity of the masses towards goals set up by the bourgeoisie." See Ranajit Guha, "Discipline and Mobilize," in *Subaltern Studies VII: Writings on South Asian History and Society*, ed. P. Chatterjee and G. Pandey (Delhi: OUP, 1992), 69-120; quote from p.111.

[70] See D.N. Dhanagare, "The Bardoli Satyagraha: Myth and Reality," in *Peasant Movements in India: 1920 - 1950* (Delhi: OUP, 1983), 88-110, for a critical appraisal of this *satyagraha* that did not achieve any tangible results for the lower castes in terms of liberation from caste oppression.; quote from p. 107.

[71] Sengupta et al., 60.

[72] See Dhanagare, 104, regarding the *Dublas* (bonded labourers) who were adivasis – called *raniparaj* (those living in the wilderness) by Gandhi – who began trusting their masters instead of confronting them.

[73] See David Hardiman, "Adivasi Assertion in South Gujarat: the Devi Movement of 1922-3," in *Subaltern Studies – III: Writings on South Asian History and Society*, ed. R. Guha (Delhi: OUP, 1992), 196-230.

[74] *Ibid.*, 217. Hardiman disagrees that such behaviour is indicative of M.N. Srinivas' '*Sanskritization*'.

[75] *Ibid.*, 225-9. See esp. the speeches of Vallabhbhai Patel and Kasturba Gandhi urging adivasi submission.

[76] One of the recent mobilisations among adivasis is the foundation of the '*Adivasi Mahasabha*' that seeks to fight for the entitlement to their own lands and forests in defiance of Gujarat's Inspector General of Forest's (IGF) order of May 3, 2002, for eviction of tribals who do not possess the land in their own name.

[77] Sengupta *et al.*, 60.

[78] For details on the *KHAM* mobilisation in Gujarat, see Atul Kohli, *Democracy and Discontent: India's Growing Crisis of Governability* (Cambridge: CUP, 1991), 40, 238-66.

[79] See Francine R. Frankel, "Decline of a Social Order," in *Politics and the State in India*, ed. Z. Hasan (New Delhi: Sage Publications, 2000), 239.

[80] See Yagnik, "Pathology of Gujarat," 21.

[81] The 1985 riots were against the State Government's decision to raise the quota for the SEBC to 28%.

[82] Clashes between *savarnas* and Dalits developed into caste wars in 18 of Gujarat's 19 districts. Interestingly, only the Dangs district, with more than 90% adivasi population remained unaffected.

[83] Sengupta *et al.*, 62.

[84] Yagnik, *ibid.* However, the subaltern move to identify with *savarna* society was, as mentioned earlier, not connected with their obsession for 'ritual purity', but with their desire to *share power* with others.

[85] Yagnik, *ibid.*, points out that in the 1990 riots after L.K. Advani's arrest on account of his *rath-yatra*, for the first time there were violent clashes between Muslims and Dalits in the industrial areas of Ahmedabad.

[86] See Ghanshyam Shah, "Caste, Hindutva and Hideousness," *EPW* 35 (April 13, 2000): 1392.

[87] Sengupta et al., 66, report that in many villages of Gujarat each household was asked to contribute one brick and one rupee towards construction of the Ram *mandir*. Trucks loaded with the bricks first went to the Taluka town and from there, to Ahmedabad.

[88] *Ibid.* It is important to note that the adivasi religious worldview is distinct from that of both, Hinduism and Christianity; thus, these groups can be referred to as 'Christianized adivasis' and 'Hinduized adivasis'.

[89] As mentioned in endnote no. 2 of the 'Preface', the word 'field' is used in the nuance given by Bourdieu.

[90] See Roshni Sengupta, "Communal Violence in India: Perspectives on Causative Factors," *EPW* 40 (May 15, 2005): 2046-50, for a discussion on some causes of communal clashes especially in Gujarat context.

[91] See S.K. Chaube, "The Scheduled Tribes and Christianity in India," *EPW* 34 (February 27 - March 5, 1999): 524-6, for an overview of the demographic breakup of the Hindu-Christian STs in India.

[92] For a lucid description of the debates on conversion see Sebastian C.H. Kim, *In Search of Identity: Debates on Religious Conversion in India* (New Delhi: OUP, 2003), especially chs. 7 & 8 for our purposes.

[93] See M.V. Nadkarni, "Ethics and Relevance of Conversions: A Critical Assessment of Religious and Social Dimensions in a Gandhian Perspective," *EPW* 38 (January 18, 2003): 227-35, for Gandhi's views.

[94] See, for e.g., Arun Shourie, *Harvesting Our Souls: Missionaries, their Design, their Claims* (New Delhi: ASA Publications, 2000); P.A. Augustine, "Conversion as Social Protest," *R&S* 28/4 (December 1981): 51-7; B.K. Roy Burman, "The Other Side of 'Conversion'," *Mainstream* 37/8 (February 13, 1999): 7-11; Dev Dutt, "Conversions: A Viewpoint," in *Politics of Conversion*, ed. D. Swarup (New Delhi: Deendayal Research Institute, 1986), 35-46; HVK, *Religious Conversions: Frequently Asked Questions* (Mumbai: HVK, 1999); Joseph Mattam and Sebastian Kim, eds., *Mission and Conversion: A Reappraisal* (Mumbai: St. Pauls, 1996); Ebe Sunder Raj, *The Confusion Called Conversion* (Chennai: Bharat Jyoti, 1998); Vasant Sathe, "Reform Hindu Society to Stop Conversion," *Times of India*, 22 January 1999, M.N. Rao, "Religious Freedom – Legal Restrictions on Conversions," *The Hindu*, 8 July 2003, 16, and Francis Gonsalves, "Debating Conversions," *Indian Currents* XI/6 (February 8-14, 1999): 35-6, among others.

[95] Article 19 (1) of the Indian Constitution reads thus: "Subject to public order, morality and health and to the other provisions of this Part, all persons are equally entitled to freedom of conscience and the right freely to profess, practise and propagate religion."

[96] Manjari Katju, "Conversions and Reconversions," in *Vishva Hindu Parishad and Indian Politics* (New Delhi: Orient Longman, 2003), 127-41, who discusses the issue with special focus on Gujarat.

[97] G.S. Ghurye, *The Scheduled Tribes*, 2nd ed., (Bombay: Popular Press, 1959), 20.

[98] Ganesh Devy, "Tribal Voice and Violence," *Seminar* 513 (May 2002): 46, mentions other differences.

[99] This is the view of Ghanshyam Shah, "Conversion, Reconversion and the State," 314.

[100] It is becoming increasingly common in the south Gujarat area to propagate Hanuman (monkey-god) as the *ishta-deva* (patron) of the adivasis. *Hanuman-Chalisa* is a booklet with prayers to Hanuman. Describing the ritual

of *'gharvapasi'* the *"Citizens' Commission Report on the Incidents in Dangs District, 1999,"* reads: "He [adivasi undergoing *gharvapasi*] was given a *'Hanuman Chalisa'* booklet and made to recite it in a prayer room. From Waghai they [adivasi and his family] were taken to the Unai hot springs, which is also a place of Hindu worship. There they were made to buy coconuts and offer them to the local *'Mataji'* deity, and wear *'tilaks'* and a Hanuman amulet around their necks. They were given a laminated picture of Hanuman, as well as one depicting Rama, Lakshman and Shabri. [*Shabri*, according to local lore, was a tribal girl who offered local berries to Rama and Lakshman]."

[101] P.R. Ram, *In the Name of Religion: Truth Behind Conversions and Acts of Violence* (Mumbai: EKTA, 1999), 12, terms this, "Brahmanisation of Adivasis".

[102] This is also mentioned in the Citizens' Report of the Dangs' Violence, 1999.

[103] In *Outside the Fold: Conversion, Modernity, and Belief* (New Delhi: OUP, 2001), 232.

[104] See Gail Omvedt, "Buddhism, Bhakti and the VHP – I," *The Hindu*, 23 December 2002, 10.

[105] See Gail Omvedt, "Buddhism, Bhakti and the VHP – II," *The Hindu*, 24 December 2002, 10.

[106] For some examples of this see Joshi, *ibid.*, 2670, 2673, 2675.

[107] *Mahuda* is a local alcoholic drink (*daru*) – made from the flowers of the *mahua* tree (*Madhuca Indica*) – used for all adivasi celebrations and even in rituals of reconciliation (*beda-bedi*) or to seal social contracts.

[108] Rudolph C. Heredia, *Changing Gods: Rethinking Conversion in India* (New Delhi: Penguin Books, 2007), 303-11, sees conversion as a process in which those who covert must be left totally free, and must be assured of their right to affirm their identity and to seek change.

[109] See Shah, "Conversion, Reconversion and the State," 315.

[110] In the houses of many adivasis in south Gujarat, one sees images of Hindu gods like Hanuman, Ram and Parvati coexisting with those of Jesus and Mary. Besides this, white flags on trees, stones smeared with *kumkum* (red) powder, earthen vessels along the boundary, etc., are all part of subaltern religious expression.

[111] See Viswanathan, *ibid.*, xix. On p. 228 she explains this dynamic in the case of the conversion of Ambedkar to Buddhism.

[112] See Kullu, 94.

[113] A sense of the common origin of all of visible creation, as well as the attitude that everything belongs to *all* and thus, must be shared by *all* is very strong among adivasis. The assertion that *jal-jungle-jamin* belongs to *'baap-dada'* (ancestors) is indicative of this. See also Mundu, 36 who stresses: "Human beings must share the land with all living beings," and again, 43: "The absence of the ownership of the forest signifies that it belongs to everyone."

[114] See *Citizens' Report on the Dangs*, 1999.

[115] Details of this section on forests are taken from Shah, "Conversion, Reconversion and the State," 312-3.

[116] A recent circular of the *'Adivasi Mahasabha'* states that the crops of 21 adivasi families were destroyed in the Dangs district.

[117] See Mihir Shah, "Governance Reform for India's Forests," *The Hindu*, 20 May 2005, 10, for the provisions and implications of this proposed Bill. See also Vikram Soni, "Tribal People and Preserving Prime Forests," *The Hindu*, 29 November 2005, 14, for a counter point of view.

[118] Shah, "Conversion, Reconversion and the State," 318.

[119] Chakraborty, *ibid.*, shows how lopsided development especially with regard to the Narmada Dam has led to conflicts, which are now covered up by resorting to violence in the name of religion.

[120] Medha Patkar and the NBA have fought long battles against the WB and IMF for funding capital-intensive projects that are beneficial only to the rich, but are a disaster for Nature and for the poor adivasis.

[121] Chakraborty, 951

[122] See Joshi, *ibid.*, 2672-3 on 'Politicisation of Religion' and 2675 'Conclusion'.

[123] See *The Gujarat Pogrom: Indian Democracy in Danger* (New Delhi: Indian Social Institute, 2002).

[124] See Ram Nath Sharma, *Gujarat Holocaust: Communalism in the Land of Gandhi* (Delhi: Shubhi Publications, 2002).

[125] See "Gujarat Genocide: 2002," *Communalism Combat* (March – April, 2002). Also Asghar Ali Engineer, "Three Years After Genocide in Gujarat," *Secular Perspective* (March 1-15, 2005).

[126] Sajeda Momin, "In the Ghetto: Gujaratis Live in a Segregated Society," *The Statesman*, 4 April 2002, 4; also, Ajai Sahni, "Gujarat: Communal Ghetto or Global Enterprises?" in *The Black Book of Gujarat*, 53-68.

[127] In *Communalism: A Primer* (New Delhi: Anamika Publishers, 2004), 7; italics added.

[128] See Bipan Chandra, *Communalism in Modern India* (New Delhi: Vani Educational Books, 1984), for a good analysis of Indian communalism

[129] See T.K. Oommen, *State and Society in India: Studies in Nation-Building*, 112-3.

[130] Gyanendra Pandey, *The Construction of Communalism in Colonial North India* (Delhi: OUP, 1990), 2.

[131] Dipankar Gupta, "Ethnicity and Politics," in *Politics in India*, ed. S. Kaviraj (Delhi: OUP, 2000), 232.

[132] See Peter van der Veer, *Religious Nationalism: Hindus and Muslims in India* (Delhi: OUP, 1998), 22-3.

133 See John Zavos, *The Emergence of Hindu Nationalism in India* (New Delhi: OUP, 2000), 4-5.

134 For instance, Peter Gottschalk, *Beyond Hindu and Muslim: Multiple Identity in Narratives from Village India* (New Delhi: OUP, 2001), 3-5, argues that scholars rely too heavily on the Hindu-Muslim communal polarity whereas community identities can also coalesce around other economic, social and political interests. Pandey, *ibid.*, 6-9, also holds a similar view

135 For e.g., one can think of ethnic, territorial, linguistic or religious nationalisms. Chatterjee, *The Nation and its Fragments*, holds that scholars have mistakenly been looking for nationalism only in the political domain of the state. But anti-colonial nationalists in India claim a special domain of culture where a new 'national' modernity is to be created around institutions of language, religion, literature, art, education, etc.

136 I take 'ideology' to mean social practice involving: [a] discourse (language, ideas, symbols, theories, etc.) and [b] activity (specific actions, gestures, behavioural patterns & institutions). These are constantly 'realized' in social life and embodied in human institutions. Thus, ideologies interpellate human subjects and communities and form them as social subjects.

137 See Benedict Anderson, *Imagined Communities: Reflections on the Origin and Spread of Nationalism.* (New York: Verso, 1996), and Sudipta Kaviraj, "The Imaginary Institution of India," in *Subaltern Studies VII: Writings on South Asian History and Society*, ed. P. Chatterjee & G. Pandey (Delhi: OUP, 1992), 1-39.

138 James Mill's work, "A History of British India" proved useful for communal ideology. See Romila Thapar, "Communalism and the Historical Legacy: Some Facets," in *Secular Challenge to Communal Politics: A Reader*, ed. P.R. Ram (Mumbai: VAK, 1998), 7-8, for a brief critique of this approach. This book will hereafter be abbreviated as *SCCP*.

139 See Romila Thapar "Imagined Religious Communities? Ancient History and the Modern Search for a Hindu Identity," in *History and Beyond* (New Delhi: OUP, 2000), 75.

140 See Zavos, *Emergence of Hindu Nationalism*, 68-98, for developments in this period.

141 As quoted by Zavos, *Emergence of Hindu Nationalism*, 74.

142 This dovetails with the hypothesis of Anderson, *Imagined Communities*, 163-85, that, nationalist 'imagined communities' were products of the census, map and museum which formed "a totalizing classificatory grid which could be applied with endless flexibility to anything under the state's real or contemplated control: peoples, regions, religions, languages, products, monuments, and so forth. The effect of the grid was always to be able to say of anything that it was this, not that; it belongs here, not there. It was bounded, determinate, and therefore – in principle – countable" (p.184).

[143] See John Zavos, "Searching for Hindu Nationalism in Modern Indian History: Analysis of Some Early Ideological Developments," *EPW* 34 (August 7, 1999): 2272.

[144] Christophe Jaffrelot, *The Hindu Nationalist Movement in India 1925 to the 1990s: Strategies of Identity-Building, Implantation and Mobilisation* (New Delhi: Viking Penguin, 1996), 13, sees this as a cultural-religious ideological strategy to defend Brahmanical hegemony.

[145] Thomas Blom Hansen, *The Saffron Wave: Democracy and Hindu Nationalism in Modern India* (New Delhi: OUP, 2001), 90-133, argues how Hindu 'organization', a product of modernity, was essential for effective mobilisation of the masses.

[146] See Zavos, *Emergence of Hindu Nationalism*, 213-4.

[147] Hereafter, whenever the word Other ('o' capitals) is used, it will refer to the other as community.

[148] See Rafiq Zakaria, *The Widening Divide: An Insight Into Hindu-Muslim Relations* (Delhi: Viking-Penguin, 1995), 46-127, for details of this period of upheavals and insecurity for the common Muslims.

[149] See Asghar Ali Engineer, "Re-Emergence of Communalism in Post-Independence India," in *SCCP*, 58.

[150] *Ibid.*, 63.

[151] See *ibid.*, 69-71, for details of the manipulation of subaltern groups by Indira Gandhi and the Congress.

[152] *Jan Sangh* is an earlier political avatar of the present BJP, the political wing of Hindu nationalism. There is evidence of the Jan Sangh's role in the 1969 riots as mentioned in the report of the Justice Jagmohan Reddy Commission; see, P.R. Ram, "Crime and (No) Punishment: Communal Violence, Inquiry Commissions and Deliverance of Justice," in *SCCP*, 127.

[153] See Ghanshyam Shah, "The 1969 Communal Riots in Ahmedabad: A Case Study," in *Communal Riots in Post-Independence India*, ed. A.A. Engineer (Mumbai, 1991), 181-2.

[154] See Frankel, "Decline of a Social Order," 239, who, in the context of *KHAM* points out: "These events not only polarized Gujarat's society between the upper and lower castes, but perhaps more dangerous for social cohesion in large areas of the country, led to communal riots between Hindus and Muslims."

[155] See P.R. Ram, "Hindutva Offensive: Social Roots and Characterisation," in *SCCP*, 103.

[156] See A.D. Moddie, "Understanding the Demonization Process," *Seminar* 484 (December 1999): 62-5, for understanding this demonization process and how it is characteristic of all religious fundamentalisms

[157] Peter van der Veer, "Riots and Rituals: The Construction of Violence and Public Space in Hindu Nationalism," in *Riots and Pogroms*, ed. P.R. Brass

(Macmillan Press, 1996), 154-76, highlights how the Ayodhya campaign has been built up through the use of rituals and other symbolic activity.

[158] Romila Thapar, "The Ramayana Syndrome," *Seminar* 353 (January 1989): 74, holds that the serial showed not the ideas of a majority of Indians but "the middle class and other aspirants to the same status."

[159] See Richard H. Davis, "The Iconography of Rama's Chariot," in *Making India Hindu: Religion, Community, and the Politics of Democracy in India*, ed. D. Ludden (Delhi: OUP, 1996), 27-54, for details. See also my article "Advani's Yatra," *The Hindu*, 6 April 2004, 19, for a critical view of the *yatra*.

[160] See Zakaria, *The Widening Divide*, 128-79, for details of the eco-socio-political and educational condition of Indian Muslims.

[161] See K.N. Panikkar, "Religious Symbols and Political Mobilization," in *Communal Threat Secular Challenge* (Madras: Earthworm Books, 1997), 159-60, for statistics of the same.

[162] See Zakaria, *The Widening Divide*, 245.

[163] See Katju, 166-8, tables 6 to 9, for the success of the BJP in the Lok Sabha elections from 1984 to 1996.

[164] Please refer to the "List of Abbreviations" for the full form of these abbreviations.

[165] The term *'minorityism'* is synonymous with 'minoritarianism'. The majority-minority polarity is problematic in the Indian context since neither the Hindu nor the 'minorities' (Muslims, Christians, Sikhs or others) are homogenous communities. See, for e.g., Madhu Kishwar, "Politics of Majoritarianism vs. Minoritarianism," in *Minority Identities and the Nation-State*, ed. D.L. Sheth and G. Mahajan (New Delhi: OUP, 1999), 138-68. Also see other articles in this edited work for insights into this polarity.

[166] See, for e.g., Gyanendra Pandey, "Community and Violence: Recalling Partition," *EPW* 32 (August 9, 1997): 2037-45, who demonstrates that narratives of the painful days of the Partition are constructed in retrospect domains of 'inside' and 'outside' for defining violence.

[167] The term 'Hindu' derives from the Indo-Aryan word for sea, *sindhu*, used also for the Indus River. The Persians to the west of the Indus picked up the term to refer to the land of the Indus valley. From Persian it was borrowed into Greek and Latin, where India became the geographical segment of the unknown lands beyond the Indus. Muslims used Hindu to designate those of south Asia who did not convert to Islam.

[168] Ilaiah, *Why I Am Not a Hindu*, is a strong critique of Brahmanic Hinduism.

[169] Nonica Dutta, "Are the Sikhs Hindus?" *The Hindu*. 4 March 2003, 10, claims that Sikhs are not Hindus.

[170] It is not uncommon to hear a Northeastern tribal say, "I'm going to India!" referring to traveling from one of seven Northeastern states to, say, Delhi or Kolkata. Affinity is with the tribe and not any 'nation'.

171 See "Myths About the Adivasis," in *Facts Against Myths* 1/11 (Mumbai:VAK, June 1995), for clarifications of the misunderstandings related to the adivasis in India.

172 See A.J. Philip, "Hindutva, the Lexical Way: Delegitimising the Adivasi," *Indian Express*, 8 March 1999. M.S. Golwalkar, *Bunch of Thoughts*, 3rd ed., (Bangalore: Sahitya Sindhu Prakashana, 1996), 115, reads: "But those forest-dwellers, the *vanvasis*, are now called *adivasis*, aboriginals, as if all others are upstarts and settlers coming here from somewhere outside!"

173 See Devy, 47.

174 Golwalkar, *Bunch of Thoughts*, 54, states: "I can define a 'Mussalman' or a 'Christian', but I cannot define a 'Hindu'" ... "How do you define Hindu culture? Well, we feel it, though we cannot define it."

175 See "An Enumerative Tool or a Communal Implement? The Myths behind Census Data 2001," in *Facts Against Myths* (Mumbai: VAK, August-September 2004), for a clarification on the various myths spread about massive increase in the population of Muslims, decline rate of Hindus, etc.

176 Golwalkar, *Bunch of Thoughts*, 362.

177 One can observe that many Hanuman *mandirs* have sprung up in villages of the Dangs' district.

178 Devy, 47.

179 Assimilation seems to be the preferred option, and exclusion is resorted to when assimilation fails. See, for e.g., Golwalkar, *Bunch of Thoughts*, 171, interpreting Nehru's views on Hindu philosophy writes, "[I]t is necessary to assimilate Muslims and Christians into Hindu society in the same manner as invaders like Shakas and Hunas were assimilated in the past." Also see Dattopant Thengadi, *Nationalist Pursuit* (Bangalore: Sahitya Sindhu Prakashana, 1992), 130, 139 who claims: "In a way we have assimilated Christ. For there is nothing he has said that our seers have not already said," and "People say the Hindus assimilated other communities, but it is far from easy to assimilate Muslims. But, provided the politicians do not prove a hindrance, it is not difficult. Even today we can assimilate them. This is the specialty of our culture, as also its capacity."

180 The worst riots before the 2002 carnage were those that took place in Ahmedabad in 1969 which took an estimated 660 human lives, left 1,084 persons injured, rendered 27,750 Muslims homeless, who were pushed into refugee camps. See, Darshini Mahadevia, "Communal Space Over Life Space," in *Fascism in India: Faces, Fangs and Facts*, ed. C. Krishna (New Delhi: Manak Publications, 2003), 401.

181 See, Sumeet Sarkar, "The Fascism of the Sangh Parivar," in SCCP, 77-89; also Abinash Lahker and Uma Dhanushkodi, *Troubled Times: Communal Fascism Arrives* (Bangalore: Bhoomika, 2002).

182 V.D. Savarkar, *Hindutva* (Bombay: Veer Savarkar Prakashan, 1969), 3-4, considered Hindutva deeper than Hinduism: "Hindutva is not a word but

a history. Not only the spiritual or religious history of our people as at times it is mistaken to be by being confounded with the other cognate term, Hinduism. Hinduism is only a derivative, a fraction, a part of Hindutva ... Hindutva embraces all departments of thought and activity of the whole being of our Hindu race."

[183] Golwalkar, *Bunch of Thoughts*, 177-201.

[184] *Ibid.*, 127, 138, 164, 209, referring to Muslims and Christians.

[185] *Ibid.*, 117.

[186] See M.S. Golwalkar, *WE, or, Our Nationhood Defined* (Nagpur: Bharat Prakashan, 1947), 52, 56.

[187] See Pralay Kanungo, *RSS's Tryst with Politics: From Hedgewar to Sudarshan* (Delhi: Manohar Publications, 2002), for an insightful analysis of how, beneath the avowed intentions of the RSS to foster cultural and religious renewal, there is a strong focus on getting political power.

[188] See Hansen, *ibid.*, 77-89, for interpreting the strands of the Hindu Nationalist movement in the writings of V.D. Savarkar, M.S. Golwalkar, Deendayal Upadhyaya and the founders of the RSS.

[189] See Satish Deshpande, "Hegemonic Spatial Strategies: The Nation-Space and Hindu Communalism in Twentieth-century India," in *Community, Gender and Violence: Subaltern Studies XI*, ed. P. Chatterjee and P. Jeganathan (Delhi: Permanent Black, 2000), 167-211; also, "Communalising the Nation-Space: Notes on Spatial Strategies of Hindutva," *EPW* 30 (December 16, 1995): 3220-7.

[190] Deshpande, "Hegemonic Spatial Strategies," 170.

[191] Momin, *ibid.*, states: "There are very few mixed societies like the Gulmarg in Ahmedabad, established by secular people like former MP Ehsan Jafri who did not approve of ghettoisation. Jafri paid for his beliefs with his life when he with his family members was brutally killed in February."

[192] Mahadevia, 381.

[193] See interviews of refugees and victims in films on the Gujarat Carnage by filmmakers Suma Josson, *Gujarat: A Laboratory*, and Rakesh Sharma, *The Final Solution* – Parts I & II.

[194] See Jan Breman, "Communal Upheaval as Resurgence of Social Darwinism," in *Fascism in India*, 367-76, for the stages of ghettoisation and also for the socio-economic problems especially of the labourers.

[195] See "We Have No Orders To Save You: State Participation and Complicity in Communal Violence in Gujarat," *Human Rights' Watch* 14/3c (April 2002): 31.

[196] See *Human Rights Watch* 15/3 (2003): 47.

[197] See Sudhir Kakar, *The Colours of Violence* (New Delhi: Viking & Penguin Books, 1995), 239-53, for details of these processes. Kakar's analysis is also used to contest the images that many Indians have of the Sangh Parivar; for e.g., see Ramesh N. Rao. *Secular 'Gods' Blame Hindu 'Demons': The Sangh Parivar Though the Mirror of Distortion* (New Delhi: Har-Anand Publications, 2001).

[198] Kakar, "Some Unconscious Aspects of Ethnic Violence in India," in *Mirrors of Violence: Communities, Riots & Survivors in South Asia*, ed. V. Das (Delhi: OUP, 1990), 137; also Kakar, *Colours of Violence*, 244

[199] See Rashna Imhasly Gandhy, "Shadow: The Archetypal Enemy," *Seminar* 513 (May 2002): 53.

[200] The Muslims are regarded as the *'tamasic'* people who do things that good Gujaratis should not do: illegal bootlegging, eating meat, practicing polygamy and forming part of the underworld. Such prejudices were very evident from the interviewees in the films by Josson and Sharma. See also, Ashis Nandy, "Obituary of a Culture," *Seminar* 513 (May 2002): 16 and Bhiku Parekh, "Making Sense of Gujarat," *Seminar* 513 (May 2002): 29.

[201] See, for instance, *Communalism Combat* (March-April 2002): 114-22; "We Have No Orders To Save You: State Participation and Complicity in Communal Violence in Gujarat," *Human Rights Watch* 14/3c (April 2002); "Compounding Injustice: The Government's Failure to Redress Massacres in Gujarat," *Human Rights Watch* 15/4c (July 2003); "The Gujarat Carnage 2002: A Report to the Nation," called the violence a "planned assault" with the police "colluding with the mobs." See *The Hindu*, 11 April 2002, 12; also Manas Dasgupta, "Saffronised Police Show Their Colour," *The Hindu*, 3 March 2002, 8; Devy, 42; Nandy, "Obituary of a Culture," 16; Parekh, "Making Sense of Gujarat," 27, who all hold the state machinery and the police responsible for what happened.

[202] See Steven I. Wilkinson, "Putting Gujarat in Perspective," *EPW* 37 (April 27, 2002): 1579-83 for details

[203] Lancy Lobo and Biswaroop Das, *Geography of Gujarat Riots, 2002: Causatives and Spatial Spread Patterns of Related Factors* (Vadodara: Centre for Culture and Development, 2004), 18, write "Dalits carry a curious mix of 'macro images' of Muslims that correspond with their prevalent image of being violent, reckless, aggressive and anti-social, but at the same time within the context of their immediate micro environs they talk of the Muslims differently." Thus, there is some ambivalence in their perceptions.

[204] See Ghanshyam Shah, "Caste, Hindutva and Hideousness," 1391-2.

[205] See Joshi, *ibid.* 2673-4, also Shah, "Conversion, Reconversion and the State," 316.

[206] Shah, *ibid.*, 316.

[207] *Ibid.*, 317-8. In my earlier interviews of those affected in the Dangs, I was told that those who were leading the mobs "wore saffron head-bands

and were issuing instructions in Gujarati." This shows that they were not adivasis who normally speak Dangi, their mother tongue.

[208] Joshi, *ibid.,* 2675.

[209] Shah, "Caste, Hindutva and Hideousness," 1391.

[210] *Ibid.*

[211] *Ibid.,* 1392.

[212] *Ibid.*

[213] Yagnik and Sheth, *ibid.,* testify: "On the west side of the Sabarmati, in posh Ahmedabad, Muslim shops and business establishments were systematically looted and then set on fire. Frenzied groups of middle and upper class men and women could be seen with armloads of shoes, clothes and kitchen equipment, making their getaway on scooters, motorcycles and cars before our very eyes."

[214] As quoted by Roshni Sengupta, *ibid.*

[215] See Kalpana Kannabiran, "Adivasis and the Genocide," *The Hindu,* 24 April 2002, 10, who shows how the adivasis were mobilized into carrying out the schemes of the upper castes and classes.

[216] See Mohandas Namishray, "The Violence in Gujarat and the Dalits," in *Gujarat: The Making of a Tragedy,* 267-70, who makes a distinction on p.268: "The Dalits who were adherents of Ambedkar's ideology continued helping the Muslims. On the other hand, the Dalits influenced by Gandhi and his ideas got mobilized into attacking the Muslims. Thus, this violence is the result more of the vitiated thinking among those who organized the violence rather than the Dalits."

[217] Devy, 48.

[218] See Kancha Ilaiah, "Trishuls, Lathis and Books," *The Hindu,* 16 May 2003, 10.

[219] See Lalita Panicker, "Saffron Sisterhood: An Illusory Promise of Power," in *The Times of India,* 25 March 2002, 10, for what she terms "communalisation of women" through Hindutva indoctrination.

[220] See Nonica Dutta, "Gujarat and Majority Women," *The Hindu,* 15 June 2002, 10. See also interviews of Hindu women in Rakesh Sharma's film, *The Final Verdict,* part I.

[221] See *At the Receiving End: Women's Experiences of Violence in Vadodara* (Vadodara: People's Union for Civil Liberties and Vadodara Shanti Abhiyan, May 31, 2002), 19-24; also, *The Gujarat Pogrom: Indian Democracy in Danger* (New Delhi: Indian Social Institute, June 2002), 75-81, for first-hand accounts of survivors and narrations of victims.

[222] See *"How Has the Gujarat Massacre Affected Minority Women? The Survivors Speak,"* Fact-Finding by a Women Panel sponsored by Citizen's Initiative (Ahmedabad, 2002).

[223] See Barkha Dutt, "The Rape of Reason," *Outlook*, 13 May 2002, 30.

[224] See Asghar Ali Engineer, "Three Years after Genocide in Gujarat," *Secular Perspective* (March 1-15, 2005), who reflects upon the events, the callousness of the State and the need to restore democracy.

[225] See Cohen, *Symbolic Construction of Community*, 19-21.

[226] As quoted by Upendra Baxi, "The Second Gujarat Catastrophe," *EPW* 37 (August 24, 2002): 3521.

[227] 'Symbolic violence' is a term used by Bourdieu; quoted by Joe Painter, "Pierre Bourdieu," in *Thinking Space*," ed. M. Crang and N. Thrift (London and New York: Routledge, 2000), 246.

[228] See Kancha Ilaiah, "Needed, a Transformation," *The Hindu*, 23 April 2002, 10.

[229] See Pierre Bourdieu, *Language and Symbolic Power* (Cambridge: Polity Press, 1991), 167.

[230] See Paula Richman, "Introduction: The Diversity of the Râmâyana Tradition," in *Many Râmâyanas: The Diversity of a Narrative Tradition in South Asia*, ed. idem (Delhi: OUP, 1994), 3-21, as well as the other articles in the book for insights into the diversity of the Râmâyana tradition.

[231] See B.R. Ambedkar, *Riddle of Rama and Krishna* (Bangalore: Dalit Sahitya Akademy, 1988), 5-18.

[232] Lord Ram has today been transformed from benign deity to belligerent warrior out to wreck havoc for the reclamation of his *janmabhoomi*. Mark Juergensmeyer, *Terror in the Mind of God: The Global Rise of Religious Violence* (New Delhi: OUP, 2001), 146, points out how mythical struggles (what he calls 'cosmic war') can be placed at the service of worldly political battles. Khare, *ibid.*, writes: "The Gujarat carnage became a modern day equivalent of *Mahabharata*, a battle of almost epic proportions, pitting the Hindus and their civilizational values against a host of external forces – the international church, the Islamic world and its terrorist outfits – all out to deny Mother India its moment of security and glory."

[233] See Ilaiah, *Why I Am Not a Hindu*, 114-32, for the definition and distinctions between the two.

[234] Ilaiah, *ibid.*, 115-6.

[235] See Hansen, 203-14, especially 210-4, for an analysis of this phenomenon.

[236] The world has witnessed this in the rise of Fascism, Nazism, ethnic nationalisms in Africa and the Balkans, those fighting for religious nationalisms and theocracies, etc.

[237] Lahker and Dhanushkodi, 138.

[238] See "Communalism as a Political Strategy," in *Human Rights Watch* 15/4 (July 2003): 51-64, which shows how communalism is used as a political strategy to get support from people by fragmenting groups, creating divisions and getting votes as in the December 2002 Gujarat elections; also, Harish Khare, "After Gujarat," *Seminar* 521 (January 2003): 30-3, for an insightful

post-election analysis of the Gujarat situation. Academics like Ghanshyam Shah argued that communal politics was not sufficient to win elections in his "Contestation and Negotiations: Hindutva Sentiments and Temporal Interests in Gujarat Elections," *EPW* 37 (November 30, 2002): 4838-43. However, this was not to be the case because the communal card has reaped rich dividends at the polls.

CHAPTER THREE

Principles and Representations: Creating Subaltern Space

3.1 Ethical Positioning, Establishing Principles and Exploring Spaces

We have studied the conflicts threatening two subaltern communities in Gujarat – namely, the adivasis of south Gujarat and the Muslim minority – and analyzed some of the causes and consequences of such conflict in terms of what 'space' they allotted to these communities, and what meaning can be drawn from such conflicts. We saw that, on the one hand, the state did not address the spatial concerns of subaltern groups (evidenced in its failure to ensure adivasi ownership over the *jungle-jal-jamin*); and, on the other, the powerful groups in the state exercised influence to define nationhood on the basis of religion and ethnicity, leading to de-territorializing and ghettoisation of Muslims. These conflicts were heightened not only by use of overt, brute force, but also by covert 'symbolic violence'. Broken as these communities are, they are not crushed. Subaltern groups also have the power to protest and resist. Hence, there is need to explore and evolve 'counter spaces' of resistance and to offer alternative models of community.

This chapter offers hermeneutical principles or interpretative keys that will help the building of community, taking into account the handicaps of underprivileged groups. This community-building exercise, evidently, will involve all communities in India with a view to assuring all communities their legitimate space. I deal here with spatiality to the extent that I will explore the *representations of space* (conceived space) and *representational spaces* (lived space) also termed *secondspace* and *thirdspace*, respectively.[1] However, speaking of 'representation' the questions arise: Who represents whom? Or, who can speak for whom? I had earlier established the grounds for adopting a subaltern perspective and took upon myself the task of interpreting the tribal world – its texts, contexts and oral traditions – in conversation with Scripture and Catholic Tradition. However, one might question both, my legitimacy as well as my competence to represent the subalterns. An assessment of this book might help one to comment about the latter; but, for the former, I draw attention to a query of Spivak.

Gayatri Spivak has raised the question, "Can the subaltern speak?"[2] in connection with both, the subalterns' capacity, as well as the validity of the 'non-subalterns' to represent subaltern concerns. Spivak argues that, at first sight, a subaltern might seem to be the best 'representative' to represent her or his group at any forum. However, it is likely that the subaltern's capacity to adequately represent her or his group in changing contexts is affected – or even diminished – since the dynamics of power changes in diverse contexts. But, if agency is truly to be restored to subaltern groups, then it must be the subalterns themselves who should seek ways and means of adequate and effective self-representation. Till such time, there is no reason to deny the possibility of the non-subaltern 'speaking for' the subalterns. This 'speaking for' does not entail replacing or substituting the subalterns, but it means methodological positioning alongside them. Rather than seek to replace or substitute the subalterns, I position myself alongside them so as to identify issues that are vital to subaltern community and to critique dominant discourses detrimental to their welfare.

In methodologically privileging the subalterns, I will first adopt a clear communitarian focus, since, as seen earlier, the sense of solidarity and community is strong among disprivileged groups. Second, I hold that all texts – social, political, cultural or religious – are always coloured by particular perspectives, personal prejudices and ideological biases,[3] and therefore I shall read them with a hermeneutic of suspicion.[4] Third, I recognize the 'distance' between the context of the author and that of the subalterns who read or interpret a text.[5] This will insure against any 'substantialisation' or 'essentialisation' of texts that contradicts the subalterns' freedom and creativity, and will, possibly, produce new meanings. Fourth, I take cognizance of the cleavages and 'silent spaces' of history, as well as the continuities and discontinuities of the old and the new, so that a 'fusion of horizons' might enrich our understanding.[6] Finally, in consonance with my transdisciplinary approach, I shall retain an ethical focus in all interpretations.[7]

While evolving what I call a 'hermeneutic of community' from subaltern perspective, I do not dichotomize between 'secular' and 'sacred' texts since such dichotomy is alien to the subaltern imagination. Moreover, as hermeneutists have shown, even the sacred texts (scriptures of religions) are products of history and require constant interpretation.[8] Indeed, one cannot dispense with hermeneutics,[9] for our theologizing must "deideologize our language and our message about God."[10] Thus, I now propose 'hermeneutical keys' or 'interpretative principles' that will create counter spaces for disprivileged communities in India.

3.2 The Principle of Equality

Equality is the most basic principle for the formation of community. If any life in common is to exist, persons must *be-in-relationship* of equality. *Being-in-relationship* shapes our humanity,[11] and the ideal of relationship can neither be over-dependence, nor independence, but *interdependence*. But, there can be cases of 'unequal interdependence' or '*de facto* interdependence',[12] as when two groups are interdependent and yet function on a principle of inequality. India still has traces of feudalism, casteism and bonded labour. Here, the dominant group's socio-economic status 'depends on' the loyalty and labour of the subordinate group, and the latter, due to deprivation and subordination, has no choice but to 'depend on' the upper class/caste or master/employer for survival. Such interdependence is unethical since the relationship is based on power, inequality and exploitation. Conversely, in an ethical interdependence, there is solidarity and reciprocity.

Solidarity and reciprocity flow from relationships of parity. In a community of equals, everyone is treated as a subject, a *Thou*.[13] In this case, as seen in the ethos of subaltern groups, many possibilities of support, sharing and mutual enrichment arise because of the equal terms and conditions within which communities encounter each other and cooperate in ventures that affect their common well-being. Conversely, when groups are consciously or unconsciously treated as unequal and inferior, the result is exclusion, isolation or even aggression and violence as the 'test cases' of Gujarat amply indicate. The principle of equality does not require elaboration, since "it does not arise from political compulsions or compromises but is derived from the core of human nature itself."[14] At the ontological level, every human being and every community deserves dignity and respect, and desires to be treated as equal to other individuals and communities, respectively. But, this does not happen where caste inequalities exist.

3.2.1 *The Caste-System and (In)equality*

Caste-structuring has been a feature of Indian society from ancient times down to the present. Indeed, "India was seen as a collection of castes; the particular picture was different in any given time and place, but India was a sum of its parts and the parts were castes."[15] Dumont too typified the Indian as basically being *Homo Hierarchicus*. But, one can contest a static 'essentializing' of caste since, due to socio-political pressures and the process of modernity, caste configurations have assumed new forms.[16] Besides, the adivasis and members of other religious communities either do not come under caste-categories or have discarded their caste-identity for socio-political or religious reasons.

The practitioners of caste either argue that although there is differentiation in the caste-system, it is merely functional, or hesitate to critique its inherent inequalities since caste belongs to the realm of *rta*, the cosmic order, based on the *Dharmasastras* and the law of *karma* that ought not to be disturbed. Gandhi subscribed to this line of thinking, which Dr. Ambedkar disagreed with, argued against, and opposed with strong words: [17]

> [I]n my opinion, unless you change your social order you can achieve little by way of progress. You cannot mobilize the community either for defence or for offence. You cannot build anything on the foundation of caste. You cannot build up a nation, you cannot build up a morality. Anything that you will build on the foundations of caste will crack and will never be a whole.

Dr. Ambedkar was aware that caste was a major obstacle in the nation-building process because, at heart, its very way of conceptualizing society depended on hierarchy and inequality. Thus, Ambedkar condemned it and opted out of the system as a protest.[18]

The innate principle of inequality in the caste-system creates conflict. After Independence and especially when Mandal 'reservations' were to be implemented, there were battles in Gujarat between the so-called 'higher' and 'lower' castes. Yet, this is not only a post-Independence trend. Caste has created conflicts during past centuries too when, for e.g., Jainism, and more so Buddhism, critiqued Brahminical hegemony.[19] Thus, Béteille holds that, "from whatever angle we view the case, the modern principle of equality was largely absent in traditional Indian society. True enough, equality was acknowledged on the metaphysical plane, but it had hardly any place on the plane of everyday social and political existence."[20]

Dichotomizing the metaphysical and the socio-political plane is problematic for subaltern groups; for, no matter what is considered to be the 'ideal' at a religious-metaphysical plane (*conceived space*), unless this 'ideal' finds expression in 'real' life (*lived space*), ethical norms like equality, justice, tolerance and so on will be mere platitudes and conflicts will continue.[21] Caste, we note, is practised even in Christianity – often with great force since, behind the façade of Christianity being a religion of equals, blatant forms of discrimination are practised, which often go unnoticed. Thus, caste-inequality is a problem cutting across religions, and so, besides critiquing caste at the ideational and metaphysical level (*secondspace*), there is need to tackle it at the socio-political plane (*thirdspace*) – where the question of democracy becomes pertinent.

3.2.2 *Democracy as a Safeguard for Equality*

The socio-political arrangement that best concretizes the principle of equality and benefits subaltern communities is democracy. Democracy is not only some form of governance where 'all' people count, but where 'all people count equally'.[22] If all people do not count equally, and if democracy serves only the interests of the 'many' even if they be a large majority, it would not be different from what Bhargava terms *mobocracy* – "the rule of the whims and fancies of a large number of people, possibly the majority."[23] The real test of democracy is its treatment of the minority. In the light of democracy's principle of equality, any form of majoritarianism, based on race, sex, caste, creed, class and the like, endangers democracy. Conversely, minority groups should not be appeased,[24] and allowed to further their particular, communal interests to the detriment of the common good of the body politic. Thus, "democracy means neither the rule of the majority nor of a minority, but primarily the acceptance of a common framework that prevents the concentration of power in either."[25]

Democracy recognizes all as equal and distributes to all the power to decide matters that affect their lives through political participation, governmental responsibility, assurance of rights, universal franchise, accountability and so on. Besides giving respect, recognition and responsibility to all citizens, gauged from a subaltern communitarian perspective, democracy is ethically preferable to other forms of government – say, monarchy, autocracy, oligarchy or theocracy – since it distributes governance over the entire body politic, and does not discriminate between individuals by granting some of them special privileges on the basis of their superior economic, social, political or religious status. Although theoretically it is easy to see that democracy is based on a principle of equality, when it is applied to the *lived space* of any society, problems arise because of the very understanding of equality and the levels at which it functions.

The principle of equality can be applied at two levels: *formal* and *susbstantive*. 'Formal equality' is based on principles of 'impersonality' (all persons deserve equal treatment) and 'impartiality' (all points of view deserve equal consideration), and as such allows for no discrimination whatsoever among individuals. We are bound to strictly follow a 'one person, one vote' policy. However, in Indian democracy, where innumerable inequalities – social, economic, religious and cultural – exist, diverse communities are 'unequal' from the very start due to social, political and historical factors beyond their control. These subaltern groups suffer inequality and deprivation due to lack of basic 'primary goods'. Here, 'substantive equality' goes beyond 'procedural' or 'formal equality' in negotiating the inequalities and injustices present among communities. It will seek for 'substantial good'. In this way it engenders 'egalitarianism' and nor merely 'equalitarianism'.[26]

In India, inequality between communities creates conflict. Certain groups find it difficult to satisfy even the basic needs like food, shelter and clothing. Here, equality is not just a desirable option but an *ethical obligation*. Amartya Sen resolves such (in)equality by stressing that one should be evaluated not only on the basis of 'primary goods' that one has, but on one's *capability* to transform these goods into satisfaction of one's needs.[27] Thus, for e.g., if two individuals possess the same 'primary goods', they are not necessarily equal since one might be handicapped in some way – say, with a terminal disease – and hence, has to satisfy a larger number of basic needs which makes one really poorer than the other with no handicap.[28] Transposing Sen's *capability principle* to weaker groups, it is not enough to assess the resources that such a community has (or does not have) at its disposal, but whether, and to what extent, that community has (or does not have) the *capability* to convert these resources into improving their well being, standard of living and so on. This will require that a community be recognized as a 'political entity' with its capacities and handicaps clearly articulated and correctly addressed in the political arena.

3.2.3 *Equality, Democracy and Subaltern 'Political Community'*

For subaltern communities to survive and grow *as* community, it is vital that they are located in the public sphere as 'political communities'. Irrespective of their ethnic, caste, religio-cultural and other differences, there must be a commonality on the basis of which subaltern communities must be able to rally for rights. This is only possible if there is a certain 'politicisation' of subaltern identity. This is well expressed by Chandhoke:[29]

> [W]hen individuals who are otherwise far too preoccupied in eking out a bare and minimum subsistence in adverse conditions come together and think out how to resolve their situation they are empowered because they are politicised. And to be politicised is to be made aware that collective endeavours offer possibilities of self-realisation. To be politicised is to be made aware of the rights that accrue to every human being by virtue of being human. It means that people who have been constituted as subjects and not as citizens by the policies of the state rise to demand justice, equality, and freedom; to demand that the state delivers what it has promised in theory.

The power of subaltern communities comes from their solidarity and numerical strength in rallying for their rights. This is well known to political and other parties who mobilize underprivileged groups for their own selfish purposes,[30] and not for improving their situation. Thus, it is to the advantage of disadvantaged communities to work for their recognition as a 'political community' by the state and its functionaries.

The concept of 'political society' as earlier mentioned has been developed by Partha Chatterjee[31] to refer to political transactions that take place outside the framework of formal institutions like those of the state and of civil society.[32] The 'political society' was supposed to describe a mediating sphere between the state and civil society that would guarantee subaltern communities their 'space' and their rights. Chatterjee saw 'political society' as filling the gap created by liberal democratic institutions and theories that did not accommodate the notion of communities and collective rights, which in Indian society have always been an indispensable part of life, especially of subaltern groups. It was felt that, by the state's decentralization of some powers to communities, people would draw on community solidarities rather than on state interventions to protect their rights in certain areas of life, as for example, in the case of slum-dwellers who could collectively organize themselves to win recognition and minimal protection from the state.[33] Chatterjee argues that community mobilisation is more familiar and easier for non-westernised Indians, and that communities are now claiming welfare from the state as a collective 'right' even though their mode of struggle may be in violation of the law. Their success will depend on how well they network with other groups and political parties to exert pressure on the state.[34]

The concept of 'political society' is also useful in the debate about secularism and toleration.[35] Theorists like Madan[36] and Nandy[37] see secularism as a product of the West and hold that it has outlived its utility. These theorists believe that India will do better by learning tolerance from its ancient religious traditions valther than from alien secular ideology. While agreeing with this view, Chatterjee examines secularism within the question of rights and cautions that majoritarian agenda like that of *Hindutva* is "perfectly at peace with the institutions and procedures of the 'western' or 'modern' state."[38] Hence, to offset the oppressive homogenizing tendencies of the state, there is need not to be swept by the homogenizing logic of modernity but to draw upon "religio-cultural capital"[39] like religious toleration, cultural values and group solidarities that have been a cherished part of Indian society.[40] This communitarian "religio-cultural capital" differs from community to community, and thus, Chatterjee maintains, "Even when one expects recognition of one's 'right to culture', one must always be prepared to act within a culture of rights and thus give reasons for insisting on being different."[41] This fosters substantive democracy.

In keeping with our distinction between 'society' (political, legal structuring) and 'community' (cohesion on account of diverse factors – emotive, natural, religio-cultural, symbolic, etc.), we adapt Chatterjee's framework to conceive of subaltern community not just as 'political society' but also as *political community*. This will necessitate that subaltern groups be defined at the macro, national/global *political level,* and also at the micro particular/local *communitarian level.*[42] This will enable disprivileged groups to rally for their legitimate Constitutional rights at the former level, and also build up their own 'community capital' (namely, their unique *socio-cultural-religious resources*) at the latter level, albeit within the parameters laid down by the legislative organs of the state.

By adapting Chatterjee's 'political society' framework to conceptualize subaltern groups as 'political communities', on the one hand, the state will not be able to relinquish its responsibility towards securing the welfare of these groups, and, on the other, subaltern communities are also given the 'space' and freedom to express what is most meaningful and vital to them, thereby enabling their growth and empowerment. This will ensure that greater democratization takes place and egalitarianism is fostered. However, in stressing that underprivileged groups retain their distinctiveness, we will have to introduce a 'differential' among communities. In other words, we must move towards a more 'complex equality' that addresses issues of justice and human rights.[43] This will be based on a 'principle of difference' whose nature and ethical bases require attention.

3.3 The Principle of Difference

The principle of difference maintains that differences are a basic datum of human existence and thus must be recognized and respected in human communities.[44] India is distinguished by widespread differences among communities – linguistic, creedal, racial, cultural, regional, and so on. These differences among communities can either foster mutual sharing and growth, or create conflict and division. It is not easy to negotiate differences. Sociologists and psychosocial theorists hold that the negotiation of identity and difference begins in childhood at the individual level.[45] Individuals develop various attitudes very early in life as they interact in community.[46] Their *conceived spaces* and *lived spaces* are conditioned and controlled in such a way that borders between 'we' and 'they' are drawn. But, as Craib rightly points out, "Neither the self nor identity are simple social products, rather in the end they are areas of individual and collective freedom which are constantly threatened by the structures and ideologies of the wider society."[47] Thus, there is always a dynamic interaction among communities that leads to orienting the lives of individuals and communities, both positively and negatively.[48] As a result, the community locates its 'Self' and differentiates it from the 'Other'.[49]

Difference *per se* is a ubiquitous 'datum of existence'.[50] But, any 'ascribed differences' that *a priori* impute value of high-low and pure-impure to subaltern groups, violate the basic ethical principle of the equality of all humans beings. Therefore, such differences – as in the case of caste differences – are undoubtedly unethical, even if backed by religious belief. A critical 'hermeneutic of suspicion' must be used here to distinguish between what is 'liberative' in religion and what is discriminatory and demeaning. This was done by Ambedkar[51] and other religious reformers. Thus, rejecting the ascribed differences like those legitimized by caste, the principle of difference we seek to develop can be described by what Uberoi calls, "a unity through equality *and* difference, relations of mutuality, complementarity and exchange in society, 'unity in variety'," that can only be attained "by the reconciliation or negotiation of equality *and* difference."[52] In reconciling or negotiating difference, we now examine three possible options – i.e., (i) indifference to difference, (ii) destruction of difference, (iii) deference to difference – and show that the third option is ethically superior to the preceding two, since it is the only one that offers possibilities of constructing subaltern community and preventing conflict.

3.3.1 *Indifference to Difference*

Difference can be encountered with an attitude of indifference. Indifference might stem either from feelings of superiority, or from prejudices that the Other is so different from anything familiar that it might preclude gainful encounter, or from a belief that the life of the Other is of no value to the Self. Indifference might be manifest either in a *laissez faire* attitude or might masquerade behind values like toleration and deep respect for the Other. Such attitudes give credence to ideologies like (a) liberalism, (b) postmodernism, and (c) globalisation, which are detrimental to the survival of subaltern communities. We briefly examine the indifferentism that characterizes each of these.

3.3.1.1 *Liberalism and 'Laissez Faire'*

Due to the pressures of free-market economy, since the early 1990's, India has been adopting a Western, 'liberal ethos'. While one could grant that certain advantages might accrue to certain groups due to economic liberalization, it is necessary to critique the very rationale upon which such ideology rests. Liberalism functions on the basic premise that, since communities have differing, often conflicting, conceptions of good, the state ought to be neutral in matters pertaining to the 'good'.[53] So also public policies must be independent of any conceptions of the good or that which gives value to life whether the conception is held by individuals or by cultural, ethnic, or religious communities. Such a position – based on Rawls's concept of fairness – would imply that "justice requires a 'hands off' approach to culture and identity out of respect for the equality and freedom of individuals."[54] This might sound acceptable in principle. However, in India, where the bonds of kinship, community, culture and religion are strong, any 'hands off' approach by the state will not be effective.[55] Thus, Chandhoke suggests that the state, as well as privileged groups within the state, must not be content with minimal involvement or neutrality required by secularism, but must positively grant to the disprivileged groups certain 'rights' – in her case, she argues for minority rights.[56]

At first sight, from the point of view of 'freedom', liberalism seems an attractive option. Second, it also seems grounded on a principle of equality since the state remains 'equi-distant' from all the communities. Third, it could be argued that it is 'just' from the angle of 'rights' since it equally respects the rights of all. However, there are hidden problems that will be clear by taking a concrete example. Suppose, on the grounds of being 'community sensitive' the Indian state decides not to intervene in favour of any group, and adopts a *laissez faire* attitude;[57] and, suppose that we have two conflicting claims – for instance, the right to private property and the right to dwell upon the land that one has long cultivated – that can both be grounded on the 'principle of justice'. Now, we assume that a landlord makes the former claim, and a poor adivasi, the latter. On the above 'just' grounds of freedom, equality and rights, viewed from a liberal perspective, the state should regard both the claims as equal and remain neutral. But, here, neutrality would either imply that justice is so neutral and universal, in which case it is abstract and devoid of content, or else it carries meaning in context that can be used to resolve conflict. In this case, as in others, being neutral is, actually, being indifferent, and implies evading issues that call for moral decision and responsibility. If true justice and equality have to prevail here, we are left with no option but to fight for the right to land of the subaltern, the labouring adivasi.[58] Evidently, liberalism's ruse of respect reveals a diffidence to bear the burdens of analyzing difference and assessing claims of conflicting rights against responsibilities towards the weaker, subaltern sections of society.

3.3.1.2 *Postmodernist 'Difference' as Indifferentism*

Complementing the liberal, *laissez-faire* approach is postmodern philosophy that so values 'difference' that, ironically, it actually often endorses indifference. For example, Derrida explains 'difference' in two senses conveyed by the French verbs: *différence* and *différance*. The former refers simply to 'difference',[59] the latter is a neologism (*neographism* according to Derrida) that combines the dual meanings of the French verb *différer*, namely, to differ (in space) and to defer (put off in time/postpone presence).[60] Used in both senses, 'difference' is linked to the words 'totalitarian' and 'solicitation', claiming that the structuralists' project of totalitarianism must be shaken off by a 'solicitation' (Latin *sollicitare* meaning 'to shake the totality'). In shaking off the totality and with its suspicion of metanarratives,[61] postmodernism repudiates all forms of universalism and privileges 'difference'. Seen purely from the angle of freedom and respect for otherness, postmodern privileging of 'difference' seems to meet ethical standards. However, we must assess postmodernism not only from its avowed aims, but also by evaluating its ends: Are its ends ethical? Moreover, since we deal with subaltern groups, we ask: Does it bring hope for communities, especially the subordinated ones?

In rejecting all metanarratives and absolutes, and in privileging the personal, the particular and the playful (*jouissance*), postmodernism reduces all truth claims to merely differing interpretations of reality with no possibility of a common morality.[62] Its deconstruction borders on nihilism, aesthetics is preferred over ethics, the Other is regarded as incomprehensible and one is expected to revel over the cacophony and fragmentation that characterize our world.[63] Postmodernism does not allow for any community since the project of 'community building' itself is regarded as an oppressive, totalitarian enterprise that necessitates some commonality, responsibility and common ethic which are bane to the postmodern mind. In this way, it erodes the very epistemic and ethical foundations upon which true community ought to be built.[64] By downplaying 'value' and by overstressing the need for total freedom in situating the communitarian Self, the uncritical valorization of 'difference' actually degenerates into states of indifference.

3.3.1.3 *Globalisation's Indifferentism: Building Aesthetic Community*

The boast of globalisation is that it creates a *global village* or borderless world. But, it is vital to inquire what 'space' society's weaker sections will occupy in such a world. Today, at the global level, we have what Bauman terms 'aesthetic communities' that "conjure up the 'experience of community' without real community," solely desiring the "joy of belonging without the discomfort of being bound."[65] The 'aesthetic communities' coalesce around money and merrymaking at the transnational and global level. The superrich of the very poor countries, too, can be part of such communities that replicate exquisite – yet 'exclusive' – lifestyles anywhere in today's borderless world.

The aesthetic communities are indifferent to differences at two levels. First, these communities are 'enclaves' within which one can 'live it up' equally pleasurably in five-star hotels, casinos and clubs anywhere in the world.[66] The differences among members are ignored since money is the great leveler. Here, fidelity and responsibility are not required. At a second level, the indifference of these communities leaves no space for questions of social justice, unshakeable obligations and meaningful dialogue. Issues like solidarity with the weak, long-term commitments, inalienable rights and fraternal sharing are never addressed. Clearly, the communities that globalisation seeks to create are immoral to the extent that they anaesthetize consciences and coexist – without any sense of indignation or injustice – with realities like poverty, hunger and exploitation.

3.3.2   *Destruction of Difference*

Apart from the attitude of indifference to difference as seen in processes like liberalism, postmodernism and globalisation, there is also the possibility of destroying difference. This has often happened in encounters involving subordinated groups where the destruction is not only blatant annihilation of the Other, but also in the encountering of the Other only in terms that are 'familiar' or 'same' to the Self. Overstressing the sameness implies that the Self treats the Other as 'another Self', and thus, this is an instance of negating otherness. Here, the Other is not encountered *as* Other but as a projected image of the Self,[67] and is a form of 'veiled violence', as difference is conquered, converted or categorized for Self-interest. Let us see how the socio-historical processes in India have destroyed difference, often covertly.

3.3.2.1 *The Veiled Violence of (Neo)colonialism and Christendom*

Communities in pre-colonial India were built around the bonds of location, castes, occupations, sects, languages, etc., and were characterized by great diversity.[68] There was what has been called a 'fission and fusion' that allowed for fluidity across tribes, sects, creeds, classes, castes, cultures, rituals, art and dance forms.[69] Constructions of Self and Other derived from local conditions and there was no clear and homogenous 'Indian national consciousness' as such. But, due to colonial intervention, two trends seemed to emerge: on the one hand, the colonizers had to show that India was the 'primitive Other' that did not fit into a universal narrative of progress and modernity and hence, had to be civilized and ruled through what Chatterjee terms the 'rule of colonial difference'.[70] On the other hand, colonialism required an 'Indian Self' that would be similar to the colonial Self, but only to serve colonial interests. Thus, it bred a class of 'Europeanized Indians' who were products of the educational system introduced by Macaulay. These were, in his words, "a class of persons, Indian in blood and colour, but English in taste, in opinion, in morals and in intellect."[71] Both these options, bound to the exercise of power,[72] were destructive of otherness – the former, by showing the Indian as 'primitive Other' to be civilized, the latter, as 'similar Self' but subordinate and subservient to colonial Self whose epistemology, etiquette and ethic were the only ones to be emulated everywhere.

The colonial destruction of difference – mainly cultural, social and political, has had its echo in the religious field as well with an aggressive expansionism of Christianity that can be called 'Christendom' or 'missionary colonialism'.[73] Foreign missionaries earlier accompanied colonizers to the Indies in their God-mandated mission to 'save souls'. The soul was conceived as an abstraction from, and considered superior to, the body. This body-soul dichotomy has always been alien to the down-to-earth subaltern spirituality of *devas*, *devis* and demons which, we have seen, was connected with body/earth cycles.[74] Thus, we have seen how some fanatic Christian groups in Gujarat's Dangs district, whose worldview is not very different from the colonial one, have created conflicts not only in Gujarat, but in many parts of India.[75] These groups had a disparaging attitude towards adivasi culture. Moreover, as a result of their interventions, conversions took place at a religio-ideational plane (in *conceived space*), whereas the socio-political conditions of the converts were hardly understood, much less responded to and resolved (in *lived space*). Thus, not only did such missionaries not resolve the socio-political problems, but they also created new conflicts in the realm of identities and cultures.

3.3.2.2   The Pitfalls of the Modernist Project

Related to the destruction of difference due to colonial interventions, is the role played by Nehru's modernist project that strove to make India a unified, industrialized and prosperous nation, This did bring some tangible benefits to subaltern groups in terms of economic advancement and weakening of the stranglehold of caste of migrants to India's cities. However, since the bulk of Indians live in the rural areas with traditional, agriculture-based systems that determine most aspects of life, the uncritical endorsement of an industry-based model of development gave rise to many crises since a techno-socio framework rested uneasily over an agro-socio one. Part of the problem was that the dynamics of modernism, based on Greek logic, Roman legalism, Church authority, etc., did not match Indian traditional, social conditions and institutions, and caused conflicts.[76]

The problems that arose due to skewed industrial development affected mostly the weaker sections of society.[77] The 'unbalanced industrialization'[78] in the urban sector and a sporadic flow of poor into the cities triggered a collapse of rural economy, an erosion of indigenous administrative systems,[79] depreciation of Indian culture, handicrafts and homemade goods, massive unemployment, exploitation of workers and the emergence of slums. Modernity gave rise to a distinct geography of factories and slums. We saw earlier how this affected the subaltern groups in Gujarat. For instance, Muslims who came into the cities and began to benefit from the processes of modernization began to be perceived as a threat to the traditional power-centres of caste-ridden society. In an attempt to "put them in place," they have been systematically targeted in communal conflagrations.

Apart from these problems, the anthropology of modernism can be critiqued on the basis of it being reductionist and mechanist since people are seen not as persons-in-relationship but as objects-of-production subjected to surveillance and control. The conceptualizing, as well as the control of the modernizing processes, was in the hands of the capitalists. In Gujarat, it was the *savarnas* (mainly, Brahmins-*Banias-Patidars*) who dominated both, the urban as well as rural spaces. Thus, while modernism enabled them to increase their economic and political power, it led to alienation of groups like the Muslims who were expected to either adopt alien culture or suffer the consequences of daring to be different.

3.3.2.3 *Globalisation's New Homogenous Spaces*

Globalisation – economic, political, cultural or societal –[80] seems interested in the formation of so-called 'world community' built on homogenizing principles dismissive of differences. But analyses of the processes of globalisation indicate that the destruction of differences works in favour of the world's rich and powerful nations and to the detriment of the world's poor. Take, for example, the Structural Adjustment Programme (SAP) that is a prerequisite for globalisation that requires that differences between world economies be eradicated so that markets may function with equilibrium. The effects of SAP can be seen on India's poor. From 1991 onward, through SAP by the IMF-WB, India underwent what Chossudovsky calls 'economic surgery'. This benefited the investments of MNCs and NRIs, but killed cottage industries and rural economies leading to starvation deaths and greater inequalities among classes/castes.[81] When glaring socio-economic, structural disparities exist between rich and poor nations, how is it possible to have 'market equilibrium'? Evidently, the destruction of difference is only a ploy by the world's powerful to further extend their hegemony over the economy of the poorer countries.

The elimination of differences in economic/market conditions leads to the elimination of economic structures and ecological systems that have supported local and indigenous peoples for centuries, since the latter cannot compete with powerful global agencies. Moreover, globalisation's prime concerns are not human community, common good, human rights, equality and justice for the poor,[82] but rather free market, capital, trade, exchange, downsizing, productivity, profitability, etc. Globalisation without "a human face" has led to greater impoverishment of the world's poor and continues to create discontentment.[83] Even worse, it has also led to innumerable suicides of farmers, nationwide, unable to cope with the manipulation of markets and money.[84]

Globalisation also poses a threat to indigenous cultures, for, on the one hand, its complex processes of differentiation enable it to survive anywhere among alien cultures, and, on the other, as a result of a *'McDonaldization'* of cultures, it destroys differences and imposes the hegemony of the West over other peoples.[85] Seen from subaltern perspective, that attaches great value to community and communion, Western culture is overly individualistic and narcissistic. Moreover, globalisation's so-called 'community of equals' has inconsistencies; for e.g., when it comes to the movement of money, principles of uniformity implemented by the G-8 and MNCs, who manage world affairs, ensure that foreign funds flow undeterred across national boundaries, often wrecking local economies. But, when it comes to the movement of people, this principle of uniformity is revoked by (dis)privileged passports, visa restrictions, work permits, immigration laws, submission of fingerprints and the like that are enforced only for the world's poor.[86]

Globalisation has also led to what is termed "a new geography of centrality and marginality."[87] New power centres arise since the globalisation is creating a 'managed world' that is "mercilessly bulldozing humanity on the road to serfdom."[88] And it is the world's underprivileged communities that are invariably the serfs and victims of globalisation. Ethical issues of responsibility towards, and solidarity with,[89] these 'victims' rarely feature in debates about the (de)merits of globalisation.[90]

3.3.2.4   *Fundamentalism's Dread of Difference*

Another example of the destruction of difference is the fear that most fundamentalist groups have of differences. The fundamentalist's assertion of superiority does not stem from the foundations of any firm faith, but, on the contrary, from deep dread and insecurity to face differences. Thus, fundamentalists strive to create and inhabit a totalizing world – usually based on theocratic principles – by embracing every realm of life, both public and private.[91]   Every attempt at separating the sacred and the secular is met with suspicion if not hostility. The *conceived spaces* of the fundamentalists are replete with symbols and discourses of power aimed at forging a make-believe unity.

The fundamentalists' dread of difference is evident in Gujarat in two ways, one latent, the other, blatant. In the first case, the fundamentalists have not resorted to open aggression as much as to covert assimilation of the adivasis on the basis of spatiality of a *Hindu Rashtra*. In the second, there has been gross violence and aggressive alienation of the Other (as with the minorities). Like the aggressive spatial strategies of the *Hindu Rashtra*, the various nationalisms emerging on the global landscape[92] often seem to be powered by fundamentalist agenda.[93] Gujarat merely indicates how *Hindutva* nationalism is, at best, assimilatory, at worst, exclusionary in its efforts to destroy difference.

To conclude this section we note that the 'destruction of difference' need not always be overtly violent as in colonial conquest, communal conflict, or blatant forms of fundamentalism, but is more often covertly so, as in the case of modernity, globalisation and forced religious conversions. In all these cases, the Self does not encounter the Other with respect but manipulates or destroys the difference to suit Self-interests. This destruction of difference is detrimental to subaltern groups because, it is on the grounds of difference itself that subaltern communities can rally for their rights.

3.3.3 *Deference to Difference*

We now see how our third option of 'deference to difference' or 'respect for difference' is more suitable than the previous two options. For this we adopt what Dallmayr terms 'differential hermeneutics' or a 'hermeneutics of difference',[94] which accepts the Other *as* Other since the Other always exceeds the idea that the Self has of the Other.[95] In other words, we hold that any preconceived ideas about the Other are bound to be inadequate and will fail to fully convey who the Other truly is. This is due to the complexity and indeterminacy of human life and human communities. Thus, the principle of difference necessitates that the Self recognize, relate and respond to the Other *as* Other.

3.3.3.1 *Recognizing Difference in Spatial Trialectic*

Difference can be understood on the basis of spatiality. First, a community can perceive the Other by virtue of the fact that the Other occupies a different geographical space or *firstspace*. Next, a community can view the Other as different on the basis of how it *conceives* of the Other in terms of ideas, codes, concepts, symbols, prejudices, stereotypes, and the like. This is *secondspace* that conceptualizes people – positively or negatively – within networks of power. Thus, for example, a community may conceive of the Other as immoral or impure if the relationship between the two is strained, for whatever reason. We saw this happening in Gujarat. At a third level, *thirdspace* locates the Other not merely in *perceived and conceived spaces*, but in a wide open sphere that transcends both, *perceived-and-conceived*. We take this position since a community cannot be understood as a simple collectivity of quantifiable components but must be approached and encountered with extreme sensitivity and caution.

When Lefebvre speaks of the Other, he goes beyond any form of '*either-or*' duality. This Other is an entity that cannot be comprehended and contained in simple binaries. It necessarily involves a 'third'. Moreover, this Other goes beyond what anthropology and psychology commonly refer to as 'the other'.[96] Theorists like Bhabha too use the term 'Third Space'.[97] However, his *thirdspace* refers to a *hybridity* – an *'in-between'* that is syncretistic and characterized by negation and silence. This space is that of an apophatic *'undecidability'* in the realm of cultural description.[98] Such a position can be reached by a dialectic of thesis, antithesis and synthesis, the third term being a syncretic *hybrid* of the first two. We are not here referring to *hybridity* and *undecidability* but with 'making space' so as to recognize, respect and relate to the Other *as* Other. This entails resistance to easy absorption and assimilation, and a refusal to meet the Other by using categories of *sameness*,[99] for the Other is best encountered not by sameness but *by and in difference*. Existential philosophers like Buber earlier introduced a 'third' of encounter.[100] However, while these dealt with existence, they did not consider issues pertaining to spatiality and diversity of cultures, which is characteristic of a country like India. Thus, we deepen our reflections in the realm of culture, and see how differences in culture can be negotiated.

3.3.3.2 *Multiculturalism's Making Space for Difference*

The need to respect and recognize differences arises from the fact that one's differences are constituted by one's culture that comprises of the meaning-systems and values that mould individuals and communities.[101] A community's culture is important to it since it enables its members to organize their lives and social relations in meaningful terms.[102] These 'meaningful terms' include a vision of the good life of a community that may not appeal to other communities, and yet, deserves respect not because this will 'pay off' in the long run – which is a 'utilitarian approach' – but because it means much to its members.[103] Thus, the cultures of all communities within a nation-state require respect and must be promoted. This is possible by adopting 'multiculturalism' to suit the Indian context,[104] albeit with the following (a) condition, (b) caution and (c) corrective.

First, it is necessary to promote recognition of the diverse cultures in India, but only on condition that they meet the consensually derived provisions of the common good, in our case, those of the Constitution.[105] This will be possible if communities are articulated as 'political community' so that no community is exempt from following the dictates of the Constitution. In this way, while a 'political community' can rally for rights, it is also brought within the purview of responsibilities. This will ensure that every community not only benefits from its rights but also bears responsibility for fostering the common good.

Second, recognition of the many cultures in India must not be a ruse for (neo)liberalism but must foster the democratization process.[106] Evidently, since democracy demands the participation of *all* the citizens in public life, there is need for *all* – especially the weaker communities – to feel that their culture, language, religion and worldview is recognized by others not only as valid, but also as vital, for achieving the common good. This will enable communities to experience a sense of belonging,[107] that can be strengthened by: (a) providing the wherewithal so that the subalterns may preserve and promote what is vital and valuable to them so as to make it available to the polity, and, (b) that either stereotypes which are demeaning are dispensed with,[108] or that disprivileged groups are left free to stress or suppress their identities. We mention 'suppression of identity' since, should a person – for e.g., someone belonging to the SCs, STs or OBCs – realize that disclosure of identity will lead to any form of discrimination, s/he must be allowed to conceal it since such discrimination will violate our fundamental principle of equality.

Thirdly, and most importantly, when dealing with culture in India, there is need to decipher how this culture is inextricably tied to other forms of social, political and economic deprivation. In the West, since socio-economic conditions among communities are largely homogenous, one can separate the cultural elements (like language, religion and regional specificities). But, in India, it is difficult to isolate a purely 'cultural' identity since a person's social location and self-identity is normally over-determined by a complex, structured pattern of identities that tend to reinforce one another.[109] For e.g., the cultures of subaltern groups like Dalits and adivasis have systematically been diminished and destroyed over centuries. Given the fact that these, too, assume different contours in different regions, it is not easy to adequately provide for their recognition, or even to assume that subaltern groups – or individuals of these groups – must remain restricted to a subaltern status.[110] Thus, more than providing for recognition, the state must ensure that justice is done, reforms are undertaken and more democratization takes place.[111]

3.3.3.3 *Difference as Weapon of the Weak*

The destruction of difference is a form of veiled violence inflicted upon the underprivileged groups because an erasure of the differences at the ideational or ideological level does not ensure a changing of the ground realities of subordination and deprivation. On the other hand, deference to, and assertion of, difference, makes it possible for weaker sections of society to *retrieve their lost spaces* and counter such veiled violence. This is especially true for subalterns groups like the adivasis who have insidiously been assimilated into socio-political structures that do not address and solve their problems. In this context, one can say that difference, and the assertion of difference, becomes 'a weapon of the weak'. This difference, when asserted, becomes the ground upon which disadvantaged groups can claim their just socio-political entitlements. These claims are not illegitimate ones, but they are the means of seeking redress for historical and other discriminations that these communities have endured for centuries.

It is not enough that difference be merely recognized and respected. True respect to difference must not only be exercised in the conceptual realm by saying that the Other – and, the culture of the Other – is worthy of recognition and respect, but it must also be negotiated and ensured in the socio-political field where power-equations exist and power is actually wielded by diverse communities. Thus, there is need to introduce differentials in concrete matters pertaining to the recognition of difference, but without violating the basic principle of equality,[112] by introducing a 'principle of representation'.

3.4 The Principle of Representation

I have so far argued that it is vital to respect all communities – especially the subaltern ones – *equally*, as well as to recognize their *differences* and to provide for them 'in principle'. But, the danger is that the principle of equality and the principle of difference may remain mere principles at an ideational level unless we determine how these principles could enhance community and resolve conflict *in practice*. This can be done from the viewpoint of spatiality and subalternity by examining what are the 'representational spaces' of subaltern communities (*lived space*) and what are the 'representations of space' (*conceived space*) associated with them. For this purpose, I use a 'principle of representation' that pertains to two vital dimensions of representation, namely, (a) socio-political representation, and (b) symbolic-conceptual representation.

3.4.1 The Socio-Political Dimension of Representation

It is evident that, in order to function in society, every community must be invested with a legitimate amount of power. Being relegated to positions of subordination in Indian society, subaltern groups do not enjoy and exercise much power as compared to others. Thus, as seen earlier, unless such groups are articulated as 'political community', they are likely to be ignored in the democratic processes and in the allocation of common resources. This is what the framers of the Indian Constitution sought to avoid.[113] Thus, at the socio-political realm of representation, it was deemed necessary that *all* communities have a proportionate share of representation at the legislative, executive and judiciary levels of common, societal life. Without adequate representation, the demands and opinions of the weaker groups would be muted at the national level, and this would result in dissatisfaction and eventual conflict. It is not necessary to argue that socio-political representation is indispensable for all communities in India, especially the weaker ones, since the *need* for representation is unquestionable. However, one can question whether such representation resolves conflict *in reality* since, unless the representatives function in the interests of the groups they represent, their very *'represent-ability'* is at stake. The issue of socio-political representation raises some problems, which we must discuss.

3.4.1.1 The Problems of Socio-Political Representation

First, we asserted that recognition of difference is a crucial component for the formation and recognition of community. This being the case, it seems logically impossible for a 'few' to fully substitute and embody (i.e., to give space to) the 'many' who are absent, because such substitution and embodiment would imply that anyone can replace, substitute and speak for anybody else. Such an assertion contradicts the argument that particularity and difference demand respect and recognition, since every person/community is unique and irreplaceable. This problem is inherent and inevitable in *represent-ability* itself. However, this lacuna can be countered if: (a) the 'distance' – not merely territorial, but also mental, emotional, cultural, religious and the like – between the representatives and the represented community is minimized, and, (b) communities evolve mechanisms to monitor and maximize the working of their representatives.

A second problem arises with the functioning of democracy itself. Though, theoretically, democracy is the governance of/by/for *all* the people, in reality, its routine functioning is in the hands of a few representatives of the people. Now, these representatives form a miniscule percentage of the community they represent, and, that community can never be sure whether its representatives will adequately and effectively intervene in its interests since, being human, the representatives have many limitations.[114] Indeed, the inadequacy of representation becomes more acute in the case of those who represent subaltern groups since, as Chandhoke notes, "subalterns 'lack voice' inasmuch as they are unfamiliar with the terms of the dominant language."[115] This 'lack of voice' is neither a denial of subaltern agency nor is it suggestive of subaltern incapability of self-representation, but it is "a lack of linguistic and epistemic authority in the deliberative domain, which is arguably governed by a rule-bound set of languages, that of political modernity."[116] Thus, even when a subaltern represents the interests of her subaltern group, there might still be a 'gap' of representability.[117] This 'gap' refers to the discrepancy between who/what is to be represented and the actual representative (person) or representation (issue at stake). Thus, socio-political representation might not be as effective as people expect it to be.

Third, there are difficulties in representative democracy itself, uppermost among which is the allegiance that representatives accord to their political parties and not to the people who have elected them.[118] In India, 'party politics' takes precedence over the needs of the common polity. In this regard, Laclau – who is highly critical of the efficacy of representation – calls it a *fictio iuris* (legal fiction) since it is difficult, if not impossible, to eliminate the opaqueness in the substitution and embodiment concomitant with representation.[119] In other words, there is always the danger that representatives might not give the expected and requisite space to the communities they represent.

Another danger of representative democracy in India is that elected representatives, and the political parties to which they belong, often violate the ethics of representation. The 'mandate theory of representation' holds that an elected representative is given 'ascriptive authority' from the represented, and thus must function in place of, and in favour of, the latter.[120] The people's mandate is violated if (a) a defeated candidate is pushed into structures of governance "through the back door,"[121] or (b) a representative defects from the party s/he is elected from and joins another party with conflicting agenda.[122] In either case, the representative no longer retains the right to represent the people who have elected her/

him and ought to resign. This hardly happens in India where ministerial berths are randomly allotted and defections are rampant. Thus the need arises to closely monitor the functioning of representative democracy while providing weaker sections with rights and affirmative action to offset their socio-political handicaps.

3.4.1.2 *Empowering Subaltern Groups: Panchayati Raj and Reservations*

Aware of the preceding – and other –[123] dangers of representation, it is necessary to ensure that the risks of representation are avoided through the following: First, ensure that representational mechanisms function not merely at the macro level of governance (e.g., Parliament and State), but also at the local level (e.g., the *panchayati raj, gram sabhas, nagarpalika* and other micro units like the village *panch*), for, democracy functions best when a 'principle of subsidiarity' is applied in working for the common good.[124] Such a principle gives a sense of responsibility to citizens at the grassroots. Moreover, local bodies of governance more fully comprehend ground realities and are more easily accountable to the people. The strengthening of local bodies ensures that democracy is built upon a broader power-base with wider scope of people's participation.

Second, it is important to ensure that the Constitution's guarantees – namely, the 'rights' and 'reservations' pertaining to weaker sections of society – are implemented to support representation at the socio-political level, while also leading to the leveling of economic imbalances with greater participation and equality for all. With the rigorous enforcement of Constitutional guarantees, subaltern communities are not only protected, but their interests can be promoted. The group rights – for instance, minority rights[125] or reservations for STs, SCs and OBCs[126] – is a form of 'positive discrimination' or 'affirmative action' based on a principle of redress: "it seeks to redress the bias of past generations in the direction of greater equality,"[127] as well as to ensure that equality, justice and freedom is given to *all* citizens irrespective of caste, creed, class or culture.

Although 'reservation' in the fields of education, employment and electoral procedures is a form of socio-political representation that empowers and 'gives space' to subaltern communities, it is a contentious issue,[128] much as the issue of 'minority rights' creates controversy.[129] This is because some citizens, mainly from the upper castes and classes, either oppose reservations (as seen in the 1981 and 1985 anti-reservation riots in Gujarat) or rally for their extension to the 'economically poor' among their ranks. This opposition is not justified since the upper castes and classes already wield a disproportionately large share of power in the processes and institutions of the socio-political field. Moreover, extending reservations to the economically poor of the high castes is also not justified, for, the rationale behind providing for reservations "for socially *and* educationally backward classes" – viz., the OBCs, besides SCs and STs – granted by article 15(4) of the Constitution, is to mitigate the harmful effects of centuries of oppression due to unjust structures like that of caste; or, to quote. Dhavan, "to make 'unequals' equal."[130]

To avail of reservations, one must suffer *both*, 'disadvantage' *and* 'discrimination' or else the basic norm of 'social justice' animating the Constitution will be compromised. As mentioned when discussing 'democracy' and 'differences' above, the purpose of reservations is to go beyond formal equality and to insure substantive equity or egalitarianism;[131] for, instituting "the right to equality without the capacity and the means to avail of the benefits equally is a cruel joke on the deprived sections of society."[132] Ever since the V.P. Singh Government strove to implement the recommendations of the Mandal Commission on reservations, there have been clashes on the socio-politico scene, nationwide. These clashes were particularly violent in Gujarat. The upper castes have always opposed concessions to the SCs and OBCs, and stoutly stall efforts to introduce more reservations. For example, in 2004 the UPA Government had mooted the idea of reservations in the private sector, in addition to those in the public.[133] The move had been resented and resisted by those who already enjoyed great powers in the public sphere.

Reservations, we must admit, are also beset by weaknesses and have led to abuses:[134] first, most politicians use reservations as a pre-poll ploy to increase 'quotas' that make them 'patrons' and the polity 'paupers' with the result that many subalterns rally for reservation quotas and forget about their rights for social justice and equality.[135] Second, instead of generating solidity and solidarity among subaltern groups to challenge the repression of caste/class hierarchies, reservations have, on the one hand, given birth to a 'creamy layer' of subalterns who are assimilated into, and consolidate, caste hierarchy and hegemony,[136] and, on the other, created "Dalits among the Dalits and backwards among the backwards" whose socio-eco-political status remains largely unaltered.[137] Third, in the absence of real structural reform, reservations mask governmental inadequacies, and are thus deemed demeaning by some subaltern groups

– for example, women – who question their efficacy.[138] While accepting that there are these lacunae in the implementation of reservations, given the glaring inequalities present between the privileged and the disprivileged groups in India, I endorse the need for reservations, albeit ensuring that inherent dangers are minimized. Only when parity is restored among communities will the termination of affirmative action (like reservations) be justified.

3.4.1.3 *Minority Rights and Social Equity*

Related to the realm of reservations, the question of 'minority representation' assumes significance for the functioning of representative democracy.[139] Majoritarianism could foster the belief that minorities do not really count in matters pertaining to public policy. However, on the world scene, as in India, minority groups – linguistic, ethnic, religious and cultural – are today asserting their identities and claiming representation in the public sphere. As a response to this, many Governments and global agencies now recognize the need to invest representational political power in minority groups, for e.g., the UN, the European Centre for Minority Issues and the International Covenant on Civil and Political Rights (ICCPR) stress that, to ensure effective participation of minorities in the political sphere, there is need for a system of 'proportional representation' in legislative, administrative and advisory bodies, as well as need for ethnic, cultural and religious minorities to form their associations, establish political parties and so on.[140]

Minority rights entail power sharing, which poses a threat to the hegemony of the majority. Thus, majority groups often stir up animosity against the minorities by creating fears, for instance, by arousing a persecutory complex or by propagating myths that 'majority' will soon be reduced to 'minority'.[141] The malice and manipulation behind such moves is often exposed by demographic analyses that prove that such fears are unfounded.[142] Hence, if democracy is to retain its feature of being the governance not only of the majority, but of *all* people, and if it must abide by the principles of equality and difference, then it must address the legitimate needs of minority groups too,[143] including the provision of political power through 'minority representation'. To take an example, in Gujarat, Muslims are disproportionately underrepresented. In Gujarat's Legislative Assembly, there are 182 MLAs, of which only 4 are Muslim. There is, evidently, very little socio-political 'space' accorded to the Muslims in Gujarat.

In view of the above discussion, at the socio-political level, the insurance of rights, privileges and reservations for the weaker sections of society, is not merely a legal obligation, but an ethical one too. This is because the basic principles of equality and justice are not compromised with such legislation, but, on the contrary, they are enhanced, since glaring structural socio-economic disparities have been present for centuries down through Indian history. Providing a hitherto-denied space for socio-political activity to the subaltern communities will allow them to exercise some degree of power. Moreover, such measures allow for greater participation of *all* the people in the political processes, thus enhancing the efficacy of representative democracy.

3.4.2. *The Symbolic-Conceptual Realm of Representation*

It is not difficult to decipher the dynamics of the socio-political dimension of representation since this deals with *firstspace* and *thirdspace* that can be mapped and monitored in terms of parties and elections, visibility and voice of the representatives, number and percentage of representatives, adherence to the Constitution and seats in Parliament, rights and reservations enjoyed by communities, efficacy of representatives, etc. But, to trace the dynamics of the symbolic-conceptual realm of representation, one treads upon tenuous terrain. This is *secondspace*, the *representations of space* comprising of symbols, myths, ideas, concepts and the like. We now enter the field of *secondspace*.

3.4.2.1   *Symbols and Myths as Representations of Space*

Symbolisation cannot be equated with mere signification since the latter – carried out with the instrumentality of 'signs' – presupposes univocal correspondence between the sign and the signified.[144] In other words, signs only 'point out to' another reality and leave little possibility for ambiguity and misinterpretation. For example, a 'red' or 'green' traffic sign univocally and universally mean 'stop' and 'go', respectively. But, symbols not only point out to another reality, but also '*re-present*' it in the dual sense of (a) 'making present anew' and (b) 'taking the place of' the represented. Moreover, in the very act of representing, symbols, unlike signs, not only address the cognitive-rational-discursive faculties of the interpreter, but also the social, emotional, volitional, relational, ethical, behavioural and other realms. Thus, they have potential to create 'new spaces'. Symbols call for constant interpretation. Hence, the possibility of ambiguity arises; more so, in the case of myths.

Myths are verbally developed symbols.[145] While a symbol might be just an object, a concept or an idea, a myth is a more developed 'form of speech' or a 'system of communication' – consisting of modes of representation – that either (positively) reveals fundamental truths about the world and human life,[146] or (negatively) distorts reality through inflexion. One might argue that myths have evolved as a means to understand human existence and express the psychic unconscious archetypes and so on. Nonetheless, myths are quite literally 'man-made' and made out to be factual when they are merely semiological (being a network of signs),[147] to be natural when they are at most historical, and to be eternal when they are but contingent.[148] This leads to deception.

Symbolic representations are employed continuously in our socio-cultural interactions with others, either consciously or unconsciously.[149] Indeed, Geertz defines culture itself as a "historically transmitted pattern of meanings embodied in symbols,"[150] and Turner asserts that, "the very essence of humans and the world that they create flows from their ability to *symbolically represent* each other, objects, ideas, and virtually any phase of their experience. Without the capacity to create symbols and to use them in human affairs, patterns of social organization among humans could not be created, maintained, or changed."[151] A symbolic representation, notably, has meaning in a particular spatiotemporal context that might change, or even appear contradictory, in another spatiotemporal context. Borrowing from Lotman, let us term such symbolic spatiotemporal contexts as '*semiospheres*'[152] and see how symbols function therein.

Living in society *as* community entails functioning within several *semiospheres* that contain representations with their own dynamics and dynamism. For instance, there are social, cultural, religious and political *semiospheres* with 'representations of space' that affect our way of perceiving, thinking, knowing, relating to others, behaving, working and living. In other words, these symbolic representations – be they social, cultural, religious, political or any other – create identity, mould mentality, induce action, construct or obstruct relationships and demarcate spatiotemporal boundaries. Such representations are also 'mediators of meaning' that inform us who, what, and where we were, who, what, where we are, and who/what we can become or where we shall go.

3.4.2.2   *Symbols as Producers and Distributors of Power in Social Space*

Symbolic representations are, undoubtedly, 'mediators of meaning'. But, this meaning can only be mediated through a cultural context that carries its ideological bias and baggage of high-low, pure-impure, superior-inferior, dominant-dominated and so on. The ideological bias inherent in culture itself is neither adequately addressed by linguistic analysts nor by structural analysts who perceive meaning present either in the relationship between signs or in some pre-given invariant, respectively.[153] Such positions overlook human historicity that derives meaning from social contexts and historical circumstances not merely as 'product' but also as 'process';[154] and, in socio-historical processes, there is both, an active and a passive dimension. Thus, a community not only constructs, re-presents or locates itself in space as 'subject' (active, positive) but it is also conceived and constructed or 'subjected to' (passive, often negative) re-presentation of itself by others. We asserted in the previous chapter that subaltern communities, in particular, are often 'subjected to' representation rather than being 'subjects' of representation.

As symbolic representations, communitarian symbols, myths and narratives are *semiospheres* of a community depicting how the community conceptually represents itself, as well as represents other communities, to its members. Studying culture along Gramscian lines, Hall has called these a community's 'mental frameworks' that are – "the languages, concepts, categories, imagery of thought, and the *systems of representation* – which different classes and social groups employ in order to make sense of, define, figure out and render intelligible the way society works."[155] Accordingly, communities constantly construct and constitute themselves *as* community by taking recourse to these 'mental frameworks' that, when recognized with their symbolic-mythical dimensions and dynamism, address not merely the mental realm, but all the other realms mentioned above – viz., the social, emotional, ethical, volitional, relational, behavioural and so on.

Symbolic representations "frame relationships of social inequality and can be intimately related to structures of power and wealth. They contain ideological and hegemonic properties that represent historical and sectional interests."[156] Thus, Bourdieu speaks of the 'symbolic power' of the dominant classes who aim at imposing the definition of the social world best suited to their interests.[157] On the other hand, those without control over the symbolic-mythical representations, mostly the subalterns, even though they "*make* the world" by their labour, are subjected to the former who "conserve it and eternalize it" never allowing a language of liberation and transformation to emerge.[158] Bourdieu terms this 'symbolic violence' since one class dominates the others through "the legitimation of the established order by establishing distinctions (hierarchies) and legitimating these distinctions," resulting in a "domestification of the dominated".[159] In the Indian context of majoritarianism and *Hindutva*, this has been termed 'pedagogic violence'.[160]

3.4.2.3 *Symbolic Spatial Representations and Community (Re)construction*

We note that symbolic representations (re)construct communities by providing them with (un)pleasant memories of the past,[161] (up)rooting in the present and the force to face (or to fear) the future. It is here that 'communitarian narratives' – which weave together myths and symbols into spatiotemporal referents of cause and effect – emerge as stories and coalesce as histories that construct community. However, Kaviraj notes: "Narrative draws lines, it distributes people ... it creates a kind of 'narrative contract'. For the recipient of narrative cannot be just anybody; it is only some people belonging to particular categories who are privileged by the narration."[162] Thus, narratives – driven by ideology and rich in symbolism – unlike rational theoretical forms of discourse, categorize people and configure communities not on rational grounds but upon emotion.[163] Aware of the irrational and emotive potential of symbolic constructions, therefore, the dominant castes and classes strive to maintain a monopoly over the mental frameworks of people depriving subaltern groups of the tools of symbolic production.[164]

Not only do dominant groups control the symbolic representations of society, but, the State too – that, as in India, is often ruled by representatives from the upper classes and castes – often pushes its ideological agenda surreptitiously. This happens in many ways, as, for instance, through its division and enumeration of the polity along contested categories. We mentioned that nationalist 'imagined communities' were primarily products of the census, map and museum.[165] Colonialism created such imagined communities by dissecting India more in order to facilitate colonial control rather than to foster any form of community. Likewise, post-colonial apparatus like the national census, too, created arbitrary religious and caste categories that have led to a 'substantialisation' of hitherto fluid identities and categories. Thus, by its insistence on putting every Indian into some (sub)caste or religious category, the census misrepresents communities.[166]

To conclude the preceding discussion, we can say that symbolic representations not only 'create spaces' in society, but differentiate and divide communities within frameworks of power. Thus, they 'allocate spaces' to different groups. This is the 'symbolic violence' that creates conflict since subaltern communities are denied their freedom, their space, and their right of Self-definition and identity. Since we have been studying the conflicts in Gujarat that have used religious symbols and myths to divide communities, let us observe the dynamics of this special group of symbols, viz., the religious representations.

3.4.2.4   *Religious Representations and Absolute Space*

We have seen how, in order to conceal the socio-political problems that plague people and the inadequacies of the state, religious representations – i.e., religious symbols, myths and narratives – have been effectively employed to divide the polity and diffuse attention from the root causes. Thus, the question of (re)conversions in the Dangs, as well as the anti-Muslim propaganda that demonizes Muslims and 'de-territorializes' them, are examples of how religion has manipulated space to marginalize communities. It is vital, then, to question why religion is so potent in mobilising people, and whether, and how, its power can profitably be used to promote subaltern community.

Religion exerts great power over peoples, since, as preached by the 'big' religious traditions, it deals with the "ultimate problems of life."[167] Hence, beyond the visible, material, immanent and historical dimensions of religion, religionists stress the invisible, mystical, ethereal, transcendent and ahistorical dimensions even more. However, while the oppressed groups labour to produce the visible and material 'social space', it is the Brahmins, priests and theologians who conceptualize it and assert their authority over it with the use of mythical and mystical language. Lefebvre notes that "those who produced space (peasants or artisans) were not the same people as managed it, as used it to organize social production and reproduction; it was the priests, warriors, scribes and princes who possessed what other had produced, who appropriated space and became its fully entitled owners."[168] This appropriation of space is possible by producing complex religious representations (symbols, myths and analogies) dealing with *Absolute Space*[169] – the space that is not only earthly, but reaches out to heaven, not merely visible and real, but invisible and ethereal, and not just historical, but trans-historical. Thus, religionists produce symbols that open out infinitely in space/time, and demand absolute allegiance.

Religious representations do not only refer to images, symbols and myths, but they include ritual activity (cult) and moral encoding (conduct). The mediation of this vast space of cultic activity and ethical encoding is also usually the prerogative of the dominant classes/castes (i.e., Brahmins, theologians, *pujaris*, priests, males, etc.), and these activities are ultimately connected to Absolute Space too. These classes, castes and groups of people (mostly male) deploy symbolic, mythical language that, though always inadequate to express – much less exhaust – the divine mystery,[170] is made out to be adequate, exhaustive and eternal. In this way, religion and religionists exert great power over people.[171] Note that while society's diverse semiospheres have a determinate spatiotemporal confine that is demarcated by rules, laws, rewards, sanctions, penalties, human authority and so on, the religious semiosphere transcends all spatiotemporal boundaries by mystifying, divorcing sacred from secular, and investing ultimate authority with the Absolute.[172] This can create a 'false consciousness' among people.[173] The demand for absolute allegiance can also lead to people being ready to maim, kill and die for religion[174] – all, apparently, in God's name!

3.4.2.5 *Religion of Power and Power of Religion*

Since religionists mediate over *Absolute Space*, they are powerful in society. They also normally have access to innumerable societal resources. For instance, Gramsci argued that the ecclesiastical intellectuals "held a monopoly of a number of important services: religious ideology, schools, education, morality, justice, charity, good works, etc." However, these were organically bound to the landed aristocracy with which it shared its privileges over land and property.[175] Thus, whether it be in the West or in India, religious and social hierarchs have, historically, worked in tandem to preserve and perpetuate their power over lived space. Concretely, in India, the nexus among the upper castes – for e.g., Gujarat's Brahmin-*Bania-Patidar* nexus discussed in the previous chapter – has ensured the perpetuation of caste hegemony, much as Weber showed how Protestantism, mainly Calvinism, engendered the spread of European capitalism.[176]

We note that any ideological structuring, like that of caste and class, can be perpetuated mainly because religious beliefs bolster and legitimize it.[177] Here, one senses how social inequalities find their logic and legitimacy in myths like the *Purusha Sukta* that equate, for instance, Brahmins with the head (upper part, purity, idea-production) and *Shudras* with the feet (lowest part, impurity, manual work). Religious representations of 'celestial hierarchies' too seem to have been replicated in societal and ecclesiastical structures.[178] Thus, while it is necessary to apply a 'hermeneutic of suspicion' to critique any religionists or religious representations that strive for a 'religion of power' (meaning, religion that abuses power to perpetuate evil, inequality and injustice),[179] it is necessary to use the 'power of religion' (the positive dimension of religion that invests believers with a passion for what is right and good). This is crucial in India given the fact that religion is an important 'religio-cultural capital' of Indian communities. However, it is not easy to 'make space' for religion in public life, and also to bring it under the purview of the Constitution, since it tends to claim *Absolute Space* and allegiance for itself.

In India, religion has a 'totalizing character'[180] that encompasses every realm of the life of most Indians. Political figures of the past like Gandhi, Ambedkar and Nehru were aware of the 'power of religion' to either make or break Indian community. Thus, Nehru desired to divorce religion from politics and keep the state neutral towards all forms of religion (*dharma nirpekshata*), while Gandhi intended that all religions be treated with equal respect (*sarva dharma samâbhava*) while seeking reform within the framework of Brahmanical Hinduism. However, Ambedkar played a crucial role in the critique of religion that led to reform and creation of 'counter spaces' of assertion and resistance.

Today, Indian academics discuss anew the relevance and role of religion vis-à-vis secularism and nationalism, with opinion being divided about whether, and where exactly, religion should feature in public life.[181] We mentioned that Nandy and Madan, among others, call for a retrieval of religious resources to tide over community conflicts arising on account of an alien secularism and uncritical adoption of western models.[182] One can critique the view of these theorists regarding secularism and modernism,[183] or even show that religion could be disruptive of society.[184] Yet, the dilemma still remains, since, by merely stating or even stipulating that religion should stay separate from politics ('separation approach') or by indiscriminately conflating the two ('integration approach'),[185] there are bipolar dangers of either endorsing a neo-liberal indifferentism or fueling fundamentalism, respectively. However, in both cases, religion will enter public space through the backdoor and cause greater conflict. This has been the case in Gujarat and other parts of India. Thus, we must seek a different approach.

In consonance with our 'principle of difference', there is possibility of adopting what might be termed a *'differential approach'* that differentiates between the institution of the State as the ultimate authority for efficient governing of all peoples, and yet, provides a space and the freedom for diverse cultural groups, as well as the institutions of religion, to evolve 'religio-cultural capital' that could inform and inspire the State in the furtherance of humanitarian and democratic causes that will benefit all citizens.[186] This third approach has the potential to tap the *'power of religion'* in religious resources of peace, toleration, love, compassion, sharing, solidarity and reconciliation while, at the same time, ensuring that democratic principles are upheld.[187] We have already mentioned that this can be done to benefit subaltern communities by: (a) articulating subaltern communities as 'political community' and demanding its rights at the political realm, and (b) allowing new 'counter spaces' to emerge that, while, on one hand, are 'critical' of dominant representations of reality, will, on the other, be 'constructive' of community by bringing to the public forum that which is culturally cherished by communities and can be shared for the enrichment all. This is what we shall try to do in the next three chapters.

3.5 Conclusion: Towards a Principled Approach of 'Religious Representations'

Based on the contextual situation of conflict in Gujarat, and its effects on subaltern communities, this third chapter has attempted to establish 'hermeneutic principles' or 'hermeneutic keys' for understanding the dynamics of the construction of subaltern communities. It has done this from the viewpoint of spatiality. In other words, it has attempted to situate or relocate subaltern communities as 'political community' within the nation-space given the fact that inequalities and injustices at the local-national level, and inimical forces at the global level, work in tandem to deny such communities their legitimate social space. Note that we have seen space, here, neither as a one-dimensional geographical reality, nor as a duality embracing 'either-or' opposites, but in a *'spatial trialectic'* with a 'both-and' logic. The 'third' in this trialectic is always more than the sum of the first and second, more than the perceived and conceived, the real and imagined. This spatial trialectic is also always invested with power, overt and covert.

The three principal hermeneutic principles discussed were those of (a) equality, (b) difference, and, (c) representation. First, it was argued that equality and substantive democracy are indispensable for the construction of subaltern community. This is only possible if underprivileged communities are articulated as 'political community'. Second, in the context of India's rich diversity, we stressed that social, economic, religious or cultural differences need negotiation through the introduction of a 'principle of difference'. This would create conditions for not only acceptance of the Other *as* Other, but would also ensure that all that is valuable to communities – especially the weaker ones – would be preserved and promoted in multicultural Indian society. This principle of difference was also justified on the grounds that it was a kind of 'weapon of the weak' that could be wielded to assert differences and appeal for legitimate rights. Yet, such differences would have to find concrete representation in the public sphere.

The third principle – namely, that of 'representation' – best translates the ideals of equality-in-difference into concrete processes and structures that could strengthen the weaker and more vulnerable communities to express themselves, participate in the public forum and retrieve the space that has, hitherto, been denied to them. This principle of representation was developed at two levels: the socio-political and the symbolic-conceptual. While the former dealt with the visible and quantifiable elements of representation, the latter was tenuous, and to that extent, susceptible to manipulation. By examining the power latent in symbolic representations, we unearthed the capacity of myths, symbols and narratives to inflict 'symbolic violence' destructive of disprivileged communities. This was evidenced in the case of the conflicts in Gujarat.

Since, our focus is theological, we saw why one form of symbolic representations – namely, religious representations – are powerful in creating conflicts among communities.[188] This was because the power inherent in religious representations could either be abused in producing a 'religion of power' or used as the 'power of religion'. Since religion is so deeply embedded in the Indian psyche, this *power of religion* could become an important religio-cultural resource for informing and inspiring community. This can be ensured by adopting a 'differential approach' that would differentiate between the institutions of the State as the ultimate authority for governing of *all* peoples, and yet, provide space for diverse cultural groups to evolve 'religio-cultural capital' that would be provide meaning and motivation for community-building.

In the next chapters we enter and explore the field of religion and theologically evolve a 'religious representation' of God as Trinity by remaining true to the principles and hermeneutic keys we enunciated in this chapter, and by simultaneously using the religio-cultural resources of subaltern communities. In so doing, I hope to indicate how the 'power of religion' can strive to resolve conflict, construct community and create new spaces for subaltern assertion and action.

ENDNOTES FOR CHAPTER THREE

[1] See chapter 1, section number 1.7.1.

[2] See Gayatri Spivak, "Can the Subaltern Speak?" in *Marxism and the Interpretation of Culture*, ed. C. Nelson and L. Grossberg (Urbana: University of Illinois Press, 1988), 271-313, who contests the very ability of a subaltern to represent her group since the equations of power change when she translates the problems of her group into another context wherein that which constitutes her as a subaltern is changed.

[3] Juan Luis Segundo, "The Hermeneutic Circle," in *Third World Liberation Theologies: A Reader*, ed. D.W. Ferm (New York: Orbis, 1986), 64-92, maintains: "Every hermeneutic entails conscious or unconscious partisanship. It is partisan even when it believes itself to be neutral and tries to act that way."

[4] See, for e.g., Purushottama Bilimoria, "The Hermeneutic of Suspicion and Religion," *JOD* 23/3 (1997): 247-74, who cautions about Orientalism in the West's interpretation of Eastern texts, cultures and religions

[5] Paul Ricoeur, "Intellectual Autobiography," in *The Philosophy of Paul Ricoeur*, ed. L.E. Hahn (Chicago & La Salle, Illinois: Open Court, 1996), 35, terms this 'distanciation'.

[6] See Hans-Georg Gadamer, "The Historicity of Understanding," in *The Hermeneutics Reader: Texts of the German Tradition from the Enlightenment to the Present*, ed. K. Mueller-Vollmer (Oxford: Basil Blackwell, 1986), 272. Gadamer has termed this process a 'fusion of horizons' in his *Truth and Method*.

[7] I make a minor distinction between 'morals' and 'ethics'. The former proceeds from organized religion and 'society' and is legal and contractual; the latter arises from the natural bonds of our humanness and 'community' and is consensual and substantive. Enrique Dussel, *Ethics and Community*, trans. R.R. Barr (New York: Orbis, 1988), 28-9, proposes a similar distinction.

'The Declaration of the Parliament of the World's Religions' in *A Global Ethic and Global Responsibilities: Two Declarations*, ed. H. Küng and H. Schmidt (London: SCM Press, 1998), 7-36, can be cited as a model of trying to evolve a common ethic.

[8] See Gadamer, *Truth and Method*, 156, who defines history as: "the great dark book, the collected work of the human spirit, written in the languages of the past, the text of which we have to understand."

[9] This is stressed by Jeanrond, 181-2; also Joseph Putti, *Theology as Hermeneutics: Paul Ricoeur's Theory of Text Interpretation and Method in Theology* (Bangalore: Kristu Jyoti Publications, 1991), 211-2

[10] Segundo, "The Hermeneutic Circle," 71, speaks of the need to 'deideologize' our language about God.

[11] Existentialists like Emmanuel Levinas and Franz Rosenzweig develop such philosophy. See Michael Barnes, *Traces of the Other: Three Philosophers & Inter-faith Dialogue* (Chennai: SNP, 2000), 20-2, 50-3.

[12] Pope John Paul II, *Sollicitudo Rei Socialis* (Bandra, Mumbai: St. Paul Publications, 1988), 43-6, n. 26, distinguishes between 'de facto interdependence' and 'moral interdependence'.

[13] See Martin Buber, *I and Thou*, 2nd ed., trans. R.G. Smith (Edinburgh: T & T Clark, 1994), 15-7, who explains the *I-Thou* as the primary word of relation. In *Between Man and Man*, trans. R. G. Smith (Boston: Beacon Press, 1957), 26, Buber considers human relationship as a spiritual act opening out to eternity.

[14] Imtiaz Ahmad, "The Right to Equality," *The Hindu*, 17 January 2001, 12.

[15] See Bernard S. Cohn, "Notes on the History of the Study of Indian Society and Culture," in *Structure and Change in Indian Society*, ed. idem and M. Singer (Jaipur and New Delhi: Rawat Publications, 1996), 16.

[16] See, for instance, Partha Chatterjee, "Community in the East," *EPW* 33 (February 7, 1998): 277-82, who argues that the common interest of urban workers, and not only factors like caste, is creative of community.

[17] Dr. Babasaheb Ambedkar, *Annihilation of Caste: With a Reply to 'Mahatma' Gandhi* (Bangalore: Dalit Sahitya Akademi, 1987), 60-2.

[18] The golden jubilee of Ambedkar's conversion to Buddhism was celebrated in October 2006. The site of his conversion, *Deekshabhoomi*, in Nagpur, Maharashtra, still remains a symbolic site where many of those belonging to the low castes convert to Buddhism. See, Subodh Ghildiyal, "50 Years after Ambedkar, Another Conversion Wave," *The Times of India*, 21 October 2005, 1.

[19] See Bhiku Parekh, "Some Reflections on the Hindu Theory of Tolerance," *Seminar* 521 (January 2003): 48-53.

[20] André Béteille, *Antinomies of Society: Essays on Ideologies & Institutions* (New Delhi: OUP, 2000), 203

[21] Parekh, "Hindu Theory of Tolerance," argues that, on the basis of historical experience, Hinduism has not been as tolerant as it professes to be, one reason being that 'caste' has not been sufficiently challenged at the existential level.

[22] For the argument on democracy and equality, I am indebted to Chandhoke, *Beyond Secularism*, 118-65.

[23] See Rajeev Bhargava, "What is Democracy?" *Seminar* 389 (January 1992): 37.

[24] There are allegations of 'minority appeasement' by former governments. Bhargava, *ibid.*, 37, makes a finer distinction between *occasional appeasement* during elections and *persistent appeasement* that is unjustified. The question of the appeasement of minorities, however, is contested by C. Rammanohar Reddy, "Facts on 'Appeasement'," *The Hindu*, 14 September 2002, 10, and Mushirul Hasan, "Myths of Appeasement," *The New Indian Express*, 7 February 2001, 8.

[25] Bhargava, "What is Democracy?", 39.

[26] Chandhoke, *Beyond Secularism*, 149-65, problematizes 'formal equality' and endorses 'substantive equality' as the only appropriate option. The *equalitarianism* (formal) versus *egalitarianism* (substantive) distinction is helpful in seeking special rights for subaltern groups.

[27] See Amartya Sen, "Capability and Well-Being" in *The Quality of Life*, ed. M.C. Nussbaum and A. Sen (Oxford: Clarendon Press, 1993), 30-53; also, *On Economic Inequality* (New Delhi: OUP, 1999), 195-219.

[28] The 'basic needs' vary from community to community, from East to West, etc. David Miller, *Principles of Social Justice* (Cambridge & London: HUP, 1999), 203-29, argues at the level of 'needs' for true justice. He defines need as "what is minimally necessary." In India, the 'minimally necessary' remains ambiguous.

[29] Neera Chandhoke, "Governance and the Pluralisation of the State: Implications for Democratic Citizenship," *EPW* 38 (July 12, 2003): 2966.

[30] Wilkinson, "Putting Gujarat in Perspective," for e.g., argues that the problems in Gujarat are primarily due to the manipulation of subaltern groups by political parties for their narrow electoral purposes.

[31] See Partha Chatterjee, "Beyond the Nation or Within?" *EPW* 32 (January 4, 1997): 30-4; "Community in the East," and "On Civil and Political Society in Post-Colonial Democracy," in *Civil Society*, ed. S. Kaviraj and S. Khilnani (Cambridge: CUP, 2001), 165-78.

[32] See Sarah Joseph, "Society vs State? Civil Society, Political Society and Non-Party Political Process in India," *EPW* 37 (January 26, 2002): 299-305, for an overview of the issues involved in 'political society'.

[33] Chatterjee, "Community in the East," 281-2, gives the case of a colony of squatters who successfully rallied for their right to live on encroached land due to their recourse to rights' theory and networking.

[34] See Chatterjee, *On Civil and Political Society*, 177.

[35] See Partha Chatterjee, "Secularism and Toleration," *EPW* 29 (July 9, 1994): 1768-77, and also Rajeev Bhargava, ed., *Secularism and its Critics* (Delhi: OUP, 1998), for diverse viewpoints on the debate.

[36] See T. N. Madan, "Secularism in its Place," in *Politics in India*, ed. S. Kaviraj (New Delhi: OUP, 2000), 342-8; also *Modern Myths, Locked Minds: Secularism and Fundamentalism in India* (Delhi: OUP, 1998).

[37] See Ashis Nandy, "A Critique of Modernist Secularism," in *Politics in India*, 329-41.

[38] Chatterjee, "Secularism and Toleration," 1768.

[39] The term 'cultural capital' comes from Richard Roberts, "Globalized Religion?" in *Theology and Sociology*, ed. R. Gill (London: Cassell, 1996), 472, who sees religion as effective 'global cultural capital'. I have used the term "religio-cultural capital" to specifically suggest that religion is an important part of Indian culture so much so that the dividing line between religion and culture is often regarded as tenuous.

[40] Sarah Joseph, "Politics of Contemporary Indian Communitarianism," *EPW* 32 (October 4, 1997): 2517-23, gives a good overview of these debates from the various viewpoints of Indian communitarian thinkers.

[41] See Partha Chatterjee, "Secularism and Tolerance," in *Secularism and its Critics*, 369.

[42] Anupama Roy, "Community, Women Citizens and a Women's Politics," *EPW* 36 (April 28, 2001): 1441-7, makes a similar distinction in discussing the rights of women in a communitarian framework.

[43] Michael Walzer, *Spheres of Justice: A Defense of Pluralism and Equality* (New York: Basic Books, 1983), 17-30, argues for the need of 'complex equality' to offset the injustice of tyrannies and hierarchies.

[44] Thinkers like John Rawls too speak of a principle of difference arising from differences among communities. These can be negotiated by evolving an 'overlapping consensus' for formulating just laws for the smooth functioning of society. However, I develop the principle of difference in a different way.

[45] See Peter L. Berger and Thomas Luckmann, *The Social Construction of Reality: A Treatise in the Sociology of Knowledge* (New York: Anchor Books, 1967), 163-73, on internalization and social structure.

[46] See, for instance, Erik H. Erikson, *Childhood and Society*, 2nd ed., (New York: W.W. Norton & Co., 1963), 247-74, for his theorizing on the 'eight stages' of psychosocial development.

[47] Ian Craib, *Experiencing Identity* (London: Sage Publications, 1998), 176.

[48] See Sudhir Kakar, *The Inner World: A Psychoanalytic Study of Childhood and Society in India* (New Delhi: OUP, 1982), 113-39; also *The Colours of Violence* (New Delhi: Viking & Penguin, 1995), 239-53.

[49] Here, 'Self' and 'Other' refer to the images that a community has of itself and of other communities, respectively. The Self/Other terms do not refer to a metaphysical entity like *Atman* or *Brahman* although this sense is strongly present in classical Hindu thought. See, for e.g., Hajime Nakamura, *Ways of Thinking of Eastern Peoples: India-China-Tibet-Japan* (Honolulu: University of Hawaii Press, 1985), 93-106.

[50] Richard M. Zaner and H. Tristram Engelhardt, Jr., *The Structures of the Life-World* (Evanston: Northwestern University Press, 1973), 59, speak of this 'life-world' as: "a structured social and cultural world historically already given to me and my fellow(wo)men." Diversity, thus, is a datum of existence.

[51] In the confrontation between Ambedkar and Gandhi, for instance, Ambedkar writes, "Not to question the authority of the *Shastras*, to permit the people to believe in their sanctity and their sanction and to blame them and to criticize them for their acts as being irrational and inhuman is an incongruous way of carrying on social reform." See Ambedkar, *ibid.*, 63. In reply, Gandhi wrote in *Harijan*, August 15, 1936: "[I]f the *Shastras* support caste as we know it today in all its hideousness, I may not call myself or remain a Hindu since I have no scruples about interdining or intermarriage." As quoted in Ambedkar, *ibid.*, 85.

[52] See J. P. S. Uberoi, *The European Modernity: Science, Truth and Method* (Delhi: OUP, 2002), 119-20.

[53] For details on the liberal view see John Rawls, *A Theory of Justice* (Oxford: OUP, 1972) and *Political Liberalism* (New York: COUP, 1993). In a nutshell, the liberal approach accords primacy of 'rights' over the 'good' in trying to establish a societal ethic. The State refrains from entering into issues of 'good'.

[54] See Joseph H. Carens, "Justice as Evenhandedness" *Seminar* 484 (December 1999): 46.

[55] As an exception, a 'hands off' approach must be adopted by the state when divergent moral values arise as in religious conflicts where the state must not arbitrarily favour one set of beliefs over another. See Chatterjee, "Secularism and Toleration," 1773, who cautions about this.

[56] See Chandhoke, *Beyond Secularism*.

[57] Dipankar Gupta, "Survivors or Survivals: Reconciling Citizenship and Cultural Particularisms," *EPW* 34 (August 14, 1999): 2321, warns about the inaction of the state to specially provide for the underprivileged on the pretext of being 'community sensitive' and not interfering with the internal issues of communities.

[58] David Hollenbach, *Claims in Conflict: Retrieving and Renewing the Catholic Human Rights Tradition* (New York: Paulist Press, 1979), 175, argues that when conflicts arise between the claims of the rich and poor, 'discerning love' grants priority to the claims of the poor, as such prioritization becomes their *right*.

[59] As in Jacques Derrida, *Writing and Difference*, trans. A. Bass (Chicago: UCP, 1978).

[60] Derrida does not define *'différance'* but, in *Margins of Philosophy*, trans. A. Bass (Chicago: UCP, 1982), 11, explains: *"Différance'* is the non-full, non-simple, structured and differentiating origin of differences."

[61] Jean-François Lyotard, *The Postmodern Condition: A Report on Knowledge*, trans. G. Bennington and B. Massumi (Minneapolis: University of Minnesota Press, 1984), xxiv.

[62] See Madan Sarup, *An Introductory Guide to Post-Structuralism and Postmodernism* (Athens: The University of Georgia Press, 1993), 150. See also Michael Luntley, *Reason, Truth and Self: The Postmodern Reconditioned* (London & New York: Routledge, 1995), for a good critique of postmodernism.

[63] See David Harvey, *The Condition of Postmodernity: An Enquiry into the Origins of Cultural Change* (Oxford: Basil Blackwell, 1989), 116.

[64] Ernest Gellner, *Postmodernism, Reason and Religion* (London & New York: Routledge, 2002): 22-72, argues that postmodernism's relativism is a form of both, moral nihilism and cognitive nihilism.

[65] Zygmunt Bauman, *Community: Seeking Safety in an Insecure World* (Cambridge: Polity Press, 2001), 69

[66] See Aijaz Ahmad, "Globalization and Culture," in *On Communalism and Globalization: Offensives of the Far Right*, 2nd ed. (New Delhi: Three Essays Collective, 2004), 102.

[67] Maurice S. Friedman, *Martin Buber: The Life of Dialogue* (New York: Harper & Row, 1960), 61, judges such a relation not as *'I-Thou'* but *'I-It'* (i.e., making the Other an object for manipulation and control).

[68] See Romila Thapar, "Early India: an Overview," in *History and Beyond* (New Delhi: OUP, 2000), 114-36; R. Champakalakshmi, "Caste and Community in Pre-modern South India," in *Jeevadhara* 31/181 (January 2001): 5-15, and McKim Marriott, ed., *Village India: Studies in the Little Community* (Chicago: UCP, 1955) for the diversity seen in studies of 8 villages in 7 linguistic areas of 5 provinces in India.

[69] See Richard Lannoy, *The Speaking Tree: A Study of Indian Culture and Society* (New Delhi: OUP, 1971), 135-242, also A.L. Basham, *The Wonder That Was India* (Delhi: Rupa & Co., 1997).

[70] In *The Nation and its Fragments: Colonial and Postcolonial Histories*, 16-22.

[71] As quoted by Benedict Anderson, *Imagined Communities: Reflections on the Origin and Spread of Nationalism*. 2nd ed. (New York: Verso, 1996), 92.

[72] Edward Said, *Orientalism: Western Conceptions of the Orient* (New Delhi: Penguin Books, 2001), 332, writes: "The construction of identity – *is* finally a construction – and involves establishing opposites and "others" whose actuality is always subject to the continuous interpretation and re-interpretation of their differences from "us". ... It should be obvious in all

cases that these processes are not mental exercises but urgent social contests involving such concrete political issues.... In short, *the construction of identity is bound up with the disposition of power and powerlessness in each society;*" italics added.

[73] See Robert Eric Frykenberg, ed., *Christians and Missionaries in India: Cross-Cultural Communication since 1500* (Michigan & Cambridge: William B. Eerdmans and London: RoutledgeCurzon, 2003), 12.

[74] For e.g., Kancha Ilaiah, *Why I Am Not a Hindu*, 91, says village gods/goddesses, "function to create a common cultural ethic, one that re-energises the masses so that they can engage in productive activity."

[75] See Antony Copley, *Religions in Conflict: Ideology, Cultural Contact and Conversion in Late Colonial India* (Delhi: OUP, 1997), who illustrates with examples how the exclusivism and inclusivism that was the result of conversions to Christianity was rarely a fruitful encounter between Christianity and Hinduism

[76] See Saberwal, *Roots of Crisis*, 52-82, for a further detailed analysis of this problem.

[77] Jain, "Securing Their Future," argues that it was Nehruvian economic development that disrupted the Indian economy and paved the way for present day globalisation.

[78] Omvedt, *Dalits and the Democratic Revolution*, 324-42, argues that the lot of Dalits, adivasis and peasants did not improve, as the post-1947 modernist project resulted in 'unbalanced industrialization'.

[79] See Milton Singer, *When a Great Tradition Modernizes: An Anthropological Approach to Indian Civilization* (Delhi: Vikas Publishing House, 1972), 245-71, for details of the conflicts that arose in the encounter between modernization and traditionalism.

[80] Globalisation is a complex phenomenon conceptualized though various perspectives, mainly, economic, political, cultural and societal, whose main proponents are Immanuel Wallerstein, John Meyer, Roland Robertson and Niklas Luhmann, respectively.

[81] See Michel Chossudovsky, *The Globalisation of Poverty: Impacts of IMF and World Bank Reforms* (Goa: The Other India Press and New Delhi Madhyam Books & Research Foundation for Science, Technology and Ecology, 1997), 125-35, for details on the ruinous effects of globalisation on India's poor; also see C.T. Kurien, *Global Capitalism and the Indian Economy* (New Delhi: Orient Longman Limited, 1994), 94-104, for details on the adverse effects of globalisation on India, especially in its debt traps.

[82] Noam Chomsky, *Profit Over People: Neoliberalism and Global Order* (Delhi: Madhyam Books, 1999), 25-8, points out that the results of globalisation are always harmful for people – especially the poor — since it contains an inherent dynamic of placing profit over people.

[83] See Joseph Stiglitz, *Globalization and its Discontents* (London: Penguin Press, 2002), 247-52.

[84] P. Sainath, among others, has documented the alarming rise of suicides of farmers. See his "When Farmers Die," *The Hindu*, 22 June 2004, 10; and, "Seeds of Suicide – I & II," *The Hindu*, 20 & 21 July 2004, 10.

[85] George Ritzer, *The McDonaldization of Society: An Investigation into the Changing Character of Contemporary Social Life* (California: Pine Forge Press, 1993), 147, speaks of the "iron cage of McDonald-ization"; yet, it is seen "as a valued end in itself ... attuned to various changes taking place within society."

[86] See, for e.g., Rustom Bharucha, "Politics of Culturalisms in an Age of Globalisation: Discrimination, Discontent and Dialogue," *EPW* 34 (February 20, 1999): 481, who mentions the inequalities involved here.

[87] See Saskia Sassen, "The Global City: Strategic Site/New Frontier," *Seminar* 503 (July 2001): 30.

[88] See Frederic Clairmont, "The Global Corporation: Road to Serfdom," *EPW* 35 (January 8, 2000): 27.

[89] Thomas R. Rourke, "Contemporary Globalization: An Ethical and Anthropological Evaluation," *CICR* 27/3 (Fall 2003): 490-510, critiques globalisation devoid of ethics about common good, solidarity, etc.

[90] See Michael Amaladoss, ed., *Globalisation and its Victims as Seen by its Victims* (Delhi: Vidyajyoti & ISPCK, 1999); "Globalization and its Victims," ed. J. Sobrino and F. Wilfred, *Concilium* 5 (2001), and Arjun Appadurai, "New Logics of Violence," *Seminar* 503 (July 2001): 14-8, for the globalisation debate from the perspective of the victims of society.

[91] See *Fundamentalisms and the State: Remaking Polities, Economies, and Militance*, ed. M. E. Marty and R. Scott Appleby (Chicago & London: UCP, 1993), for analyses of diverse cases of fundamentalisms.

[92] See T.V. Sathyamurthy, "Nationalism in the Era of Globalisation," *EPW* 33 (August 15, 1998): 2247-52, for an analysis of the manifestation of nationalisms in the context of globalisation and neo-capitalism.

[93] See, for instance, Lancy Lobo, *Globalisation, Hindu Nationalism and Christians in India* (Jaipur: Rawat Publications, 2002), 104-34, for an analysis into the dynamics of globalisation and Hindu nationalism.

[94] Fred Dallmayr, *Alternative Visions: Paths in the Global Village* (Maryland: Rowman & Littlefield Publishers, 1998), 7; also his "Gadamer, Derrida, and the Hermeneutics of Difference," in *Beyond Orientalism: Essays on Cross-Cultural Encounter* (Albany: State University of New York, 1996), 39-62.

[95] This idea is in line with Emmanuel Levinas, *Totality and Infinity*, trans. A. Lingis (Pittsburgh: Duquesne University Press, 1969), 31, who sees the other (albeit, individual) as a 'face' that invites ethical response.

[96] Sundar Sarukkai, "The 'Other' in Anthropology and Philosophy," *EPW* 32 (June 14, 1997): 1406-9, taking insights from Levinas, argues for an ethical and 'participatory' knowing of the other in ethnography.

[97] See Homi K. Bhabha, *The Location of Culture* (London & New York: Routledge, 2000), 38.

[98] *Ibid.*, 127-38.

[99] See Jürgen Moltmann, "Knowing and Community," in *On Community*, ed. L. S. Rouner (Notre Dame: NDUP, 1991), 162-76, who argues that the other must be known by difference rather than by 'likeness'.

[100] See Buber, *Between Man and Man*, 204.

[101] See Charles Taylor, "The Politics of Recognition," in *Multiculturalism: Examining the Politics of Recognition*, ed. A. Gutmann (Princeton: PUP, 1994), 25-73. For an Indian perspective see Neera Chandhoke, "The Logic of Recognition?" *Seminar* 484 (December 1999): 35-9.

[102] See Bhiku Parekh, "What is Multiculturalism?" *Seminar* 484 (December 1999): 14.

[103] Susan Wolf, "Comment," in *Multiculturalism*, ed. A. Gutmann, 84-5, is critical of Taylor's justification of multiculturalism on the grounds that it has some special aesthetic or intellectual contribution to make and will 'pay off' in terms of an enlarged understanding of the world or a heightened sensitivity to beauty.

[104] Amir Ali, "Case for Multiculturalism in India," *EPW* 35 (July 15, 2000): 2503-5, claims that multicultu-ralism can be an effective counter to the homogenizing project of majoritarianism, as well as lead to greater democratization; also, Ananta Kumar Giri, "Promoting Multiculturalism." *The Hindu*, 3 February 2001, 12.

[105] See Marc Galanter, "The Indian Constitution and Provisions for Special Treatment," in *Democracy, Difference & Social Justice*, ed. G. Mahajan (New Delhi: OUP, 2000), 565-77.

[106] Multiculturalism differs from pluralism as it stresses equality: "It asks whether different communities living peacefully together, co-exist as equals in the public arena." See Gurpreet Mahajan, *The Multicultural Path: Issues of Diversity and Discrimination in Democracy* (New Delhi: Sage Publications, 2002), 12.

[107] See Parekh, "What is Multiculturalism?" 16-7, who points that although a particular community might be assured of its rights, it might not feel part of larger society in case its sense of 'belonging' is hampered by the demeaning or patronizing way it is treated by other groups.

[108] See Chandhoke, "Logic of Recognition," 38; also, Parekh, "What is Multiculturalism?"

[109] See Sarah Joseph, "Of Minorities and Majorities," *Seminar* 484 (December 1999): 32.

[110] Rajeev Bhargava, "On the Majority-Minority Syndrome," *The Hindu*, 9 July 2002, 10, writes: "The majority-minority syndrome is disastrous for Indian Muslims. It can hardly do any good to Hindus. It divides the nation,

mindlessly detracts from welfare and development, breeds hierarchy and, by inhibiting reforms, restricts freedom, stultifies communities and emboldens a morally obnoxious conservatism."

[111] Joseph, "Of Minorities and Majorities," 33.

[112] See Bhiku Parekh, *Rethinking Multiculturalism: Cultural Diversity and Political Theory* (New York: Palgrave, 2000), 243-8, terms this an "equality of difference"; also Mahajan, *The Multicultural Path*, 23, writes: "Different but equal: this is the leitmotif of multiculturalism."

[113] See Shefali Jha, "Representation and Its Epiphanies: A Reading of Constituent Assembly Debates," *EPW* 39 (September 25, 2004): 4357-60, who shows how the members of the Constituent Assembly engaged in extensive debate to ensure that fair and adequate representation was given to all the people.

[114] Sri Aurobindo, *The Human Cycles. The Ideal of Human Unity, War & Self-Determination* (Pondicherry: Aurobindo Ashram, 1962), 279, asserts: "[The] modern politician does not represent the soul of people or its aspiration. What he usually represents is all the average pettiness, selfishness, egoism, self-deception in him. ... Yet, it is by such minds that the good of all has to be decided .. to such an agency calling itself the State that the individual is being more and more called upon to give up the government of his life."

[115] See Chandhoke, *The Conceits of Civil Society*, 185.

[116] *Ibid.*, 186. Chandhoke gives the example of an adivasi who when asked to 'prove' that a piece of land belonged to him said, "I know for sure that this land is mine since the bones of my forefathers are buried along the boundary!" What the Government official wanted to see was a written *patta* (entitlement deed).

[117] See, for e.g., Gopal Guru, "Politics of Representation," *Seminar* 508 (December 2001): 29-32, who raises the question: "Who can validly represent a subaltern group?" In many cases, subaltern groups are represented by the non-subalterns, as evidenced at the UN Conference on Race and Xenophobia held in Durban, South Africa, in 2001, where issues of caste were raised by non-Dalits.

[118] See Neera Chandhoke, "Crisis of Representative Democracy," *The Hindu*, 19 June 2004, 10.

[119] See Ernesto Laclau, *Emancipation(s).* (London & New York: Verso, 1996), 84-104, ch. 6 entitled "Power and Representation" discusses the problems of representation.

[120] See David Miller, ed., *Blackwell Encyclopaedia of Political Thought* (Oxford: Blackwell, 1987), 432.

[121] Chandhoke, "Crisis of Representative Democracy" shows the illegitimacy of offering defeated candidates ministerial berths or nominating them for the Rajya Sabha.

122 See, for instance, Peter Ronald de Souza, "Whose Representative?" *Seminar* 506 (October 2001): 57-61, who discusses the tension between the 'mandate theory' and 'independence theory' of representation in the light of the many defections of representatives in Goa.

123 Besides the problems of representation mentioned here, there are other problems affecting the poorer sections of society; for e.g., John Harriss, "Political Participation, Representation and the Urban Poor," in *EPW* 40 (March 12, 2005): 1041-54, shows that urban poor (here, in Delhi) are not always successful in obtaining effective political representation and consequently finding solutions to their collective problems.

124 Antony Black, "Communal Democracy and its History," *Political Studies* 45/1 (March 1997): 5-20, argues that democracy will function better if power is distributed among smaller communities.

125 See, for e.g., K.S. Durrany, *State Measures for the Welfare of Minorities* (Bangalore: CISRS & Delhi: ISPCK, 1997), who highlights problems of religious minorities vis-à-vis the issue of Constitutional rights.

126 See Gurpreet Mahajan, *Identities and Rights: Aspects of Liberal Democracy in India* (New Delhi: OUP, 2001), 115-48, who argues for affirmative action so as to include subalterns in the socio-political arena. In this regard, articles 330 and 332 of the Indian Constitution stipulate that the SCs and the STs should be given reserved seats in the Parliament and in the state Legislative Assembly.

127 See André Béteille, *Antinomies of Society: Essays on Ideologies & Institutions* (New Delhi: OUP, 2000), 214-21, for details on the rationale and problems of 'positive discrimination'. See also Granville Austin, *The Indian Constitution: Cornerstone of a Nation* (New Delhi: OUP, 2004), 113-4, who argues that, "[T]he Fundamental Rights and the Directive Principles were instruments designed to bring about great reforms of the social revolution like social, economic and political justice for all.... Fundamental Rights have both created a new equality that had been absent in traditional Indian (largely Hindu) society and have helped to preserve individual liberty."

128 The question of reservations is highly complex. See, for e.g., Rajeev Dhavan, "Reservation for All?" *The Hindu*, 13 June 2003, 10; Neera Chandhoke, "A Quota-driven Polity," *The Hindu*, 18 February 2003, 10, "Justifying Affirmative Action," *The Hindu*, 4 June 2003, 10, "Reservations about Reservations," *The Hindu*, 16 August 2004, 10; also S.S. Gill, "Diluting Mandal," *The Hindu*, 24 June 2003, 10, among others.

129 See Chandhoke, "Why Minority Rights?" *The Hindu*, 27 July 2002, 10; Pratap Bhanu Mehta, "Minority Institutions and the State," *The Hindu*, 10 August 2002, 10; Rajeev Dhavan, "The Minorities Case," *The Hindu*, 15 Nov. 2002, 10; Amrik Singh, "After the Minority Rights Verdict," *The Hindu*, 30 May 2003, 10.

130 Dhavan, *ibid.*

131 See Gill, *ibid.*

132 See P.B. Sawant, "The Constitution and Reservations," *The Hindu*, 2 July 2003, 10.

133 See Nivedita Mukherjee, "Playing With The Future," in *The Week* 22/36 (August 8, 2004): 32-40; also, Kancha Ilaiah, "Demanding a Share" in *ibid.*, 36-7, for a brief response from the Dalit perspective.

134 See, for e.g., Dipankar Gupta, "Recasting Reservations in the Language of Rights," in *Democracy, Difference & Social Justice*, 509-11, who discusses the Mandal reservations in relation to those envisaged by Ambedkar who saw reservations as temporary, and vital to end untouchability and bring equality.

135 Chandhoke, *ibid*; Gill, *ibid.*, also P. Radhakrishnan, "Sensitising Officials on Dalits and Reservations," *EPW* 37 (February 16, 2002): 653-9, discusses the crisis of inequality in the case of Tamil Nadu's Dalits.

136 See Pradipta Chaudhury, "'The Creamy Layer': Political Economy of Reservations," *EPW* 39 (May 15, 2004): 1989-91, who argues that this assimilation has also diffused attention from burning economic issues.

137 Pradeep Kumar, "Reservations within Reservations: Real Dalit-Bahujans," *EPW* 36 (Sept. 15, 2001): 3505-7, discusses the complexities of 'social backwardness' reservations in the case of UP and Karnataka.

138 See, for instance, Meena Dhanda, "Representation for Women: Should Feminists Support Quotas?" *EPW* 35 (August 12, 2002): 2969-76, who points out to the lacunae of merely asking for quotas for women.

139 Granville Austin, *Working a Democratic Constitution: The Indian Experience* (New Delhi: OUP, 1999), 634, indicates that this is especially so since in India, "[T]raditional forms of hierarchy and privilege have licensed exploitation .. but, the rules of representative, constitutional democracy have given power to minorities and 'weaker sections of society'."

140   See Iqbal A. Ansari, "Minority Representation," *Seminar* 506 (October 2001): 37-8.

141 For instance, A.P. Joshi, M.D. Srinivas, and J.K. Bajaj, *Religious Demography of India* (Chennai: Centre for Policy Studies, 2003), divide the polity into 'Indian Religionists' (mainly Hindus) and 'Other Religionists' (Muslims and Christians) and show how the former will become a minority in the near future (p.38). Earlier there was also release of census-figures according to religions in which the growth rate of the Muslims (2.5%) was shown to be higher than that of other religions. Fanatics used this to warn people that the Muslim population would soon exceed that of Hindus. See *Times of India*, September 7, 2004, 2.

142 See, for instance, D. Jayaraj and S. Subramanian, "Abusing Demography," *EPW* 39 (March 20, 2004): 1227-36, who, with detailed statistical data, demonstrate that the book *Religious Demography of India* is "intellectually trivial" (p.1236), for, it is the outcome of: "exploitation, abuse and inappropriate application of statistical techniques in the cause of an

unsustainable demographic thesis" (p.1227). See also, C. Rammanohar Reddy, "Statistics and Demography," *The Hindu*, 30 March 2004, 10, for a similar argument.

[143] See Chandhoke, *Beyond Secularism: The Rights of Religious Minorities*, for arguments in favour of this.

[144] See Susanne K. Langer, *Philosophy in a New Key: A Study in the Symbolism of Reason, Rite, and Art* (New York: New American Library, 1951), 42-63, for a lucid exposition on the logic of signs and symbols.

[145] Louis Dupré, *Symbols of the Sacred* (Michigan & Cambridge: William B. Eerdmans, 2000), 92.

[146] Gerald Arbuckle, "Communicating through Symbols," *Human Development* 8 (1987): 7-12, views myths as "fundamental truths" that "provide a framework for comprehending phenomena outside ordinary human experience." The positive aspect of myths is also described by Mircea Eliade in *Myth and Reality* (London: George Allen & Unwin Ltd, 1964), 5, who understands myth as a narration of sacred history, i.e., relating events that took place in primordial Time. Eliade's view of history, however, is contested by Ivan Strenski, "Mircea Eliade: Some Theoretical Problems," in *The Theory of Myth: Six Studies*, ed. A. Cunningham (London: Sheed & Ward, 1973), 40-78.

[147] See, for instance, Anthony P. Cohen, *The Management of Myths: The Politics of Legitimation in a Newfoundland Community* (Manchester: Manchester University Press, 1975), 99-114, how two groups of political leaders manage myths to compete for legitimacy. Such manipulation is possible by using myths.

[148] See Roland Barthes, *Mythologies*, trans. A. Lavers (London: Paladin Books, 1989), 117-74, who lucidly analyzes the dynamics of how the myth works to distort and falsify reality.

[149] William A. Van Roo, *Man the Symbolizer* (Rome: GUP, 1981), 304, holds that, "all human operation is *symbolic*, but only consciously, intentional operation is *symbolizing*."

[150] See Clifford Geertz, *The Interpretation of Cultures* (New York: Basic Books, 1973), 89.

[151] Jonathan H. Turner, *The Structure of Sociological Theory*, 4th ed., (Jaipur: Rawat Publications, 1987), 334-5; italics added.

[152] Yuri Lotman, *Universe of the Mind: A Semiotic Theory of Culture*, trans. A. Shukman (Bloomington: Indiana University Press, 1990), 124-5, coins the word from the Greek *semeion*, meaning 'sign'.

[153] See, for instance, Claude Lévi-Strauss, *Myth and Meaning* (London & Henley: Routledge & Kegan Paul, 1978), 8, who holds: "[T]he structuralist approach is the quest for the invariant, or for the invariant elements among superficial differences." Here, as with other structural, cultural theories, what matters most are the underlying structures, systems and rules of a semiotic system as a whole rather than the specific practices which are merely instances of its use.

[154] See Valentin N. Voloshinov, *Marxism and the Philosophy of Language*, trans. L. Matejka and I.R. Titunik (New York: Seminar Press, 1973), 61, who holds that the meaning of a sign is not in its relationship to other signs within the language system but rather in the social context of its use. See also Geertz, 17: "Whatever, or wherever, symbol systems 'in their own terms' may be, we gain empirical access to them by inspecting events, not by arranging abstracted identities into unified patterns."

[155] In "The Problem of Ideology: Marxism without Guarantees," in *Stuart Hall: Critical Dialogues in Cultural Studies*, ed. D. Morley and K-H Chen (London: Routledge, 1996), 26.

[156] See *Social Construction of the Past: Representation as Power*, ed. G. C Bond and A. Gilliam (London: Routledge, 1994), 2. In this regard, in the Indian context see Nandini Rao, "Interpreting Silences: Symbol and History in the Case of Ram Janmabhoomi/Babri Masjid," in *ibid.*, 158, who sees in symbols employed in this controversy what she terms, a "symbolic legitimization of power", also see Said, *Orientalism*, 349, who mentions the complicity between understanding and power.

[157] Pierre Bourdieu, *Language and Symbolic Power* (Cambridge: Polity Press, 1991), 167.

[158] Barthes, 162.

[159] Bourdieu, *ibid.* Such a view is contested by James C. Scott, *Weapons of the Weak: Everyday Forms of Peasant Resistance* (Delhi: OUP, 1990), 234-40, who maintains that the subalterns – in this case, the peasants of Sedaka – have their own mechanisms for assertion and rejection of a symbolic world.

[160] See Jayant K. Lele, "Hindutva as Pedagogic Violence," in *Hindutva: The Emergence of the Right* (Madras: Earthworm Books, 1995), 81-103.

[161] For e.g., Robert N. Bellah et al., *Habits of the Heart: Individualism and Commitment in American Life* (New York: Harper and Row, 1985), 153, refer to 'community of memory' where immigrants, despite differences, construct themselves as community through remembering a shared ancestry, history, etc.

[162] See Sudipta Kaviraj, "The Imaginary Institution of India," in *Subaltern Studies VII: Writings on South Asian History and Society*, ed. P. Chatterjee and G. Pandey (Delhi: OUP, 1992), 33.

[163] It is important to note that emotions, too, are socially constructed, as shown by Rajeev Bhargava, "Community Sentiment and the Teaching of History," *Seminar* 522 (February 2003): 35-7, "since emotions, like beliefs, unlike sensations, have an intention." See also David L. Scruton, "The Anthropology of an Emotion," in *Sociophobics: The Anthropology of Fear*, ed. idem (Boulder & London: Westview Press, 1986), 7-49, who shows that though privately felt, emotions are culturally created, derived and used.

[164] Bourdieu, *ibid.*, 169, shows how this happens in the religious realm where a type of 'division of labour' takes place with religionists ensuring that the laity is robbed of the instruments of symbolic production.

[165] See Anderson, *Imagined Communities*, 163-85.

[166] Satish Deshpande and Nandini Sundar, "Caste and the Census: Implications for Society and the Social Sciences," *EPW* 33 (August 8, 1998): 2157-9, discuss the problems of census enumeration in India. This danger is arising once again with India embarking upon the 2011 census.

[167] J. Milton Yinger, *The Scientific Study of Religion* (New York: Macmillan, 1970), 7, defines religion as "a system of beliefs and practices by means of which a group of people struggles with *the ultimate problems of life.*" Rajeev Bhargava, "Religious and Secular Identities," in *Crisis and Change in Contemporary India*, ed. U. Baxi and B. Parekh (New Delhi: Sage Publications, 1995), 347, footnote 11, considers the 'ultimate ideals' of religion as: "… values that are incomparably higher than desires, and even than other values. They are of *ultimate importance*, override all other values and desires under all circumstances and all times. These command our fundamental, deepest commitment;" italics added.

[168] *The Production of Space*, 48.

[169] I use the term 'Absolute Space' more in the sense of 'eternal space' encompassing all spaces and times. It is defined and demarcated by religionists. This is slightly different from Lefebvre's understanding of the same, which is "religious and political in character"; see *ibid.*, also 229-91.

[170] Dupré, 66, argues that symbolic religious representations are inadequate to contain the divine mystery since they are polysemous, and yet, they are the only language available for such purposes.

[171] See, for instance, Matthew Schoffeleers, "Religion and Power: Introduction," *Social Compass* 32/1 (1985): 10, who points out that not only does power produce meaning, but systems of meaning also produce political power.

[172] Francis Gonsalves, "Wars of God and Gods of War: Religion and Violence in Contemporary Society," in *Yearbook of Contextual Theology* (Frankfurt: IKO Verlag fur Interkulturelle Kommunikation, 2001), 36.

[173] Peter L. Berger, *The Social Reality of Religion* (Norwich: Penguin University Books, 1973), 88-107, holds that religion can be alienating and creative of 'false consciousness'. He writes, "All human productions are, at least potentially, comprehensible in human terms. The veil of mystification thrown over them by religion prevents such comprehension." (p. 96).

[174] See Wilfred, "Religions and Martyrdom Today," in *The Sling of Utopia*, 164-81, for related issues.

[175] See Gramsci, *Selections from the Prison Notebooks*, 7.

[176] See Max Weber, "Religious Affiliation and Social Stratification," in *The Protestant Ethic and The Spirit of Capitalism*, trans. T. Parsons (New York: Charles Scribner's Sons, 1976), 35-46, for details of his thesis.

[177] See Hendrik M. Vroom, "Religious Hermeneutics, Culture and Narratives," in *SID* 4/2 (1994): 189-213, who shows how religious narratives

interpret human existence and affect community interactions; also, James M. Gustafson, "Possibilities and Problems for the Study of Ethics in Religiously Pluralistic Societies," in *Culture, Religion and Society*, ed. S. K. Chatterji and H. P. Mabry (Delhi: ISPCK, 1996), 240-59, shows how religious symbols & myths construe the meaning of life in the world and initiate action.

[178] See, for instance, Dionysius the Areopagite, *The Mystical Theology and the Celestial Hierarchies* (Surrey: The Shrine of Wisdom, 1949), 30, that asserts that God discloses the celestial hierarchies to us by "consecrating our hierarchy as fellow-ministers, according to our capacity, in the likeness of their Divine ministry...." Such assertions run the risk of legitimizing human hierarchies as modeled upon the Divine.

[179] Ambedkar, *Annihilation of Caste*, is a noteworthy example of this.

[180] T.N. Madan, "Secularism in its Place," 344, speaks of the *totalizing character* of Asia's major religions.

[181] See, for e.g., Rajeev Bhargava, ed., *Secularism and its Critics*; Arvind Sharma, ed., *Hinduism and Secularism After Ayodhya* (Hampshire & New York: Palgrave Publishers, 2001); Antony Copley, ed., *Hinduism in Public and Private: Reform, Hindutva, Gender, and Sampraday* (New Delhi: OUP, 2003); T.N. Madan, *Modern Myths, Locked Minds: Secularism and Fundamentalism in India* (Delhi: OUP, 1998); and Ainslie T. Embree, *Utopias in Conflict: Religion and Nationalism in Modern India* (Delhi: OUP, 1990), among others.

[182] See Nandy, "A Critique of Modernist Secularism," 329-41 and Madan, "Secularism in its Place," 342-8.

[183] See, for e.g., Anwar Alam, "Secularism in India: A Critique of the Current Discourse," in *Competing Nationalisms in South Asia*, ed. P.R. Brass and A. Vanaik (New Delhi: Orient Longman, 2002), 85-93; also Rajeev Bhargava, "Religious and Secular Identities," in *Crisis and Change in Contemporary India*, ed. U. Baxi and B. Parekh (New Delhi: Sage Publications, 1995), 317-49, who finds Nandy's views on modernity and secularism as "too simplistic".

[184] See A.R. Desai, "National Integration and Religion," in *Sociology of Religion in India*, ed. R. Robinson (New Delhi: Sage Publications, 2004), 54-67, who holds that religion will disrupt nation-building processes

[185] I borrow this insight from David Hollenbach, *The Common Good & Christian Ethics* (Cambridge: CUP, 2003), 117-20.

[186] See Bhiku Parekh, "Making Sense of Gujarat," also, Antony Copley, "Has Religion a Future in India?" *R&S* 44/2 (June 1997): 23-52, who argue along these lines.

[187] See M.S. Gore, "Secularism and Equal Regard for all Religions," ch. 9, in *Unity in Diversity: The Indian Experience in Nation-Building* (Jaipur and New Delhi: Rawat Publications, 2002), 189-203, for details.

188 Kaviraj, *Politics in India*, 24, asserts that: "[T]he religion that is causing intense problems in the realm of politics is a religion constantly reduced, thinned down, diminished, depleted." Hence the need to critique its representations, as well as the injunctions about time, space and rituals dealing with the 'sacred'.

CHAPTER FOUR

God is Tribe: Trajectories of Subaltern Trinitarian Theology

4.1 One is a Rock and an Island, Two is Company and Comfort

I have entitled this chapter 'God is Tribe' for the simple reason that the etymological root of the English word 'tribe' is *tribus*, derived from the root *tres*, meaning, 'three'. A 'tribe' was formerly used for a grouping of 'three' – originally, a third part of the Roman population who were divided as the 'tribe' of Ramnes, Tities and Luceres.[1] Although God is One and Undivided, Jesus has also revealed to us that God is Three, *Tria*, *Tribus* (Father, Son, Spirit) while always remaining *Unus*. One might desist from calling God 'tribe' or 'tribal' for, in common parlance, the word has a pejorative nuance for primitive, uncivilized peoples. Although I believe that our 'God of the poor/*anawim*' would rejoice at being called by some pejorative appellation consonant with the divine option, while personally considering God as 'Tribe' or, better still, as 'epitome of tribe,' I will not insist on foisting one and only one name onto God, for God is, certainly, above all names. God's Name or names notwithstanding, I begin my reflections with very basic and simple illustrations and observations on human relationships.

A Jesuit colleague once remarked, "It's better to be alone than to be in the best of company!" Not known to be one who enjoyed the company of his peers, and being a recluse of sorts, he lived in a Jesuit house and unconsciously enjoyed the comforts concomitant with being part of a Jesuit community even if, apparently, living and working alone. In other words, he was assured of his board, lodge and other expenses though he preferred to be alone. So, he was not really 'alone'. A community covertly dwelt in him although he was unaware of it. His sentiments have found expression in song, too. One might remember the lyrics of Simon and Garfunkel's popular 1970's song: "I am a rock, I am an island … hiding in my room… safe within my womb … I touch no one and no one touches me." The loner goes on to sing, "I have my books and poetry to protect me," and ends with: "and a rock feels no pain, and an island never cries." It's clear that the songster lives alone, feels like a rock and an island, has no friends, suppresses his emotions and 'protects' himself with books and poetry. It's likely, today, that one could protect oneself from entering into any meaningful relationship with others and yet mitigate one's loneliness by surfing TV channels or chatting in cyberspace. Such cases are rare, border on the pathological, and do not require much comment.

"Two is company, three is a crowd," is surely one of the popular sayings used when one wants to spend time or getaway with a loved one. The underlying assumption is that a relationship between two persons is perfect, whereas inclusion of a 'third' implies imperfection or excess. Much as I agree with this axiom theoretically, experience has taught me that there's much selfishness and self-seeking in most one-to-one relationships. The selfishness or self-seeking I refer to is, of course, often unconscious; meaning, when two people are in love or seek to enter into an exclusive one-to-one relationship, there is often an unconscious, hidden "you scratch my back and I'll scratch yours" agenda that can function quite well for two partners, even if ultimately it does not ensure their true welfare. I make this observation on the basis of my dabbling in youth and family counseling. Let me elaborate what I mean by giving examples.

In English theatre, the classical Romeo-Juliet couple or the modern 'Love Story' pair, or, nearer to us the *deshi* Laila-Majnu lovers drive home a message that love is eternal, immortal and faithful-unto-death. Perhaps. However, there's another equally evergreen Bollywood or Kollywood theme, i.e., the "*hum-tuum-whoh*" or "I-you-s/he" one that attracts greater attention and is usually pepped with plenty of poignancy. Here, the hero falls madly in love with the heroine and the two swear to love each other exclusively and eternally. Songs, dances and poetry aplenty make this out to seem a heaven-on-earth. Suddenly, a 'he' or 'she' – the 'third' – appears on the scene and creates heartache or heartbreak for one or the other of the friends. This 'third' transforms what seemed like heaven into a veritable hell. Interestingly, philosopher Sartre's famous axiom, "Hell is other people" comes from his play 'No Exit' wherein three unknown and unrelated persons are locked together in a room with no possibility of escape.[2] In the course of their conversations and interactions, each one realizes how unpleasant, even loathsome, the company of the 'other' is and how each of them creates hell for the other two. So, while 'two' is certainly 'company' isn't there also the possibility that this twosome relationship is more one of mere comfort and convenience since it does not accommodate another person? That brings me to a briefly examine the 'three' or the 'third', which I believe constitutes community, and yet, can also cause conflict.

4.1.1 *Three as Community, Three as Conflict*

While the above examples suggest that "three creates conflict," it is also true that "three creates community," meaning, one is never sure that a one-to-one relationship is mature and truly open to Life in all its complexity unless the two persons involved in such a relationship are open to a 'third' – be it in the form of someone or something 'beyond' what the twosome presently accommodates, imagines or expects. This can be demonstrated in the case of a married couple that enjoys marital bliss for many years. The attention and energy of each spouse is entirely and exclusively directed towards the 'other'. The birth of a child could initially be a source of great joy, but could also lead to conflict; because now, besides giving time and attention to each other, the couple must care for the child. There is the possibility of either spouse giving so much of attention to the child so as to neglect the 'other' spouse, leading to resentment and conflict. Or, it could also happen that the husband and wife are so lovingly lost in each other so as to neglect the child. Seen from anyone's viewpoint – i.e., father or mother or child – it is easier to relate only to just one 'other' rather than to relate to two others at the same time. Indeed, it's not easy to include a 'third'. Yet, it is only when the love of two opens out to a 'third' that true love is tested and 'company' (that can often be self-seeking comfort, at best, or selfish utilitarianism, at worst) blossoms into what I would call 'the first moment of community' with the possibility of either communion (positive) or conflict (negative).

The possibilities as well as the problems inherent in a relationship of 'three' can also be illustrated in the field of human communication. For example, when two people enter into a conversation, they can either find some common topic to discuss, on which they might agree or disagree with each other; or, they might choose to remain silent. Suppose another person, the 'third', enters into the conversation, a new situation arises whereby whoever is talking must make sure that the other two are drawn into the conversation. If not, it will happen that only two persons will be involved and the 'third' will be left out. Now, what happens if a fourth person arrives? The numbers four, five, six or 'many' can be broken up into smaller units of twos and threes and are not problematic since, if, for example, a fourth person arrives, there's the possibility of the group of four breaking up into two sets of 'couples' and some level of 'comfort' can again be reached.

The reason for my insistence of testing authentic relationships on the basis of the 'three' and not 'two' is simple: what often appears to be true love between two persons might not really be so, for, what is initially a close relationship could really degenerate into a 'closed relationship' unwilling to accommodate the 'third' – be it in the form of children, or other people, or varied viewpoints very different from what the 'two' hold as ultimate in their limited vision, or, even as Absolute in their image of God. The danger of an 'exclusive two' is that each one is likely to so totally depend – or 'over depend' – on the 'other' so as to lose one's freedom and personal identity and seek to control and manipulate the 'other' for one's 'needs', even if unconsciously. We will later enter into discussion of the dynamics of the 'third', but, with this little 'prologue', so to say, on trinitarian thinking, we now move on to evolve trinitarian theology by tapping the religio-cultural resources of subaltern communities. I explore the possibility of reinterpreting a traditional religious representation, namely, the Christian conception of God, the Trinity, by positioning myself in the *'lived space'* of disprivileged communities to seek new contextual meaning for what is termed 'subaltern trinitarian theology'. To do so, I first locate the starting-point for this subaltern trinitarian theology.

4.2 The Starting Point of Subaltern Trinitarian Theology

Every theology is shaped by its starting-point, context and assumptions. So too, as trinitarian theology evolved through the Christian centuries,[3] it was particular and contextual insofar as the socio-historical-ecclesial contingencies necessitated explications that were apt and adequate for that particular period, but not necessarily so for another. Thus, for instance, no theologian will today belabour to explain traditional trinitarian terms like *homoousios* (consubstantial), *circumincessio* or *perichoresis* (mutual penetration) or *ekporeusis* (procession) not only because the present philosophical and theological climate is different from the Patristic and Medieval times in which these terms were used, but also because people are asking different questions about God in diverse times and places, worldwide.[4]

In the initial pages of this book, I stressed that context is indispensable for theology. The question of context is important; for, context determines content. When speaking about context in trinitarian theology, one could either refer to place – for instance, Asian,[5] African,[6] European,[7] Australian,[8] Latin American[9] or North American;[10] or, to time[11] – post-VC II,[12] modern,[13] postmodern,[14] and so on; or, to variations in religious conceptions;[15] or, to special global issues – ecological,[16] ecumenical,[17] scientific,[18] tribal,[19] or gender-related,[20] – that have necessitated newer interpretations and reinterpretations of trinitarian doctrine.

In my conversations with people about the Triune God, I have sensed a tendency in many people to dismiss the Trinity as being too 'classical' a conception of divinity to be meaningful to underprivileged groups who are poor, often illiterate, and exploited. This line of thinking is already prejudiced against the subalterns' capacity to seek theological meaning on their own terms and with their own terminology. Contrary to this line of reasoning, I will attempt to show that a subaltern trinitarian theology not only provides possibilities for fostering the life of underprivileged communities – be they adivasis, Dalits, women, or minorities like the Indian Christian community itself – but can also serve as an example of how esoteric theological expressions could be divested of their ideological trappings and rooted in experience and praxis to foster true liberation.

Rather than begin with dogmatic or metaphysical assertions of who/ what God is in Godself, I begin with what we know about God through a particular revelation – here, mediated by Jesus – expressed in Scripture and Tradition in language that is symbolic, metaphorical, analogical and based on models.[21] I read Scripture and interpret Tradition through the lens or prism of the 'subaltern hermeneutic of community' so that theology influences life, and life influences theology. In other words, subaltern trinitarian thinking will move 'from below upwards';[22] or, as Schoonenberg succinctly states:[23]

> All our thinking moves from the world to God, and can never move in the opposite direction. Revelation in no way suspends this law. Revelation is the experienced self-communication of God *in* human history, which thereby becomes the history of salvation. With reference to God's Trinity, this law means that the Trinity can never be the point of departure. There is no way that we can

draw conclusions from the Trinity to Christ and to the Spirit given to us; only the opposite direction is possible.

This line of thinking, popularized by Rahner's oft-quoted, "from the economic to the immanent Trinity" dictum, will underscore my trinitarian theology, although I shall preserve the immanent mystery of God *per se*, *in* Godself,[24] who is *Deus semper maior*,[25] ever transcending human efforts at comprehension. Before exploring subaltern trinitarian theology, I point out landmarks in the landscape of Indian trinitarian theology, in general.

4.3 A Brief Overview of Indian Trinitarian Theology

Indian Christian trinitarian theology began to develop in a dialogical encounter with classical Hinduism. Keshub Chandra Sen (1838-84), a pioneer in this venture, described the Trinity as "the loftiest expression of the world's religious consciousness."[26] His synthesis comprised of triadic attributes and functions identifiable with the three 'persons'. Thus, Father (Creator/Still God), Son (Exemplar/Journeying God) and Spirit (Sanctifier/ Returning God) were associated with the attributes of Truth (*sat*, being, force), Good (*cit*, love, wisdom) and Beauty (*ânanda*, joy, holiness), respectively. Brahmabandhab Upâdhyây (1861-1907) gave further deeper meaning to the term *Saccidânanda*,[27] extolling the divine attributes in a 'canticle'.[28] He saw Christianity not only as the fulfillment of Judaism but also of Hinduism. He felt that, as Greek philosophy inspired Western theology, so must Vedanta enlighten Indian Christian theology.[29]

Among foreign scholars who made India their home and contributed to Indian trinitarian theology, Jules Monchanin (1895 -1957) pioneered a contemplative-monastic approach to the Trinity. Monchanin believed that the Reality in which both Christianity and Hinduism can meet is the mystery of God as Trinity. This meeting will be facilitated if Christians can emphasize the fact that God's being (*esse*) is being together (*co esse*) and Hindus can rethink their equation that *Atman* is *Brahman*. The Hindu experience of God as *Saccidânanda* and India's search for "One-without-a-second" finds its fulfillment in the Christian understanding of the Trinity. He wrote:[30]

> Are we not entitled to expect that, through acknowledging the 'Indwelling God', the mystery of the universal and deifying presence of the Holy Ghost, India, in rising upwards to the "One without a second," *Ekam eva advitiyam* (*Chândogya Up.* 6.2.2), will find at length the mystery of the Father's Love overflowing into the Plentitude of His Incarnate Son?

Bede Griffiths (1906-93) later explained the Father as *nirguna Brahman*, the Son as *sadguna Brahman* and the Spirit as *Shakti* the "feminine principle in the Godhead."[31] He believed that the central Christian insight of 'God is love' is indicative of relationship in Godhead itself, and viewed the Upanishads in this light of God's love. He held that Hinduism and Christianity could meet at the point of 'God is love'.[32] Likewise, Swami Abhishiktânanda (1910-73) was fascinated by the Hindu *advaitic* experience of the Upanishads and tried to show that it is compatible with the Christian experience of Trinity.[33] The *advaitic* experience is found also at the root of the Christian experience that holds that God and the world are not two. This *advaitic* dimension of Christianity finds an eminent expression in the revelation of the Trinity where the Father, Son and Spirit are alike in non duality (*advaita*) of nature and in communion (*koinonia*) of Persons.[34] This is not just theoretical knowledge, but experiential awareness of God:[35]

> [T]here is no question of theological theorizing or of academic comparison between the terms of the Christian revelation and those in which India has expressed its own unique mystical experience. It is rather a matter of an awakening, an awareness far beyond the reach of intellect, an experience which springs up and erupts in the deepest recesses of the soul. The experience of *Saccidânanda* carries the soul beyond all merely intellectual knowledge to her very centre, to the source of her being.

Comparisons between such experiences have been drawn up even recently.[36]

Scholars of foreign origin like Michael von Brück,[37] Hendrik M. Vroom,[38] and John B. Carman[39] have also explored the philosophical aspects of classical Hinduism and Buddhism, drawing parallels with the Christian Trinity. In particular, insights were drawn from Mahayana Buddhism and the Buddhist *shûnyatâ*, relating them to classical Trinitarian doctrine.[40] While the Buddhist *shûnyatâ* is sometimes equated with Christian '*kenosis*'[41] on the grounds that both are translated as 'emptiness', scholars caution against either simplistic parallelisms or derogatory reductionisms; for instance, von Brück writes: "[S]*hûnyatâ* as Buddhists announce and Westerners often fail to hear, has nothing to do with nihilism. Nor is it a concept, for it is not meant to determine anything. *Shûnyatâ* is a symbol of non-determinism."[42] Such explorations have also had their impact in the field of dialogical spirituality between religions.[43]

Raimundo Panikkar's trinitarian theology is significant because it provides a framework for dialoging not only with classical Hinduism but also for understanding the dynamics of the prophetic, as well as the mystic, religions.[44] He maintains that the Trinity is the ultimate paradigm of personal relationships. Between Word and Spirit – intelligible structure or form and fluid or dynamic life – there is a never ending process of interchange that reflects what is experienced in everyday interpersonal relations. Just as the human person is neither monolithic oneness nor disconnected plurality, so the Trinity as pure relation epitomizes the radical relativity of all that there is. In sum, the diversity of human experience is not to be totalized into an overarching universal theory; it is only to be discerned by entering into the *de facto* proliferation of different putative experiences of God in the world's religions. Panikkar's trinitarian theology has been commended,[45] as well as critiqued on various counts.[46] It is beyond the scope of this book to evaluate Panikkar's theology; but it has undoubtedly been influential in shaping Indian trinitarian theology for almost four decades.

Besides explorations into the conception of God as *Saccidânanda* – which is a metaphysical and impersonal notion of God (*nirguna* Brahman) – there have also been attempts to draw parallels between the Hindu *Trimurti* (Brahma-Vishnu-Siva or *sadguna* Brahman) and the Christian Trinity.[47] Although the Hindu *Trimurti* seemingly resembles the Christian Trinity to the extent that God is considered in deist terms, there are basic differences with regard to the question of the unicity and historicity of the divine manifestation, the soteriological aspects, the question of Trinitarian missions and so on. Nevertheless, the *Trimurti* has inspired Indian Christian art as in the work of artist Jyoti Sahi (see picture 1).[48] He has also creatively combined traditional Eastern symbols like the classical dance *mudras* and the *mandala* with Christian trinitarian themes (see picture 2).[49]

In the field of what is called 'social trinitarianism'[50] – where the three persons of the Trinity are perceived as the ideal or 'model' of the human community – Geevarghese Mar Osthathios initially used the analogy of the nuclear family to explain the Trinity and the consequent demands of establishing a classless society.[51] Though his approach to the world situation of inequality and injustice incorporates Marxian insights, the society he envisages is more Gandhian since he sees *sarvodaya* (development of all) as the ideal of classless society.[52] In a later work, Geevarghese develops his trinitarian theology in terms of a 'Sharing God' by using

Picture 1: Jyoti Sahi's adaptation of the *Trimurti* to depict the Trinity

Picture 2: Jyoti Sahi's adaptation of *mudras* and *mandalas* to portray the Trinity

traditional concepts like *koinonia* and *agape*, borrowing from Moltmann and Boff, and incorporating insights from Scripture and Tradition.[53]

4.3.1 *A Critical Appraisal of Indian Trinitarian Theology*

The preceding, bird's eye view of Indian trinitarian theology indicates that all these attempts were dialogical mainly with regard to classical Hinduism.[54] They can be termed contextual since they developed within differing spatiotemporal contexts whether it was Bengal's pre-Independence Indian Renaissance (Sen and Upâdhyây) or the Catholic church's post-VC II context that inspired Christian *advaitins* (Abhishiktânanda, Griffiths and Monchanin) to reinterpret doctrine consonant with changing times. All the above Indian trinitarian theologians concentrated on dialoguing with what is called the 'Great Tradition' be it Hindu or Buddhist, partly because they assumed that only the 'Great Tradition' seemed rich in philosophical or theological content. Consequently, these theologians failed to recognize the richness of the 'little traditions' with their wide variety of *devas*, *devis*, demons, myths, stories, symbols, forms of *bhakti* and cultic practices that abound with images of divinity far divergent from the so-called 'classical' traditions.

Indian trinitarian theology has so far forwarded frameworks for viewing God as Trinity in cognitive mystical terms like *Saccidânanda* drawn from Vedanta. Such conceptions can be critiqued on certain counts. First, even though it is claimed that such cognitive mysticism is not merely of the intellect but 'experiential', one can question 'whose' experience and 'what' experience goes into formulating conceptions of divinity, and whether *sat-cit-ananda* (truth-consciousness-bliss) is the most adequate Indian way of understanding God. Second, the danger of advaitic philosophy is that it speaks of unity at the metaphysical and theoretical level (*conceived space*); however, the problems at the existential, practical, socio-political levels (*social space*) persist, for, attractive spiritual principles of unity/harmony do not automatically destroy the ground realities of discrimination and exploitation fed by hierarchical principles of high-low, pure-impure. Third, a privileging of the cognitive-mystical realm, we have seen, leads to class/caste-based division of people that results in the so-called upper classes/castes controlling the intellectual-cognitive realms thereby representing others on their terms and convenience.

Another danger in comprehensive frameworks for understanding the Trinity like the *theandrism*[55] or *cosmotheandrism*[56] of Panikkar is that reality is seen as a harmonious whole encompassing God, human beings and nature. Here, the cleavages and conflicts of human communities are not sufficiently recognized. These cleavages and conflicts that appear in subaltern histories, cultures and religions have been 'buried' and 'disguised' by dominant traditions.[57] Likewise, the religio-cultural worldview and everyday experiences of subaltern communities have never found adequate expression in Indian theology, and this lack needs to be filled. Articulating the need for a break with Brahmanical theology and the development of Dalit Theology, Prabhakar writes: "It will represent a radical discontinuity with classical Indian Christian Theology [in] the Brahmin tradition which needs to be challenged by the emerging Dalit Theology. This also means that a Christian Dalit Theology will be a counter-theology."[58] The need to evolve such a 'counter theology' is evident, especially in the field of trinitarian theology.

Still another lacuna of Indian trinitarian theology is that it has hitherto developed as a result of dialogue with other religions and has sought to incorporate the best of what religions offer. However, theology has not sufficiently dialogued with the disciplines and incorporated insights from the academia. This lacuna is significant at a time when much attention is paid to interdisciplinary and trans-disciplinary approaches. Furthermore, with swift and sweeping changes taking place at the national and global levels, theology cannot afford to distance itself from the other sciences that can provide it with contextual analyses of Indian society, thereby fostering theological reflection. Reflection on the Trinity from a contextual base, with the assistance of the disciplines, has not been undertaken by Indian theologians in the past two decades or so, and yet, these past two decades have seen religion in India gaining salience – although we often see manifestations of the *'religion of power'* eclipsing the *'power of religion'*.

Finally, in the context of current debates on nationalism, the Indian Church faces many problems regarding its identity and mission. Christians are identified as a "minority community that forcibly converts others." This has many repercussions. The 'minority' label also embraces many communities of Christian tribals and Dalits who face problems peculiar to their own situation. In addition, the so-called Christian 'missionaries' and 'missions' face conflicts on various fronts and from many forces. In view of this ferment, not much of contextual theology addresses current problems. This is also true for Indian trinitarian theology wherein the major works were developed about three decades ago.[59] Hence, I try to fill a lacuna by developing trinitarian theology from a subaltern perspective against the background of current contextual crises and conflicts.

4.4 Towards a Subaltern Trinitarian Theology

I develop subaltern trinitarian theology in the light of the subaltern ethos and religio-cultural capital that, as described in the second chapter, is characterized by: (a) situations of subordination, coupled with a quest for agency and 'contradictory consciousness', (b) a strong sense of equality and solidarity, community and communion, (c) an all-pervading sense of the sacred, devoid of duality and dichotomies, encompassing 'three levels' or 'worlds' envisaged as (d) three 'dimensions of communion' – primordial, ancestral and natural – that make (e) religion down-to-earth, this-worldly, here-and-now, practical, and accommodative of diversity. Moreover, religion is manifest in many indigenous forms that reconcile play and dance, pain and pathos. Apart from the Gujarat subaltern context, these traits are common among other disprivileged groups, as well.[60] I now trace trajectories along which, I believe, subaltern trinitarian theology could be developed in terms of *three interrelated theses* summarized as:

1. Trinity is a Representation of Relationship, Communion and Solidarity

2. Trinity is a Representation Reaffirming the Sacredness of Subaltern Space

3. Trinity is a Representation Revealing 'Counter Spaces' of Subaltern Power

Let us go into details of each of these.

4.4.1 *Trinity is a Representation of Relationship, Solidarity and Communion*

The idea of 'Trinity' is neither some self-evident truth about God that was always held and believed by the early Christian community, nor is it a name of God found in the Bible.[61] However, it evolved in Christian Tradition as a *theological, symbolic re-presentation* of God's nature. In simple terms, the new community of disciples of the crucified-risen Jesus felt the need to *re-present* God symbolically because they had new, firsthand religious experiences in the very life, death and resurrection of Jesus who not only claimed to be God's Son, but whose death was vindicated and claims were validated by his resurrection. To evolve such a theological, symbolic representation, they used a new *Jesus narrative* with 'traces of trinitarianism' revolving upon three 'personal' axes:

a.   God, who Jesus addressed as *Abba*, Father;

b.   The Holy Spirit, who Jesus promised would be their teacher and counselor, and

c.   Jesus himself, whose self-awareness seemed to be that of the 'Son' claiming a unique and unprecedented relationship to God.

There is no well-developed trinitarian theology in the Second Testament,[62] and Paul, for example, can at best be called a 'latent trinitarian' whose main purpose was to proclaim God's salvation through the *experience* of Christ and the Spirit.[63]

Trinitarian thinking arose in the nascent Christian community not as abstract metaphysical principles about God descending *from above*, but as a process of reflection on communitarian experiences emerging *from below*. The first Christian believers' experiences of calling God *Abba* in prayer, and the power they received from the Holy Spirit, were not only expressed in the creedal confessions of scripture, but also in their cultic and liturgical celebrations now focused upon Jesus Christ. Thus, on the one hand, we see that the trinitarian passages in the Second Testament are not dogmatic assertions but descriptive theological affirmations; and, on the other, these were being widely used by newborn Christian communities in their sacramental and liturgical practices, uppermost among which was the baptismal liturgy. For instance, the presence of Mt 28:16-20 in scripture and its incorporation into the baptismal liturgy of the early Church indicates the significance of the Trinity for the community.[64]

Common to early trinitarian confessions is the aspect of their relevance for communion and community life. This new life was possible only through their 'experience of salvation'[65] in the Holy Spirit and in Jesus who taught them that God is *Abba*,[66] Father – intimate and approachable (Gal 4:4-7; Rom 8:15-6). This relationship of nearness and intimacy animated their own teaching and liturgy (*leitourgia*), as well as their community life (*koinonia*) overflowing into service (*diakonia*). Thus, from earliest times, the trinitarian focus was always soteriological and practical, namely, stressing God's salvation *in practice* of liturgy, sacraments and life, rather than seeking precise articulation in theory or in dogmas. This reasoning resonates well with the subaltern reality insofar as divinity has bearing on *soteriology and praxis* rather than divinity being grasped as some abstract theories about God. And the bedrock of soteriology is that *"God saves"* not by demanding strict adherence to rules and regulations, but by entering into a relationship of love, solidarity and communion with humankind. This is basically what Christ's Incarnation is all about. What would this mean, in concrete terms, for a subaltern community, who do not really have a trinitarian conception of God, as such?

4.4.1.1 *Trinitarian Relationship as Persons Being-in-Communion*

Neither the adivasi nor the Dalit worldview seems to have a clear conception of God as Trinity in terms of three persons sharing one divine life or having three attributes.[67] Nonetheless, there is a very strong stress on relationships and interdependence in the community. We saw in the second chapter how, unless a newborn infant undergoes the rites of initiation and name-giving ceremony, it is not recognized as a member of the clan or tribe. However, after the initiation rites, it is not only a child of its parents, but a child of the whole tribe, so to say. In the event of the death of its parents, it will not be dumped in some orphanage but will be looked after by the tribe. In other words, the socialization process ensures that the infant moves from being a 'non-person' to being a 'person' and from being a 'non-tribal' to being a 'true tribal'.

The understanding of 'personhood' needs some clarification. But, before entering into understanding the usage of the word in trinitarian theology, we could reflect upon an event reported in the newspapers some years ago. A 27-year old woman, Rochom P'ngieng, who disappeared in the jungles of Cambodia at the age of eight, suddenly reappeared, and an elderly couple claimed that she was their long lost daughter.[68] Rochom reportedly got lost while herding buffaloes and lived in the jungles for almost twenty years without any contact with human beings. Journalists who saw Rochom said: "She can't speak any intelligible language," "She's half-human and half-animal," and "She's weird; she sleeps during the day and stays up at night." This was probably due to the fact that Rochom neither had any contact nor relationships with human beings for a long time. She lived in the jungle, totally isolated from human beings; and so, it wasn't surprising that she could neither communicate in any intelligible language nor live as a normal human being and was described as being "half animal".

Based on this rather unusual case of Rochom, we can assert that, a human being is not really a 'person' and almost resembles an animal if the human being is not in relationship with others. It is only when one enters into fruitful relationships with others that one grows into being a true 'person'. Indeed, every human being is necessarily born from relationship – irrespective of its quality – since the basic sexual union between man and woman causes the birth of a child. At birth, except for the genetic factors that could lead to differences in the development of different infants, all newborns equally have the potential to grow up to be responsible citizens in society or irresponsible, animal-like antisocial elements. This is the whole 'nature-nurture polarity' that depends largely on the quality of relationships that a child has and the degree of acceptance or non-acceptance it receives from the family and the community, at large.

The idea of 'personhood' has been studied and discussed in various disciplines. For instance, psychologists like Erik Erikson (and his eight-stages of development), Harvey, Hunt and Schroder (and their studies on cognitive development) and Lawrence Kohlberg (who researched moral development), among others, have tried to explain psychosocial stages of development on the basis of a child's interactions with its family and environs. In India, Sudhir Kakar studied how Indian children are schooled in the Indian – mainly Hindu – context with interactions with family members and the larger landscape of Indian culture.[69] Without entering into details, we observe that, from an infantile stage of dependence, children grow through an adolescent, reactionary stage of independence and finally settle for 'interdependence' with the realization that one only survives in society through processes of mutuality, reciprocity, sharing and cooperation.

Moving from general, human experience to the Christ event, one can conclude that, much as one analogically comes to understand the love and acceptance of the larger community only if one has concretely experienced the love and understanding of one's nuclear family, so did the early Christian community come to grasp the relationships in God. Based on the life, love, liberation they concretely experienced in Jesus; and, drawing meaning from the analogical language of love and the imagery he used, Jesus' disciples would evolve God-talk. The analogies and images that Jesus used for talking about God were drawn from the human person and from the nature of love.[70] We must note that trinitarian experience was always being articulated in Christian Tradition in analogical language.[71] Indeed, "we have no choice whatever but to speak of God in terms derived from our experience of creaturely reality – that is, by analogy."[72] However, what was spoken about the Trinity was not about love as some abstract philosophical notion, but as a concrete attribute that fostered interpersonal and interdependent relations.[73]

In Jesus' person and life, the early community fully *experienced* the love of Jesus-Father-Spirit, *expressed* it in word (Jn 3:16; Rom 8:38-9) and *emulated* it in their everyday living (Acts 2:42-7; 4:32-7). The focus here was on love, service, caring, sharing, solidarity and communion with God and with one another. However, in later development of trinitarian doctrine, the aspect of love, sharing and true relationship was eclipsed by philosophical terms and concepts consonant with the contexts of the times.

In his efforts to describe how God can be *tri-une*, Tertullian [160-220] used the word 'person' (*persona*) in the sense of an 'actor's mask' or a 'face' or to signify a juridical subject (*homo, vir*).[74] The focus here was on individuality and legality. Boethius's [480-524] definition: "an individual substance of a rational nature" added the dimension of rationality.[75] Later, Aquinas held that 'person', with regard to God, signified a 'subsistent relation' in the inner life of God.[76] More recently, and in consonance with Aquinas, Rahner substituted 'person' with "distinct manner of subsisting" and added that this conveys, "exactly as much as the formulation which uses the word 'person'"[77] All these theologians were employing philosophical concepts and technical terms that were intelligible to people of their times and places;[78] yet, they created difficulties for understanding the mystery of the Trinity in other times and contexts. This seems especially true for subaltern communities in India.

The terminology of earlier trinitarianism seemingly derives from concepts that are individualistic, legalistic and rationalistic. Tertullian's and Boethius's understanding of 'person' evidently do not account for the communitarian dimension and the inter-relatedness of persons. So also, Rahner's explanation does not take full cognizance of true personhood, which has not so much to do with 'subsistence' as with love, support, solidarity and relationship. In today's context, the problem of understanding personhood becomes acute with the (post)modern concern with 'self' and 'person'.[79] This task is even more difficult in the light of current debates on 'trinitarian persons and personhood'.[80] Thus, for our purposes, we revert to an understanding of person and personhood amenable to subaltern imagination.

In the adivasi context, person and personhood is understood only in the light of relationship with community. In other words, to be a person one must be bound in relationship with one's community.[81] However, there is a difference between saying 'human persons are relational' and 'God is relational'. In the former case, we are referring to the *capacity* or *potentiality* to enter into relationships and thereby to develop 'personality', which is the sum total of the moral, attitudinal and behavioural qualities one imbibes and possesses. Here, the more and better relationships that a person *'has'*, the more and better are that person's chances of actualizing her/his personhood into a balanced personality.[82] In this sense, when we speak of anyone being relational, we mean that one *has* relationships or is relational in a secondary sense. But, when we say 'God is relational' and speak of 'person' in God, we assert that being relational is the very *essence* or *nature* of God.[83] Thus, while we *have* relations, God *is* the relations that God has.[84] Or, for God, 'to be' and 'to be in relation' is one and the same thing.

Unlike in Western, modern and postmodern societies that foster independence and individualism to a large extent, the subaltern communities that are bound together by relations of interdependence, sharing, caring and community-spirit are more likely to resonate with the image of a God-in-communion. In these communities, the primacy of the community is stressed over the individual, but that does not mean that the individual is unimportant, for, there is deep respect for the life of all members. This is not exactly so when we speak about the Trinity since, in the Triune God, 'person' and 'community' coincide.[85] The multiplicity of three persons does not in any way imply a division of the divine nature since the three divine persons coinhere; and, the entirety of divine nature is in each of them.

From the preceding discussion, we can affirm: "God's being is communion"[86] or God is personal *Being-in-Communion*, meaning, God eternally exists as a 'communion of persons'. In other words, God does not exist as some substance or as some abstract principle but as a relationship of persons.[87] Each member of the Trinity "is a person, a distinct person, but scarcely an *individual* or *separate* person. For in the divine life there is no isolation, no insulation, no secretiveness, no fear of being transparent to another."[88] Thus, 'person' becomes a primary ontological category, and the 'being-in-communion' of divine persons becomes a model for the being of human community. This being-in-communion, we've seen, is already present to a large extent in disprivileged communities; but, there is always scope for more deeply living out this communion. This becomes a challenge for subaltern communities; indeed, for each and every Christian community, as well.

4.4.1.2   *Sophia and Shakti in Intra-Trinitarian Relationship*

We have seen that the only way one can talk about God is through language that is analogical. While analogy enables us to conceive of God in terms that are intelligible to human beings, it also runs the risk of being inadequate and inappropriate. This has been so with trinitarian terminology, too, that has suffered distortions and misrepresentations. For example, one basic question that arises today is that of the adequacy of only male terms to express the mystery of God. The issues involved here range from the dynamics of religious language[89] to feminist debates of trinitarian terminology.[90] Since we have already dealt with the dynamics of religious, symbolic representations in the previous chapter, we shall now only examine the gender debate from two angles so as to question: (a) whether the current language is appropriate to express the trinitarian mystery, and (b) whether there are possibilities for employing terms that are not gender-specific.

Traditional Father-Son terminology might make it seem that God is exclusively male or the Trinity is a 'male community'. In this regard, some theologians argue for the retention of these terms since Father-Son-Spirit language is reflected in the *Jesus narrative* that is firmly grounded both, in Scripture and Tradition.[91] Conversely, it is alleged that such androcentric language has led to patriarchy and to the subordination of women,[92] for which, alternative terms have been suggested that are personal but not androcentric, for example, Creator-Redeemer-Sanctifier,[93] or God-Christ-Spirit, or Parent-Child-Spirit, or Mother-Lover-Friend.[94] Rather than enter into any discussion of the pros and cons of each of these triadic terms,[95] it would be better to see what could be the consequences of altering traditional language and adopting new terminology from the point of view of disadvantaged communities like adivasis, Dalits and women.

A change of terms might succeed in eliminating androcentric language when speaking about the Trinity, but it is unlikely that the problems of patriarchy will ipso facto be resolved. Such problems must rather be addressed at two levels, namely, (a) the ideological level, with a 'feminist hermeneutic of suspicion', and, (b) the existential, practical level, by creating appropriate ecclesial, representational structures.[96] A second reason for retention of the current terminology is that liturgical and sacramental practice has a fairly long history of traditional Father-Son-Spirit invocations that cannot easily be dispensed with without creating confusion.[97] Furthermore, sacraments incorporate individuals "into the power and essence of God, into the history and story of God, into the life and heart and identity of God,"[98] and thus *relationship with God* must be stressed rather than interpreting these as ascribing gender or mere functionality to God.[99]

The question of relationship and communion – that we have stressed earlier – is vital in our discussion since the *Jesus narrative* explicitly expresses what can be called "the trinitarian history of God" that makes human history a *history of salvation* as "poor, sinful and dying people are taken up into the history of the Son, and the Spirit with the Father to find in it divine life."[100] Thus, although God,[101] or even Jesus,[102] might analogously – and even appropriately – be called 'mother' when referring to divinity in general, it is necessary to be extremely cautious when deviating from traditional trinitarian terminology, which we shall attempt to do, but only after stressing a crucial corollary stemming from the Father-Son relationship.

Viewing the Trinity from tribal perspective, the Father-Son relationship can be seen as analogous to the *Singbonga/Dharmes*-human relationship where God is pictured as Father or Grandfather thereby indicating a relationship of intimacy, concern, nearness, providence and protection. The *Varle Dev* of Gujarat's Vasavis is similarly evocative of feelings of security, protection, providence and affection.[103] Such conceptions make it possible for underprivileged communities (a) to stress the inner bonds of equality and solidarity among themselves, (b) to perceive God's nearness, solidarity and participation as Grand/Father in their daily life, and (c) to assert their identity as God's grand/children who will not passively accept their being conceived of as emanations from the feet of an abstract, corporate entity like *Purusha Sukta*. Thus, the personal, parental or grand-parental images covertly create 'counter spaces' for subaltern protest and resistance. But, the question still remains whether these parental or grandparental images create sufficient space for a feminine aspect in the Trinity.

Divine Wisdom or *Sophia*[104] (Greek) or *Hokmah* (Hebrew) has strong foundations in Scripture and Tradition.[105] Wisdom is identified with the Spirit and has feminine characteristics attributed to it.[106] This thinking is found in some traditions, for instance, the Syriac Christian tradition.[107] Together with Word (*Logos*), Wisdom could effectively be used to develop a trinitarian theology with feminist and relational overtones.[108] However, in the Indian context, the use of Wisdom-terminology is risky. This could lead to an intellect-inspired, esoteric Theism that will, at best, seem sterile to subaltern imagination, and, at worst, lend itself to further exploitation bolstered by Brahmanical belief that the head/mind – as in the *Purusha Sukta* myth – is superior to other parts of the body.[109] Although we are critical about Wisdom terminology, the feminine dimension of Trinity can be captured by *Shakti* that is an important component of subaltern religion.[110]

Shakti refers to power, ability, strength and energy.[111] It is the supreme female principle, the divine primordial energy which is personified as female divinity and is responsible for the creation and preservation of the cosmos. Indian Christian tradition has avoided associating the personified concept of *Shakti* with the Spirit because the myths connected with it could create conflict with the strongly male Biblical monotheism.[112] However, in the Gospels, we are told that Jesus' ministry is always accomplished in the energizing power of the Spirit (*dynamis*),[113] and, the Pentecostal power of the Spirit is indicated by symbols of power like fire and wind.[114] Besides these symbols being native to the subaltern imagination, the subaltern association of the 'world of spirits' with power and energy could lead us to reinterpret the Spirit as *Shakti*. Note that this is different from the widely accepted – though static and sterile – *Atma* or *Atman* which, while perhaps expressing the Trinity's immanence to some extent, fails to capture the power and energy characteristic of *Shakti*.[115] Thus, I hold that the Spirit as *Shakti* could be perceived as a maternal, loving, protective, as well as an energetic and powerful divine presence that empowers the weak and emancipates those captive to societal evils.

I think that the use of female imagery for God does not distract, detract or deviate from traditional belief in the one God, but "opens up the possibility of new religious experience of the one Holy Mystery."[116] Moreover, besides being appropriate for subaltern groups like Dalits and adivasis, such *Shakti*-imagery enforces the dignity of women who have suffered centuries of exploitation on account of the use of exclusively male images and also from the abuses arising from patriarchal structures built upon the manipulation and misinterpretation of such images. The question of images and symbols, then, still remains unresolved. And I propose that the adivasi *naach/nu* or *akhra* (dance) could be a dynamic symbol for perceiving (*firstspace*) and conceiving (*secondspace*) of Trinity. Furthermore, I shall attempt to show that this symbol of the *naach/nu* or *akhra* (see picture 3) could relate the experience of God's revealed *tri-une-ness* to the daily life of adivasi community (*thirdspace*).

4.4.1.3 *Trinitarian Solidarity in the Naachnu (Dance) of Tribal Life*

We have ascertained that the Trinity is a symbolic, theological representation of relationship. It expresses the fact that God is relational and can be understood and related to only in terms of categories of relationship like person, family, parent/daughter/sonship, community, love, support, solidarity, interdependence, etc. In the strict sense, Trinity tells us something *about* God rather than being a proper name or *avatar* of God like Ram, Vishnu, Allah, Jesus or Yahweh. Since Trinity reveals something *about* God, it is an aniconic image of the Divine insofar as it is symbolic but does not impute any particular anthropomorphic form to God.[117] Moreover, while we are dealing with the Christian Trinity, here, the term 'trinity' can loosely be used for any threesome like the metaphysical *Sat-Cit-Ânanda*, or the *Trikâya* of Mahayana Buddhism,[118] or the deist, personal *Trimurti* of Hinduism.[119]

As an *aniconic* representation of the Divine, the Trinity is acceptable to subaltern imagination. Aniconic images of God abounded in India – especially in rural India – prior to iconic images that were later introduced in shrines and temples.[120] We have seen earlier how the adivasi worldview is replete with aniconic images of divinity, as well as a few icons of some *devas* and *devis*. Thus, in Gujarat's adivasi villages, for instance, it is not uncommon to see a white flag atop a tree, or a smeared stone besides a

Picture 3: The adivasi *naachnu* or *akhra* (dance)

river, or mud pots at the village boundary to symbolize the presence and action of gods or spirits. These symbols *re-present* a 'personal dimension' of divinity since divinity is perceived in *personal* terms of protector, healer, sustainer, destroyer, reconciler, and so on.

Subaltern symbols of divinity are also *transpersonal* in the sense that objects like a flag, stone, earthen pots, rivers and trees also symbolize divinity.[121] Thus, while *Varle Dev* or *Ucchaliyo Dev* (of Gujarat's adivasis) or *Singbonga, Dharmes* or *Haram* (of Chotanagpur adivasis) symbolize the *personal* dimension of divinity, natural elements like the sun, moon, rivers and sacred groves, are *transpersonal* images amenable to the adivasi imagination. In the 'conceived spaces' of adivasi imagination, natural and *transpersonal* symbols like 'sun-rays-energy' or 'source-wellspring-living water'[122] aptly convey God's triune nature and can be effectively used to express God's *tri-une-ness*.[123]

As a symbolic religious representation of divine *tri-une-ness*, the Trinity has often been represented in the Christian Tradition in the field of art with diverse approaches or versions, for example, triadic, incarnational and societal.[124] One of the most popular depictions of the Trinity, based on the 'hospitality of Abraham' (Gen 18), is that of Andrei Rublev (see picture 4).[125] The evocative power of this representation is such that it addresses different thinkers differently. For instance, it may suggest mutual indwelling of the three persons in one Godhead,[126] or it may indicate the aspect of self-giving and sacrifice,[127] or it may tell the story of salvation,[128] or symbolize the Eucharist and the Church-community.[129] While this representation is considered an *icon* in that it represents a divine reality in anthropomorphic form, it is also *aniconic* because its many symbols – like table, cup, tree – go beyond the *personal* and express the *transpersonal* without ever exhausting the trinitarian mystery.[130] This is precisely so because of the power of symbols, since they, (a) reveal mysteries without exhausting them, and (b) open up reality in its multi-faceted complexity and thereby address all the realms of human existence.

In the subaltern religious world – especially in the adivasi worldview, with a strong focus on play and dance –[131] the *naach/nu* or *akhra* is a vibrant symbol of life. The *naach/nu* (or *akhra*) symbolically expresses life, energy, rhythm, harmony, equality, movement, familiarity and solidarity. People dance around in a circle, arms intertwined, supporting each others' bodies, while repeating a refrain that echoes joy, awe, gratitude, worship, sorrow,

Picture 4: Andrei Rublev's 'Hospitality of Abraham'
reminiscent of the Trinity

pain, suffering, petition and so on. There is no 'leader' or 'first person' in the dance and similarly no 'last' since all move around in a circle, from left to right and then from right to left. The body and feet-movements synchronize with the beating of a *dholak* or *mandar* (drum) with the drummer standing in the centre, who also dances while drumming (see picture 5).[132] Often, the songs are accompanied by an indigenous wind instrument called *pipudi* made of bamboo and birds feathers. A variation of the *naach/nu* is done with the women and children standing on the shoulders of the menfolk, who entwine their arms at shoulder-length and then once again go round in a dancing circle exuding ecstasy, energy, harmony and happiness (see picture 6).[133] While evoking the joy, cooperation, solidarity and vibrancy of adivasi society, the *naach/nu* best expresses what has traditionally been termed trinitarian *perichoresis*,[134] but with marked differences.

John of Damascus [675-749] first used the word *perichoresis* (Greek, for *co-penetration* or *co-inherence*) to describe the relationship between the three divine persons: Father, Son and Spirit. Its Latin equivalents, *circuminsessio* or *circumcessio* used by Thomas Aquinas [1125-74] and Bonaventure [1221-74], respectively, convey the same meaning.[135] Down the centuries these terms have been used to indicate co-communion, inter-relationship, 'moving around' and 'sitting around' without any concrete or meaningful reference to any visible, cultural symbol. There are hardly any dances in the Western, and even classical Indian tradition,[136] where the whole community is involved in dancing-*and*-singing in close communion with nature and with the intertwining of human bodies. Conversely, the *naach/nu* and *akhra* are richly evocative of trinitarian 'differentiated oneness', as well as the energy, harmony and 'reciprocal delight' that is the essence of divine communion.[137]

There are striking differences between the *naachnu* and the majority of Western and Indian classical dances. The latter are performed by an individual or a couple who need practice to master a dance and an audience to enjoy and appreciate their art. In such dances, there is also need of an auditorium and stage, and accompanying musicians or an orchestra or choir to complete the performance. This is not the case with the *naachnu* or *akhra* that is not an individual performance but a communitarian, spontaneous participation in Life itself enacted in the open *perceived space* (centre) of the village. There is neither need for any audience nor any practice since everybody dances and everybody learns the movements

Picture 5 : Vasavi adivasi drummer playing the *dholak*

Picture 6: Variation of the adivasi *naachnu*

just as one learns one's native language. Moreover, the lyrics reecho the moods, and the movements replicate the flow of adivasi life in its interpenetrations of ups and downs, pleasures and pains, triumphs and travails. Thus, *naach/nu is* Life reenacted in dance. And, Life *is* a dance in solidarity and communion.

With the Christianization of adivasis in south Gujarat, many religious and biblical themes have been transposed and woven into *naach/nu*.[138] Thus, besides symbolizing the fact that every member supports the community and is supported by the community, the image of God in *naach/nu* can suggest three things: (a) that the divine persons are intertwined in an eternal dance as *Creator, Re-creator* and *Trans-creator*,[139] (b) that the divine dancers are invisible, yet indispensable, partners in the dance of adivasi life, and (c) a Triune God inheres and animates the *lived spaces* of human life. In this way, God is not viewed as distant in heaven and unaffected by peoples' lives, but is *one-with* them, an *insider* fully attuned to the moods and movements of life, enhancing relationships, creating community, inspiring communion, and ever in solidarity with the subalterns.

Not only is the *naachnu* evocative of the joyful side of life, but it is also echoes struggle, pathos and pain. Moreover, unlike the *perichoresis*, which is a mental construct or idea without an equivalent in the field of experience, the *naach* or *akhra* is existential and experiential for adivasi communities. Thus, for now, while I adopt this indigenous image to symbolize the inner life of the Trinity, I will have to show that its adoption is relevant to subaltern community and consonant with Christian Tradition. Moreover, although this symbol gives us an idea of and insights into Trinitarian relationship *ad intra* (immanent) and *ad extra* (economic), we will have to assess its limitations; for, ultimately, God will always be *Deus semper maior*, God ever 'more' than what the human mind can imagine and what human language can possibly express.

I sum up my first thesis by reiterating that the Trinity is a representation of relationship, a symbol of God's *Being-in-Communion* (immanent) and in solidarity and communion with the disprivileged groups (in the economy), arm-in-arm, step-in-step, with them in the *naachnu* of Life. Adivasi communities already have an understanding of God as Grand/Father. Thus, the trinitarian 'Father-Son' terms can meaningfully be retained since it gives historical rooting to the *Jesus narrative*. However, it must be stressed that 'Father-Son' does not in an essentialist way refer to the maleness of God but to an analogical relationship marked by parental-filial intimacy, a maternal fatherliness[140] so to say, of tender love, sharing and self-giving.[141] This analogical relationship is complemented by understanding the Spirit not as Wisdom or *Atman*, but as *Shakti*, who loves, sustains, energizes and empowers disprivileged groups. These personal, relational and communitarian aspects of the Trinity reinforce the sense of egalitarianism, solidarity, sharing and communion prevalent among disprivileged communities.[142] This is not only true for the tribals of India, but also for tribes elsewhere.[143] Thus, conceiving of God in personal, relational, communitarian terms is not only meaningful but also necessary to foster the communitarian concerns of underprivileged communities by stressing inner relationships that become for them sources of strength, identity, meaning and power.[144]

4.4.2 *Trinity is a Representation Reaffirming the Sacredness of Subaltern Space*

We have seen that the 'symbolic violence' that the subaltern groups undergo is largely due to a violation of their 'social space' or 'lived space' (real-*and*-imagined space). The *bin-adivasis* or so-called *ujjaliyats* either fail to comprehend the wholism underpinning the subaltern view of reality, or, manipulate it to serve their own interests. By unjust legislation and exploitation of *jungle-jal-jamin* (*perceived space*), or by devising devious and alien concepts and symbols to subjugate subaltern groups (*conceived space*), the producers of space wield power to wreck weaker communities. In this case, the disadvantaged groups are neither treated with respect nor given the recognition required to foster community on their own terms and with their own resources. Consequently, conflicts arise. It is thus vital to explore the possibility of evolving 'counter symbols' that will facilitate the creation of community. I hold that the Trinity is one such symbol that could reaffirm the wholism and sacredness of subaltern spatiality.

Symbolic violence often arises since the dominant groups tend to dichotomize between the pure/impure and sacred/secular spaces, and between *lived-life* and *afterlife*, in order to legitimize various forms of exploitation and violence. Conversely, as we have seen earlier, subaltern religion and spirituality is coterminous with Life itself. Hence, in the organized religions, while rectitude of creed and cult is stressed, one's 'secular' life can run parallel to, and totally divorced from, the 'sacred'.

But, in subaltern religion, belief and life go hand-in-hand, and it is the concrete existential life of the people that is the source of their beliefs. Thus, for e.g., in the adivasi world, concrete materialization of beliefs in life is more important than creedal or cultic expressions of belief that have little bearing on lived life.[145] Hence, religious representations that can bridge the gap between secular/sacred, visible/invisible, historical/ahistorical, and *perceived/conceived spaces* could empower subaltern groups, as well as provide them with the means to critique other religious representations that dichotomize, deceive and destroy.

4.4.2.1   *The Primordial-Historical- Spiritual as Triune Spatiality*

In the second chapter, we saw that there are three 'levels' of being, namely, visible, invisible and primordial, that correspond to three 'dimensions' of communion: (i) with nature, (ii) with spirits and (iii) with the Supreme Being, respectively. The latter two dimensions pertain to the invisible world, while the first refers to the visible. We also saw that each of these levels and dimensions is important and deeply in communion with the other two. Each 'needs' the other two and lives *with-in-for* the other two, and yet, each is distinct and differentiated from the other two. All spaces therefore, whether perceived, conceived or lived, are not only inseparably interlinked and invested with an inherent sacredness, but they also retain their difference. Thus, while recognizing the unity, interdependency and communion of the three levels/dimensions and also respecting their differences, the community lives and acts within what we might call a *'tri-une* spatiality', which can help us to understand the Trinity. We could see it in the following way.

4.4.2.1.1 The Father: The Primordial in Tri-Une Spatiality

The primordial dimension is indicative of origin and depth. In time, it can be considered as 'origin' since it is anterior to, and creative of, everything and everyone else. In space, it can be conceived of as 'depth' since it is the foundation or substratum that supports everything and everyone else. It can be symbolized by aniconic, transpersonal images like foundation, source, wellspring, root,[146] and, it has been personified with names like *Varle Dev, Ucchaliyo Dev, Singbonga*[147] and *Haram*,[148] by the Vasavas, Hos and Mundas, respectively; or, can simply be called *Great Spirit*.[149] The anthropomorphic image that corresponds to this primordial reality is that of Grand/Father. Consequently, the Supreme Being's or Great Spirit's work is to create, support, protect and provide.

Since the primordial level is invisible, and neither constrained by space nor by time, the divinity associated with this level can equally, and validly, be conceptualized as abiding high up in the sky,[150] or deep down at the centre of the cosmos.[151] So also, there is no beginning and no end, here.[152] Moreover, we note that, divinity is not an isolated and indifferent monad, but is kind, compassionate, caring, and creates the cosmos as an intercommunion, an interdependence of all beings. However, although the Supreme Being is an integral part of this intercommunion, it is not wholly identifiable with it. Thus, we can neither conceive of divinity as 'The One' without any relationship to 'the many', nor can we consider it identical with the many; for, it is the very substratum upon which all beings rest.[153] Given the personal attributes, the transpersonal images, and the activities associated with the primordial level of reality – namely, creation, providence and sustenance – we notice a close resemblance to the trinitarian person called 'Father'.

It is apt to draw a parallel between *Abba*, the Father of Jesus and the primordial level/dimension of reality for the following reasons. First, it conforms to what has long been asserted about the Father in the Christian Tradition, namely, that the Father is the 'uncreated origin' (*agennesia* or *ingenerateness*).[154] Since the Father is spatiotemporally prior to all else, He is the creator, provider and sustainer of the cosmos comprising of all that is visible and invisible. Second, as substratum, the Father could be conceptualized not as God *up* in the heavens, but more as God *down below* who is easily accessible, ever present, entwined and in-step with, and eternally supportive of His children in their daily life, labours and struggles. Third, while remaining differentiated from other visible and invisible entities, the primordial Father always remains united to all of creation and all creatures; and thus, everything and everyone is invested with the sacredness that comes from being daughters and sons of the Father. However, lest this remain just an idea or mental construct, there is need for visibility, which leads us to another level.

4.4.2.1.2 The Son: The Visible of Tri-Une Spatiality

In subaltern imagination, the visible world comprising of nature and human beings is the 'real world', the 'perceived space' or *firstspace* wherein people live, work, relate to each other and find fulfillment in life. This visible space is that which flows out from, and depends on, the primordial. Thus, while the primordial is regarded as root or source, the visible dimension can be regarded as shoot/tree or wellspring. While the primordial is ahistorical, the visible can be mapped within a spatiotemporal framework. Thus, it is spatial, social and historical. The visible world is always in communion with the eternal primordial, and thus bears its characteristics. Yet, it is also distinct, and can be differentiated, from it. The visible and primordial are bound by a relationship just as root and tree (transpersonal images) or parent and child/offspring (personal images) are intimately connected.[155] In view of these characteristics, it would seem apt to draw correspondence between the 'Son' of the Trinity and the visible dimension of reality.

The Son, Jesus, or the second person of the Trinity, is the visible manifestation of God. Jesus is sent and comes from God, *Abba*, Father, and reveals himself as 'Son'. In the biblical world to be a son connoted three things, namely, obedience, revelation and agency.[156] First, a true son was obedient to his father, and, in this sense Jesus was true son, always attentive and obedient to his *Abba*'s will (Jn 4:34, 5:19, 8:28, 10:37, 14:31). Secondly, since instruction was not institutionalized, the father taught his son the Torah, imparted knowledge and entrusted other trade secrets of the family business, and therefore, only the son knew the father (Jn 5:20, 14:8-10). Finally, the son was agent of his father, his 'representative' acting on his behalf. In this sense, too, Jesus was son of the father (Jn 5:21-2, 3:35, 6:40).[157] In this schema, the unity between Father-Son is not about abstract metaphysical principles but about parental-filial intimacy, agency and action.

Parental-filial intimacy, agency and action are suitable ways of describing adivasi relationship with the primordial. The appearance of God's Son in human history ensures that religion and spirituality remain incarnated in everyday life and are not transported to some abstract, ideological realm susceptible to manipulation. Moreover, as visible, active 'representative' of God, the son gives meaning to subaltern history and spatiality by being born on the 'borders' and dying "outside the camp."[158] I shall elaborate this later. However, here, I feel that, not only does such thinking dovetail with Christian Tradition, but it can also empower underprivileged groups to recover lost social space. This assertion can be supported by some good reasons that I now highlight.

First, Scripture reveals that Jesus is the "image of the invisible God, the first-born of all creation" (Col 1:15) and "bears the stamp" of God's nature (Heb 1:3). Indeed, "all things were made through him, and without him, was not anything made that was made." (Jn 1:3). Second, the 'coming forth' of the Son from the Father has traditionally been termed 'generation' (*gennesis* or *generateness*).[159] In the adivasi worldview, the process of differentiating the visible (offspring) from the primordial (root, source, wellspring) can also be seen as a process of generation. Moreover, third, the motif of Son coming forth from the Father has parallels among the Vasavis of Gujarat who believe that the *Pahelo Vasavo* (literally, the first Vasava) or 'first-born' leaves his father's house to establish a new household. Such imagery empowers adivasi groups since God's 'first-born' who bears God's image can be understood as coming forth from the primordial level in order to establish a new house (*oikos*) at the visible level (*jungle-jal-jamin*). Thus,

(a) The whole cosmos can be considered sacred and suffused with divine life,

(b) God's first-born or divine image/offspring[160] becomes the blueprint of all created realities, and

(c) This first-born reveals what living in communion with God and with others truly entails.

4.4.2.1.3 The Spirit: The Invisible of Tri-Une Spatiality

The space or level of the invisible beings can be called *secondspace* or 'conceived space' replete with ideas and conceptions of spiritual/ancestral beings. These invisible beings are related to, as well as differentiated from, both, the primordial being and well as visible beings. The invisible beings are of three types: ancestral, benevolent and malevolent. More than being celestial, they are terrestrial in the sense that, being ancestral, they once were socio-historical part of the community. Moreover, they are now still present, though imperceptibly, either to aid or to assail the community. Thus, the invisible spirits inhabit particular geographical spaces like the hills, rivers, forests, village-borders and so on,[161] and the effects of such habitation are concretely experienced in people's lives.

We note that the invisible spirits and ancestors share invisibility – and some degree of divinity – with the primordial being, and yet, can be said to share visibility with the physical world not by virtue of being perceived by the senses, but by their concrete effects being felt and experienced. These effects – both, helpful and harmful to the community – can be mapped spatially, and are recognized either by expressions of gratitude like setting aside food and drink for the ancestors, or, by rituals of appeasement.

The encounter with, and the effects and appeasement of, spirits, can be spatially located not in temples or shrines (as in organized religion), but upon mountains, besides rivers, in fireplaces, within groves/fields, and even in graveyards.[162] Inherent in both, the action of the spirits, as well as their appeasement, is the question of *power*. The community conceives of this power in terms of air, breath, fire and water, and while there may be special mediums, *buvas* or *pahans* who negotiate this power, such power is neither considered hereditary nor associated with ideas of purity/impurity as in the case of Brahmanism. Air, breath, fire and water are common Biblical symbols for divinity, especially corresponding to the Spirit (*ruah* or *pneuma*).[163] Moreover, the Bible associates power with God's Spirit. Thus, we could conceive of this world of invisible spirits as corresponding to the third person of the Trinity, *Shakti*-Spirit, but with caution.

God's Spirit is invisible, but its effects are experienced in creation and in the consecration of certain individuals/communities who are empowered and entrusted with mission. For instance, in the Bible, the Spirit is the power of God in creation (book of Genesis), the breath of life (Ezek 37; Jn 20:20), the water of life (Is 44:3; Jn 4:10, 7:37-9, 19:34), the wind and fire (Acts 2:3-4) and so on. More precisely, the life of God's son, Jesus, is inseparably united with the Spirit-*Shakti* whose power is manifest in mighty deeds (*dynamis*). After the ascension of the historical Jesus, and at the Pentecost, the Spirit-*Shakti* consecrates the community and empowers it to "turn the world upside down".[164] The community realizes that the *Shakti*-Spirit "blows where it wills" (Jn 3:8). This gives certain universality to the Spirit's presence and activity.

The universality of the Spirit's presence and action imbues all spaces – perceived and conceived – with inestimable power. Indeed, the Spirit-*Shakti* inheres in all times and inhabits all spaces. In the *thirdspace* (*lived space*) of subaltern life, She invests the 'counter spaces' of resistance and revolt with power, wisdom, motion and direction. The Spirit has traditionally been described as 'proceeding' from God (*ekporeusis*).[165] In a subaltern worldview, we could conceive of the Spirit not only as 'procession' from God, but also as the invisible and inexhaustible *Shakti* of all social-historical-spatial 'processes' that foster benevolence (joy, love, faithfulness, community spirit, etc.),[166] and fight against the malevolence of evil structures, injustice, inequality and exploitation.

In sum, the *tri-une spatiality* we have so far seen – involving the primordial, visible and invisible – has been reinterpreted as corresponding to the three Persons of the Trinity, i.e., *Abba*-Father, Jesus-Son and *Shakti*-Spirit, respectively. We have provided skeletal scriptural references to substantiate our claim that the Trinity is a representation that reaffirms the sacredness of subaltern spatiality. However, in the *Jesus narrative*, the central spatial symbol of 'Kingdom of God' can give us a deeper understanding of how the trinitarian God proposes a 'counter space' for the underprivileged of society.

4.4.2.2 *Kingdom of God and 'God of the Kingdom' as 'Counter Spaces'*

The Kingdom of God – referred to in Mt 4:23, 9:35; Mk 1:14-5; Lk 4:43, 8:1, 16:16 – can be understood as new spatiality, a trinitarian 'counter space' that Jesus announces, activates and animates. In the Judaic tradition, the king was seen as 'son of God' in the sense of representative of God, and Kingdom of God meant the 'reign of God'.[167] This concretely meant that, if God reigned, God's people – in particular, the *anawim*, or, in our context, subalterns – would enjoy a whole, healthy and prosperous life. This would entail peace, equality, justice and solidarity; in sum, a 'new society'.[168] In our terms, this 'new society' that Jesus was inaugurating would more be 'community' rather than 'society' since it would not be founded upon rigid rules and regulations, but on the natural, familial bonds of being children of the same *Abba*, Father, sisters and brothers of God's Son, Jesus, sharing common life and power made possible by the Spirit-*Shakti*.

The Kingdom of God has often been considered as a Christological revelation. This is only partly true, since the Kingdom is more fully a Trinitarian revelation, as it involves all the three persons of the Trinity. This can be seen from the fact that, in Jesus' Kingdom *kerygma*, there is no recorded instance of Jesus calling for faith *in himself*; rather, it was a call to faith in the power of God (Spirit-*Shakti*) and to a filial relationship with God (*Abba*-Father), with Jesus as God's representative, mediator or agent.[169] Thus, when we look at Jesus' praxis with regard to the Kingdom of God, we ought to always examine it from the viewpoint of trinitarian relatedness and the *tri-une spatiality* discussed earlier, so as to more fully comprehend what the Kingdom actually meant and could mean, today

The Kingdom of God's spatiality was disturbing to the religious, social and political hierarchs of Jesus' time. In the realm of 'perceived space' (*firstspace*), it destroyed the distorted and devious conceptions of space that had led to the creation of categories like sacred/secular, insider/outsider pure/impure, righteous/sinner and so on. Two examples illustrate this point: (a) Jesus' cleansing of the Temple; (b) Jesus' table-fellowship. In the first instance (Jn 2:13-22), Jesus shifts the sacral sanctuary and the site of sacrifice from the Temple of Jerusalem to the "temple of his body" (v.21). His point of reference is "my Father's house" (v.16). In another striking passage, Jesus announces that: "The hour is coming when you will worship the *Father* neither on this mountain nor in Jerusalem" (Jn 4:21); for, "*God is spirit,* and those who worship him must worship in spirit and in truth" (Jn 4:24). To the receiver of this revelation – an 'outsider' and 'impure' Samaritan woman – who says, "I know that the Messiah is coming" (Jn 4:25), Jesus announces: "I am he" (v.26). Besides revealing trinitarian traces of his life and mission, Jesus' cleansing of the Temple and his encounter with the woman of Samaria is fine example of Jesus' contestation of *firstspace* and *secondspace*.

Jesus' table-fellowship also subverted sacrosanct laws of Jewish commensality.[170] By dining with the tax collectors and so-called 'sinners' (Mt 9:10-3; Lk 7:36-50, 19:1-10), Jesus was destroying structures built upon injustice, hypocrisy, domination and power. The demands of table-fellowship are deepened in the gospel according to John when Jesus illustrates a new spatiality by positioning himself at his disciples' feet, washing them at his 'last table' (Jn 13:1-15). This passage has erroneously been interpreted as a lesson in humility. It is, rather, a realigning of social relationships based on a new understanding of power.[171] Here, Jesus rightly asserts that he is Master, for by not doing so, he would be untruthful; yet, he establishes a new order wherein one with knowledge and power is not just seated at the 'head' of the table, but bends down at the 'feet', as servant, ready to use knowledge and power in the loving service of those divested of it. In these table-fellowships, then, Jesus is, so to say, re-creating God's family and re-laying God's table to include, empower and feed those who have hitherto unjustly been left out or *dis-membered* from filial communion with the Divine.

In the realm of *secondspace*, the *conceived space*, Jesus goes beyond the physical, visible manifestations of the Kingdom (perceived in and through his cleansing of the temple, table-fellowship, the healing of diseases, the calming of storms and so on), to provide a *conception* of the 'God of the Kingdom'. This picture is trinitarian in that it discloses the three persons, each of whom has a specific role to play, beginning with Jesus himself who proclaims it, inaugurates it, and is its unique and incomparable image or icon: the '*Autobaseilia*'.[172] As God's 'representative' Jesus *re-presents* God not as Almighty King but as *Abba*-God, a God of nearness, intimacy and solidarity. Rather than any traces of patriarchy and authoritativeness, *Abba*-King symbolizes maternal tenderness and paternal providence, as seen earlier. Indeed, the God of the Kingdom is more mother than King, not lordly but loving, not commanding but compassionate, ever calling all people to filiation.

Besides revealing who the *Abba*-King is, Jesus also reveals himself as Kingdom representative, full of God's Spirit-*Shakti*, bringing good news of Messianic promise (Is 35:3-6, 58:6-10; 61:1-2) to concrete historical fulfillment (Lk 4:21). He proclaims good news specifically to the poor and oppressed (Lk 4:18, 7:22; Mt 11:2-6), the subalterns who are heavily burdened (Mt 11:28). He works miracles and displays power in favour of the weak, the suffering and the marginalized through his intimate union with the Spirit, *Shakti* (Mt 12:28). Empowered by this *Shakti*, he promotes among these 'least' a freedom *from* sickness, sin, evil and death, as well as a freedom *for* living "the glorious liberty of the children of God,[173] by making them like himself, in fellowship with him."[174] Thus, liberation and freedom are integral parts of the Kingdom vision and Kingdom project.

The Kingdom of God, as well as the God of the Kingdom, is revealed in *thirdspace* (real-*and*-imagined) in a comprehensive framework embracing the *already* and the *not-yet*,[175] the past-present-future, since the Kingdom is "at hand" (Mk 1:15; Mt 10:7; Lk 21:31), and yet, like mustard-seeds or leaven-in-dough it is in the process of growing into final fullness. The Kingdom of God is already "in the midst" of Jesus' hearers (Lk 17:21), a *here-and-now* reality that precludes postponement of God's salvation to some unreal space and future time. This thinking resonates with the subaltern religio-cultural worldview. It also opens up 'counter spaces' for subaltern assertion against exploitative ideologies and worldviews that postpone salvation simply to some future, esoteric spatiotemporal reality. It stresses the salvation of the *here-and-now*. It also has a cosmic dimension since, as Paul asserts, "creation waits with eager longing for the revealing of the children of God" (Rom 8:19).

In its final fulfillment, in a kind of 'reverse narrative of history', Christ "delivers the Kingdom to God the Father" after destroying every evil, including death, so that "God may be everything to everyone" (see 1 Cor 15:20-8). Therefore, God in Jesus Christ and through the Spirit-*Shakti* sustains human history (Kingdom of God's *already*) and carries it towards final fulfillment (Kingdom of God's *not-yet*). When the point of final fulfillment is reached, there will be no question of Kingdom since God's purposes will be accomplished, but there will be a full and perfect communion with God. Thus, we see that Kingdom of God is simultaneously revelatory of the God of the Kingdom, or, "The Kingdom of God is the trace of the Trinity … and the Trinity abides 'behind' the Kingdom of God and gives itself to us in cooperating with God in bringing about God's rule."[176] The human cooperation entails being *faithful* to the historical project envisaged by the Kingdom of God, being *affiliated* to the God of the Kingdom as children and consequently, working with the Spirit-*Shakti* for the *freedom* of those bound in situations of oppression. Thus, a Kingdom ethic can be evolved in terms of the triad of *fidelity-filiation-freedom*, [177] without which it is impossible to make the Kingdom a reality.

4.4.3 Trinity is a Representation Revealing 'Counter Spaces' of Subaltern Power

Jesus' life is not devoid of conflict. At every stage of his ministry, he enters into conflict with diverse groups functioning in various fields – with the rich whom he said would be condemned if they did not share their wealth (eco-social field), with the hierarchs whom he castigated for their hypocrisy, ritualism and legalism (religious field) and with leaders like Herod and Pilate who were afraid of his growing influence over the masses (political field). Jesus does not evade conflict but faces it courageously, always seeking meaning from his *Abba* relationship and strength through his empowerment by Spirit-*Shakti*. Thus, the conflict that Jesus faces is not merely a Christological mystery but a trinitarian one, involving Father-Son-Spirit in dynamic intercommunion.

4.4.3.1 Trinitarian Conflict as God's Suffering in Subaltern Solidarity

Conflict can be dealt with in three ways: first, by evading conflict and passively submitting to the Other who dominates; second, by unleashing violence on, and wiping out, the dominant Other; third, by resolutely responding – with all of one's resources – to the dominant Other so that values like truth, justice, equality and lasting peace might prevail. The first case is an instance of cowardice, and the violence will increase since the one who dominates will be emboldened and will continue exploiting the weaker ones. In the second instance, the dominant Other will be destroyed through violence, but this is bound to arouse vengeance; and since the causes of conflict are not resolved, problems will persist. The third case seems to be the only viable option that, while confronting the root causes of violence also seeks to bring the Other to see the truth and to reach a lasting and just solution. However, this third option is fraught with dangers and difficulties.

The *Jesus narrative* indicates that Jesus rejected the first and second options but chose the third. He criticized and confronted exploitative powers – social, political and religious – whenever he encountered them or saw their evil effects on the poor and the powerless of his time. Simultaneously, he stayed in solidarity with the sick, the suffering and the subordinated ones. Deeply aware that the *new Kingdom-space* he was creating implied the filiation of all *Abba*'s children, he stood arm-in-arm, and journeyed step-by-step with these victims and the *least*, unleashing the overpowering effects of *Shakti* in the many signs and wonders he worked in their favour. By doing this, Jesus was proposing a new God-image, a God of *pathos*, abounding with *com-passion*, thereby attributing to God the ability to "suffer with, to be present with"[178] victimized communities.

The early evangelizers of Christianity persistently proclaimed a suffering, crucified God. Their *kerygmata* (preachings, in the plural)[179] unfailingly converged on this one point that God had become visible in Jesus. And if God's son/representative Jesus suffered, then, in some way, God also suffered and suffers. Such a conception was diametrically opposed to the influential Greek philosophy of the time and would have met with opprobrium and opposition. In fact, God's greatness lay precisely in God's apathy (Greek, *apatheia*) since God was believed to be unchangeable, unaffected by external influences and incapable of feeling pain and sorrow, which were all expressions of frailty and finitude. An apathetic God, it was believed, was absolutely free and perfect.[180] Rejecting this, and other similar conceptions of divine impassibility that informed Judaic, Gnostic and Stoic imagination, the *kerygmata* of the apostolic community were images of "a Christ crucified" who is "stumbling block to Jews and folly to Gentiles;" yet, these images were experienced as "the power and wisdom of God" (see 1 Cor 1:23-5) for the Christian community.

For marginal communities, solidarity is power. Centuries of injustice and exploitation have purged them not only of socio-eco-political power, but also burdened them with religio-cultural universes that are oppressive and alienating to them. By contrast, a God who is in solidarity with them in their situations of struggle, suffering and pain can also reveal a way to confront and negotiate the negativities of life. Conversely, the predominant conceptions of divinity of the 'big traditions' – including Christianity – that extol God's *fullness* are often alien and alienating, and have little to contribute to subaltern life and liberation.

The Trinity has often been interpreted in terms of divine *fullness* (*plerosis, pleroma*),[181] which has its roots in Aristotle's 'unmoved mover'. This was developed by Aquinas for whom God was *actus purus* (pure act).[182] The *fullness* aspect is also stressed in classical Hinduism as *purnam*. Applying a 'hermeneutic of suspicion' to constructions of *fullness* that are cognitive conceptions, often esoteric and alienating, we consider them inappropriate for our purposes. But, from subaltern perspective, we appropriate and reinterpret the God who suffers in solidarity with the disprivileged and displays a new paradigm of power by himself walking the path of emptiness. It is the emptiness of the persecuted, crucified Jesus that leads the subaltern into the mystery of God. It is thus necessary to undertake what could be called a 'subaltern hermeneutic of the cross'[183] to more fully understand what Jesus' death and resurrection reveal about the trinitarian God.

4.4.3.2 *'Outside the Camp' Subaltern Hermeneutic of the Cross*

Jesus' birth, life, death and resurrection must always be seen as trinitarian events or else we will miss the significance of Christian revelation. God's Self-emptying does not take place only on the cross, but is present as a process right from the first moment of the Incarnation when primordial divinity (*Abba*) sends his visible agent or representative (Son) in the power of the Spirit (*Shakti*).[184] While accepting that *kenosis* – in the sense that God empties Godself or 'makes space' to assume human form –[185] is present all through the Christ-event, we hold that God's *kenosis* is most visible at the end of Jesus' life and ministry, i.e., in his passion and death.[186] I attempt to reinterpret this event using a 'subaltern hermeneutic of the cross'.

Jesus' mission is specifically directed towards the poor and the oppressed (Lk 4:18-21) and thus he strives to bring them the fullness of life (Jn 10:10) that has been denied them. His mission of loving and serving them is based on the prophet Isaiah's messianic servanthood (chs.53, 61) that is lived out to the point of total self-sacrifice (Mk 10:45). This sacrifice involves two dimensions: (a) *action,* since it is the outcome of his *activity* leading to confrontation, conflict and death at the hands of the powerful, and (b) *passion,*[187] since his solidarity and *com-passion*[188] for the powerless make him walk the whole way of victimization and death that is their real, *lived space.* Both these aspects are indispensable, and it would be wrong if either were ignored. Moreover, *passion* is not coterminous with passivity, but is the stage when, as a result of one's conscious choices and actions, one 'hands over' one's whole life as an act of faith in that which one believes to be of ultimate significance.[189] Lastly, since Jesus is revealed as *theanthropos,* his death must be seen not only as the death of a human being, but also as the death of God.[190]

Spatially, the crucified Jesus hangs between sky and earth as if he neither belongs to the 'up' that could be the *conceived space* of heavenly beings nor is he rooted in the 'down' of earthly, human beings. Scripture describes the space of Jesus' *kenosis* as "outside the camp" (Heb 13:11-3). Primarily this is the space beyond the religious world of Law and the cult,[191] the space where the defiled victims of sacrifice are burned.[192] But, it is also a space despised by the social and political powers. Calvary, outside Jerusalem, is the space of desolation, defilement and death. During his passion and death, apart from the shame and physical pain, his disciples and friends desert him. Thus, from human viewpoint, Jesus' death has all the elements of pain, shame, failure, frustration and forsakenness. It is the worst of conflicts that seems to shatter his lifetime ambitions and actions related to the Kingdom of God or the *Abba-*community of equality, love, peace and justice. Evil, ultimately, seems to triumph. Thus, Jesus could only hope for *Abba*'s intervention, and for courage from Spirit-*Shakti,* both of whom had never forsaken him.

Jesus' ultimate act of faith is to be faithful to his mission to the end with the certainty that it is his *Abba*'s will.[193] But, when his *action* leads to his *passion,* the conflict he faces is transferred, so to say, to 'God's camp'. *Abba* suffers Jesus' pain and enters his passion. On the one hand, admitting 'the pain of God'[194] seems like a limitation; on the other, God has been revealed as love (1 Jn 4:8), and, the greatest love is manifest when one suffers with, and dies for, a loved one (Jn 15:13; 1 Jn 3:16).[195] Thus, the suffering that God endures is not an unwilled, passive suffering, but "an active suffering motivated by love, a voluntary sacrifice in order to be affected by others."[196] Indeed, the more perfect love is, the deeper will suffering be. Hence, if God is Absolute Love, then God must, in an infinite degree, be able to identify with and suffer the pain of everyone who is a 'child of God', more so, of the One revealed as God's Son. This gives us insight into the cross.

A father's readiness to sacrifice his son is prefigured in the Abraham-Isaac biblical narrative (Gen 22). This motif is also present in adivasi myths of the Chotanagpur region. For instance, *Singbonga* appears on earth in the guise of a boy covered with scabies.[197] As expiation for human pride and greed, this boy offers himself as a vicarious sacrifice. The *Jesus narrative*, however, differs from the preceding two examples in that God not only allows his son to be sacrificed in the vilest form of crucifixion, but also 'forsakes'[198] and 'rejects'[199] him prior to his death. This can be seen from Jesus' cry of abandonment from the cross: "My God, my God, why have you forsaken me?" (Mk 15:34). This cry can be interpreted in two ways: (a) as the cry of a forsaken child of God, and (b) as an accusation of *Abba*'s infidelity in forsaking his Son who remained faithful to his will till the very end. In the former case, as we have already seen, it can be interpreted as referring to human forsakenness – i.e., Jesus is "placed outside the community," so to say;[200] in the latter case, it can be interpreted as 'divine impotence', as we shall now seek to explain.

Jesus' *passion* begins with his Gethsemane *agony* (Greek *agôn*, means 'battle' or 'conflict'). The *agonizing battle* (interior) at Gethsemane is completed in the *pathetic conflict* of Jesus' cross (interior-exterior). The latter conflict is of 'divine impotence' and the 'victory of evil'. Here, God no longer seems Father because *Abba* is the one who forsakes, Son seems no better than any common crucified criminal because his claims and actions are frustrated, and the power of *Shakti* seems sterile to save the Son from death. Ironically, it is here that the dynamic of self-sacrificing love emerges in pain and separation because in sacrificing and abandoning Jesus, *Abba* sacrifices and abandons Godself. The Son experiences the total *pain of abandonment* before death (since he cannot feel pain after death), while, by not sparing his Son and giving him up, *Abba* experiences the death of his Son in the infinite suffering of his love.[201] The Father's *pain of separation* from the Son is not *patripassianism*,[202] since it is the Son who dies. So also, the pain of separation is not weakness, but on the contrary, it is the power of love. Spatially, it can be conceived as *Abba* standing behind the cross, offering up his own Son as the supreme manifestation of love. It is the primordial, divine love made visible and tangible. This is, so to say, *Abba's* "love soaked in blood."[203]

From the preceding discussion, we can conclude that Jesus' *passion* is his Father's willed *action*. It is a trinitarian act since: first, Jesus does not escape his *passion* but surrenders to his Father's will; second, the Father silently suffers through the passion and refuses to free Jesus from the cross, and third, from the core of this act of sacrificial love there is the offering (Heb 9:14)[204] and the outpouring of the Spirit (Jn 19:34).[205] The historical abandonment and the eschatological surrender coincide on the cross as "unity in separation and separation in unity."[206] In the cross, *Abba* and Son are totally, *spatially separated* by Jesus' abandonment, and yet, intimately united in surrender. It is a deeply trinitarian event because, between the Father who forsakes and the Son who is forsaken, between the loving Father and the beloved Son, there proceeds the sacrifice itself, the Spirit, who justifies the ungodly, rescues the forsaken, forgives and reconciles the sinner, and, as we shall see, vindicates the victim and raises the dead. Besides being backed by Scripture,[207] this sequence of *action-passion* in the Trinity reveals how conflict ought to be effectively faced – neither in passivity nor with violence – but with a courageous, confrontational stance that, in adherence to the truth, dares make the ultimate act of faith.

Trinitarian *kenosis* on the cross and Jesus' cry of abandonment reveal both, God's pain, as well as the pain of suffering, broken and dying communities.[208] This symbolizes not only the physical pain of subaltern groups, but also their mental anguish at being the *non-peoples*, their forsakenness at being socially ostracized, their moral degradation at being abused, and their spiritual angst at being confined to corners in certain churches and denied entry into temples. Nirmal holds:[209]

> [H]is (Jesus') Dalitness is best symbolized by the cross. On the cross, he was the broken, the crushed, the split, the torn, the driven as under man – the Dalit in the fullest possible meaning of that term. "My God, my God, why hast thou forsaken me?" he cried aloud from the cross. The Son of God feels that he is God-forsaken. That feeling of being God-forsaken is at the heart of our Dalit experiences and Dalit consciousness in India. It is the Dalitness of the divinity and humanity that the Cross of Jesus symbolizes.

Besides the Dalits and women,[210] the adivasis of south Gujarat, too, identify with the symbol of the crucified Jesus in their emptiness, sufferings and struggles, and also see it as a manifestation of God's power.[211] Nonetheless, if, as Paul asserts, the *kenosis* truly reveals God's "wisdom and power," then this trinitarian *action-passion* cannot terminate in the triumph of evil over good and of death over life. If such were the case, God would be negating Godself and the powers of evil and death would have to be considered more powerful than goodness and life, respectively. It is here that we must look beyond the cross and enter into the trinitarian dimension of the resurrection. In other words, *kenosis* will be incomplete unless we reflect upon its concomitant – divine *plerosis*.

4.4.3.3   *Kenosis-Plerosis as Power and Promise of a New World*

I have, so far, posited a dual surrender of Father-Son and the outpouring of the Spirit in Jesus' sacrifice itself. Jesus' surrender is the ultimate act of faith. His cry of surrender – "Father, into your hands I commit my spirit" (Lk 23:46) – seems to emerge from within the darkness of the evil and injustice that envelopes his passion; and yet, it is uttered in the light of Jesus' love and knowledge of his *Abba*, and trust and faith in *Abba*'s will and actions. This cry of surrender is one of refuge, and for deliverance, just as one seeks anchoring on a rock or security within a fortress.[212]

God raises Jesus from the dead by the power of the Spirit (see picture 7).[213] Thus, Jesus' resurrection or *plerosis* is the vindication of Jesus' victimization. The *plerosis* confirms the authenticity of Jesus' life, actions and *kenosis*. On the one hand, it signifies the Father's stamp of approval upon Jesus' praxis and his fidelity as son even unto death, and, on the other, it reveals that even in the forsakenness and silence, the Father was always present behind the cross together with the Spirit, the bond and outpouring of divine love, surrender and sacrifice. The resurrection, therefore, like Jesus' passion and death, is fully a trinitarian event.

The trinitarian *kenosis-plerosis* paradigm of conflict resolution and power negotiation is not only evidenced in the Christ event, but also in tribal mythology. To take the aforementioned example of *Singbonga* who appears on earth disguised as a boy covered with scabies, we note that the boy not only offers himself as a vicarious sacrifice, but also rises resplendent after the immolation. In this myth, there is "an identification between the sacrificer, the victim and the Spirit it was offered to. He accepted to be immolated. There was to be a perfect immolation: a holocaust. This immolation, however, did not turn out into a destruction but into a transfiguration."[214]

Picture 7: Painting of the Father raising the Son at
the prompting of the Spirit

Evidently, while we cannot draw simplistic parallels between the *Jesus narrative* and the adivasi myth, the motif of self-sacrifice for the Other stands out as a recurrent theme. This sacrifice is not a compromise of conflict but a confrontation of evil; it is not weakness but strength; not passivity but activity; not meek resignation to fate but an ultimate act of faith that challenges death. Moreover, it is vicarious – not done for self-interest, but for the Other *as* community.

Trinitarian *plerosis* provides hope for underprivileged communities since, in Jesus' *action-passion*, they see in their own suffering and pain not only God's solidarity and *passion*, but also God's *action* for righting wrongs, vindicating victims and giving new meaning to history. This is well expressed by Prabhakar from a Dalit perspective:[215]

> Suffering becomes redemptive when we suffer with God who in his divine self suffers with his people, particularly "the least and last" of them. That is what God did on his cross and through his resurrection, defeating decisively the power of sin, death and Satan thereby bestowing upon us the freedom to struggle against suffering which destroys humanity. The cross and resurrection of Jesus vindicated God's purposes of redemptive suffering for the oppressed and all humanity. This divine redemption liberated the oppressed (Dalits), freeing them from being controlled or determined by their own suffering. Our belief that God was in Jesus and defeated suffering will not be true unless Jesus rose again from the dead and is alive and present with us in our struggles for freedom. In the resurrection of Jesus, we have received the vision of the divine future and the gift of a new humanity, without which we the oppressed (Dalits) cannot go forward, transcending and transforming the present, to move into the future, for the full realisation of our humanity, under God.

The "gift of a new humanity" asserted here is not one that comes from conflict resolution on the terms of the dominant Other, but on the *subordinated community's own terms*, articulated in a language of resistance to oppression and struggle for life and liberation.

Not only does trinitarian *kenosis* take place "outside the camp" but the *plerosis* too irrupts among lowly peoples faraway from Jerusalem's centre-space of temple and palace. Moreover, it opens up subaltern 'counter spaces' in many ways: first, in a society in which only males could testify in a court of law, all the evangelists record that the risen Jesus appears first to women and instructs them to be witnesses of his resurrection (Mt 28:1-10; Mk 16:1-11; Lk 24:10-2; Jn 20:1-18); second, it breaks through in the midst of sadness and hopelessness (Lk 24:13ff); third, the early disciples who experience the resurrection and work through the power of the Spirit initiate a new movement at the margins, a socio-religious reawakening of peripheral peoples for whom the crucified-risen Christ becomes "the power and wisdom of God" (1 Cor 1:24).

The trinitarian dynamic of *kenosis-plerosis* is vital for vulnerable communities since many movements at the margins are often suppressed; yet, it is these that, amidst the darkness of evil and death, indicate that God is, ultimately, a God of Life. Thus while the *passion* or *kenosis* of such communities is the pain, struggles and sufferings they undergo, their *action* or *plerosis* is manifest in their protests and resistance to oppression, their songs and *naach/nu* (dances) that echo life, and their movements and organizations that already promote a liberation ever open to the promise of a new world. However, such a world can only be built from *kenosis* to *plerosis*, and not from *plerosis* to *plerosis*.

A final point must be made here that, apart from its relevance for underprivileged communities, the divine *kenosis-plerosis* also becomes a blueprint for human society at large, plagued by secularization, narcissism and perverse displays of power.[216] Such a 'weak ontology' of divine *kenosis* stands out strongly against society's violence and power play.[217] It provides a paradigm to resolve conflicts caused by injustice and evil:[218]

> [T]he human-divine Son of God becomes the link between *kenosis* and *plerosis*. That the Son is the link can be seen in the fact that the human Jesus voluntarily realizes creativity and justice in an ideal way. Not only this, but the New Testament records also affirm God fully suffered concretely in the Christ the diabolic effects of conflict. ... We grasp perhaps most clearly in Christ a vision of the God who loses his life in order that he may take it up again, and the God whose inexhaustible power is poured out eternally for the sake of his Other.

Indeed, the cross rises up "outside the camp" and in the *in-between* space of sky-earth: (a) as a critique and condemnation of the powerful who fill themselves while being the cause of the Other's emptiness, nakedness, suffering and death, and (b) as a banner of battle for the powerless, symbolizing courage to confront evil, as well as the faith to live, and even die, for the creation of a new humanity/world built on equality, justice and truth.

4.5 Conclusion: Trinitarian Trajectories of Relationship- Spatiality- Power

In this chapter I have proposed trajectories for a trinitarian theology by positioning myself alongside subaltern communities. The chapter began with preliminary reflections on the contours of community – twos and threes – and showed how the 'third' seems to be the starting point for both, community and conflict. I then determined the starting-point for trinitarian theologizing, namely, situations of subordination, and thus stressed the need to start 'from below'. Providing an overview of the *status questionis* of Indian trinitarian theology and pointing out the lacunae in this area, in a move away from post-VC II initiatives of dialoging with the 'big traditions', I developed 'subaltern trinitarian theology', using the spatiality and the religio-cultural resources of the 'little traditions'. I condensed *subaltern trinitarian theology* into three main theses:

- Trinity is a representation of relationship, solidarity and communion
- Trinity is a representation reaffirming the sacredness of subaltern space
- Trinity is a representation revealing of 'counter spaces' of subaltern power

I argued that, first, the disprivileged communities believe in God not in the abstract, but as a Parental God who walks in step with it, protecting it and empowering it. *Being-in-communion* thus becomes an ideal that animates the community, which can best be symbolized by the adivasi *naachnu* where the whole community dances arm-in-arm and step-in-step to melodies echoing the ups and downs of life. Second, this God reaffirms subaltern *tri-une spatiality* as sacred – with *Abba* (primordial), Son (visible) and *Shakti* (invisible) conceived as representing not only the relationships in God, but also relationships concretely lived out in the *social space* of disadvantaged communities. Here, Jesus' conception of the Kingdom of God and God of the Kingdom become the 'counter spaces' for new life and liberation. Third, in fostering communion, retrieving lost space or in the construction of the Kingdom of God, there is bound to be conflict. Contrary to the power games and violence of society, trinitarian *kenosis-plerosis* traces a trajectory to confront evil and opens possibilities for the creation of a new world. We shall discuss the 'How' of this new world in the next two chapters.

ENDNOTES FOR CHAPTER FOUR

[1]   See *Cassell's Latin Dictionary* (London: Macmillan Publishing Co., 1993), s.v. *'tribus'*.

[2] See Jean Paul Sartre, *No Exit and Three Other Plays*, New York: Random House, 1955.

[3] See Bertrand de Margerie, *The Christian Trinity in History*, trans. E. J. Fortman (Massachusetts: St Bede's Publications, 1981) and Edmund J. Fortman, *The Triune God: A Historical Study of the Doctrine of the Trinity* (Philadelphia: Westminster Press, 1972), among others, for concise histories of trinitarian theology.

[4] See William J. La Due, *The Trinity Guide to the Trinity* (Harrisburg, Pennsylvania: Trinity Press International, 2003), for easy reference to the main periods and persons involved in trinitarian theology.

[5] See, for e.g., Jung Young Lee, *The Trinity in Asian Perspective* (Nashville: Abingdon Press, 1996); Albert Sundararaj Walters, *We Believe in One God? Reflections on the Trinity in the Malaysian Context* (Delhi, ISPCK: 2002); Salai Hla Aung, "Relational Trinity and its Conceptual Implications for Asian Community," *AJOT* 14/1 (April 2000): 82-92, and Paul Chung, "Trinity and Asian Theology of Divine *Dukkar*," *AJOT* 6/1 (2001): 131-47, among others.

[6] See, for e.g., Brian Gaybba, "Trinitarian Experience and Doctrine," in *Doing Theology in Context: South African Perspectives*, ed. J. W. De Gruchy and C. Villa-Vicencio (New York: Orbis Books, 1994), 77-88; Charles Nyamiti, "Divine Immanent Responsibility: An African Approach to the Mystery of the Trinity," *ACS* (1998): 1-46 and "The Trinity as Source and Soul of African Family Ecclesiology," *ACS* (1999): 34-92; Mika Vähakängas, "African Approaches to the Trinity," *ATJ* 23/2 (2000): 33-50.

[7] The trinitarian theologies from Europe are numerous. The theology of Karl Rahner, *The Trinity*, trans. J. Donceel (Kent: Burns & Oates, 1986) and Karl Barth, *Church Dogmatics*, vol. I (Edinburgh: T & T Clark, 1936) represent the most popular Catholic and Protestant positions, respectively. For a more contextualized and local European theology see, for e.g., Gerry O'Hanlon, "The Trinitarian God: Towards a New Ireland," *TITQ* 55/2 (1989): 99-113, who develops a 'mystery approach' to trinitarian theology for Irish Christians.

[8] For e.g., Anthony Kelly, *The Trinity of Love: A Theology of the Christian God* (Wilmington, Delaware: Michael Glazier, 1989), and Kevin Hart, "The Kingdom and the Trinity," *TACR* 73/3 (July 2001): 321-39.

[9] See, for e.g., Leonardo Boff, *Trinity and Society*, trans. P. Burns (New York: Orbis, 1988) and *Holy Trinity, Perfect Community*, trans. P. Berryman (New York: Orbis, 2000), and Juan Luis Segundo, *Our Idea of God* (New York: Orbis, 1974), among others.

[10] See, for e.g., Joseph A. Bracken, *The Triune Symbol: Persons, Process and Community* (Lanham: UPOA, 1985); Ted Peters, *God as Trinity. Relationality and*

Temporality in Divine Life (Louisville, Kentucky: John Knox Press, 1993); Sallie McFague, *Models of God* (Philadelphia: Fortress Press, 1987), among others.

[11] Duane Larson, *Times of the Trinity: A Proposal for Theistic Cosmology* (New York: Peter Lang, 1995), sees the Trinity as a theologically productive way to address the issue of how eternity relates to time; also Michael Welker, "God's Eternity, God's Temporality & Trinitarian Theology," *TT* 55/3 (Oct 1998): 317-28.

[12] See, for e.g., Peter Drilling, "The Genesis of the Trinitarian Ecclesiology of Vatican II," *Science et Esprit* 45/1 (January-April 1993): 61-78.

[13] See, for e.g., Colin E. Gunton *The One, The Three and The Many: God, Creation and the Culture of Modernity*, vols. I & II (Cambridge: CUP, 1993) and Thomas Finger, "Modern Alienation and Trinitarian Creation," *Evangelical Review of Theology* 17/2 (April-June 1993): 190-208, among others.

[14] See, for e.g., Graham Ward, ed., *The Postmodern God: A Theological Reader* (Oxford: Blackwell Publishers, 1997); Michael P. Jensen, "Is There Anything in What We Say? A Trinitarian Response to the Challenge of Postmodernism," *RTR* 60/1 (April 2001): 18-29; and Martin Henry, "God in Postmodernity," *ITJ* 63/1 (1998): 3-21.

[15] See, for e.g., Michael von Brück, *The Unity of Reality: God, God-Experience and Meditation in the Hindu-Christian Dialogue* (New York: Paulist Press, 1991); Jason J. Yoder, "The Trinity and Christian Witness to Muslims," *Missiology* 22/3 (July 1994): 339-46, and *Buddhist Emptiness & Christian Trinity: Essays and Explorations*, ed. R. Corless and P. Knitter (New York: Paulist Press, 1990), among others.

[16] See, for e.g., Denis Edwards, *Jesus, the Wisdom of God: An Ecological Theology* (Homebush, N.S.W.: St. Paul's, 1995); David T. Williams, "Trinitarian Ecology," *SBET* 18/2 (Autumn 2000): 142-59; Sallie McFague, *The Body of God: An Ecological Theology*. Minneapolis: Fortress Press, 1993), among others.

[17] See E.L. Mascall, *The Triune God: An Ecumenical Study* (Sussex: Churchman Publishing Ltd., 1986).

[18] See, for e.g., John Russell, Nancey Murphy, and Arthur R. Peacocke, eds. *Chaos and Complexity: Scientific Perspectives on Divine Action* (Vatican City: Vatican Observatory Publications and California: The Center for Theology and the Natural Sciences, 1997); S.L. Jaki, *The Road of Science and the Ways to God* (Edinburgh: Scottish Academic Press, 1978), and Diarmuid O'Murchu, *Quantum Theology* (New York: Crossroad, 1998), among others.

[19] See, for e.g., Sudhir Kumar Kujur, "Tribal Concept of the Divine: A Trinitarian Perspective," *Sevartham* 21 (1996): 115-31, and A. A. Yewangoe, "The Trinity in the Context of Tribal Religion," *SID* 13/1 (2003): 86-105, among others.

[20] See, for e.g., Elizabeth A. Johnson, *She Who Is: The Mystery of God in Feminist Theological Discourse* (New York: Crossroad, 1992); Catherine Mowry LaCugna, *God For Us: The Trinity and Christian Life* (New York: HarperCollins,

1991); Rosemary Radford Ruether, *Sexism and God-Talk: Towards a Feminist Theology* (Boston: Beacon Press, 1983), among others.

[21] See "On Human Language for God, Simile, Metaphor, Parable, Analogy, Name," in James B. Torrance, *Worship, Community, and the Triune God of Grace* (Carlisle, U.K.: Paternoster Press, 1996), 111-5.

[22] See, G. Aloysius, "The Study of Religion-in-Society: A View From Below," *R&S* 42/1 (March 1995): 5-16, who argues that the religion of the oppressed emerges from below, from their situations of oppression.

[23] P.J.A.M. Schoonenberg, "Trinity – The consummated covenant: Theses on the doctrine of the trinitarian God," *SIR* 5/2 (1975-6): 111. This quotation combines the first three of the thirty-six points of his theory.

[24] See Javier Prades, "From the Economic to the Immanent Trinity: Remarks on a Principle of Renewal in Trinitarian Theology" (Parts I & II), *CICR* 27/2,3 (Summer & Fall 2000): 240-61, 562-93, who stresses that Jesus is the entryway to the Trinity for he cannot be understood without reference to the Father and the Spirit; yet, cautions about a reductionist view of the mystery of God; also Joseph A. Bracken, "Trinity: Economic and Immanent," *Horizons* 25/1 (Spring 1998): 7-22, cautions about the current indiscriminate move away from ontology to phenomenology and suggests a new look at a 'metaphysics of becoming' and 'social ontology' so as to retain the healthy tension between immanence-transcendence, being-becoming; also Eberhard Jüngel, "The Relationship between Economic and Immanent Trinity," *TD* 24 (1976): 179-84.

[25] Patristic and Medieval Trinitarian Tradition kept this insight of God's Absoluteness (the always 'more') alive. See Augustine, *Sermo* 117/5; Aquinas, *Summa Contra Gentiles* 1/5, 34; Anselm, *Proslogion* 15.

[26] See his lecture on January 21, 1882, "That Marvellous Mystery: The Trinity," in *Keshub Chunder Sen: A Selection*, ed. D.C. Scott (Madras: CLS and Bangalore: UTC, 1979), 217-47.

[27] See *The Writings of Brahmabandhab Upadhyay*, vol. I, ed. J. Lipner and G. Gispert-Sauch (Bangalore: UTC, 1991), 125-30, for his development of the term. See pp. 94-145, for his understanding of God.

[28] See Julius Lipner, *Brahmabandhab Upadhyay: The Life and Thought of a Revolutionary* (Delhi: OUP, 1999), 199-204, for the text, translation, as well as discussion on the deep thought contained in the hymn.

[29] See Joseph Mattam, *Land of the Trinity: A Study of Modern Christian Approaches to Hinduism* (Bangalore: TPI, 1975), 18.

[30] Jules Monchanin, *A Benedictine Ashram* (with H. le Saux) rev. ed., (Douglas: Times Press, 1964), 37. See also his *Ermites du Saccidânanda: Un Essai d'Intégration Chrétienne de la Tradition Monastique de l'Inde* (with H. le Saux) (Paris: Casterman, 1957), 175-6, wherein he stresses that the experience of the Christian mystic and the Hindu sanyasi meet in *Saccidânanda* where, for the Christian, *Sat* is *"le Principe sans Principe"* (Father), *Cit* is *"l'Image intellectuelle consubstantielle à l'Existant"* (Son), and *Ananda* is *"l'Amour Absolu"* (Spirit).

[31] See Bede Griffiths, *Return to the Center* (Springfield, Illinois: Templegate, 1976), 126-9.

[32] See Bede Griffiths, "The Advaitic Experience and the Personal God in the Upanishads and the Bhagavad Gita," *ITS* 15/1 (March 1978): 71-86.

[33] For a concise summary of Abhishiktânanda's trinitarian theology see his "Notes on Christology and Trinitarian Theology," *VJTR* 64/8 (August 2000): 598-612.

[34] See Abhishiktânanda, *Saccidânanda: A Christian Approach to Advaitic Experience* (Delhi: ISPCK, 1974); also J. Glenn Friesen, "Abhishiktânanda: Hindu Advaitic Experience and Christian Beliefs," *HCSB* 11 (1998): 31-8.

[35] Abhishiktânanda, *Saccidânanda*, 178.

[36] See, for instance, Jojo Joseph. "Trinitarian Experience of a Christian and Advaitic Experience of a Hindu," *JOD* 27/2 (April-June 2002): 207-31.

[37] See von Brück, "*Advaita* and Trinity: Reflections on the Vedantic and Christian Experience of God with Reference to Buddhist Non-Dualism," *ITS* 20/1 (March 1983): 37-60; also, "Trinitarian Theology: Hegelian vis-à-vis *Advaitic*," *JOD* 8/3 (July–September 1983): 283-95.

[38] See Vroom, *No Other Gods: Christian Belief in Dialogue with Buddhism, Hinduism, and Islam*, trans. L. Jansen (Michigan & Cambridge: William B. Eerdmans Publishing Company, 1996); also, "Religious Hermeneutics, Culture and Narratives," *SID* 4/2 (1994): 189-213.

[39] See Carman, *Majesty and Meekness: A Comparative Study of Contrast and Harmony in the Concept of God* (Grand Rapids, Michigan: William B. Eerdmans Publishing Company, 1994).

[40] See, for instance, Michael von Brück, "Buddhist Shûnyatâ and the Christian Trinity: The Emerging Holistic Paradigm," in *Buddhist Emptiness and Christian Trinity: Essays and Explorations*, ed. R. Corless and P. Knitter (New York: Paulist Press, 1990), 44-66; also David Tracy, "Kenosis, Sunyata, and Trinity: A Dialogue with Masao Abe," in *The Emptying God: A Buddhist–Jewish–Christian Conversation*, ed. J. B. Cobb, Jr., and C. Ives (New York: Orbis, 1990), 135-54, and John P. Keenan, "A Mahâyâna Understanding of the Trinity," in his *The Meaning of Christ: A Mahâyâna Theology* (New York: Orbis, 1989), 240-59.

[41] See, *The New Dictionary of Theology*, ed. J.A. Komonchak et al., (Bangalore: TPI, 1993), 556, s.v. 'kenosis'; also O'Collins and G. Farrugia, *A Concise Dictionary of Theology*, 116. For a theological development, see, Lucien J. Richard, *A Kenotic Christology: In the Humanity of Jesus The Christ, The Compassion of Our God* (Washington, D.C.: University Press of America, Inc., 1982). For a contextual interpretation, see Francis Gonsalves, The Implications of Kenosis Christology for Contextual Christology," *VJ TR* 66/1 (January 2002): 7-17.

[42] Von Brück, "*Advaita* and Trinity," 47.

[43] See, for instance, Donald W. Mitchell, *Spirituality and Emptiness: The Dynamics of Spiritual Life in Buddhism and Christianity* (New York: Paulist Press, 1991).

[44] See Raimundo Panikkar, "Toward an Ecumenical Theandric Spirituality," *JOES* 5/3 (Summer 1968): 507-34; also, *The Trinity and World Religions: Icon-Person-Mystery* (Bangalore: CISRS, 1970).

[45] See, among others, Rowan Williams, "Trinity and Pluralism," in *Christian Uniqueness Reconsidered*, ed. G. D'Costa (New York: Orbis Books, 1990), 3, who judges Panikkar's book on the Trinity to be "one of the best and the least read meditations on the Trinity in our century"; also, S. Mark Heim, *The Depth of the Riches: A Trinitarian Theology of Religious Ends* (Grand Rapids, Michigan/Cambridge, U.K.: William B. Eerdmans Publishing Company, 2001), 148, says that Panikkar has offered, "probably the most thought-provoking recent attempt to interpret the religions in trinitarian terms." Ewert Cousins, "The Trinity and World Religions," *JOES* 7/3 (Summer 1970): 476-98, also builds upon Panikkar's basic framework.

[46] See for instance, Stephen Williams, "The Trinity and 'Other Religions'," in *The Trinity in a Pluralistic Age: Theological Essays on Culture and Religion*, ed. K.J. Vanhoozer (Grand Rapids, Michigan/ Cambridge, U.K.: William B. Eerdmans Publishing Company, 1997), 26-30; also, Eckman P.C. Tam, "The Trinity and World Religions Reconsidered," *SID* 8/2 (1998): 52-66.

[47] See, for instance, Kurian Mathothu, *The Development of the Concept of Trimurti in Hinduism* (Bangalore: St. Paul's Press, 1974), 119-38, for details on how the concept of *Trimurti* developed in the Hindu tradition. There is also an attempt to compare the *Trimurti* with the Trinity.

[48] Sahi told me that he had adopted "The 3 heads as in the *Trimurti* of Elephanta Caves [base of picture], with one central face representing *Ishwara*, the Lord, and on one side the Masculine aspect or *Purusha* (God the Father) and on the other side the Feminine aspect, *Shakti*, which could be understood also as the Spirit. The figure below is Moses. The tear is because God said from the Burning Bush, "I have seen the sufferings of my people." The tree is the Burning Bush. The feet, as in the image, which we find in the Buddhist tradition, are meant to represent the presence of the Lord, and that the place is Holy Ground."

[49] A *mudra* is a hand-gesture in classical Indian dance. Sahi informed me that, "The 3 gestures or *mudras* represent the Trinity. These gestures are as follows: 1. *Abhaya Mudra*, hand raised in a gesture of protection and "do not fear", conveys the idea of the Father. 2 The gesture pointing down with two fingers, is a traditional Christian image found in many icons, and is meant to represent the Word, which has two natures: Divine and human. 3. The gesture with the index finger joined to the thumb, is called the *Dhyana Mudra*, or gesture of meditation. In the Christian tradition this gesture is also sometimes associated with Beauty. This gesture is used by the priest celebrating the Eucharist, at the time of Consecration and the *Epiclesis* when the Spirit descends on the elements. I have associated this *mudra* with the Holy Spirit."

[50] There are many proponents and opponents of 'social trinitarianism'. The earliest proponents of the social analogy were the 4th cent. Cappadocian Fathers who likened Father, Son and Spirit to three human persons. The social analogy reappeared in the 12th cent. in Richard of St. Victor's trinitarianism based on inter-personal love. The 19th cent. Russian Orthodox theologian Nikolai Fedorov said, "The Trinity is our social programme." In the 20th cent., the works of Leonard Hodgson, *The Doctrine of the Trinity* (London: Nisbet & Co., 1944) and Claude Welch, *In This Name: The Doctrine of the Trinity in Contemporary Theology* (London: SCM Press, 1953) were seminal works. Today, well-known proponents of social trinitarianism are Jürgen Moltmann, *The Trinity and the Kingdom: The Doctrine of God*, trans. M. Kohl (Minneapolis: Fortress Press, 1993); Leonardo Boff, *ibid.*; Cornelius Plantiga, Jr., "Social Trinity and Tritheism," in *Trinity, Incarnation and Atonement*, ed. idem and R. Feenstra (Notre Dame, Indiana: NDUP, 1989), and Joseph A. Bracken, "The Holy Trinity as a Community of Divine Persons – I & II," *THJ* 15/2, 3 (April-July 1974): 166-82, 257-70, among others. For critiques see, Brian Leftow, "Anti Social Trinitarianism," in *The Trinity: An Interdisciplinary Symposium on the Trinity*, ed. S.T. Davis et al., (New York: OUP, 1999), 203-49; Mark D. Chapman, "The Social Doctrine of the Trinity: Some Problems," *ATR* 83/2 (Spring 2001): 239-54; Karen Kilby, "Perichoresis and Projection: Problems with Social Doctrines of the Trinity," *NBF* 81/956 (October 2000): 432-45, and James P. Mackey, "Are there Christian Alternatives to Trinitarian Thinking?" in *The Christian Understanding of God Today*, ed. J Byrne (Dublin: Columbia, 1993), 66-75, among others. Also see John L. Gresham, Jr., "The Social Model of the Trinity & its Critics," *SJOT* 46/3 (1993): 325-43, and John J. O'Donnell, "The Trinity as Divine Community: A Critical Reflection upon Recent Theological Developments," *Gregorianum* 69/1 (1988): 5-34.

[51] See Geevarghese, *Theology of a Classless Society* (Madras: CLS, 1980).

[52] *Ibid.*, 132-3.

[53] See Geevarghese, *Sharing God and a Sharing World* (Delhi: ISPCK & Tiruvalla: CSS, 1995).

[54] See Dominic Veliath, "The Trinity in Indian Theology," *Kristu Jyoti* 8/2 (June 1992): 1-24, for a brief comparative study on four trinitarian theologians: Upâdhyây, Abhishiktânanda, Griffiths and Panikkar.

[55] See Panikkar, *The Trinity and World Religions*, 69-80, where: "*Theandrism* is the classical and traditional term for that intimate and complete unity which is realized paradigmatically in Christ between the divine and the human and which is the goal towards which everything here below tends – in Christ and the Spirit." Panikkar prefers this term to 'Trinity' since it is not specifically Christian. However, the term seems weak since it lacks historicity and does not convey what is central to the Christian revelation.

[56] Panikkar, *The Cosmotheandric Experience: Emerging Religious Consciousness* (Delhi: Motilal Banarsidass Publishers, 1993), 54-77, describes this experience as the original and primordial form of consciousness embracing divine,

human and earthly. See also "The Cosmotheandric Intuition," *Jeevadhara* 14/
79 (January 1984): 27-35.

[57] See Foucault, *Power/Knowledge: Selected Interviews and Other Writings*, 81.

[58] M.E. Prabhakar, "Christology in Dalit Perspective," in *Frontiers of Dalit Theology*, 410.

[59] Geevarghese's *Sharing God and a Sharing World* (1995) is a notable exception.

[60] See Wilfred, *The Sling of Utopia*, 137-63, and James Ponnaiah, "Spirituality of the Subalterns," *Vaiharai* 9/3 (September 2004): 32-58, for details of some of the characteristics of subaltern religious experience; also *Dalits & Women: Quest for Humanity*, ed. V. Devasahayam (Madras: GLTCRI, 1996), for the specificities of the Dalit socio-eco-political-religious context and contours for Dalit theology. For case studies on Popular Catholicism, see *Popular Catholicism in a World Church: Seven Case Studies in Inculturation*, ed. T. Bamat and J-P. Wiest (New York: Orbis, 1999), especially Francis Jayapathy, "Mukkuvar Catholicism," in *ibid.*, 183-214. See also P.T. Mathew, *We Dare the Waters: The World & the Worldview of the Mukkuvar* (Chennai: UOM, 2001), for popular religion in an Indian fisher community.

[61] The non-occurrence of the word 'Trinity' in the Bible does not mean that a trinitarian dimension of God is absent from Scripture and is, therefore, a later addition of the post-apostolic Church. Any such assertion is disproved by Scriptural texts that are trinitarian in character; for e.g., Mt 28:19; 2 Cor 13:14; Gal 4:4-8, etc.

[62] It can be said that: "The NT contains no doctrine of the Trinity;" see, Donald H. Juel, "The Trinity and the New Testament," *TT* 54 (1997): 313; also, Fortman, 32.

[63] See Gordon D. Fee, "Paul and the Trinity: The Experience of Christ and the Spirit for Paul's Understanding of God," in *The Trinity*, ed. S.T. Davies et al., 49-72, for details. In brief, Fee argues that Paul has an 'economic trinitarian' idea of God, and perhaps an 'ontological trinitarian' one, as well, although its philosophical and theological nuances are unclear to theologians.

[64] This emerges from the arguments of de Margerie, 39-44. He also discusses other NT trinitarian texts

[65] Fee, "Paul and the Trinity," 52, stresses that Pauline trinitarianism emerges out of Paul's 'experience' of 'salvation'. Footnote 9 says that Paul's God/Christ/Spirit triad is changed to God/Spirit/Son in Gal 4:6.

[66] See Luis M. Bermejo, *Abba, My Dad!* (Anand: GSP, 2003), for a good scriptural and systematic exposition of God as *Abba* of Jesus *and Abba* of all human beings.

[67] Although this seems to be true of both, the Gujarati, as well as the Jharkhand adivasis, John Lakra, specifies in a questionnaire sent by me to him: "According to the Oraon religious myth *Dharmes* has a consultation with a female counterpart in the course of creating the world. Except for the

consultation she has no role whatsoever of a wife, nor does she figure anywhere else in the tribal life of worship. I consider this person as God's *Wisdom* personified. This could perhaps be considered a divine community or communion of two persons." Lakra, however, states that there is no conception of trinity among adivasis.

[68] This news item appeared in *The Hindu*, Friday, January 19, 2007.

[69] See Sudhir Kakar, *The Inner World: A Psychoanalytic Study of Childhood and Society in India*, New Delhi: Oxford University Press, 1980.

[70] See, for e.g., how Augustine [354-430] used the analogy of love to explain the Trinity: the Father being 'lover' (*amans*), the Son being the 'beloved' (*quod amatur*) and the Spirit being the mutual love (*amor*) passing between the Father and the Son, proceeding from both, and uniting the three divine 'persons'. See his *De Trinitate*, book IX, especially ch.8, for this point. See also J.N.D. Kelly, *Early Christian Doctrines* (San Francisco: Harper & Row, 1978), 276-9, and Eugene TeSelle, *Augustine the Theologian* (New York: Herder, 1970), 232-4, for details on Augustine's analogies.

[71] Theological language is always metaphorical, symbolic and analogical. Though 'analogy' imputes 'likeness' it also always implies 'unlikeness'; hence, never exhausts the truth contained in *reality-in-itself*.

[72] See William Hasker, "Tri-unity," *JOR* 50/1 (1974): 1-32, who develops this thesis. The quote is from p. 2; see also John A. Thurmer, "The Analogy of the Trinity," *SJOT* 34/6 (1981): 509-15.

[73] See, for e.g., Richard of St. Victor [d.c.1173] who further developed the analogy of love in terms of a movement from self-love (Father) to mutual love (Father and Son) and to shared love (Father-Son-Spirit). For further details on the trinitarian theology of Richard St. Victor, see Fortman, 191-4 and Ewert H. Cousins, "A Theology of Interpersonal Relations," *Thought* 45 (1970): 56-82. Note that while Augustine starts from nature, Richard begins from 'persons' and analyses love in human relationships.

[74] See Fortman, 113, for nuances of what Tertullian meant.

[75] *Ibid.*, 163. What Boethius stressed about 'person' was substantiality, intellectuality and incommunicability.

[76] In *Summa Theologica*, Ia.29. Note that Aquinas begins with *divine internal relations* rather than human.

[77] Rahner, *The Trinity*, 113 and 114, respectively.

[78] Joseph T. Lienhard, "*Ousia* and *Hypostasis*: The Cappadocian Settlement and the Theology of 'One *Hypostasis*'," in *The Trinity*, ed. S.T. Davis et al., 103, holds that such terms are "crafted on the workbench of theologians, and even for them, it is more of a convenient abbreviation than the last word that might be uttered."

[79] See, for instance, John McMurray, *Persons in Relation* (London: Faber and Faber, 1961); Charles Taylor, *Sources of the Self: The Making of the Modern*

Identity (Cambridge, Massachusetts: HUP, 1989); Alistair I. McFadyen, *The Call to Personhood: A Christian Theory of the Individual in Social Relationships* (Cambridge: CUP, 1990), and Elaine L. Graham, *Making the Difference: Gender, Personhood and Theology* (London: Mowbray, 1995), among others.

[80] See, David Brown, "Trinitarian Personhood and Individuality," in *Trinity, Incarnation & Atonement*, ed. R. Feenstra and C. Plantinga (Notre Dame: NDUP, 1988), 48-78; Anthony C. Thistleton, *Interpreting God & the Postmodern Self: On Meaning, Manipulation & Promise* (Edinburgh: T&T Clark, 1995); Fritz Buri, "Trinity and Personality," *Iliff Review* 40 (Winter 1983): 15-24; Thomas F. Torrance, *The Christian Doctrine of God: One Being Three Persons* (Edinburgh: T&T Clark, 1988); Alan J. Torrance, *Persons in Communion: Trinitarian Description and Human Participation* (Edinburgh: T&T Clark, 1996); Lawrence B. Porter, "On Keeping 'Persons' in the Trinity: a Linguistic Approach to Trinitarian Thought," *TS* 41/3 (September 1980): 530-48, and Norris Clark, "Person, Being and St. Thomas," *CICR* 19 (1992): 601-18, among others.

[81] See Kullu, 98-9.

[82] See Harriet A. Harris, "Should We Say that Personhood is Relational?" *SJOT* 51/1 (1998): 214-35, for an insightful analysis of the questions of 'person', 'personhood' and 'relation'.

[83] See E. Schillebeeckx and B. Iersel, eds., "A Personal God?" *Concilium* (1977), for diverse aspects of God as person.

[84] See Nicholas Lash, *Believing Three Ways in One God: A Reading of the Apostles' Creed* (Notre Dame, Indiana: NDUP, 1992), 32.

[85] This is well expressed by William A. Barry, *Paying Attention to God* (Notre Dame, Indiana: Ave Maria Press, 1990), 72: "God is perfect community. The three persons are so united with one another that they share everything in common; the only difference between them is their mutual relationships to one another. Hence, in the community that is God there can be no disunity, no separation, no fear."

[86] See also Abhishiktânanda, 98: "God's life is indeed Communion; Being is essentially Communion." Hence, he coins the word *samsat*, meaning, 'being-with' for the divine existence.

[87] See John Zizioulas, *Being as Communion: Studies in Personhood and the Church* (London: Darton, Longman and Todd, 1985), 40-9, who stresses the relational and personal aspects of the Triune God.

[88] Cornelius Plantinga, Jr., The Threeness/Onesss Problem of the Trinity," *CTJ* 23 (April 1989): 50.

[89] See, for instance, Terrence W. Tilley, *Talking of God: An Introduction to Philosophical Analysis of Religious Language* (New York: Paulist Press, 1978); Ted Peters, "The Battle Over Trinitarian Language," in *Dialog* 30 (Winter 1991): 44-9; Christian J. Barrigar, "Protecting God: The Lexical Formation of Trinitarian Language," *MT* 7 (July 1991): 299-310; George A. Lindbeck, "Reflections on Trinitarian Language," *Pro Ecclesia* 4 (Summer 1995): 261-4;

Sallie McFague, *Metaphorical Theology* (Philadelphia: Fortress Press, 1982), and Janet M. Soskice, *Metaphor and Religious Language* (Oxford: Clarendon Press, 1985), among others.

[90] Many feminist theologians have debated the question of Trinitarian terminology: Rebecca Chopp, *The Power to Speak: Feminism, Language, God* (New York: Crossword, 1989); Rosemary R. Ruether, *ibid.*; Catherine M. LaCugna, *ibid.*; Elizabeth A. Johnson, *ibid.*, and Deborah Malacky Belonick, "Revelation and Metaphors: The Significance of the Trinitarian Names, Father, Son and Hoy Spirit," *USQR* 40/3 (1985): 31-41, among others. For alternative viewpoints see Donald G. Bloesch, *The Battle for the Trinity: The Debate over Inclusive God-Language* (Michigan: Servant Publications, 1985); Thomas F. Torrance, "The Christian Apprehension of God the Father," in *Speaking the Christian God: The Holy Trinity and the Challenge to Feminism*, ed. A.F. Kimel, Jr. (Michigan: William B. Eerdmans, 1992), 120-43; Joseph A. DiNoia, "Knowing and Naming the Triune God: The Grammar of Trinitarian Confession," in *ibid.*, 162-87.

[91] Alvin F. Kimel, Jr., "The God Who Likes His Name: Holy Trinity, Feminism, and the Language of Faith," in *Speaking the Christian God: The Holy Trinity & the Challenge to Feminism*, ed. idem, 188-208, argues that the terms Father-Son-Spirit are irreplaceable due to their grounding in Tradition and Scripture; see also Ben Witherington and Laura M. Ice, *The Shadow of the Almighty: Father, Son, and Spirit in Biblical Perspective* (Grand Rapids, Michigan & Cambridge, U.K.: William B. Eerdmans), 2002.

[92] Rebecca Oxford-Carpenter, "Gender and the Trinity," *TT* 41/1 (April 1984): 7-25, argues that a 'masculinization' of the image of God took place around the end of the 2nd century due to the political and cultural changes inside and outside the Church; such distortions having adverse psychological implications.

[93] Note that sometimes the word 'Sustainer' is used instead of 'Sanctifier'. This terminology has found wide acceptance especially in North America. See John Thompson, *Modern Trinitarian Perspectives* (New York: OUP, 1994), 115-6. Geoffrey Wainwright, "The Doctrine of the Trinity: Where the Church Stands or Falls," *Interpretation* 45/2 (April 1991): 117-32, and DiNoia, *ibid.*, 169-73, expose the inadequacies of this formulation. Wainwright argues that this formula has traces of Sabellianism, dissecting God into three functions. Conversely, Susan Brooks Thistlethwaite, "On the Trinity," *Interpretation* 45/2 (April 1991), 170, writes: "It is, in my view, the strength of the economic Trinity as Creator, Redeemer, Sustainer that it names the history of God with the world."

[94] Sallie McFague, *Models of God* (Philadelphia: Fortress Press, 1987), 181-7, argues for these appellations instead of Father-Son-Spirit since they are also more appropriate for developing an ecological theology. Oxford-Carpenter, *ibid.*, 22, argues that: "[D]esexed but personal images of God ... prevent us from falling into sexist theological traps, and they transcend our own gender-laden categories."

[95] See O'Collins, *The Tripersonal God*, 183-91, who debates the pros and cons for re/naming the Trinity.

[96] See Gregory Rocca, "The Trinity and Feminism," in *T.Th.* 57/3 (July 1993): 509-20, for a dispassionate treatment of the feminist issue in the light of Trinitarian theology.

[97] Caution is required when citing a 'long history' of Father-Son-Spirit terminology since there are some exceptions to this as pointed out, for instance, by John Dart, "Balancing Out the Trinity: The Genders of the Godhead," *TCC* 100 (February 16-23, 1983): 147-50, who maintains that there are notions of a maternal Spirit and an androgynous Jesus in early Church teachings that were subsequently rejected. Thus, a 'balancing out' theology of the Christian Godhead, informed by psychological insights has both 'modern relevance' and 'ancient precedent'.

[98] Catherine Mowry LaCugna, "The Baptismal Formula, Feminist Objections, and Trinitarian Theology," *JOES* 26/2 (Spring 1989): 248.

[99] LaCugna, *ibid.*, 235-50, discusses this issue and proposes conditions for retaining traditional terms; also Janet Martin Soskice, "Trinity and 'the Feminine Other'" *NBF* 75/878 (1994): 2-17, stresses that the Trinity tells us nothing about sexuality but that it indicates that "to be" most fully is "to-be-related."

[100] See Jürgen Moltmann, *History and the Triune God*, trans. J. Bowden (New York: Crossroad, 1992), 83.

[101] See, for e.g., Anna May Say Pa, "The Feminine Image of God," *IGI* 19/2 (June 2000): 2-9; also Alan E. Lewis, ed., *The Motherhood of God* (Edinburgh: Saint Andrew Press, 1984).

[102] John P.H. Clark, "Nature, Grace and the Trinity in Julian of Norwich," *TDR* 100/340 (July 1982): 203-20, points out that Julian of Norwich considered Jesus as 'mother' on the basis of his being God's Wisdom.

[103] It is interesting to note that the equivalent of 'Father' in the Gamit tribal language is precisely '*Abba*'. Christianized Gamit adivasis use this term in their liturgy for God, the Father

[104] Elizabeth A. Johnson, *ibid.*, 191-223, develops the analogy of 'Wisdom' for the Trinity. She speaks of God as 'Holy Wisdom' or simply as 'Sophia-God'. The relationship among the three 'persons' is explained as Spirit-Sophia, Jesus-Sophia and Mother-Sophia paralleling the traditional Spirit-Son-Father respectively.

[105] 'Wisdom' (*Hokmah*) appears as many as 318 times as noun, adjective or verb in the OT mainly in the books of Job, Proverbs, Ecclesiastes (Qoheleth), Sirach and Wisdom. Some of these have personal nuances.

[106] Also note that the Hebrew word for Spirit in Genesis, namely, *Ruah*, is also feminine.

[107] See, Emmanuel Kaniyamparampil, *The Spirit of Life: A Study of the Holy Spirit in the Early Syriac Tradition* (Kottayam, Vadavathoor: Paurastya Vidyapeetham, 2003), 203-23, who discusses the question of the Holy Spirit

as feminine in the Syriac tradition, with a sizable group of adherents in the state of Kerala.

[108] See Salai Hla Aung, *ibid.*, 90-1, speaks of God, the *Ruach*, God the Wisdom and God the *Logos*. O'Collins, *Tripersonal God*, 23-34, discusses the appropriateness of the Wisdom-Word-Spirit triad, and Harold G. Wells, "Trinitarian Feminism: Elizabeth Johnson's Wisdom Christology," *TT* 52/3 (October 1995): 330-43, appreciates Johnson's theology for expressing God's nature, albeit with some reservations. See also Donald L. Gelpi, *The Divine Mother: A Trinitarian Theology of the Holy Spirit* (Lanham, MD: University Press of America, 1984) and idem, "A Peircean Approach to Trinity as Community: A Response to Some Responses," *Horizons* 27/1 (Spring 2000): 114-30, for a defence of his theological interpretation.

[109] Besides dangers of this *Manu Smriti* terminology, such Wisdom-language also fits in with the Hindutva discourse of the supremacy of the 'Great Indian Mind' (*Manas, Buddhi*) that is oppressive to the subalterns.

[110] See, for e.g., Susan S. Wadley, *Shakti: Power in the Conceptual Structure of Karimpur Religion* (New Delhi: Munshiram Manoharlal Publishers, 1985), for the dynamics of ritual power in an Indian village.

[111] The root of *shakti* is *sak*: "to be able". For uses of *shakti* in the Hindu traditions, and possible uses in the Christian Tradition, see Niranjan S. Singh, "*Shakti*," in *Gems from India*, ed. G. Gispert-Sauch (Delhi: ISPCK & VIEWS, 2006), 60-2.

[112] Note however that artists like Jyoti Sahi have interpreted *Shakti* (feminine) as Holy Spirit in Indian art.

[113] See, for instance, Lk 4:14 and Rom 15:13, 19 where power (*dynamis*) is associated with the Holy Spirit.

[114] See Acts 2:1-4; Rom 15:19. Jesus' breathing on disciples shows empowerment by the Spirit (Jn 20:22).

[115] I am grateful to George Gispert-Sauch for enlightening insights and a discussion on this subject.

[116] See Elizabeth A. Johnson, "The Incomprehensibility of God and the Image of God Male and Female," *TS* 45/3 (September 1984): 441-65, for a good handling of the gender issue in Trinity. Quote from p. 465.

[117] *Aniconic* is distinguished from *iconic* image that has recognizable 'likeness' to God. See Diana L. Eck, *Darshan: Seeing the Divine Image in India*, 2nd ed., (Pennsylvania: Anima Books, 1985), 32-44, for examples of the distinction between *iconic* and *aniconic* in the Indian, Hindu context.

[118] See, for instance, Sybille Fritsch-Oppermann, "Trikâya and Trinity: Reflecting Some Aspects of Christian-Buddhist Dialogue," *JOES* 30/2 (Spring 1993): 245-61, for points of dialogue between the two.

[119] Christopher Kaiser, "The Ontological Trinity in the Context of Historical Religion," *SJOT* 29/4 (1976): 301-10, compares the Triadic conceptions of God in Hinduism, Buddhism and Christianity.

[120] Eck, 33-4.

[121] Note, for e.g., how Panikkar, *The Trinity and World Religions*, uses the triad "Icon-Person-Mystery" as the sub-title of his book referring to the personal, iconic, as well as the mystery-dimension of the Trinity.

[122] See David S. Cunningham, "Developing Alternative Trinitarian Formulas," *ATR* 80/1 (Winter 1998): 26-9. Such images are also present in Scripture; see, for e.g., Jn 4:10, 13; 7:37-9; Heb 6:4.

[123] I find certain transpersonal trinitarian images inappropriate for subaltern communities. For e.g., the 'Idea-Activity-Power' analogy developed by Dorothy L. Sayers, *The Mind of The Maker* (London: Methuen, 1941), 26-35, which is discussed by John Thurmer, *A Detection of the Trinity* (Exeter: The Paternoster Press, 1984), 59-73; also, Michael Downey, *Altogether Gift: A Trinitarian Spirituality* (New York: Orbis, 2001), with the trinitarian persons identified as 'Giver-Given-Gifting'. Although he supports 'person' language, it is difficult to see how the second and third appellations actually refer to 'persons'.

[124] For instance David Brown, "The Trinity in Art," in *The Trinity*, ed. S. T. Davis et al., 329-56, divides trinitarian art on the basis of three 'versions': triadic, incarnational and societal.

[125] Painted around 1411, it is in the Tretyakov Gallery in Moscow.

[126] See Geoffrey Wainwright, "Trinitarian Worship," in *Speaking the Christian God*, ed. A.F. Kimel, 221.

[127] Kallistos of Diokleia, "The Human Person as an Icon of the Trinity," in *Sobornost* 8/2 (1986): 18.

[128] See, for e.g., Gerald O'Collins, *The Tripersonal God: Understanding and Interpreting the Trinity* (New Jersey: Paulist Press, 1999), 198, who is struck by the symbols of salvation: table, chalice and tree.

[129] See Gavin D'Costa, "The Christian Trinity: Paradigm for Pluralism?" in *Pluralism and the Religions: The Theological and Political Dimensions*, ed. J. D'Arcy May (London: Cassell, 1998), 23-27, for details.

[130] See, for e.g., Jyoti Sahi, *The Child and the Serpent: Reflections on Popular Indian Symbols* (London: Routledge & Kegan Paul Ltd., 1980), 91-109, for the rich meanings conveyed by the symbols of Indian art.

[131] See Wilfred, *Sling of Utopia*, 159-60, for details of the subaltern religious experience in play and dance.

[132] Drumming is a traditional occupation of the Dalits. Sathianathan Clarke, *Dalits and Christianity: Subaltern Religion and Liberation Theology in India* (Delhi: OUP, 1998), 140-78, develops the symbol of the drum and 'Christ as Drum', pp. 179-217. Among adivasis, the drummer is any member of the group. The *dholak*-player provides rythem with the home made drum of the bark of a tree and cattle hide.

[133] I am grateful to John Rose, Rappai, Carmen Borges and Sureshbhai

for these pictures of the adivasi *naachnu.*

[134] The term is still used today. See, for instance, Robert L. Kress, "Unity in Diversity and Diversity in Unity: Toward an Ecumenical Perichoresic Kenotic Trinitarian Ontology," *DAA* 4/3 (Fall 1990): 66-70; also, Trevor Hart, "Person & Prerogative in Perichoretic Perspective: An Ongoing Dispute in Trinitarian Ontology Observed," *TITQ* 58/1 (1992): 46-57; see also Kilby, *ibid.*

[135] *Circuminsessio* (with letter 's'), proposed by Thomas Aquinas, means 'co-inherence'; while *circumincessio* (with letter 'c'), used by Bonaventure, is translated as 'mutual penetration'. De Margerie, 183, notes: "*circuminsessio* reminds us of Jn 10:38; 14:9ff; 17:21, while *circumincessio* is in the line of Jn 1:2 and 1:18." The Council of Florence [1439] opted for the spelling *circuminsessio* of Aquinas.

[136] This applies to Western dances like ballet or Indian classical dances like *Bharatnatyam, Kathakali,* etc.

[137] Athanasius [c.296-377] first used the term 'reciprocal delight' in his *Contra Arianos* (2.64); for details, see O'Collins, *The Tripersonal God*, 128, 132.

[138] This is also called *'ubhu bhajan'* (literally, standing hymn) by some Christian adivasis.

[139] I am indebted to Philip Rosato for this terminology. *Creator* refers to the Father, *Re-creator* to the Son who saves and redeems humanity thereby effecting a 're-creation' and *Trans-creator* to the Holy Spirit inherent in, and energizing, all cosmic process that are within and also beyond (*trans*) space and time.

[140] See, for instance, Jurgen Moltmann, "The Motherly Father. Is Trinitarian Patripassianism Replacing Theological Patriarchalism?" in *God as Father? Concilium* (March 1981): 51-6, who critiques patriarchical and monarchical images of God and proposes images of a God who suffers out of love for the Son.

[141] Note also how the Creed of the 11th Council of Toledo (675) speaks of the Son as coming from the *womb* of the Father – *ab utero Patris.* Thus the Father is regarded as having maternal characteristics.

[142] See, for instance, Kujur, 120, who holds that in the Trinity, tribal theology "finds an analogy so as to enable these particular groups of people to believe in the revelation of the Trinitarian mystery which gives them a distinctive identity, i.e., a peace-loving and God-fearing egalitarian community. The latter is the reflection of the Divine Community."

[143] See Yewangoe, *ibid.,* who discusses this idea in the Indonesian context; and Vähakängas, *ibid.,* who shows that relational and family (*Ujamaa*) terminology is appropriate for the Trinity in the African context.

[144] Wiel Eggen, "Religion of a Family God?" *SID* 10/2 (2000): 175-96, shows the importance of kinship and family in the African context: "Kinship relations are pivotal for the construction of one's sense of meaning, as they help form the mental operations that will underpin all cognizance." Quote from p.190.

[145] See Kullu, 90, 108-9.

[146] Van Exem, 20.

[147] See Mundu, 26-31.

[148] See Van Exem, 24-8.

[149] See Munda, 6.

[150] To cite an example, *Varle Dev* and *Ucchaliyo Dev* literally mean, 'God-above'.

[151] While Western thought largely locates divinity as 'on high', the Eastern mind more innately thinks of divinity as 'depth'. However, thinkers of Western origin are increasingly finding the category of 'depth' and 'centre' conducive to the development of their thought; see, for instance, Yves Raguin, *The Depth of God*, trans. K. England (Hertfordshire: Anthony Clarke, 1979); also, Griffiths, *Return to the Center*.

[152] Van Exem, 27; Mundu, 31; Munda, 6.

[153] Bracken, "Infinity and the Logic of Non-Dualism," 43, writes: "[F]inite entities are ... co-existent members of a cosmic society with God. The unity of the cosmic society, moreover, is not the unity of God as its transcendent member but the dynamic unity brought about by the divine nature as the underlying principle of existence and activity for all the members, God included."

[154] See Fortman, 80-3, for details. The term *agennesia* was proposed by Gregory of Nazianzus [330-89].

[155] Note, for e.g., how John's Gospel (ch. 15) uses symbols like 'vine' when referring to Jesus.

[156] See M. Eugene Boring, "John 5:19-24," *Interpretation* 45/2 (April 1991): 176-81, for further details.

[157] See A.E. Harvey, *Jesus and the Constraints of History* (London: Gerald Duckworth & Co., 1982), 159-64, for a good discussion on these three aspects of what sonship meant in the Jewish context and what being 'son of God' implied in the NT writings, especially the gospel of John.

[158] This is a term taken from the NT, namely, from the letter to the Hebrews 13:11,13.

[159] See Fortman, *ibid*. Gregory of Nazianzus proposed the term *gennesis*.

[160] Jesus as God's 'image' also is referred to in the comparison between Adam and Christ (1 Cor 15:45-9).

[161] See Mundu, 243.

[162] See, for instance, an unpublished doctoral thesis by James Ponniah entitled *Folk Religion and Ritual Power in Society: A Study on Cutalaimâtan Cult*," University of Madras, 2005, wherein divine encounter and appeasement take place in graveyards.

[163] See, for example, Gen 1:1-2; Ezek 37:1-14; Jn 3:8; 4:10; 7:38-9; 20:22; Acts 2:1-4, and so on.

[164] This term is used by the religious authorities to describe the power evident in the mission that was being done by Jesus' disciples (see Acts 17:6). Also in 1 Tim 1:7 The Spirit is the 'gift of God' and 'power' of God.

[165] *Ekpouresis* is the term used by Gregory of Nazianzus; see, Fortman, *ibid*.

[166] This can be expressed in scriptural terms as 'fruits of the Spirit' (see Gal 5:22-3).

[167] See Rudolf Schnackenburg, *God's Rule and Kingdom*, 2nd ed., (New York: Herder & Herder, and London: Burns & Oates, 1968), 77-113, for details on the 'Reign of God' in the preaching of Jesus.

[168] See George Soares-Prabhu, "The Kingdom of God: Jesus' Vision of a New Society," in *The Indian Church in the Struggle for a New Society*, ed. D.S. Amalorpavadass (Bangalore: NBCLC, 1981), 579-608.

[169] See Dunn, 15, who refers to faith as a childlike dependence on God and openness to God's power; see also Harvey, 161-4.

[170] See Jan Michael Joncas, "Tasting the Kingdom of God: The Meal Ministry of Jesus and its Implications for Contemporary Worship and Life," *Worship* 74/4 (July 2000): 329-65, for further details.

[171] See Sandra M. Schneiders, "The Foot Washing (John 13:1-20): An Experiment in Hermeneutics," *CBQ* 43/1 (January 1981): 76-92, for further details.

[172] *Autobaseilia* can literally be translated as 'Kingdom-Itself'. Origen (c.185 - c.254), for instance, so closely identified Jesus with the Kingdom of God that he called him *Autobaseilia*.

[173] See Rom 8:19-21 that conveys the idea of "the glorious liberty of the children of God."

[174] Moltmann, *The Trinity and the Kingdom*, 210, works upon Joachim de Fiore's tri-epochal framework. While accepting that the Kingdom of God comes as *freedom*, I do not subscribe to Moltmann's schema.

[175] This is the terminology of Oscar Cullman who speaks of the Kingdom as already present in seminal form, but always growing towards its final fulfillment.

[176] Kevin Hart, "The Kingdom and the Trinity," *TACR* 73/3 (July 2001): 321-39, in contrast to Moltmann holds that the Trinity comes to us in and through the Kingdom of God, which is a 'trace' of Trinity. Quote from p.337.

[177] See Hermann Häring, "Christian Belief in the Threefold God," in *The Many Faces of the Divine: Concilium* 2 (1995): 45, who speaks of a 'triadic impulse' of trust, freedom and discipleship. I rather see *fidelity-filiation-freedom* as basic to evolving what might be called a *Kingdom ethic*.

[178] See Dorothee Sölle, "God's Pain and Our Pain," in *The Future of Liberation*

Theology: Essays in Honor of Gustavo Gutiérrez, ed. M.H. Ellis and O. Maduro (New York: Orbis, 1989), 329.

[179] See the debate between C.H. Dodd and R. Bultmann, the former studying *kerygma* as 'content' the latter as 'preaching'. Through different approaches, both agree that underlying NT-diversity, there is an underlying unity or 'the *kerygma*' of Jesus. See Dunn, *ibid.*, 11-3, for the main argument of this debate.

[180] See Jürgen Moltmann, *The Crucified God: The Cross of Christ as the Foundation and Criticism of Christian Theology* (London: SCM Press, 1974), 267-70, for details of understanding God's *apatheia*.

[181] *Plerosis* and *pleroma* (Greek, meaning 'plenitude') refer to the "fullness of God" and the full measure of Christ's divinity (Col 1:19, 2:9). It is the opposite of *kenosis* or *kenoma* (Greek, meaning 'emptiness').

[182] See, for e.g., Earl Muller, "Real Relations and the Divine: Issues in Thomas's Understanding of God's Relation to the World," *TS* 56 (1995): 673-95, who addresses concerns raised about Aquinas's thought.

[183] See Robert W. Jenson, *The Triune Identity: God According to the Gospel* (Philadelphia: Fortress, 1982), 465, uses the term 'hermeneutics of the cross'. However, my interpretation is not the same as his.

[184] Hans Urs von Balthasar speaks of three moments of *kenosis*: (a) creation, (b) covenant, and (c) the incarnation. He holds that only the *third kenosis* is wholly trinitarian. See his *Theo-Drama: The Action*, vol. IV (San Francisco: Ignatius Press, 1994), 331. However, *ibid.*, 319, he also holds that: "The full doctrine of the Trinity can be unfolded only on the basis of a theology of the cross ... we must see the doctrine of the Trinity as the ever-present, inner presupposition of the doctrine of the cross." In his *Mysterium Paschale: The Mystery of Easter* (Michigan: William B. Eerdmans, 1990), 41, he describes the cross as "the acme of the entire redeeming and revealing work of the triune God."

[185] This is best expressed in Phil 2:5-11: The 'Lord' (*kyrios*) becomes 'slave' (*doulos*). See also 2 Cor 8:9.

[186] Moltmann has dealt extensively with this theme. In his "The Crucified God: A Trinitarian Theology of the Cross," *Interpretation* 26/3 (1972), 295, he holds that, "The material principle of the doctrine of the Trinity is 'the cross', and the formal principle of the theology of the cross is the doctrine of the Trinity."

[187] The word 'passion' is derived from the Greek '*pathos*' referring to "that which happens to a person or thing," or "what one has experienced," or, "experience, emotion, passion, suffering, misfortune, calamity, etc." Its Latin equivalent '*patior*' meaning 'to suffer' or 'to undergo' is etymologically related to the Greek '*páskho*' (again referring to suffering, enduring, undergoing) that gives us the word 'paschal', which is so central to the Christian understanding of Jesus' death.

[188] Note that the original Greek word, '*splagchnizomai*' conveys more aptly

what the English 'compassion' does. It is a churning from within, a gut-level feeling of oneness with the pain and suffering of the victim

[189] W.H. Vanstone, *The Stature of Waiting* (London: Darton, Longman & Todd, 1982), explains the passion of Jesus as the supreme act of Jesus' waiting whilst being 'handed over' for a vicarious death.

[190] Here, 'death of God' neither refers to *'Patripassianism'* nor to the Nietzschean nuance, but to God – the Father and the Spirit – being involved in the Son's (Jesus') passion, death and resurrection.

[191] See Dom Aelred Cody, "Hebrews," in *A New Catholic Commentary on Holy Scripture*, ed. R.C. Fuller et al., (London: Thomas Nelson and Sons, 1969), 1238, who interprets this as the world outside of institutional and cultic religion.

[192] Myles M. Bourke, "The Epistle to the Hebrews," in *JBC*, ed. R. E. Brown et al., (Bangalore: TPI, 1968), 402, sees this as referring to the Day of Atonement where the flesh of the victims was burned outside the camp. In Jesus' case, he was crucified outside the gates of Jerusalem, the holy city.

[193] Note that we saw earlier that the character of a son in Jewish tradition lay in obedience to his father.

[194] Kazoh Kitamori, *Theology of the Pain of God* (London: SCM Press, 1966), 120, sees the pain of God in dual dimension: "First, it is God's pain in the sense that he forgives and loves those who should not be forgiven; secondly, it is his pain in the sense that he sends his only beloved Son to suffer, even unto death."

[195] Frans Jozef van Beeck, *God Encountered: A Contemporary Catholic Systematic Theology, vol. 2/2, part II: One God, Creator of All That Is* (Collegeville, Minnesota: The Liturgical Press, 1994), 159, writes: "In relation to creation, God has the absolute ability to 'un-be'."

[196] Moltmann, "Crucified God," 288.

[197] Mundu, 70-6, explains the myth of the boy called *Toro Kora* who sacrifices himself and rises resplendent as a lesson against the greed of the *Asurs* (an avaricious tribe of iron-smelters).

[198] In the passion narratives, the Greek word for 'forsake', i.e., *paradidonai* – seen in the context of Jesus' life – clearly has a negative tone, meaning, to betray, hand over, deliver, give up, kill.

[199] Rejection is an extreme form of suffering since Jesus dies alone. Dietrich Bonhoeffer, *The Cost of Discipleship* (London: SCM Press, 1959), 76, writes: "In the Passion, Jesus is a rejected Messiah. His rejection robs the Passion of its glory."

[200] See Michael Jinkins and Stephen Breck Reid, "God's Forsakenness: The Cry of Dereliction as an Utterance within the Trinity," *HIBT* 19/1 (June 1997): 48.

201 See Moltmann, "Crucified God," 292.

202 *Patripassianism* (Latin, meaning "suffering of the Father") is a term coined by Tertullian for that form of *Monarchianism* called *Modalism* proposed by Praxeas and Noetus who believed that it was the Father who became incarnate and suffered on the cross.

203 Bermejo, 29.

204 Here there is mention of Jesus offering himself up to God "through the eternal Spirit." Although the 'eternal Spirit' is sometimes understood as the Holy Spirit, the text itself does not warrant such an interpretation. Cody, 1231, sees it as the "divine principle behind Christ's saving work." Bourke, 398, sees it as "Christ's life which cannot be destroyed." By either interpretation we can assume that it is a power that proceeds from Jesus' inner life shared with God. In this sense, it could be understood as Spirit, *Shakti*.

205 This passage speaks about "blood and water" flowing out of Jesus' pierced side. In John's gospel, water is the sign of the Holy Spirit (see 3:5; 4:10,14; 7:38-9). This symbolizes Jesus giving up the Spirit

206 Moltmann, "Crucified God," 293.

207There are many Scriptural passages that support this interpretation; for instance, "God so loved the world that he gave [up] his only Son" (Jn 3:16). Paul, likewise, alludes to its eschatological dimension: "He who did not spare his own Son but gave him up for us all, will he not also give us all things with him?" (Rom 8:31). God abandons his son in the darkness of sin, evil and death. Christ is "made *to be* sin" (2 Cor 5:21) and he became "a curse for us" (Gal 3:13). In the cross, not only does the Father give up the Son, but the Son also gives himself: "[T]he Son of God, [who] loved me and gave himself for me" (Gal 2:20)

208 See Jose Comblin, *Cry of the Oppressed, Cry of Jesus* (New York: Orbis, 1984), for details of this.

209 In "Towards a Dalit Christian Theology," in *A Reader In Dalit Theology*, ed. idem (Madras: GLTCRI, n.d.), 69.

210 See, Elizabeth A. Johnson, "Suffering God: Compassion Poured Out," in *She Who Is*, 246-72, ch. 12.

211 This observation is based on my conversations with adivasis of south Gujarat. Among Hinduised adivasis there is use of scornful words like "naked god" and "helpless god"; but Christianized adivasis find strength in it. Concretely, Poslabhai D. Vasava of Karotha village, Mandvi taluka, Surat district, once remarked: "The cross of Jesus gives me strength to face all pain and sufferings in my life."

212 The evangelist Luke interprets Jesus' last cry as one of hope and confidence. This verse, taken from Ps 31:6, must be seen in the light of the psalmist viewing God as "rock of refuge" and "strong fortress" (v.2).

213 Picture 7 is a painting of the Trinity where the Father raises the Son from the grave at the prompting of the Holy Spirit. The Spirit is seen whispering into the Father's ear. The picture is taken from Eugene F. Rogers, Jr., *After the Spirit: A Constructive Pneumatology from Resources outside the Modern West* (Grand Rapids, Michigan/Cambridge, U.K.: William B. Eerdmans Publishing Company, 2005)

214 See van Exem, 168. Ibid., 166-71, explains the various symbolisms of this sacrifice. It would be too simplistic to equate this to the death of Jesus. However, the dynamic of sacrifice, suffering and victory is striking in the two cases. See also Mundu, 87-8, for a prophetic interpretation of the *Asur* legend.

215 Prabhakar, 422-3.

216 See, for instance, Sebastian Moore, *The Crucified Jesus is No Stranger* (New York: Paulist Press, 1977), 63-70, who sees in the death of Jesus an antidote to narcissism and self-absorption.

217 See Gianni Vattimo, *Belief*, trans. L. D'Isanto and D. Webb (Cambridge: Polity Press, 1999), 20-68, who develops the idea of *kenosis* within a secularist context, albeit reaching contestable conclusions. Vattimo's understanding of *kenosis* is also premised on a nihilism inspired by Nietzsche

218 Randall B. Bush, *Recent Ideas of Divine Conflict: The Influences of Psychological and Sociological Theories of Conflict upon the Trinitarian Theology of Paul Tillich and Jürgen Moltmann* (New York: Edwin Mellen Press, 1991), 271.

CHAPTER FIVE

'Performance' Challenges of
Subaltern Trinitarian Theology

5.1 Trinity and Subaltern Spatial Trialectic

In the previous chapter, we laid down three interrelated trinitarian theses – pertaining to (a) relationship-solidarity-communion; (b) subaltern spatiality, and (c) 'counter spaces' of subaltern power – that could be called 'trajectories' towards which subaltern trinitarian theology must move and gain momentum. I have developed these three theses as the fruit of conversations between the subaltern (mainly adivasi) religio-cultural universes and Christian Scripture and Tradition. During the course of these conversations, I have mainly moved in and out of the perceived space (*firstspace*) and conceived space (*secondspace*) of subaltern communities in a fairly limited manner.

Up to this stage, our trinitarian thinking is still *intra*-communitarian in the sense that we have been working at only two levels: first, the local-subaltern; and, second, the parochial-Christian. This is not enough. Today, no community can afford to remain merely at an *intra*-communitarian level since, beyond the narrow confines of a particular community, it must also consider *extra*-communitarian factors, which often have global ramifications. This is especially true for weaker communities; for, as I earlier asserted, unless these communities are articulated, and function, as *'political community'*, they are neither likely to secure their socio-political rights nor get their religio-cultural resources recognized by society, at large. Hence, we must evolve a larger socio-religio-political and national-global framework within which to articulate finer distinctions and further functions of subaltern trinitarian theology. This is consonant to our option to do 'public theology' that will meaningfully get involved in civil society, thereby voicing subaltern concerns.

I think that Lefebvre's *spatial trialectic* is helpful to situate subaltern groups in the larger national space. In his trialectic thinking, although Lefebvre makes mention of the Christian Trinity, he sees it as a symbol of authoritarian, masculine power. Though I disagree with his observation, it would help us to hear him verbatim. Lefebvre writes:[1]

> [R]epresentations of space ... were borrowed from Aristotelian and Ptolemaic conceptions, as modified by Christianity: the earth, the underground 'world' and the luminous Cosmos, Heaven of the just and of the angels, *inhabited by God the Father, God the Son, and God the Holy Ghost*. A fixed sphere within a finite space, diametrically bisected by the surface of the Earth; below this surface, the fires of Hell; above it, in the upper half of the sphere, the Firmament – a cupola bearing the fixed stars and the circling planets – and a space criss-crossed by divine messages and messengers and *filled by the radiant Glory of the Trinity*.

Here, God is conceived as being *up* in the cupola-firmament of the heavens, a God who produces spaces and inhabits the isolated, luminous, highest regions. Elsewhere, Lefebvre also asserts that conceptions of Trinity have led to the usurpation of power through control of space. This space, he opines, is "the space of the triune God, the space of kings, no longer the space of cryptic signs but rather the space of the written word and the rule of history. The space, too, of military violence – and hence a *masculine* space."[2]

There is some truth in Lefebvre's criticism of Trinity since Western trinitarianism in early Christianity seems influenced by the homogenizing trends of the Roman Empire. When Christianity spread through the Mediterranean basin, it was influenced by a political-religious ideology that had monarchy as an ideal.[3] Thus, God was perceived as a tyrannical ruler hidden in the upper spheres like the Persian king; and power, authority and sovereignty were prime attributes associated with Trinity. This notwithstanding, I part company with Lefebvre since, in the subaltern scheme of spatiality, God need not only be located *up* in the heavens, and God's power need not necessarily be masculine. I've already shown that God can equally aptly be the primordial substratum *below* and *within* historical processes, and God's Spirit can be expressed in powerful, yet, feminine terms like *Shakti*. Thus, rather than merely critique representations of Trinity that have led to what we saw as 'symbolic violence', I shall use Lefebvre's framework in exploring how the Trinity, and 'spatial trialectic' could enable subaltern communities to understand their relationship with the Absolute, as well as with society, at large.

5.2 Trialectic Development of Trinitarian Theology

Lefebvre's insight of seeing life neither as a one-dimensional reality, nor as a double-dimensional reality, but in terms of three dimensions or *spatial trialectic*, enables us to view all contexts and circumstances with, so to say, a *'Tri-angled Lens'*. While taking note of both, the Self and the Other, a tri-dimensional overview or *trialectic of space* accommodates also the *Third* or, we could say, *produces a thirdspace*. This *thirdspace* is similar to both, *firstspace* and *secondspace*, and yet, it is also dissimilar and is not a *hybrid* or simple synthesis of the first two. *Thirdspace* is characterized by a *'both-and'* logic. Applying this logic to trinitarianism, we could say that God is *Tri-Une*, Three-*and*-One or One-*and*-Three.[4] While being particular, trialectic always retains universality, while being equal to its antecedents, it always recognizes and respects difference. Such a trialectic, we shall now see, has not been alien to the development of trinitarian thought.

The Christian community has, from earliest times, tried to avoid both, a unitarian conception of God, as well as conceiving of God in terms of dualities like pure spirit (God, mainly Father) and divine image (Jesus). While unitarian thinking led to heresies like *modalism* and *monarchianism*,[5] dualistic conceptions led to *subordinationism*, another form of which was *tritheism*.[6] These two broad orientations have been considered as typographies or prototypes of Western and Eastern trinitarianism, respectively.[7] One must be cautious in simplistically subsuming all of Western or Eastern trinitarianism into these two, convenient categories. Aware of this danger, we only note that the errors and exaggerations arising out of unitarianism and dualism were condemned,[8] and rightly so. Conversely, without using numerals, the community strove to profess that: (a) God is eternally a unity, and yet is also Father-Son-Spirit,[9] and (b) this Father-Son-Spirit is the model or paradigm or archetype according to which community was to be fashioned. Interestingly and significantly, one of the most important events of the basic foundational experience of Christianity, i.e., the Pentecost, was one of "*many* people, from *many* nations, hearing *one* message in their own native language" (Acts 2:5-12).

Early apostolic exhortations for maintaining unity apparently appear against a horizon of universality as seen, for example, in Paul's advice to Christians at Ephesus:[10]

> [Be] eager to maintain the unity of the Spirit in the bond of peace. There is one body and one Spirit, just as you were called to the one hope that belongs to your call, one Lord, one faith, one baptism, one God and Father of us all, who is above all and through all and in all (Eph 4:3-6)

The context is an exhortation for the community "to lead a life worthy of the calling to which you have been called." The text is trinitarian in a primal sense,[11] and expresses the call to a "unity of the Spirit" but under the universal parentage of the "God of *all*". This trinitarian dynamic is a *foundation of Christian experience*[12] and unites-in-universality, particularizes-in-difference. Here, this unity-in-diversity is not derived from any abstract philosophy or ideology, but from the basic experience that the community had of Jesus Christ[13] – an experience that led them to harmonize the *particular* (Jesus, as God's definitive revelation), the *universal* (God, as *Abba* of *all*), and what might be called a *transversal* (Spirit, in all, through all, and yet, *beyond all*).[14] This trinitarian typology gives us the impetus to think in terms of what might be called a '*subaltern trinitarian theology of religions*,' the contours of which I now trace.

5.3 Subaltern Spatial Trialectic in the Realm of Religion and Politics

I earlier interpreted the three dimensions or levels of being, i.e., the primordial-visible-invisible, as corresponding to *Abba*-Son-*Shakti*, respectively. By so doing, I argued that the Trinity reaffirms sacred spatiality and reflects the *intra*-communion that underlies all relationships *within* subaltern community. However, now, by further asserting that the Trinity inseparably links *particular-universal-transversal*, I broaden the parameters of discourse to embrace not only spatiality and *intra*-communitarian bonding (as done earlier), but also to consider *sociality-historicity-spatiality* as a whole, and stress *extra*-communitarian ties. I do this since, no community – and this particularly applies to the underprivileged ones – will succeed in forming itself *as* community in any socio-political formation, unless effective relationships with other communities are fostered, albeit, in varying ways and diverse degrees. To cite an example, if a subaltern community desires to protect its rights as 'minority', it is juxtaposing itself to some 'majority', and thus, it will have to consider what the minority-majority labeling will socially and politically imply for both communities defined by this binary. I consider the spatial trialectic as being vital in two fields or realms, namely, (a) religious and (b) socio-political.

5.3.1   Spatial Trialectic and Subaltern Theology of Religions

In the religious realm, the triadic experience of particularity-universality-transversality is not alien to subaltern imagination since there has always been wide acceptance of diverse beliefs, rituals and ethical practices.[15] Thus, on the one hand, the underprivileged groups easily accept, and even adopt as their own, what are often considered the 'prophetic religions' or the 'word religions' (mainly, Judaism and Islam). These can be seen as representing *universality* in the sense that God (Yahweh, Allah) is viewed as Supreme Being of *all* – the One, Indivisible, Absolute and the Perfection of every conceivable human attribute – mercy, love, fidelity, goodness and truth – while also being formless and faceless.

Further, on the other hand, there has also been acceptance of the so-called Indic, 'mystic' or 'cosmic' religions (Hinduism, Buddhism and Jainism); and thus, many have adopted Buddhism as a means of protest against the caste-system. These religions can be seen as representing *transversality* with divinity conceived of as *Brahman*,[16] or seen as *sanatana dharma* (eternal religion, Hinduism) or based upon *dhamma* (eternal law, Buddhism).[17] Finally, although Christianity stresses the *particular*, namely, Jesus as the fullness of revelation, it endorses the universalism of Judaism and Islam, but gives God a form and face: Jesus Christ. Moreover, it also shares the transversality of Hinduism and Buddhism since the Spirit's presence and action that "blows where it wills" (Jn 3:8) is recognized as mystery-beyond-history; and yet, it cannot but be firmly rooted in history since it takes the *Jesus narrative* as the definitive story of salvation. Christianity, too, has found acceptance, accommodation and adoption by Dalits and adivasis.

The subaltern capacity to accept and adopt, reform or reject, diverse religions and religious expressions is remarkable. This capacity has historically been exercised to overcome their local situations of subordination and exploitation (as in their adoption of Buddhism),[18] or even for socio-economic advantage (as is allegedly the motive for their conversion to Christianity). Assessing religions from the viewpoint of their practical relevance to life can thus be the basis for evolving an 'indigenous trinitarian theology of religions'.

A 'subaltern trinitarian theology of religions' will differ from other similar attempts,[19] since, ideational and mutually incompatible *isms* like *exclusivism-inclusivism-pluralism* become irrelevant,[20] their being derived through abstract thinking and judgments on the issue of salvation.[21] In these, the Other would be considered as 'saved' based on the *either-or* 'confession' of Christ as saviour, irrespective of whether such confession actually leads to true faith, Christic praxis and commitment to Life, in general. In contrast, rather than choose *either-or* of apparently conflicting positions, 'subaltern trinitarian theology of religions' could opt for a *both-and* third option which, while stressing the unity, on the one hand, will carefully and critically negotiate the differences, on the other. Such thinking is echoed in some Asian theologies too.[22] Moreover, it opens up possibilities for the liberation of communities.

As a consequence of *spatial trialectic,* in the field of religion, there is the possibility of subaltern groups evolving religio-cultural capital divergent from – and even opposed to – the aforementioned 'big' religions. This is perhaps more clearly seen in the case of Dalits who, through centuries of being oppressed in hierarchical social structures, have been following a religion that is not of their making, not serving their interests, and not fostering their life in community.[23] Many such oppressed communities are today expressing their religion and culture neither merely as 'divergent from', nor only as 'opposed to', but also in terms of a unique *thirdspace* creative of new forms of resistance and protest.[24] Examples of this are the *Valmiki* religion of Ludhiana, Punjab,[25] the *Khristbhakta* movement of Varanasi,[26] the *Dalitization* that is gaining momentum in many places,[27] and the Ambedkar movement mentioned earlier.[28]

While recognizing that a *spatial trialectic* opens up possibilities for subaltern protest and assertion, it is not enough that such affirmations be limited to the religio-cultural field. The weaker communities coexist with other more powerful groups, and hence, it is necessary to seek recognition and the adoption of an equality-difference principle in the socio-political field as well. This is where the Trinity and trialectic spatial logic can be helpful in terms of inspiring *'political community',* while also ensuring that Christian theology truly embraces the public sphere wherein God is ever alive and active.

5.3.2   *Spatial Trialectic and Subaltern Political Community*

In the third chapter we discussed how religion could be a source of great power either for (a) legitimizing unjust structures, or (b) liberating peoples. In the latter case, there is use of the *'power of religion'* that promotes community, and, in the former, religion's power is abused to appropriate more power for the producers and interpreters of religious symbols, while alienating those who are their passive recipients. I showed how this covertly happens with *Hindutva*. However, Western trinitarianism itself has formerly been suspected of supporting the imperialism and authoritarianism of Christian emperors rather than of leading to the development of a liberating God-image that creates community and empowers the poor. An example will substantiate this allegation.

Eusebius of Caesarea [c.265-339] developed the idea that the Kingdom of God was replicated on earth as 'image' in Constantine's empire. As a result, Constantine was regarded as an image of *Logos*-Christ-King, reproducing the image of God, the Father,[29] on earth. Eusebius set the Church so firmly within the Christian empire that the two became difficult to distinguish. Later, though he did not identify the City of God with the earthly city besieged by evil, his theology became a 'political Augustinianism' that inspired a political monotheism.[30] Here, the conflation of religion and politics distorted the God-image. It neither respected the equality-difference aspect of trinitarianism nor did it promote the cause of those who sought true empowerment in religion.

As opposed to attempts to promote a *religion of power*, a representation like the Trinity can unleash the *power of religion* by being the basis for working along the lines of unity-*and*-difference. Jesus has been described as "the only and the unsurpassable expression of the mystery of the *unity of identity and difference between God and human beings*."[31] In other words, *Abba*'s representative, the *Shakti*-filled Jesus stands at the interstices of the divine-*and*-human and reveals equality-*and*-difference with both, God and human beings. Thus, being the image and likeness of God, Jesus strives to restore the "divine image and likeness"[32] that is destroyed by situations of domination and deprivation forced upon subaltern groups. This injustice results in such communities living a 'diminished humanity'. Here, the *Abba*-Son-*Shakti* God stands *before* them as Saviour/Liberator empowering them to fight for a socio-political unity and equality with other communities.

One might critique my Scriptural interpretations as being too 'secular' or 'political'. Such a critique does not hold much weight in the context of subaltern religion and spirituality that does not dichotomize between sacred-versus-secular and political-versus-apolitical. Moreover, refusal to read the Bible so as to critique and combat dehumanizing socio-political contexts is a denial of God-given Life, a subversion of the history of salvation,[33] and, a dereliction of the duty of any theologian whose sacred task it is to respond to the public sphere where God's *anawim* struggle for Life.

Apart from standing *before* the disprivileged communities as Creator-Liberator-Sustainer, Father-Son-Spirit stand *beside* and *behind* them since, at the visible level of reality, Jesus is prototype of the victimized one, suffering, supporting, and in solidarity with the victims of society. Jesus becomes the representative of both, the Dalits,[34] as well as the adivasis.[35] In this role, he 'identifies' with their sufferings and struggles, and yet, he empowers them to 'differ' with the status quo, to protest and challenge it, in order to transform and redeem it. The praxis of Jesus clearly indicates the adoption of an *equity-with-difference principle*: unless wealth was shared, it would be the cause of damnation (Lk 16:19ff), wages would be given equally to those employed in the first hour or the last, since their willingness to work and their needs were the same (Mt 20:1-16), etc.

In his 'identification with' the poor and powerless, and in his 'differentiating from' the rich and powerful groups like the Jewish nobility, the Pharisees, the Sadducees, members of the Sanhedrin, the priestly class, teachers of the law, and those who wielded political power like Herod and Pilate, Jesus was not only making moral-religious options, but also creating 'new spaces' for fuller life and proposing guidelines for an eco-socio-political programme indispensable for the realization of God's Kingdom. In other words, all this was aimed at building a more egalitarian, caring and sharing community.[36] And, the 'model' of this community and communion seemed to be the profound union between him and his *Abba*-Father, shared in the Spirit-*Shakti* of love and power.

Jesus' identification with poor victims, his restoration of wholeness to the dehumanized and condemnation of the rich, the powerful, the socio-religious hierarchs and their structures of exploitation, were signs of what we termed a 'new society': the Kingdom of God. However, in inaugurating the Kingdom and restoring spaces for the subalterns of his time, Jesus was disturbing power-equations and had to face conflicts, even death. Nonetheless, in the very process of disturbing and destroying Man-made structures of the *'religion of power'*, he was tapping the *'power of religion'*, which we have seen as a 'counter space' of subaltern power that overflows far beyond the visible boundaries of Christianity; indeed, leaving nothing or no one outside its embrace. It is for this reason that subaltern trinitarian theology has potentiality to fulfill what Peter Beyer calls the 'performance' role of religion. A cursory glance at what Beyer means will help us to broaden the scope of our trinitarian theology.

5.4 Religion's 'Performance' Role in Global Society

India is characterized by rich religio-cultural diversity and religion exerts great influence over almost all Indian communities. Like other social systems, religion has its own logic, dynamics, structures and processes, but it is not easy for religion to build a united community, albeit retaining the diversity that, as we have seen earlier, is a source of enrichment.[37] This is so because religion deals with ultimate questions of life, and, a particular religion has its specific worldview, philosophy and theologies that differ from those of another religion.[38] Yet, since all religions professedly seek to promote the life of people, building a better society/world will remain a challenge that must be faced by all.

Theorists have tried to determine what role religion could play in global society. In line with Niklas Luhmann's theorizing on globalisation, Beyer distinguishes between 'function' and 'performance' as regards the role of religion in global society. He writes:[39]

> Function is the pure, 'sacred' communication involving the transcendent and the aspect that religious institutions claim for themselves, the basis of their autonomy in modern society. Religious performance, by contrast, occurs when religion is 'applied' to problems generated in other systems but not solved there, or simply not addressed elsewhere. Examples of such problems are economic poverty, political oppression, familial estrangement, environmental degradation, or personal identity.

Awareness of this distinction between 'function' and 'performance' is vital because most religionists seem overly concerned about matters pertaining to their own autonomy, identity, mission, religious beliefs, cultic practices, moral norms, community rights, etc., without seeking to be of service to other religions, other groups of people, or welfare agencies who are also committed to improving the quality of life for all. Rather than being preoccupied with asserting their own identity or rallying for their own rights or converting others to their particular beliefs, if religions in India worked for the common good, we would have less of the conflicts we analyzed earlier. Hence, I stress *religious performance* as vital to religion since we are dealing not only with the welfare of underprivileged communities, but also of community in India, at large.

Although I adopt Beyer's distinction between 'function' and 'performance', and privilege the latter, it is evident that the two are not mutually exclusive, for, if a "real tension exists between the two," the two are also "inseparable and mutually reinforcing."[40] This is even truer when we deal with underprivileged groups where there is no dichotomy between secular-sacred, this-life versus afterlife, or between immanent-transcendent. Thus, within this framework, I will first explore how subaltern trinitarian theology – with its central symbol of the *naachnu* or *akhra* – could inspire communities to start and support movements in the line of their 'performance' role. Then, in the sixth and final chapter, I shall discuss how the 'minority' Indian Christianity's 'functional role' can better be accomplished as outcome of its trinitarian theology.

5.5 Subaltern Movement(s) as Offspring of Subaltern Trinitarianism

In the fourth chapter, I explained how the adivasi *naach/nu* or *akhra* (dance) could be the most appropriate symbol for representing and reinterpreting trinitarian communion, which "brings to mind the image of the divine dance, a dance of unthinkable intimacy and mutual love, a dance which freely overflows in creation and becomes expressed in the dance of the universe."[41] The adivasi *naach* symbolizes joy, life, energy, support, harmony and spontaneity. Moreover, it always suggests *movement*. For subalterns, life is not stagnant, but full of *movement* – i.e., ups and downs that harmonize with earth's cycles and the ocean's tides, for, underprivileged groups earn their livelihood by working upon the earth and transforming it with their toil. So, too, the fisher communities have a bonding with the seas and life therein. Thus, subaltern trinitarian theology can foster the life and liberation of disadvantaged groups by weaving *triune spatiality* with *three movements* of the *naach*: (a) *circular*, (b) *counter*, and, (c) *supportive* movement. The word *movement* is used here in two senses: (a) *spatiotemporal*, as for example, there are movements in a dance or an orchestral, musical composition, and (b) *socio-historical*, referring to organized efforts to promote or attain an end, e.g., the 'Dalit movement' or '*Jai Adivasi* movement'.[42] The movements we highlight are distinct and yet not separated, they are *tri-une*, being simultaneously one-*and*-three. We now discuss this.

5.5.1 The Circular Movement: Relationship and Redemption of The Son

The first movement of the *naach/nu* or *akhra* is the *circular movement*. The community members move arm-in-arm and step-in-step with each other to the rhythm of the *dholak* and their songs of sowing and reaping, sorrow and joy, ebbs and flows (see picutre 8).[43] This is the most basic movement

Picture 8: South Gujarat adivasi *naachnu* in a circular movement

of the *naach*. In this movement, we can think of the community as *re-presenting* the basic fact that they exist not in isolation as individuals, but *as community in relationship*. Relationship – with nature, one another and God – is so vital to disadvantaged communities that, without relationship, there is no community. Here, the relationship is not theoretical, but practical; not exclusive, but inclusive; not invisible, but visible; not dealing with afterlife but with the here-and-now. Moreover, this relationship is not of inequality and domination, but of equality and cooperation.

The subaltern circle, first and foremost, embraces and relates to the earth. The earth is the visible and tangible *perceived space* comprising of *jungle-jal-jamin*. Unlike the so-called 'high castes' and privileged groups who have sought to manipulate markets, exchange goods, make money, produce ideas, define concepts, interpret scriptures and so on, the Dalits, adivasis, and the fishing/farming communities till the land, tap the forests and toil at sea. They are the *true producers* (providing grain, fruit, vegetable, fish, etc.) who sustain the life of all people. By stressing the sacredness of the earth and all its visible elements and spaces, subaltern trinitarianism supports ecological concerns and poses a challenge to the degradation of nature concomitant with so-called 'development' and 'progress'. Reflecting upon the trinitarian mystery in creation John Paul II said:[44]

> In beholding the glory of the Trinity in creation, man [*sic*] must contemplate, *sing* and rediscover wonder … The discovery of a transcendent presence in created things must lead us also to rediscover our *kinship with the earth*, to which we have been linked since our own creation (cf. Gen 2:7) … If nature is not violated and degraded, it once again becomes *man's* [*sic*] *sister*.

Here, there is a call to *sing* – and, we could add, *dance* – for joy at the rediscovery of our *kinship with the earth* and our *sisterhood with nature* pregnant with the presence of the Trinity. If nature is wo/man's sister, then she is an animate, vital part of the family circle.

Post-Newton and post-Einstein, the circle of scientists holds that the basic stuff of the created world is neither atoms/particles nor *wavicles*,[45] but *quarks*.[46] According to quantum scientists, today, the ultimate building blocks of reality seem to be quarks that "prove to be highly elusive, making sense only in groupings of *two* or *three*, displaying an elegant versatility to manifest their existence only *in relationships*. The capacity to relate seems to be at the heart of the quark world!"[47] Stressing this, O'Murchu adds:[48]

> What science – for long the perceived enemy of religion – reveals and confirms is what many belief systems have been struggling to articulate in their trinitarian doctrines: God is first and foremost a propensity and power for relatedness, and *the divine imprint is nowhere more apparent than in nature's own fundamental desire (exemplified in the quarks) to relate – interdependently and interconnectedly.* The earthly, the human, and the divine are in harmony in their fundamental nature, in their common propensity to relate and to enjoy their interdependent coexistence. .... For the *quantum theologian,* the doctrine of the Trinity takes on a very vibrant meaning, intensifying the *call to relate, in love and justice, to all life on Planet Earth and beyond.*

Interestingly, what the community of scientists and quantum theologians has taken centuries to formulate in *word* and *theory,* namely, that human beings and nature exhibit an innate propensity for interrelatedness and interdependence, the community of subalterns – farmers, fisherfolk, Dalits, adivasis and other labouring communities – has, for centuries, been formulating through their *work* and *praxis.* Their manual work has transformed the world's *perceived spaces.* This is *'religious performance'* par excellence that the labouring communities and classes have been committed to for many centuries.

Subaltern communities relate to the earth (*jungle-jal-jamin*) as if to a living being.[49] This attitude is often disparagingly dismissed as being 'animistic'.[50] Such a dismissal not only reveals ignorance of the subaltern worldview, but also ignorance of the meaning of the Biblical creation story. Christianity has understood humankind's relationship with nature as 'mastery over nature' on the basis of the creation story's texts like: "[F]ill the earth and subdue it; and have dominion over the fish of the sea and over the birds of the air and over every living thing..." (Gen 1:28). Westermann argues that dominion, in some sense, does refer to 'mastery'; but the mastery is not to be understood as subjugation, but as the mastery of one who "masters an art or a craft or a language. Strictly speaking, what is meant is *a relationship to a living being.*"[51] This shows that adivasi communities cannot simplistically be called animists, for, even if they were unaware of this Biblical truth as *theory,* they live it in their *praxis* of *kinship with the earth.* This praxis of right relationship leads to restoration of balance between human community and the cosmos.[52]

The circular movement of the *naach* also embraces and represents the relationship among human beings. We can speak of a 'trinitarian anthropology',[53] in general, that not only seeks *oneness* of diverse peoples but also accentuates *differences* without destroying a basic unity. This involves interrelatedness in a creative tension involving the harmony of many-*and*-one or three-*and*-one.[54] Here, we could consider Jesus, the Son, as the prototype of relationship. In his incarnation, life, death and resurrection, he becomes the one who reconciles the invisible One and the visible many. He *re-creates* the diminished "image and likeness of God" (Gen 1:26-7) in the *perceived* and *lived spaces* of society, and rectifies the distorted "God image" in the *conceived space* of human thinking.[55]

The *imago Dei* theology of the Genesis-passage – i.e., "Let *us* make man *in our image,* after our *likeness* … so God created man in his *own image, in the image of God* he created him: male and female he created them" – does not warrant deduction that the original writer intended the "let *us*" and "*our* image" to imply that God is essentially a communion of persons or eternally triune. Any such deduction will be anachronistic and belie the demands of biblical, historical criticism. Yet, from the 2nd century onwards, Christian thinkers have been interpreting this text as indicative of the Trinity.[56] Furthermore, two important theological corollaries can be drawn from this passage:[57]

I.   [T]he uniqueness of human beings consists in their being God's counterparts. The relationship to God is not something which is added to human existence; humans are created in such a way that *their very existence is intended to be their relationship to God,* and

II.   [T]his is valid for all people. God has created all people "to correspond to him," that is so that something can happen between creator and creature. This holds despite all differences among people; it goes beyond all differences of religion, beyond belief and unbelief. *Every human being of every religion and in every place, even where religions are no longer recognized, has been created in the image of God.*

Jesus, God's Word and *image,*[58] reveals new relationships of these two corollaries as *two movements*: (a) a *vertical* circular movement since all human beings can address God as *Abba,*[59] since God creates new relationship with human beings as daughters/sons in the Son, Jesus,[60] (b) a *horizontal* circular movement since what is asserted of our forebears equally applies to *all* people of *all* times, places, cultures, religions, ideologies and so on.

The Genesis passage and Jesus' praxis reveal that God's inner relationship is 'replicated', so to say, in women and men so that they can *re-present* God, being moulded in the divine *image* (icon), and enter into relationship with God, being created in God's *likeness* (as daughters and sons). We note that in the Biblical world, as also in the subaltern worldview, the *image* (icon) was and is the 'representative' of the deity.[61] Thus, a trinitarian understanding of God will lead us to assert that not only do human beings *re-present* God as individual image, but they also *re-present* God as equal persons and partners created for community. This being the case, any assertion of superiority or inferiority and purity or impurity, any practice of discrimination and inequality, or any form of exclusivism is not only a distortion of the community God intended to create, but is in itself a negation of God. Thus, the Trinity becomes a critique of dehumanizing systems like caste practised within the Indian Church and in Indian society, at large.

At its deepest level, the circular movement of the *naach* embraces the divine. In Jesus joining life's dance (i.e., *kenosis* of the Incarnation),[62] seen from divine perspective, the space is created for the community to be adopted and located arm-in-arm and step-in-step with the Trinity; from the human angle, the community experiences and realizes that *in Jesus* the Trinity is arm-in-arm, step-in-step with it as it dances in *social space*. However, since Jesus is not only the icon of the human, but also the icon of God in an irreplaceable way, his cross, which is the final visible moment of his life's movement, brings the *naach*'s circular movement to an abrupt and agonizing halt. This frozen and frightening movement – symbolized by Jesus' arms still outstretched in relationship – fully and finally reveals what relationship with nature,[63] humankind and Trinity entails.

With the circular *naach* movement brought to a halt, *thirdspace* is created 'outside the camp'. Jesus' *naach* has always been *action*-laden with songs and movements of love, sharing, caring, justice, compassion, equality and forgiveness. However, in Jesus' *passion* these tunes are transposed into dirges of hate, evil, sin, injustice, betrayal, selfishness and vengeance echoed, finally, by Jesus' cry of forsakenness. This is not only the space of conflict and rupture in the *perichoretic* human dance, but it is also the point of conflict in the trinitarian *perichoretic* dance where, as we have seen, the space between *Abba*-Son-*Shakti* seems so infinitely large and unbridgeable that Godself is negated, or, God dies, or, as Christian Tradition and faith assert, "God dies out of love *to redeem us/me*."[64]

To say "God *dies* out of love *to redeem us/me*" seems absurd unless we simultaneously assert, "God also *lives* beyond God's death-out-of-love." The latter statement asserts that: (a) a vicarious death out of love for others is redemptive, more so, if it is the death of God's Son, and (b) since God's Son died as an outcome of his goodness that was negated by the powers of evil, God *must* vindicate his death by transforming it into some form of life. To explain this, we must assert that the demands of love must meet and match the demands of justice.[65] If this does not happen, the *perichoretic* dance circle remains ruptured and God will be guilty of acquiescing in evil and being impotent in the face of injustice.[66] This is a tautology as this goes against the very nature and goodness of God.

The last step of the circular movement of the *naach* is the resurrection, the Lord's *plerosis*. It is life, not death; good, not evil; and *plerosis*, not *kenosis*, which completes the dancing circle of subaltern trinitarian *perichoresis*. The victimized Son of God, Jesus, is not only the emptied one, but also the glorified one: Victim-*and*-Victor. Thus, here, the conflict in the human circle, as well as the conflict in the divine community, is resolved.

> The humanity of God in Jesus supremely points to the *kenosis* that was begun in creation. [T]his *kenosis* does not reach its deepest point until the martyrdom of Christ, where God chooses to allow his Son to be forsaken in order to bring about an end to all illegitimate political institutions that exploit human beings. The resurrection of the crucified, on the other hand, points to God's inexhaustible *power* as that dimension of his transcendence in origin.[67]

In the *kenosis-and-plerosis,* God provides *third space* for humankind to enter into trinitarian *relationship* and to experience *redemption*, through the exercise or emptying of power. Here, salvation is to build relationships of redeeming love and familial equality in ever widening circles; and, conversely, sin and evil is a refusal to join the dance circle and enjoy the space created by God in Jesus. It is a failure to move in interrelatedness and interdependence with others in the circle and refusal to pay the price of *kenosis* before reaping the plenitude of *plerosis*. Seeing in the circular movement of the *naachnu* the relationship and redemption revealed by Jesus, we proceed to another movement.

5.5.2 *The Counter Movement: The Shakti of Communion and Conflict*

Another movement in the adivasi *naach* might be called a *counter movement*. After the completion of a stanza, or at the end of a particular mood, the row of entwined dancers suddenly reverses direction. Normally, the circular movement is from left to right; but the counter movement is from right to left (see picture 9). The *dholak* and *pipudi* player in the centre also begin to move around in the reverse direction. The visual effect is that of a break, a new mood, a 'going against the current'. However, in this movement, too, there is relationship and interdependence, for the *naach* goes on uninterruptedly, but now, in reverse spatiality. This new spatiality and movement can be conceived as the counter movement or the *counter space*, which is the domain of the Spirit, *Shakti*.

The counter movement also follows a circular trajectory, but in its very dynamics and direction, it suggests novelty, change, contrast, disruption, reversibility and power. It also indicates conflict in its reversal of the regular rhythmic circularity of everyday life. Normally, a reverse movement would indicate retreat and regression. But, in the adivasi *naach*, there is no question of retreat and regression since everyone is located in a circle. Thus, with the movements of Son, Jesus, seen in radical relationships and redemption, there is the counter movement of Spirit-*Shakti*. This movement sustains intercommunion, and highlights contrasts, ruptures, conflicts and power. *Shakti* pervades Jesus' being and work; and so, he too is a symbol of contrast and conflict, as already explained earlier.

The Spirit-*Shakti*'s presence is encountered and experienced in *movement* at three levels: (a) in creation and nature as fire and water.[68] While fire and water are vibrant, visible, primal symbols,[69] at times, *Shakti*'s effects are imperceptible to the human eye, but are felt as breath,[70] or experienced in phenomena like thunder and whirling winds[71] that rejuvenate spaces of 'hot' or 'cold',[72] or sacred, etc.; (b) in human beings who, on receiving *Shakti*-power, launch out in mission-movement as prophets, kings, evangelists and martyrs armed with divine power;[73] and (c) in God. We get a glimpse of this third level in Scriptural references to the Spirit who "searches the depths of God" (1 Cor 2:10) and "comprehends the thoughts of God" (1 Cor 2:11). Moreover, God's *Shakti*, we have argued, is powerfully manifest in Jesus' signs and wonders (*dynamis*).

The Spirit-*Shakti* fosters *communion* and *creation* – being "the primal energy of creation, the pressure of God towards goodness"[74] that fills all creatures and abides in all spaces. She works in natural processes and within human freedom, never substituting for it, but animating it. She groans with alienated nature, as if in travail, waiting to receive divine

Picture 9: South Gujarat adivasi *naachnu* in a counter movement

adoption (Rom 8:18-25), pours divine love into human hearts (Rom 5:5), and unifies communities and cultures without destroying their difference as evidenced at Pentecost (Acts 2:5-12). As promised by Word-*Logos*, Spirit-*Shakti* "brings to remembrance"[75] God's redemptive events in Jesus and *is* Wisdom, Teacher, Counselor and Comforter (Prov 8; Jn 14:16,26; 15:26).[76] She also unifies human beings with God in their weaknesses with "sighs too deep for words" (Rom 8:26), and, when people are in trouble and rendered speechless, *Shakti* puts words into human mouths (Mt 10:20; Lk 12:11-2).

Much as Spirit-*Shakti* is creative and fosters communion, She is also *destructive* in prophetic acts of breaking chains and opening prisons (Is 61:1; Lk 4:18). She destroys fears and cowardice and transforms people to "turn the world upside down."[77] Amidst chaos, conflict and contingency, She inspires human discernment to seek truth by judging between good and evil, and She empowers human decision to right wrongs. Much as *kenosis-plerosis* of the cross epitomizes God's love and justice, Spirit-*Shakti* enables both principles to be harmonized *in praxis* in concrete cases. "Justice and mercy in themselves look back, the Holy Spirit's creative appropriation of these principles looks forward."[78] In other words, the Spirit opens up *thirdspace* – beyond regarding justice and mercy as mere dualities – that calls for effective integration and implementation of the two. Thus, She never avoids conflict but takes it to a realm where it is resolved through processes and structures that ensure restoration, retribution, reconciliation and redemption.

The counter movement in the trinitarian perichoretic *naach* inspires underprivileged groups to move ahead with the prompting and under the power of *Shakti*. In the religion of the oppressed there is already awareness of the pervasive presence of *Shakti*, identified by movement and power. This is found in the *perceived space* of nature, as well as in *social space* when certain wo/men get possessed by *devas*, *devis* or *matas* who invest them with superhuman strength seen in their unintelligible cries, prophetic utterances, dangerous actions, physical strength, vigourous body movements, etc.[79] These are counter movements opening up *counter spaces* that, while unifying what is good, true, beautiful and liberative, simultaneously denounce evil, disrupt the status quo, defend the weak, disturb the comfortable and destroy the forces of oppression.[80]

From the viewpoint of *Shakti's counter space*, there is an important *'religious performance'* that subaltern trinitarianism can inspire, namely, evolving and empowering social movements,[81] peasant movements,[82] Dalit movements,[83] women movements,[84] and the like, that (a) emerge *from below*, (b) are able to *mobilize masses*, (c) can *create*, as well as *destroy*, and (d) will *resist institutionalization*.[85] If these elements are present, the 'contradictory consciousness'[86] among subaltern communities will enable them to effectively confront all oppressors and forms of oppression. Here, subaltern trinitarian religion will not be alienating, but empowering, for, *Shakti*-Spirit too counters evil, brings justice, and dances in counter movement in *counter spaces* of life.

In the 'subaltern trinitarian theology of religions' that I developed, I showed how Spirit-*Shakti* invests the community with the power of wisdom, discernment, judgment and integration. These values, associated with Spirit-*Shakti*, enable weaker sections of society to approach and adopt other religious traditions in a spirit of openness and with a view to forming larger community. However, should the need arise, this same Spirit also enables oppressed communities to maintain a distance from, resist, reject and protest against, or ensure a differential in matters related to the furtherance of their socio-eco-cultural and political ends. In this way, subaltern communities will ensure that no creed is accepted in the abstract, but is adopted only if there is congruence between the symbolic (*conceived*) and the actual (*social space*), and between the professed and the practised.[87]

5.5.3 *The Supportive Movement: Abba's Creation and Solidarity*

The adivasi *naach* has a third movement, which could be called the *supportive movement*. In this movement, the physically stronger members of the community – usually, the men – dance the steps of the circular and counter movements, but another ring of dancers stands on their shoulders.[88] The lower rung, holding their arms entwined shoulder-high, support the upper rung of dancers who also have arms entwined and sway according to the singing and the rhythm of the *dholak*. The upper layer of dancers always has smaller-built, lighter and weaker members of the community – usually, women and children (see picture 10). There is balance, sensitivity and perfect harmony between the two or three rungs. The overall picture is one of solidarity, synchronization and support. And, since the stronger ones bear the weight of the lighter ones on the top, one sees the adivasi community symbolically *re-presented* in *naach* since the community is supportive of, and stands in solidarity with, all its members, especially the weaker, disadvantaged ones.

Picture 10: South Gujarat adivasi *naachnu* in
a supportive movement

In *triune spatiality*, a parallel was drawn between the primordial dimension of reality and the trinitarian person revealed as *Abba*,[89] Father of Jesus. Here, we could see the supportive movement of the *naach* as symbolizing *Abba*, our Father, too. We noted that 'Father' – used for the first person of the Trinity – is not a term that ascribes sexuality and gender to God, but primarily indicates relationship. Moreover, *Abba*, we stressed, indicates a relationship of tenderness and intimacy, a *motherly fatherliness*. This roughly parallels adivasi parental figures like *Varle-Dev* or *Ucchaliyo-Dev* (Gujarat) or *Dharmes, Singbonga* or *Haram* (Chotanagpur). In the supportive movement, God is not spatially located *up there* or *high above*, but rather *down here* or *below/ beneath* the community.

The Father's specific role in traditional trinitarianism is creation. God, Father, is revealed as Creator whose creative action extends far beyond the creation of human beings to all of nature. Thus, the Creator God is concerned about every tiny creature – 'clothing' grass that dries so swiftly and 'feeding' even sparrows.[90] In subaltern trinitarianism, this Creator God, *Abba*, is associated with the primordial dimension of reality, the *substratum, the uncreated origin* from whom all else comes. The Yahwist Biblical account of the creation of humanity, which reads: "God formed man of dust from the ground, and breathed into his nostrils the breath of life" (Gen 2:7),[91] uses imagery from the potter's craft of moulding from mud.[92] God is not a philosopher or ideologue who *conceives* or *wishes* human beings into existence, but is *re-presented* as a potter –[93] oppressed in Indian caste hierarchy – who *moulds* humans from mud and breathes into wo/man divine breath.[94] Furthermore, in the same account, the destiny of human beings is shown to be ground, dust (Gen 3:19). A brief note on these two passages is required here.

These verses from the Yahwist account of Genesis indicate that: (a) God is creator of *all* human beings, (b) the origin, as well as the destiny, of all human beings is the earth, soil, dust, (c) human beings are directed to the earth in their work and the earth is directed to the work of humans,[95] (d) the person is created *as a living person*. Westermann argues:[96]

> The person created by God is *a living person* ... The person as a living being is to be understood *as a whole* and any idea that one is made up of body and soul is ruled out. A person created as a living being means that one is a person only in one's living state. A *person cannot be made into an object of study apart from the living state*

in which that person exists. An 'image of humanity' or a doctrine about humanity cannot comprehend human existence as it is.

Earthy symbolisms like the potter's act of moulding earth, the animation of humans from dust and God's living breath, as well as non-dichotomous thinking with regard to body-soul fully conforms to the subaltern worldview and contests the 'image of humanity' of Brahmanism that is dichotomous, otherworldly, oppressive and generative of inequality.

With *Abba*'s creative action firmly embedded in the earth, animated by *Shakti*'s living breath, imaged according to the Son whose arms, cruciform, are outstretched in limitless, 'reckless'[97] love and selfless sacrifice, vulnerable communities can feel supported upon God's shoulders. God is a solid, primal cause named *Abba* symbolizing the indestructible power of being, "which conquers chaos like a warrior and has the strength to ensure that [God's] purposes will ultimately be achieved."[98] The *conceived space* that *Abba* creates for his subordinated children is upon his shoulders that raise up, support and launch out into action. This is very different from caste-conceptions that relegate the so-called 'lower castes' at the feet of the eternal *Purusha*. Note that the upper rung (community) depends for its rhythm and movement on the lower rung (God) that moves it forward, while also maintaining the equilibrium, creativity and continuity of the *naach*. On the other hand, there is need for cooperation and coordination from the lighter dancers in the upper rung or else there will be collapse and chaos, and the dance will be disrupted.

Conceiving of God dancing the supportive movement of solidarity goes against either the oppressive, hegemonic 'One', or, against 'many' deities who dominate or deceive. The former could refer to various processes that professedly create oneness – for instance, globalisation, fundamentalism, neocolonialism and Western imperialism – but actually destroy that *weapon of the weak* called 'difference'. And, the latter could refer to those who play "a politics of power" – those "human kings aspiring to be 'divine beings',"[99] or also to ideologies like liberalism and postmodernism[100] with little regard for anything that universally unites or for anyone who stands in unyielding solidarity. Here too, *Abba*'s solidarity enables the balancing of love and justice. Moreover, as the primordial and "divine principle of direction and determination in history," *Abba* will ensure that the Son's circular movements and *Shakti*'s counter movements will renew, redeem, reconcile and resurrect dying and broken humanity in the spaces and power of *kenosis-plerosis*.[101]

Assisting *Abba's* action in the supportive movement of the *naach*, we can think of NGOs and the agencies of civil society that may not have subalterns as direct members, but are nonetheless *supportive of*, and *in solidarity with*, them and committed to their cause. Yet, this commitment cannot be 'from above' as patrons and benefactors, but *'from below'* as supporters and catalysts. Symbolically and spatially, these will have to "bear the burdens" of the weak and the victims of society so that creation might continue to be carried forward with deep faith that this is being done shoulder-to-shoulder and step-by-step with *Abba* who ensures *plerosis* in "the dance of the universe, a dance led by the trinitarian persons in ever new improvisations, which touch each creature and embrace the whole."[102]

To sum up, from the viewpoint of oppressed groups, subaltern trinitarianism can fulfill a *performance role* by conceiving of Trinity as a *God-of-movement* (eternally inhabiting all times, creating new spaces) and a *God-in-movements* (animating all life-giving and liberative eco-socio-historic-political processes), whose eternal perichoretic dance embraces the *here-and-now naach* of subaltern communities with the rhythm of *kenosis-plerosis*. Symbolically, this can be seen as the Son who begins circular movements, the feminine *Shakti* who initiates counter movements, and a parental *Abba* figure arm-in-arm, dancing step-in-step at the bottom rung of dancers. While being *iconic*, since the Son has a face and his arms, outstretched, *re-present* the cross, such a symbolic representation will also be *aniconic* since the swirling and swaying of the powerful, feminine *Shakti* will be held in creative harmony in the loving embrace of *Abba* in earthy *naach* movements (see plate 12)

5.6 Subaltern Trinity's *'Performance'* Challenges to Indian Christianity

Three corollaries that follow from the three basic trinitarian theses we developed in the previous chapter are: (i) conflicts among communities can be forestalled if communities exist in *communion* and *right relationship*, (ii) the relationships among communities depend on their shared, common *space* – perceived, conceived and lived – that deals with the exercise of *power*, and, (iii) in subaltern trinitarian theology, the exercise of power is revealed and realized in the mystery of divine/human *kenosis-plerosis*. In the light of these basic insights, then, we consider what performance role Indian Christianity can play in Indian society and how it can be of service to India, and the world, at large.

5.6.1 Spatial Trialectic and 'Outside-the-Camp' Communion

Our world is characterized by individualism, selfishness and competition. In sharp contrast, the Trinity is a representation of relationship, communion and solidarity. Thus, while global forces promote the 'I' (individual) or the 'We' (one's own community) as the *centre*, subaltern trinitarianism evolves from the *periphery* – from what our subaltern trinitarianism has demarcated as 'outside the camp' – creating *thirdspace* that, while taking cognizance of the self and the other, offers fuller possibilities for both.

Thirdspace is the space beyond monism[103] and dualism. Monism in its various forms – for instance, unitarianism,[104] imperialism, neocolonialism, globalisation and fundamentalism – seeks the hegemony of the 'I' or the 'We' over and against the 'Other'. This might not be so evident at first sight. However, in chapter three, we argued that these processes lead to conflicts and violence. Conversely, dualism in its diverse forms either has a dichotomous view of reality, for instance, spiritual-material (Gnosticism)[105] or light-darkness (Manichaeism),[106] or, divides humankind on the basis of simplistic binaries like pure-impure (casteism), white-black (racism), superior-inferior (fascism), *deshi-pardeshi* (*Hindutva*),[107] bourgeoisie-proletariat (Marxism) and so on. However, reality is far too complex to either be reduced to some homogenous One, or to be seen as a conflict between two opposing camps. Therefore, we must look for other alternatives. Here, pluralism has always been an attractive option. Nonetheless, we have cautioned about the dangers inherent in ideologies propped by pluralist premises, for e.g., liberalism and postmodernism, since they (a) innately eschew ethics and issues of justice and group rights, and (b) tend to either be dismissive of difference or fail to seriously consider its value in the socio-religio-cultural field. Instead of any uncritical pluralism, we *valorized difference* and opted for a *spatial trialectic*, which, I believe, retains a conflictive tension, and yet, is constructive of community. Let us view the *naachnu* to understand this.

Using our subaltern trinitarian symbol of the *naach*, we can think in terms of three persons who dance shoulder-to-shoulder in circular and counter movement. Here, although there are actually six entwined arms, to the outside viewer, there appear to be *only three*;[108] and, the dancing insider *always* holds on to *both*, her/his partners, but to *only one arm* of each of them. Therefore, if all three dancers desire to sustain the beauty and balance of the dance, each must *equally* give her/himself *fully* to the other two, aware that s/he gives-and-receives *only one hand* to-and-from each of the other two, respectively. The dance would be disrupted if any one of the three were to get so engrossed in a second dancer forgetting that, "We are three!" This illustration could be transposed to the most basic unit of community, i.e., the family (mother-father-child), where the most 'balanced' family is one where any one of the three equally, fully and simultaneously responds to the other two. This *tri-une* situation has been represented elsewhere in Christian art (see picture 11)[109] and could serve as an illustration for *extra-ecclesial communion* in the following manner.

When the Indian Christian community moves 'outside the camp' of its *lived space*, it encounters the so-called *Other*, whereupon, it can (a) convert the Other to its own, familiar spatiality, (b) disregard, despise or destroy the Other,[110] or (c) create a *thirdspace* that, while including the spaces of both, is far more extensive than mere syntheses of both, Self-and-Other. This *thirdspace* is possible because, although Self (first) consciously encounters the Other (second), this encounter, *always*, consciously or unconsciously, unfolds within the larger landscape of *An-Other*,[111] i.e., a *Third*.[112] While this involves an element of transcendence, we are not referring to God or some Absolute, (although, for the religious believer, this is taken for granted). But, we *do* stress that all encounters between communities take place within so many horizons or *scapes*,[113] that naïve divisions, definitions and descriptions do not convey what something or someone truly *is*. Thus, effective, extra-ecclesial relationships can only be formed and fostered in a spirit of openness and extroversion,[114] thereby making spatiality a challenge to be faced. Indeed, "spatiality is not, primarily, what makes distance possible, but what makes nearness possible. Spatiality enables us to stand in creative tension with one another, i.e., it makes us neighbors."[115] Nonetheless, we said that spatiality is always *produced* and involves concomitant elements of power and knowledge that require careful negotiation.

5.6.2   *Spatiality, Knowledge and Power of Indian Christianity*

If Indian Christianity is to fulfill a *performance role* in society, it must critically consider the triad of *space-knowledge-power*. All spaces in society are invested with power and have been *produced* as an outcome of some form of knowledge. As far as the *perceived space* of Indian Christianity is concerned, the Indian Church is a mighty institution on the Indian landscape comprising of huge church buildings, prestigious educational

Picture 11: The 'Hare Window' suggestive of trinitarian intercommunion

institutions, elite hospitals and comfortable formation houses built upon, and possessing, large tracts of land in big cities and towns. Even in so-called 'mission centres', for e.g., in adivasi areas of Gujarat, near to the cheaply built indigenous adivasi houses of bamboo, cow dung, mud and leaves, the 'official' Christian community is *perceived* and identified by concrete structures – chapels, hospitals, residences of clergymen, religious wo/men and boarding schools – that disclose money and power.

While the *perceived space* of Indian Christianity gives the impression of power and money to those 'outside the camp', the public face of Indian Christianity clamours for consideration as a 'minority community' guaranteed of special rights, reservations and privileges by the Indian state. In chapter three I argued that 'reservations' must always be premised on a 'lack'. The Indian Christian community argues that, by virtue of its numerical insignificance, its interests run the risk of being swamped by the majority Hindu community. However, when the *perceived space* of Indian Christianity conspicuously *does not indicate any lack*, but on the contrary, an *excess* of finance, land, immovable properties like institutions, church buildings, etc., doubts are raised whether the community really needs special privileges or whether it is just an 'appeased minority'.

Moving from *perceived space* to *conceived space*, or from the material to the field of ideas, some discrepancies arise. First, in consonance with the *perceived space* of Indian Christianity described above, the corresponding *knowledge* that has produced such space, and the knowledge (i.e., the ideas, concepts, symbols, myths, stories, narratives, ideologies, philosophies, theologies, etc.) that such space produces (present) and will produce (future) is bound to be elitist and alienating to disadvantaged and working communities who directly work upon the earth, soil, forests and seas.[116] In this regard, one could question whether those who pass out from Christian colleges and schools are equipped with knowledge that could be profitably used in their native contexts, or even whether the skills they gained enable and empower them to carry on their family trades, with greater competence and confidence.

Second, there is often incongruity between *centre-periphery*. Church documents, theological statements[117] and the directives of religious congregations always profess their 'option for the poor'[118] and 'solidarity with the broken' (i.e., marginal ministry), but, when it comes to actual involvement or *praxis* with marginal peoples, Christian religionists inevitably start constructing concrete so-called 'centres' that are, clearly, 'centre' only to the Church hierarchy. The gates, landscape, walls, watchmen, furnishing, etc., that form part of Indian *Churchscape*[119] serves as a deterrent for 'peripheral' communities to enter such space, and, ironically, for Christian religionists to leave the comforts of such so-called 'centres'. As a consequence of this spatiality, thirdly, most Indian Christians consider themselves located 'above' others and 'work for' others as patrons/benefactors, not 'work with' them as friends/sisters/brothers, thereby behaving like *sahibs*,[120] not Christ-like servants. Fourthly, if one sees the 'products' of Indian Christianity in terms of the powerful alumni of Christian institutions, one is likely to be disappointed, since, many of these ex-students neither seem committed to serving the poor nor to forming inclusive Indian community.[121]

Many more discrepancies can be cited between the *perceived* and *conceived space* of Indian Christianity, but examining the triad of space-knowledge-power from the vantage point of *social space* is far more challenging. Here, diverse communities share a common space invested with all kinds of knowledge and power, and inclusive of diverse, often conflicting, eco-socio-religio-cultural-political processes, institutions and structures. This *shared social space* is problematic in a populous country like India where over a billion people from backgrounds of striking diversity vie with each other for what they consider to be "an equal and just share of national resources" in terms of land ownership, rights, opportunities, educational and job benefits, etc. Conflicts undoubtedly arise here, and this must lead a community to assess its *geopolitical space* vis-à-vis other communities.

5.6.3 *Reconstructing Indian Christians as 'Political Community'*

Negotiating the triad of space-knowledge-power in any society or 'polis' necessarily involves going public and being political. Thus, despite arguments that religious communities ought to shun politics, be *apolitical*, and concentrate on 'purely religious matters', we observe that, in India, such thinking is idealistic, dualistic and impractical. This is so because (a) most Indians are innately religious and their religiosity is unlikely to remain confined to some private space, and (b) communities are granted 'minority rights' and 'reservations' on the basis of their *religious affiliation*. Seen from the viewpoint of the state or from that of any 'minority religion', these are *political concessions* given by, or received from, the state.[122] Hence, conflicts are bound to arise in the allocation and appropriation of 'affirmative action', and also discontentment especially from groups that suffer eco-socio-political disadvantage but, for some reason, cannot avail of such benefit.

To legitimately seek benefits from the state, the Indian Christian community – and, especially subaltern groups – must be articulated as *'political community'*. But, a 'principle of difference' must be applied here, namely, since subaltern communities *actually suffer* the effects of various forms of discrimination, rallying for their rights *as community* becomes a prime issue.[123] In the case of the Indian Christian community, however, there is need not only to rally for rights, but also to realize its *responsibilities* towards others. In the present case of 'minority rights', it must: (a) be mindful of its 'minority' status and use the benefits that accrue thereby for truly allowing it to assume its role as *servant* of society, (b) be aware of many other oppressed groups – within itself and 'outside the camp' – that require similar benefits, and be ready to work for the procurement of these for other weaker groups, too, and, (c) readily forego such rights when it realizes that it does not require them, especially in areas where Christians, though numerically a minority, do not suffer from disadvantages that necessitate such rights.[124] By so doing, the Indian Christian community will be fulfilling its *performance role* by its very engagement in the public sphere with other concerned groups who will respect it. .

Besides the issue of 'minority rights' that is often the core concern of Indian Christian communities, it is vital that the Church bridge the gap between what it possesses as property (*firstspace*) and what it professes in its pronouncements (*secondspace*). "To change life is to change space; to change space is to change life."[125] Before any change or conversion of others, this is a call for Self-conversion – a challenge to be aware of, and active in, *thirdspace* (lived space) inhabited by *peripheral peoples* 'outside the camp' with whom the Trinitarian Community abides, animates and activates in circular-counter-supportive movements that are concerned about economics, politics and social structures. *The Compendium of Social Teachings of the Church* exhorts it to:[126]

> [P]*ermeate this world* in the realities of the economy and labor, of technology and communications, of society and politics, of the international community and the relations among cultures and peoples (n.1). ... [T]he salvation offered by Christ *is of the whole person in all dimensions*, personal, social, spiritual and corporeal.

> This *salvation is also universal*. Thus, there is a link 'between the relationship that the person is called to have with God and the *responsibility* [s]he has towards her/his neighbor in the *concrete circumstances of history* (n. 40).

This text is revelatory and revolutionary, but it will be sterile – like many Church documents – unless Indian Christianity internalizes at least three injunctions it contains.

First, the opening words *"permeate this world"* succinctly suggest the Scriptural symbols of 'leaven in the dough' and 'salt in food',[127] i.e., the idea of an invisible, tiny-yet-indispensable ingredient flavouring the great mass. These are appropriate symbols for the insignificant 'minority' Indian Christian community that, imperceptible, must incisively influence the great Indian masses. Indian Christian spatiality, today, seems inconsistent in that an insignificant minority wants others to come to its self-proclaimed 'centres' to avail of its services. This incongruity is like that of a little girl making a dolls' house in the garden and asking her whole family to stay therein with her as 'head' of the family! If Indian Christians are to *permeate the world*, they must do it as leaven and salt, not with cement and bricks – i.e., expecting others to come to them, but by *working with others*.

Second, the text speaks of the *whole person* in all the dimensions of life: personal, social, spiritual and corporeal. This dovetails with the subaltern worldview that is integral and does not admit of any duality. Moreover, this text – like others in the Second Testament –[128] also stresses that *salvation is universal*. These two propositions ought to inspire Christians to reject dichotomous thinking of body-soul, earth-heaven, material-spiritual, and so on, and learn from subaltern trinitarianism and *tri-une spatiality* that God is present everywhere as goodness, truth, beauty, song, dance and the like. But, where there is sin, evil, death, selfishness and injustice, it becomes the duty of Indian Christians to network with peoples and movements already engaged in life-giving and liberative activity that is aimed at making everyone daughters and sons of God.

Third, (and related to the second), the text does not talk about the Church's *rights* but it speaks of *responsibility (response-ability)*[129] seen as inseparable relationship between (a) God, and (b) *"neighbour in the concrete circumstances of history."* Jesus understood 'neighbour' as the wounded victim lying forsaken by the roadside.[130] Thus, everyone 'outside the camp' is the Indian Christian's *neighbour* for whom every Christian, and the Indian Church as community, is *responsible*. Besides being a *performance* religious task, working for the life and liberation (i.e., integral salvation of all)[131] *with others*, becomes Christianity's 'leaven role' in the Indian Kingdom of God:[132]

> The trinitarian life of God as a *perichoresis* of the "persons" embraces *the struggle for community* as well as the achievement of communion ... Classical theology has often obscured the meaning of the Divine Trinity instead of allowing it to revolutionize the very notion of "God" and by extension, *the political form of community* in which God's life is expressed as the salvation of creatures. ... The *struggle for community is the struggle for a political form of life* in which friendship between persons and groups is based on justice and where justice is fulfilled in friendship.

This 'struggle for community' and 'struggle for political form of community' (the Kingdom's *already-and-not yet*) must materialize not in 'concrete' churches and institutions, but in the conflictive, yet *concrete, circumstances of history* – rather, 'histories', especially of the borderlands. Such a *performance task* requires dynamic interactions usually termed 'dialogue', but what I term '*trilogue*'. What does *trilogue* entail? Who does it embrace? What could be if effects?.

5.7 Spatial Trialectic and *Trilogue* of Subaltern Trinitarianism

Whether in general terms,[133] or as literary form,[134] or in a more technical sense as used in the academy or by the disciplines,[135] 'dialogue' refers to an exchange between two subjects or groups/communities, most commonly identified by the binary *I-Thou*,[136] or *Self-Other*.[137] Even if, at times, more than two persons/parties are involved in this exchange, the 'more-than-two' factor is again either identified as *Thou-Other* or simply as *Plural* or *Many*. In other words, '*Thirdness*', if one might call it that, is not accorded special attention. Barring Bhabha and Buber, who explain '*thirdspace*' or '*Third*' as *hybridity* or some Absolute, respectively,[138] i.e., different from Lefebvre, I am unaware of any other thinker who uses 'spatial trialectic' or 'Thirdness' the way Lefebvre does.[139] Besides, the *an-Other* in the Lefebvrian sense does not refer to duality or to a 'second' but to a 'third'. It is unique. Indeed, in a later work when he explores the triad of *melody-harmony-rhythm*, Lefebvre writes:[140]

> Triadic analysis distinguishes itself from dual analysis just as much as from banal analysis. It doesn't lead to a *synthesis* in

accordance with the Hegelian schema ... [it] links three terms that it leaves distinct, without fusing them in a *synthesis* (which would be the third term).

Thus, while the aim of dialogue normally seems to be some *synthesis* or *consensus*,[141] *trilogue* maintains a *three-one tension* and *always* holds together reality within a *thirdspace*. Further elaboration, and a couple of examples from the 'field' of music, might clarify the concept of *trilogue* more.

A 'trilogy' is a combination of *three* dramas, literary works, musical compositions or dance movements *closely related* into a *single* theme. The important words are: (a) three, (b) closely related, and (c) single. One can also think of three *distinct things* like: (a) a piece of wood called 'violin', (b) a length of wire called 'string' and (c) some hairs from a horse's tail drawn into a 'violin bow'. When an accomplished violinist draws the bow over violin strings, the ensuing music is nothing like wood, wire or a horse's tail, but while the audience enjoys the melodious music (One), it can point out where the violin's wood is, what the string does, and how a horse's tail makes good bows (Three). Note that there is *tension* (*conflict*) in this triad, for, if the violinist were to release the tautness of the strings, or the tension in the bow, he would be unable to make music. Thus, though the word '*trilogue*' has been used before,[142] I wish to explain it a little differently with three important characteristics that distinguish it from mere dialogue.

5.7.1   Trilogue and the Primacy of Praxis

Subaltern trinitarianism stresses that what is important for community is relationship, communion and solidarity. These three terms are intimately related to the *here-and-now*. In subaltern imagination the *primordial-visible-invisible* do not refer to afterlife or some future spatiotemporal reality, but to reality as it *lived-perceived-conceived* in the *concrete* circumstances of history. This history has been one of silencing and subjugation precisely because theory has been divorced from praxis, and while the dominant groups *produced* theory (*conceived space*), the subordinated communities were reduced to merely *re-producing* what others had *conceptually produced*. Herein lies the danger of mere dialogue divorced from the *thirdspace* of lived life or *social space*.

Subaltern trinitarianism asserts that, "The life of God is our life too,"[143] for, just as the *kumbhar* (potter) moulds pots from the mud of the earth, so have *all* human beings been fashioned. But, the difference between the potter's work and God's creation is that *Abba* blows *Shakti*-breath into human beings and thereby enters into relationship and adopts them as children – sisters and brothers of his Son, Jesus. It is within this *tri-une* presence and action of Son-*Abba-Shakti,* identifiable with the *tri-une* spaces of the *visible-primordial-invisible,* respectively, that revelation makes meaning. Thus, the 'matter' of any interfaith *trilogue* must include all three spaces beginning with *the visible* – the subaltern sense of communion with *jungle-jal-jamin,* as well as its ownership, the power of people and their further empowerment through movements, the equality of all as sisters/brothers with *Abba*-God, vis-à-vis present inequalities and injustices they face.

Together with this 'matter' (i.e., the content and context) of *trilogue,* its 'form' (i.e., its nature or character) derives from the revelation of God's *tri-une-ness.* Theologians have held that,[144] "The internal life of the Trinity may be characterized as one of dialogue."[145] This means that there are dynamic exchanges among the three persons that arise on account of their relatedness,[146] shared divine nature and perfect communion. Human beings understand this internal divine relationship neither as monistic nor dualistic, but as *Tri-Une.* This fact gives *trilogue* its nature of *triuneness.* Concretely, this implies that *interfaith trilogue* will include not only two parties who 'have faith' (understood as certain beliefs or ideas about God locatable in *secondspace*), but also a *third* party who 'may not have faith' as per this 'religious' understanding, but who is *faith-full* in the sense that Jesus staked his life for the Ultimate which he saw as *Abba*'s will. Subaltern trinitarianism needs one to be *faith-full* in this sense. This faith is neither the prerogative of the Christian,[147] nor of the 'religious believer',[148] but is shared by all those who dare to act, trust, dance, challenge, suffer and die for what they in their right conscience consider as Ultimate or Absolute – called by whatever name.

In the realm of praxis (*social space*) there is a complex dynamism between the real-and-imagined, *perceived-and-conceived.* Hence, in these *real life-situations* true knowledge comes, *primarily,* from immediate involvement or 'experience' (action) rather than from the mediation of ideas and concepts (reflection).[149] For example, in times of tsunami or flood, it is scandalous for believers to discuss the role of water in religion or whether the victims were baptized and would go to heaven, and the meaning of this disaster from the viewpoint of God's love, religious faith, etc. The 'crucified ones' are the victims and their families deprived of God's Life. The trajectory through which *trilogue* would progress would be first, experience (action); second, evaluation of the conflicts and tensions involved, for e.g., between love and justice, between charity and structural approach, reconciling the demands of justice and love, etc. (reflection); and third, placing faith on the side of justice, truth, etc. (enlightened, trinitarian action).[150]

A final point that can be made in the realm of *trilogue as praxis* is that, whereas dialogue usually seeks the reconciliation of opposites or two positions at a higher/deeper level of harmony, synthesis, integration or consensus, *trilogue* always seeks a *Third* point, which is *not necessarily synthesis or consensus*. Moreover, in any situation it neither looks at reality as one-dimensional nor two-dimensional, but so to say, as *tri-dimensional*. Triads like the one we have dealt with, namely, space-knowledge-power, and within this, still others like spatial-historical-social, or space-time-energy, are the stuff of *trilogue*. By looking at reality in its trinitarian complexity, and in seeking solutions with peoples of other religions, other disciplines and ideologies, Indian Christianity will be undertaking a *performance role* fuelled by the fundamental fact: "Trinity is our social programme."[151]

5.7.2   *Trilogue and Trinitarian Tension*

Subaltern trinitarianism *always* involves an element of tension. Since the trinitarian relationship, solidarity and communion is presently consciously denied to a great majority of India's oppressed masses,[152] and since God is present in the *naach/nu* of these oppressed communities – in their ups and downs, circles and ruptures – God continues to suffer *pathos*, and will continue to do so until the *least* of Jesus' sisters and brothers is given her/his rightful space in God's Kingdom. In other words, what we saw as the divine mystery of *kenosis-plerosis* in the cross of Jesus is replicated and replayed in the world today. *Trilogue* must remain aware of, and respond to, this perennial tension.

I have discussed the dynamics of conflict among communities. This conflict cannot be merely the lot of humankind created by God, while this same God enjoys perfect communion in Godself unaware of, and unaffected by, the evils and injustices inflicted upon those who *Abba* moulded with his hands and breathed into, who the Son, Jesus, accepted and adopted as his sisters and brothers, and in whom the Spirit-*Shakti* abides. If this were true, the passion-death of Jesus would have been, quite literally, 'divine drama' that would have nothing to offer to human beings cruelly condemned to suffer several passions-deaths not as drama, but as daily experience. But, since we have explained the *kenosis-plerosis* as God's concrete participation in history and God's promise of a new world,[153] this *kenosis-plerosis* becomes the privileged point where each divine 'person' reveals a 'word' (*logos*) about God's plans for humankind.

We must remember that God is not only *pleroma* or *plerosis*, but also undergoes *kenosis* at various times, visible in creation and in the Incarnation.[154] Put together like a trilogy, these *tri-logoi* present in the trinitarian mystery of *kenosis-plerosis* reveal the particular missions of *Abba* (creation and solidarity), the Son (circular relatedness and redemption), and *Shakti* (communion, as well as conflict). In this regard, we can assert that, "*kenosis-plerosis* is the *basic grammar* of trilogue;" or, in every *performance* attempt to relate Indian Christianity – or, for that matter any religion – to peoples' problems, the *triloguers* must undergo *kenosis* if they expect *plerosis*. Within the tensions of freedom-and-finitude, sin-and-salvation and love-and-justice, all those committed to Life *movements* have to make options and take decisions that, while struggling for trinitarian *plerosis* will have to meet the demands of *kenosis*. Commenting about *kenosis* Amaladoss writes:[155]

> This fullness is not given, but to be achieved (Eph 1:3-14). In this perspective, we are aware of our own limitedness on the one hand, which makes us open to and receptive of others. On the other hand, we are impelled to dialogue [*trilogue*][156] with others so that through mutual interpenetration we can converge toward unity and reconciliation, purifying in the process what is merely human as limitation and sin, in ourselves and others. Kenosis, then, refers not merely to a personal attitude, but also to the Word's self-manifestation in Jesus.

To achieve an interpenetration or intercommunion of all religionists, ideologues, religious believers or even those who profess no religion or ideology at all, *kenosis* would seem to be a uniting principle albeit understood with diverse nuances.[157] This is because *kenosis* is an attitude that 'creates space' by virtue of self-emptying for the welfare of *the Other* and *an-Other*, especially the oppressed communities who have been denied their space for centuries. If different groups are truly committed to liberative praxis, it would matter little whether one joined the *movement(s)* because one felt inspired by the *shûnyatâ* and compassion of Buddhism,[158] or was moved by *kenotic* love of Christ, or considered this as an act of *karuna* (mercy) or *tyaga* (sacrifice) enjoined by Hinduism, or opted for a *weak ontology*[159] amidst the evils of secularization out of concern for suffering humanity. Indeed, all those committed to such *interfaith responses*[160] will not only empower those they *work with*, but will experience the spatial power of *kenosis-plerosis* in their own praxis of intercommunion that will always bear some traces of creative trinitarian tension.

5.7.3   *Trilogue and Decentralization of 'Christian Centres'*

There is no 'centre of *trilogue*' as there are *centres of dialogue* because: First, since *trilogue* privileges praxis over theory, action over reflection, *lived space* over *conceived space*, and *interfaith*,[161] instead of interreligious encounters, it desists the easy option of appealing for finances from the rich to build big, concrete 'centres' faraway from peoples' struggles so that their problems might be reflected upon and solved therein. Conversely, *trilogue* is undertaken in *lived spaces* of *bastis*, fields, hills, riversides, kitchens, fireplaces, college campuses, neighbourly committees, village squares, etc., where life is shared in reality and praxis, first; and only later, as on outcome of this lived life, there could be exchange, expression and mutual enrichment by means of news' articles, social analyses, theological articulations, street plays, public meetings to discuss further action, evolve movements, etc.

Second, when a minority religion in India like Christianity starts a '*centre* of dialogue', it implies that what is *not-centre* is, in some sense, the *periphery*. Here, there is an implicit arrogance, which seems 'presumptuous', looked at from the prism of India's religious composition. Since only two Indians out of a hundred are Catholic, does it not seem audacious for a 'minority-within-a-minority' (i.e., Catholic clergymen who start centres) to be inviting ninety-eight percent of the country to come to its self-styled 'centre' to seek solutions to problems that exist elsewhere? Moreover, often underlying the financing of institutions, hospitals and 'centres of dialogue' is an effort to engage more intellectuals to continue *producing* alien and elitist ideas and concepts, at best, divorced from subaltern life, and at worst, directed towards further alienation and oppression of the subalterns.

Third, the two trinitarian *kenoses* that are the foundations of subaltern trinitarianism – namely, Jesus' incarnation and death,[162] unfolded in the *counter space* of what I call 'outside the camp'. The *first kenosis* takes place at Nazareth and Bethlehem and "the Word" becomes flesh and dwells among us (Jn 1:14) in the form of a vulnerable child who is first revealed to a despised social group on the periphery, the shepherds. Later, Jesus reveals the Trinity's *second kenosis* at Calvary among criminals with a cry symbolizing total forsakenness, yet, tinged with trustful surrender. And between these two *kenoses*, there is the *kenotic* movement of the poor, yet powerful *Shakti*-Word, Son, proclaiming *Abba* and initiating a Kingdom-movement by sermons from hillsides, *signs* over seas and during storms, healing sessions on Sabbaths, meals with the marginalized, scandalous *interfaith trilogue* with a woman beside a well and her kinsfolk, critiques of hypocrites, etc., despite having "nowhere to lay his head" (Lk 9:58). The overall image that one gets is of mobility at the margins, liberative movements, denouncement of rigid religious 'centres' and the irruption of 'outside the camp' as wellspring of a new world. Indeed, subaltern trinitarianism poses a challenge to all so-called 'centres' of Indian Christianity.

Fourth, given the overall 'new geopolitics of globalisation'[163] it is, quite literally, 'burdensome' to be pinned down to a plot of land, with a building and immovable assets, as well as libraries, discussion-rooms, administrative staff and so on. By contrast, the space generated by globalisation and the InfoTech revolution is *cyberspace* and a vital pathway of *trilogue* is the network or the web. Like a predator prowling around for the unsuspecting victim, globalisation's giants roam worldwide through websites to create and capture markets, multiply money and marginalize peoples subsisting upon *jungle-jal-jamin* produce. These giants guide anti-poor, anti-God *movements of Mammon* in myriad manifestations,[164] often difficult to decipher. But, they must be discovered and destroyed.

In keeping with Christ's command to be "as wise as serpents"[165] wise *triloguers* will counter Mammon by using the very websites it creates to expose its anti-God, anti-poor policies and geopolitics. Thus, *triloguers* reject Mammon, but with effective apparatus like 'group-websites'[166] they network with movements, worldwide, to prophetically proclaim, "another world is possible" – a 'mother world' –[167] where the poor and powerless are protected, nurtured and empowered to protest and resist all manifestations of Mammon. Evidently, instead of a 'centre of dialogue' *trilogue* would, at most, require a 'computer of *trilogue*' – a laptop, preferably – that could be carried everywhere to gauge global geopolitics in the womb of history and to generate *subaltern counter cyberspaces*.

It is not expedient to reject globalisation fully, for it has brought us some benefits that could be used for the common good of humankind.

Thus, *trilogue* demands the use of global technological advances with a *'both-and'* logic to highlight the concerns and advance the movements of the world's oppressed communities. Moreover, given the undeniable fact that the world and Indian Church is another potent MNC, it is only apt that it fulfills its *performance role* by webbing with Life-giving and liberative movements, worldwide. This movement would be consonant with the ever-widening circular, counter and supportive movements of the subaltern trinitarian *naachnu* or *akhra*.

5.8. Conclusion: Trinitarian Movements and Trinitarian Triloguers

This chapter has primarily focused on the 'performance' role that religion can play in global society. First and foremost, I explored the possibility of a 'subaltern trinitarian theology of religions' and emphasized the need for disprivileged communities to be articulated as 'political community'. Second, tracing out three 'movements' – circular, counter and supportive, corresponding to Father, Son and Spirit, respectively – of the adivasi *naachnu*, I tried to show how the adivasi dance can both, express the presence and power of God in its midst, as well as energize and empower itself to rally for its rights in the larger national landscape. Third, expanding the embrace of our discussion, I proposed that a 'spatial trialectic' be used in all Indian Christian involvements and interventions in the public or socio-political sphere. Fourth, I discussed the possibility of entering into *'trilogue'* – as opposed to mere 'dialogue' – so as to more complexly and comprehensively include the views and visions of diverse groups and communities.

Without wanting to theorize 'up in the air', I have situated my reflections in the down-to-earth *'Churchspace'* of India so that the subaltern trinitarian theology that evolves may critique much of what we have constructed and cherish, and more importantly, re-construct Indian Christian community and 'church' in consonance to the will of a subaltern God who always plants Godself in mystical, liberative movements – always on the margins. The sixth and final chapter will be in the nature of 'functional footnotes' to all that I have said earlier.

ENDNOTES FOR CHAPTER FIVE

[1] In *Production of Space*, 45; italics added.

[2] *Ibid.,* 262; emphasis in the original.

[3] See Yves Congar, "Classical Political Monotheism and the Trinity," *God as Father? Concilium* (March 1981): 31-6.

[4] Plantinga, "The Threeness-Oneness Problem of the Trinity," 41-3, strives to give an understanding of this oneness-threeness dilemma by explaining it in simple terms using the analogy of a human family.

[5] *Modalism* was the heresy that so stressed the divine unity as to deny that Father, Son and Spirit are personally distinct. They are merely three manifestations or ways in which the one God is revealed and acts in creation and redemption. Starting in Asia Minor with Noetus (c.200), the heresy was propagated in the West by Praxeas (c.200), Sabellius (early 3rd cent.) and others. *Monarchianism* also so stressed the unity of God as to deny a truly divine Son with a distinct personal existence. Both heresies were condemned.

[6] Dualistic thinking arose due to the influence of Greek – mainly Platonic – thought, and could be seen in Patristic theology of the East where the idea prevailed that the one God is the Father, and the Son and the Spirit share with him his divine life. Though this seems scriptural, it led to *subordinatist* ideas that culminated in the Arian controversy, on the one hand. On the other, *unitarian* thinking was more characteristic of the Western tradition, where *modalism* and *monarchianism* failed to adequately recognize distinctions in God.

[7] See, for instance, von Brück, *The Unity of Reality*, 79, who points out that, while the West reflected on the unity, only then to include threeness, the East reversed this: it began with the three different beings (*hypostaseis*) and attempted to understand their unity. However, von Brück also warns about exaggerating such West-East typography although it does, to some extent, indicate different emphases or approaches.

[8] See, for instance, "Letter to Dionysius of Alexandria," in *The Christian Faith*, ed. J. Neuner and J. Dupuis, 6th ed., (Bangalore: TPI, 1996), 138, n.301, for the errors of tritheism.

[9] The question of not 'numbering' God is pertinent. The NT never refers to God as either 'three' or 'one' but simply speaks of God as Father-Son-Spirit. Predicating number in God runs the risk of *tritheism*.

[10] There are also other Pauline texts suggestive of the same sentiments; for e.g., Eph 2:18 and 1 Cor 8:6.

[11] Fee, "Paul and the Trinity," 55, comments that this passage: "puts into creedal form the affirmation that God is *experienced* as a triune reality;" emphasis by the author. Beside this, in his book *God's Empowering Presence: The Holy Spirit in the Letters of Paul* (Peabody, MA: Hendrickson, 1994), 827,

Fee maintains that Pauline epistles "are full of presuppositions and assertions which reveal that he [Paul] *experienced* God, and then expressed that experience in a fundamentally trinitarian way."

[12] See M. Darrol Bryant, "Recovering the Trinitarian Foundations of Christian Experience: A Pathway to Christian Unity," *DAA* 4/3 (Fall 1990): 4-20, for the idea of Christian trinitarian experience as foundational.

[13] Note that the experiences themselves were marked by unity-in-diversity; see, for e.g., Aloys Grillmeier, *Christ in Christ Tradition: From the Apostolic Age to Chalcedon (451), vol. I*, trans. J. Bowden (Atlanta: John Knox, 1975), 9-32, who outlines the various Christologies of the NT; also see, James D.G. Dunn, *Unity and Diversity in the New Testament: An Inquiry into the Character of Earliest Christianity* (London: SCM Press, 1977), for a good overview of diversity in the NT

[14] According to the Merriam-Webster's Collegiate Dictionary, 10th ed., 'transversal' is "a line that intersects a system of lines." Thus, it is here used in the sense of that which intersects the particular and the universal and yet, also transcends or goes beyond them.

[15] We have seen this in the adivasi religio-cultural worldview that admits of iconic and aniconic representations of the divine, as well as personal and transpersonal conceptions.

[16] *Brahman* is, essentially, atemporal, and has little relation with time. Thus, can be seen as 'beyond time'.

[17] Note that *dharma/dhamma* is contextual and yet refers to a principle of universal validity and value.

[18] Note that such adoption is not only limited to the past but is also widespread even today. See, for instance, Ranjit Hoskote, "For a Casteless Society," *The Hindu, Magazine Section*, 13 November 2005, 1.

[19] See, for instance, Gavin D'Costa, "Christ, the Trinity and Religious Plurality," in *Christian Uniqueness Reconsidered: The Myth of a Pluralistic Theology of Religions*, ed. idem (New York: Orbis, 1990), 16-29; also Daniel P. Sheridan, "Grounded in the Trinity: Suggestions for a Theology of Relationship to Other Religions," *T. Th.* 50/2 (1986): 260-78.

[20] Western theologians normally work within the framework of exclusivism-inclusivism-pluralism

[21] For a good summary of the various positions in the West's 'Theology of Religions', see, Jacques Dupuis, *Toward a Christian Theology of Religious Pluralism* (Anand: GSP, 2001): 180-201.

[22] See, for instance, Jung Young Lee, *The Theology of Change* (New York: Orbis, 1979), 114-9, where he explains how the Trinity can be understood in the *yin-yang* model of change that is a process of uniting and dividing; also his *The Trinity in Asian Perspective*, 213. Likewise, Chung, 139-41, also uses the symbol of *Yin-Yang* to explain the Trinity in Asian perspective

[23] See, A.M. Abraham Ayrookuzhiel, "Religion and Culture in Dalits' Struggle for Liberation," *R&S* 33/2 (June 1986): 33-44, who describes this religio-cultural universe as being alienating and oppressive.

[24] See, for e.g., Nirmal Minz, "Religion & Culture as Power in the Context of Tribal Aspirations in India," *R&S* 33/2 (June 1986): 45-54, who highlights the value and power of adivasi religion and culture, but also stresses that it must be backed by socio-eco-political structures to be effective for fostering community life.

[25] The Valmiki religion is a new religion that has a wide following in Ludhiana, Punjab. The adherents are former Dalits who protest against the caste system and do not wish to be called *Dalits* but *Valmikis*, after their deity also called *Valmiki*. The "India This Week" TV-news of Sunday, September 18, 2005 (21.00 hours) highlighted this religion with interviews of adherents who refused to be dominated by Brahmins.

[26] This is a flourishing brand of Christianity largerly found in Varanasi that seeks inspiration from the figure of Christ and the Bible. However, there is no baptism and other sacramental forms of worship, nor is there any central authority.

[27] Ilaiah, *Why I Am Not a Hindu*, 114-32, discusses an indigenous and assertive Dalit religio-cultural programme called *Dalization* that opposes the oppressive structures and programmes of Brahmanism; see also his *Buffalo Nationalism*, 101-20, part 5: "On the Right to Religion"; see also Michael Amaladoss, "Folk-Culture as Counter Culture: The Dalit Experience," *Jeevadhara* 24/139 (January 1994): 31-42.

[28] See, for instance, Omvedt, *Dalits and the Democratic Revolution*.

[29] See Remi Brague, "On the Christian Model of Unity: the Trinity," *CICR* 10 (Summer 1983), 153

[30] See Congar, 33-5. See also Moltmann, *The Trinity and the Kingdom*, 194-7 and Gunton, vol. I, 25. Eusebius's *De laudibus Constantini* [335], in which he describes the ideal of the Christian emperor, and *De vita Constantini* [337], whose first part was written for the 13th anniversary of Constantine's accession, are theological works with political overtones. God is the Father, the *Pantocrator*, resembling the Persian monarch. The *Logos*, who was the image of the Father-God, was believed to have ordered and preserved creation by his creation of a terrestrial empire as *eikon*, an image of the heavenly empire

[31] Prades, part II, 591; emphasis added.

[32] The Book of Genesis 1:26-7 depicts human beings as being created in the "image and likeness" of God. Kallistos of Diokleia, 15-6, also argues for equality and intercommunion among all on the basis of this text.

[33] See, for e.g., Metz, *ibid.*, Bonino, *ibid.*, also Jon Sobrino, *Spirituality of Liberation: Toward Political Holiness*, trans. R. R. Barr (New York: Orbis, 1988), who stress the necessity for a political theology. Such theology takes God's

involvement in history seriously, as seen in the events of salvation like the Exodus.

[34] See, for instance, Prabhakar, 414, where Jesus is described as 'Dalit' in his forsakenness on the cross.

[35] See, for e.g., Mundu, 266-8, where Jesus is 'Adivasi' in the sense of 'original inhabitant' of the cosmos and a 'blood-brother' through whose blood – that is same as ours – is shed to bring us all into communion.

[36] See Boff, *Trinity and Society*; also, Geevarghese, *Sharing God and Sharing World*.

[37] See, Boris Klyuev, *Religion in Indian Society: The Dimensions of 'Unity in Diversity'* (New Delhi: Sterling Publishers, 1989), for some of the characteristics of the Indian situation of unity in diversity.

[38] See, for instance, Philip L. Quinn, and Kevin Meeker, eds., *The Philosophical Challenge of Religious Diversity* (New York: OUP, 2000); Terrence W. Tilley, *Postmodern Theologies: The Challenge of Religious Diversity* (New York, 1995).

[39] In *Religion and Globalization*, 79-81; quote from p. 80.

[40] *Ibid.*

[41] Denis Edwards, "The Discovery of Chaos and the Retrieval of the Trinity," in *Chaos and Complexity: Scientific Perspectives on Divine Action*, ed. J. Russell et al., (Vatican City State: Vatican Observatory Publications and California: The Center for Theology and the Natural Sciences, 1997), 161.

[42] The *'Jai Adivasi* movement' is a movement started by the adivasis of south Gujarat to assert their *adi-vasi* (original inhabitant) identity as a revolt against the *Hindutva* campaign to call them *vanvasis*.

[43] The *dholak*-player provides rhythm with the homemade drum while the dancers go around in a circle.

[44] In his General Audience on January 26, 2000. See full text, "Trinity is Mysteriously Present in Creation," in *L'Osservatore Romano*, 2 February 2000, 11; italics added.

[45] See, for instance, Ian G. Barbour, *Myths, Models, and Paradigms: A Comparative Study in Science and Religion* (New York: Harper & Row, 1974), 71-5, for details of the wave-particle duality.

[46] See O'Murchu, "Beyond Our Isolation," in *Quantum Theology*, ch. 7, for details.

[47] *Ibid.*, 79; italics as in the original text.

[48] *Ibid.*, 82-3; italics added.

[49] See, Mundu, 229-98, for differences between the Christian sense of communion and that of communion among the adivasis. Basically, whereas the former communion is *theandric*, the latter is *cosmo-theandric*.

[50] See Vidyarthi and Rai, 239-41, for details.

[51] See Claus Westermann, *Genesis 1-11: A Commentary*, trans. J.J. Scullion (Minneapolis: Augsburg Publishing House, 1984), 158-60 for the whole argument; quote from p. 160, italics added.

[52] For care of creation and restoring ecological balance along trinitarian lines, see also George E. Tinker, "The Integrity of Creation: Restoring Trinitarian Balance," *ER* 41 (October 1989): 527-36.

[53] See, for instance, one such attempt by John W. Dixon, Jr., "Toward a Trinitarian Anthropology," *ATR* 80/2 (Spring 1998): 169-85.

[54] See, for instance, Patricia Wilson-Kastner, "The One and The Many" A Twentieth-Century Vision," *ATR* 76/2 (Spring 1994): 232-45, who discusses the problem of identity in a fast-changing world with its variety of lifestyles, epistemologies, theologies, etc. She writes: "A Trinitarian theology open to struggles with contemporary cosmology may offer us new insights about how a God who is essentially relationship relates to the interconnected cosmos" (p. 242).

[55] See what I have asserted about the "God of the Kingdom" in the previous chapter.

[56] Kallistos of Diokleia, 15-6, points out that the Epistle of Barnabas understands these words as addressed by God the Father to the Son; so also is the exegesis of Justin. Further, Theophilus and Irenaeus interpret this text as the Father speaking this to the Son and Spirit. The three persons are seen as 'taking counsel'.

[57] See Westermann, 147-61, for a detailed explanation of the passage; quote from p.158.

[58] See Col 1:15, that speaks of Jesus as "image of God", also Heb 1:3; Jn 14:9; Rom 8:29.

[59] See Lk 11:2 and Jn 20:17.

[60] See Gal 4:4-7 and Rom 8:29.

[61] Eck, *ibid.*, also stresses this point in the Indian context.

[62] Hans Urs von Balthasar sees the *kenosis* in terms of drama, which he calls *Theo-Drama*. See his *Theo-Drama*, vol. IV, 323: "The Father's self-utterance in the generation of the Son is an initial kenosis within the Godhead that underpins all subsequent kenosis. For the Father strips himself, without remainder, of his Godhead and hands it over to the Son; he 'imparts' to the Son all that is his."

[63] Jesus' life embraces nature, as well. He speaks about God's care of birds, lilies and grass (Mt 6:25-33) and of sparrows (Lk 12:6), and many of his stories are about sheep, seeds, fish, etc.

[64] See Gal 2:20.

[65] See, for instance, David Nicholls, "Trinity and Conflict," *Theology* 96 (1993): 19-27, who discusses the conflict present in the Trinity in the polarity of mercy and justice.

[66] See, for e.g., Hans Urs von Balthasar, "Creation and Trinity," *CICR* 15/3 (Fall 1988): 292, who writes, "The endurance of evil should not be considered as a means of accentuating the ever-greater love of God in the surrender of his Son (Jn 3:16), but at most as giving play to finite freedom until its finite end in order thus to reveal the unsearchable ways of God (cf. Rom 11:33). As part of this unsearchableness one would then also have to count the unimaginable pain of the Father which is the basis of his surrender of the Son."

[67] Randall B. Bush, "Trinitarian Conflict: A Re-assessment of Trinitarian Analogies in the Light of Modern Psychological and Sociological Conflict Theories," *PIRS* 19/1 (Spring 1992): 36-7; italics as in the text.

[68] Note Biblical passages like Gen 1:2; Ex 3:2, 19:18; Jn 4:10, 7:38-9; Acts 2:3-4.

[69] In the history of philosophy, fire and water are considered as primal elements of flux and power. See Samuel Enoch Stumpf, *Socrates to Sartre: A History of Philosophy* (New York: Mc-Graw-Hill Book Company, 1975), 5-16, for details about the ancient Greek philosophers, Heraclitus, who saw fire as the most basic unit, and, Thales of Miletus, who considered water as the basic stuff of the universe.

[70] See Biblical passages like Gen 2:7; Ezek 37:5 and Jn 20:22.

[71] See Jn 3:8: "The spirit blows where it wills, and you hear the sound of it..."

[72] In the Indian conception of power, when the 'spirit of the deity' resides in certain places and symbols, they are rendered 'hot' and must be cooled with water or milk; for e.g., the *Siva-lingam*. I am indebted to Dr. James Ponniah for this observation.

[73] We can think of Moses and the anointing of the seventy elders (Num 11:16-7); the anointing of prophets and kings, the 'laying on of hands' on the apostles and their successors (Acts 6:1-6), etc.

[74] Keith Ward, *God, Faith and the New Millennium: Christian Belief in an Age of Science* (Oxford: Oneworld Publications, 2002), 38.

[75] In this sense *Shakti* is also *Sakshi* ('Witness', in Hindu terminology). See Sahi, *Stepping Stones*, 68.

[76] The word '*Parakletos*' in Jn 14:16 can be translated as both, Counsellor and Comforter.

[77] This is best seen in the total transformation of Jesus' disciples after their empowering by the Spirit that changes cowardice into courage, fearfulness into fearlessness; see Acts of the Apostles (quote from 17:6).

[78] Nicholls, 25.

[79] See, Susan S. Wadley, ed., *Powers of Tamil Women* (New Delhi: Manohar Publications, 1991), 23-4.

[80] See, G. Aloysius, "The Study of Religion-in-Society: A View From Below," 11-5, for some of the characteristics of the 'religion of the oppressed'.

[81] See, for e.g., Oommen, *Protest and Change*; also Ghanshyam Shah, *Social Movements in India*.

[82] See, for instance, Dhanagare, *Peasant Movements in India*.

[83] See, for e.g., Omvedt, *Dalits and the Democratic Revolution*.

[84] See, for instance, Padmini Swaminathan, "Some Issues Confronting 'Women's Movement' in India," in *Dalits & Women: Quest for Humanity*, ed. V. Devasahayam (Madras: GLTCRI, 1996), 179-89.

[85] Beyer, 106, points out to the danger of institutionalisation that will prevent effective mobilisation.

[86] This term of Gramsci best expresses the Spirit function of being a sign of being 'contradictory' to evil.

[87] See also Aloysius, "Religion-in-Society: View From Below," 14-5.

[88] In some cases, there can also be a third ring atop the second.

[89] For Gujarat's Gamit adivasi community that uses the word '*Abba*' for 'Father', this is very appropriate.

[90] See Mt 6:28-30 and Lk 12:6-7.

[91] For a detailed and insightful commentary on this verse, see Westermann, 203-7.

[92] Ibid., 203, quotes P. Humbert: "The use of the substantive *yeser*, like that of the verb, begins with the potter's craft, i.e., its primary and basic meaning is concrete, plastic and technical ..." Westermann argues that this image is taken from the dominant Egyptian and Mesopotamian cultures of the time.

[93] Besides the Gen 2:7 imagery suggestive of the creation of humankind akin to a potter creating out of clay, see Is 62:8, that has the same image.

[94] Note that breath is a symbol of the Holy Spirit as, for example, in Jn 20:22.

[95] Westermann, 206, quotes H. Gunkel who adds, "Man is created from the ground and he is called to till the ground; his dwelling is on the ground and he returns to the ground when he dies."

[96] Ibid., 207.

[97] Von Balthasar, *Theo-Drama*, vol. IV, 329, speaks of: "[T]rinitarian 'recklessness' of divine love, which, in its self-giving, observed no limits and had no regard for itself." Such love is manifest in Jesus' cross.

[98] See Keith Ward, 32.

[99] See Bush, "Trinitarian Conflict," 36.

[100] See, for instance, Jensen's trinitarian critique of postmodernism, for a deeper understanding.

[101] A similar thought is expressed in Bush, "Trinitarian Conflict," 37.

[102] See Edwards, 175.

[103] *Monism* comes from the Greek 'one'. The word was coined by Christian Wolff (1697-1754) for attempts to interpret reality by eliminating diversity and distinctions (e.g., between body and soul or between the visible created world and the invisible God) Monists tend to reduce everything to one basic principle. Monists include Plotinus (c.205-70), Spinoza (1632-77) and idealist philosophers like Fichte (1762-1814) who reduce everything to the '*I*'. For further details, see O'Collins and Farrugia, *A Concise Dictionary of Theology*, 146-7.

[104] *Unitarianism* refers to the view that rejects the divinity of the Son and the Holy Spirit, and in defence of strict monotheism accepts only one divine person. Unitarianism was developed by Martin Cellarius (1499-1564), Michael Servetus (1511-53) and Faustus Sozzini (1539-1604). See *ibid.*, 255, for details.

[105] *Gnosticism* was a philosophy that emerged in the 2nd century A.D. that was dualistic and drew upon Jewish, Christian and pagan sources. It presented salvation as spiritual elements being freed from an evil material environment. Christian Gnostics denied Christ's real incarnation and the *salus carnis* (Latin, 'salvation of the flesh') he effected. See *ibid.*, 84, for details.

[106] *Manichaeism*, developed by Mani (c.215), was a dualistic philosophy that borrowed elements from Zoroastrianism, Buddhism, Gnosticism and Christianity. Manichaeism sought to free the spark of light in human beings and so deliver them from matter and darkness. See *ibid.*, 133, for further details.

[107] *Deshi-pardeshi* literally means 'of the country' juxtaposed with 'foreigner'. It is *Hindutva* ideologues' way of defining who belongs to the *Hindu Rashtra* and who does not.

[108] See, for e.g., the 4 dancers on the top rung of picture 8 should have 8 arms, but we only see 4, entwined.

[109] This sculpture is on the 'Hare Window' of the Paderborn Cathedral, Germany. The three hares totally have three ears; and yet, each hare has two normal ears. This is suggestive of trinitarian intercommunion.

[110] This dynamic has already been discussed in chapter 3 dealing with the negotiation of 'difference'.

[111] Soja, *Thirdspace*, 31, uses the term 'an-Other', and cites Lefebvre's French formulation: "*Il y a toujours l'Autre*" (meaning, "There is always the Other") as central to his theorising on spatiality.

[112] As mentioned earlier, the terms 'Third' and 'thirdspace' are also used by thinkers like Martin Buber and Homi Bhaba, to refer to God and a 'hybridity', respectively. I am merely using this term as Soja does.

[113] According to the Merriam-Webster's Collegiate Dictionary, the word 'scape' means "a view or picture of a scene" and usually appears as suffix to land as "landscape." See, for instance, J. Douglas Porteous, *Landscapes of the Mind: Worlds of Sense and Metaphor* (Toronto: UTP, 1990), who, describes many 'scapes': smellscape, soundscape, escape, childscape, deathscape and so on.

[114] The stance of 'extroversion' can also be located in the adivasi *naach* (dance) when the dancers go round in a circle but with their bodies and faces turned outwards. This could be called an 'outward movement'.

[115] Raimundo Panikkar, "There is No Outer without Inner Space," CC 43/1 (Spring 1993): 73.

[116] See Ilaiah, "On Education," in *Buffalo Nationalism*, 169-200, for insightful points on this issue.

[117] See, for instance, the official 'statement' of the *ITA* (Indian Theological Association) entitled "Dalits' Concerns and an Indian Theological Response: Statement of the Indian Theological Association Twenty-Eighth Annual Meeting," *VJTR* 69/11 (November 2005): 853-69. This document is an inspiring text. But, the point is, how it will work in *praxis*.

[118] The 'option for the poor' has been a slogan of the Jesuits – a Catholic religious congregation to which I belong – ever since VC II. In the intervening period of 40 years, I am sceptical about how much the relevant documents have affected both, the Jesuits, as well as the 'poor' they work for.

[119] I take *Churchscape* to simply mean "a view or picture of the Church."

[120] *Sahib* refers to 'master' and has connotations of superiority associated with colonialism.

[121] For e.g., included in a long list of alumni of Christian educational institutions, there are many politicians, diplomats and leaders who are often seen as 'communal', as well as 'anti-poor'.

[122] The Indian Christian community has been struggling over the years to secure reservations for those among its ranks who are of Dalit origin. Unfortunately, many Christians who do not belong to this group and who are powerful in the public sphere do not use their power and influence to rally for reservations for their less-fortunate brethren. For further details see the brochure *"Let Justice be done to all Dalits!"* (New Delhi: CBCI Commission for SC/ST/BC, 2009).

[123] Satish Deshpande and Geetika Bapna, Dalits is the Muslim and Christian communities. A status Report of current sociloa scientifc knowledge (New delhi: The National Commission fro Minorities Goverment of India, 2010), Who Substantiate with statistics that Dailt Muslim and Dalit Christian Suffer great social discremination when compared two there noni Dalit counter parts. Thus, their demands for reservations is fully justified.

[124] See, Wilfred, "Minority Rights and Minority Obligations: Some Theological Reflections,' in *The Sling of Utopia*, 230-48, for an insightful discussion on the issue of minority rights as regards the Indian Church.

[125] See Merrifield, 173.

[126] See John Paul II, *Compendium of Social Teachings of the Church*, October 25, 2004. The text is taken from the Vatican's *Zenit* news agency; italics are added to stress three vital points for the Indian context.

[127] See Lk 13:20-1 and Mt 5:13, where Jesus proposes the symbols of leaven and salt, respectively. The images of fragrance and aroma are also appropriate; see 2 Cor 2:15-6.

[128] See, 1 Tim 2:4: "God desires *all* to be saved," and Jesus saying that he came to save *all* (Mk 10:45).

[129] This word is best broken up into *response-ability*, because God's judgement will be based upon each one's 'ability to respond' as in the Good Samaritan story or in the parable of the Last Judgement.

[130] See Jesus' parable of the Good Samaritan (Lk 10:25-37). Interestingly, the one who acted *responsibly* was neither the priest nor the Levite, but the Samaritan, who, in our terms, can be seen as a despised one.

[131] See, for e.g., Leonardo Boff, "Trinitarian Community and Social Liberation," *CC* 38/3 (Fall 1988): 289-308 and Daniel L. Migliore, "The Trinity and Human Liberty," *TT* 36 (January 1980): 488-97.

[132] See Thomas D. Parker, "The Political Meaning of the Doctrine of the Trinity: Some Theses," *JOR* 60/2 (April 1980): 179 & 181.

[133] 'Dialogue' (Greek, *dialogos*, meaning 'through word') commonly refers to a conversation carried on between two or more persons or to a verbal interchange of thought between them.

[134] As literary form it is "a carefully organized exposition, by means of invented conversation, or contrasting philosophical or intellectual attitudes." See *New Encyclopaedia Britannica*, 15th ed., s.v. "Dialogue."

[135] See, for instance, Sarukkai, "The 'Other' in Anthropology and Philosophy."

[136] The *I-Thou* is the term popularised by French philosopher Martin Buber in a book by the same name.

[137] See, for e.g., Barnes, *Traces of the Other: Three Philosophers and Inter-faith Dialogue*.

[138] Note that I've already referred to these terms earlier and I'm not using *'thirdspace'* in that sense.

[139] This, of course, excludes Edward Soja who coins the word *Thirdspace* for use in the Lefebvrian sense.

[140] See his *Rhythmanalysis: Space, Time and Everyday Life*, trans. S. Elden and G. Moore (London & New York: Continuum, 2004), 12.

[141] One will immediately think of Hegel's 'synthesis' and Rawls's 'overlapping consensus', respectively. While not excluding them, *spatial trialectic* transcends these two concepts.

[142] See the use of the term *trilogue* by Jung Young Lee, *The Trinity in Asian Perspective*, 217-8, who writes: "The conscientization of religious inclusivity is the beginning of trilogue. If all human beings began with the first family on earth, and all religions are part of their cultural heritage, then everyone and every religion is connected to every other just as a great river is connected to many streams. In trilogue, many religions are in one religion and one religion is in many religions, because every religion bears the image of the Trinity." This definition appears to mean 'inclusiveness'. I develop *trilogue* differently.

[143] See Michael P. Wilson, "St John, the Trinity, and the Language of the Spirit," *SJOT* 41/4 (1988): 483

[144] Theologians like Panikkar, Abhishiktânanda, Geevarghese, D'Costa, Heim, and Cousins, mentioned earlier, all see in the Trinity or God's *tri-uneness* a paradigm for dialogue. See also Jacques Dupuis, "Trinity and World Religions," *CM* 35 (1971): 77-81, and, Daniel P. Sheridan, "Grounded in the Trinity: Suggestions for a Theology of Relationship to Other Religions," *T. Th.* 50/2 (1986): 260-78.

[145] Alistair McFadyen, "The Trinity and Human Individuality: The Conditions for Relevance," *Theology* 95/763 (1992): 15, develops this thought in terms of personhood and reciprocal delight-in-difference.

[146] Pope John Paul II's 1984-Document for the "Secretariat for Non-Christian Dialogue and Mission" reads: "The Church ... feels itself called to dialogue principally because of its faith. *In the Trinitarian mystery*, Christian revelation allows us to glimpse in God a life of communion and interchange." See ND, n.1042.

[147] One can think of passages like Mt 7:21 and Jn 13:14-7 whereby Jesus asserts the primacy of *action*.

[148] I distinguish between *faith* as staking one's all in something or someone and *belief* as an expression of that faith in propositions, creed, etc. This is somewhat like the distinction made by Ashis Nandy.

[149] Jon Sobrino, "Faith, Justice, and Injustice," in *The Pastoral Cycle Revisited*, ix, stresses the importance of "'getting a grip on reality', which requires us to be truly and actively involved in reality, affected by things as they are; it is not sufficient to be intellectually face to face with their meaning and concepts."

[150] This dynamics is similar to what is expressed in *ibid.*, xvii.

[151] This is the statement of 19th century Orthodox theologian, Nicolai Fedorov, quoted by Thompson, 106.

[152] This point is developed by Boff, "Trinitarian Community and Social Liberation," 306-7, who holds that all liberative activity must begin in the sites – in our case, the *spaces* – of the oppressed communities.

[153] William Hill, "Does the World Make a Difference to God?" *T.Th.* 38/1 (January 1974): 146-64, contests the view of God's immutability, since, if God

created the world and entered it in time (incarnation), God *was* and *is* concerned about the world. Human beings, then, are dialogic partners with God.

[154] Theologians like von Balthasar, Bracken, Moltmann and others have developed this point of *kenosis* in the Incarnation, as well as in the passion-death of Jesus.

[155] Michael Amaladoss, "Syncretism and Kenosis: Hermeneutical Reflections in the Indian Context," in *The Agitated Mind of God: The Theology of Kosuke Koyama*, ed. D. T. Irvin and A. E. Arkinade (New York: Orbis, 1996), 67.

[156] While Amaladoss uses the word *dialogue*, I hold that this is more in the nature of *trilogue*

[157] See, for instance, John D. Caputo, "Toward a Postmodern Theology of the Cross," in *Postmodern Philosophy and Christian Theology*, ed., M. Westphal (Bloomington, Indiana: Indiana University Press, 1999), 214-24, who describes the meaning of the cross from the postmodernist Derrida's point of view.

[158] Mitchell, *Spirituality and Emptiness: The Dynamics of Spiritual Life in Buddhism and Christianity*, chs. 1,3,4 develop creation, redemption and sanctification as the *'kenosis'* of the Father, Son, Sprit, respectively, and see points of convergence between Christianity's *kenosis* and Buddhism's *shunyata*.

[159] See Vattimo, 65. He sees the 'weak ontology' of *kenosis* as an antidote to secularisation of the present.

[160] Note that I use the term *interfaith responses* since all those truly committed to life share a 'faith' in the sense of 'ultimate concern' that I described earlier. This faith goes beyond religions to a deep humanism.

[161] See my distinction between *faith*, in general, and *religious belief*. 'Interfaith' includes everyone committed to life while interreligious refers to those who explicitly endorse some Absolute, normally, God.

[162] See von Balthasar, *Theo-Drama*, vol. IV, 322-8, for *first kenosis* (incarnation) and *second kenosis* (death).

[163] Sassen, *ibid.*, speaks of 'new geography of globalisation'.

[164] Jesus says, "You cannot serve God *and* mammon" (Mt 6:24). This is, obviously, an *either-or* option.

[165] This mandate of Jesus (Mt 10:16) flows from the preceding mission of 'The Twelve' (vv.1-15). The number 'Twelve' stands for Jesus' close *circle* of disciples and is thus symbolic of the Church he intended.

[166] For instance, I am a member of one such network, i.e., the 'Coalition for Secular Democracy' that makes people aware of social injustices and organizes action through signature campaigns, public rallies, letters to editors and politicians, etc.

[167] "Another World is Possible," is the slogan of the World Social Forum (WSF) that is an anti-globalisation gathering of peoples, worldwide, who protest against the policies of the G-8, WB, IMF and other MNCs. See my "Making a 'Mother World' Possible," *National Catholic Reporter Online* (USA), *Global Perspective* 1/41 (January 22, 2004), for some details on WSF - 2004 in Mumbai.

CHAPTER SIX

'Functional' Roles and Responsibilities of Subaltern Trinitarian Theology

6.1 Subaltern Trinity Challenging Church 'Functions'

Our subaltern trinitarian theological explorations have so far enabled us to critique and create new spaces and movements for Indian Christian communities to orient themselves towards *'performance'* action within the larger Indian nation-space. Subaltern trinitarian theology assumes that the Church is not only the 'mystical body' of Christ, but also a 'historical body' (*political community*) of the Trinity that carries the Kingdom-project forward in vibrant movements symbolized by the *naachnu*'s circular, counter and supportive movements. These movements signify interrelatedness, solidarity, harmony, sharing, interdependence, communion, faith, sacrifice and so on. We dance not only in a 'vertical communion' with the Trinitarian Community, but also in 'horizontal solidarity' with nature and all peoples, especially the poor. I have so far dealt with *extra-ecclesial* aspects of this communion. I now explore the *intra*-ecclesial possibilities, meaning, I try to see how subaltern trinitarianism could affect and alter the way we fulfill our roles and responsibilities as members of the 'minority' Indian Christian community: the church.

It might help us to very briefly point out some characteristics of the Indian Church, today: First, the Indian church comprises of a kaleidoscopic communion of 'churches' – majority, Catholic, and also including many other denominations with dazzling diversity as regards ethnic, linguistic, cultural, geographical and ritual composition. Second, although the diversity of the Indian church is its strength, it is not uncommon to hear of division and strife in terms of interdenominational rivalry, rallying for recognition of rites, power mongering, sheep stealing, caste and class factions, and the like. Third, Indian Christians are truly a 'minority' in terms of numbers and political influence;[1] and, of these, the subaltern groups – mainly, adivasis and Dalits – account for over 70% of the total Christian population. Fourth, the Indian church is a persecuted one. In chapter two, I mainly discussed the violence against Christian adivasis of south Gujarat's Dangs district. However, persecutions go on unabated till today, presently more noticeably in the Indian states of Orissa and Karnataka.[2] Fifth, Christian missionary intervention is mostly limited to education and health care. There is also sporadic developmental and social work going on in rural areas.

Having briefly mentioned the characteristics of Indian Christianity, and after seeing (in the previous chapter) the *'performance'* role that Indian Christianity can play, we will assess its current *functional* role and suggest ways of fostering it further. As background, we note that all religions seek from its adherents acquiescence to a set of beliefs, practice of certain rituals, adoption of an ethical code and the living out of a spirituality that sustains and 'saves' believers. Beyer stresses that conformity to religious *functions* not only assures salvation but also identifies *insiders* and distinguishes them from *outsiders*. In this sense, the *functions* of religious systems generate community and protect the particular religious group from what are seen as dangers to the cohesiveness and salvation of that religious community.[3] The performance and functional roles of religion are not mutually exclusive. I see them as capable of being harmonized with a *'both-and'* logic characteristic of this book. However, I have *prioritized the performance role* since, Indian Christianity has, ostensibly, been overly occupied with its *functional* role, often forgetting that it must *responsibly serve* not only Christians,[4] but all peoples, especially the oppressed. With this basic framework, I explore how subaltern trinitarian theology can affect the *functions* of Indian Christianity.

6.2 We Believe in a *Tri-Une* God: Subaltern Trinitarian Creed

While being monotheistic, the Christian creed is always *Tri-Une* or One-Three, i.e., "We believe in One God who is Father-Son-Spirit." While God's *tri-une-ness* is in eternal harmony and perfect communion, when we, humans, try to express this in theological representations and ecclesial dogmas, we become painfully aware of human finitude and the limits of our languages vis-à-vis the immensity and incomprehensibility of who we call 'God', The One above us, below us, around us, within us, before us, after us, beyond space-time-name-form. Therein lies the tension, which can never be resolved in language that is monistic or in categories that are dualistic. The former has led to isolation, hegemony and oppression, the latter, to dichotomy, confrontation and violent conflict. Thus, the Christian community has always tried to tread a 'third' way.

Down the centuries, the Christian Tradition has tried to express its belief in God by avoiding unitarian, as well as dualistic theological terminology. However, in that *spatial trialectic* that juxtaposes a *'both-and'* in a 'tense *thirdness'*,[5] it has articulated what Jesus has revealed, namely, God eternally abides, animates and acts in-from-through an interrelatedness and communion identifiable – as Kasper and Ratzinger have shown – by the relational, dialogal and personal terms: the *I-Thou-We* of human relationship, or, the Father-Son-Spirit of Christian revelation.[6] While the first two terms *reveal* God in incarnational and immanent terms (*Deus revelatus*), the third term, in a way, *conceals* God (*Deus absconditus*) in transcendence. Yet, God is present at, and acts from, the heights and the depths of the cosmos, since, "God is automatically active and present in *each and every* place of space and time."[7] This is so because God is *Creator, Re-Creator* and *Trans-Creator*.[8]

6.2.1   *Harmonizing the Historical and the Transversal*

Scripture reveals that human beings are created in God's "image and likeness." Today, it is unfortunate that we create God in *our* image and likeness. Thus, if current Christian belief and practice either thins down God to a 'Forgotten Trinity',[9] or if the so-called 'shy member' of the Trinity (Spirit) is erased from our creed,[10] or if the *motherly fatherliness* of *Abba* is distorted to depict a male despot, then nothing remains of Christianity. Conversely, subaltern trinitarian theology firmly roots God's presence and action in history,[11] and, "we are summoned to a quest for the historical God who takes our individual stories up into the total story of God and the world."[12] Subaltern trinitarianism stresses God's historicity, and locates God's presence in its most dynamic and everyday depiction of Life: the *naach*.

Stressing the historicity of God, as well as the Father-Son language in the Christian creed is problematic, as we pointed out earlier, especially in a Jewish or Muslim context. Here, "All suggestions of paternity or sonship in the physical sense should be avoided.... Language must be employed in such a fashion as to highlight the conviction that the Trinity is not a violation of God's unity, but rather a way of understanding that divine unity."[13] This is what we attempted to do. Moreover, in trinities like Hinduism's *Trimurti* (Brahmâ-Vishnu-Siva) and *Saccidânanda*, or Mahayana Buddhism's *Trikâya* (three bodies of Buddha), trinity is understood in a cosmological and symbolic sense and the historical is not stressed. But, subaltern trinitarianism always stresses the latter since, "God is said to be ontologically triune; transcendentally three persons. If it were not for the divine names 'Father', 'Son' and 'Spirit', we too would be forced to regard God as *nirguna*, entirely without positive attributes."[14] This too would create problems.

Attributing form to God (historicity) locates the Trinity here *below-and-beneath* all human endeavours. The Indian Church must resist and reject any translocation of religion from *lived space* to the *conceived spaces* of the purely intellectual, cognitive or mental. The Kingdom of God holds the *already-and-not yet* in a *spatial trialectic* that the Indian Church must capture and confess in its creed. Thus, in the movements of its dances, the melodies of its songs,[15] and in its retelling of the *kenosis-plerosis* trinitarian story in vernacular idiom,[16] the Indian Church must reecho a *here-and-now* historical happiness and liberation that will,[17] undoubtedly, be brought to final fulfillment in the *not-yet space* when all peoples will be able to synchronize and harmonize as sisters and brothers in the eternal *perichoretic naach*. In the interim period, the Christian creed must denounce sin as refusal to enter the spaces of the Trinity's liberating love, and a subversion of Kingdom space.

Much as the Christian creed articulates in *words* what the Church believes in, it also calls for *silence* in the face of trinitarian mystery. In this sense, the creed embraces the *spatial trialectic* of history-and-mystery, word-and-silence, intelligibility-and-unintelligibility in trinitarian tension. This ought to enable Indian Christians to profess a creed with the certainty that God's life and liberation have irrupted in history in the Christ-event (*Abba*-Word-*Shakti*). Nonetheless, the Church also humbly professes that God is beyond all its dogmas, icons and symbolic representations that, while revealing God as Trinity, calls Christians to profess also God's words and *Shakti* in the transversal spaces that are always within the action of *Shakti* who blows where She wills (Jn 3:8). Barnes believes that:[18]

> The Christian relationship with the other is conceived after the particular model of Christ's relationship with the God who is called Father, who is named by Christ in the very act of abandonment, by dying to self. But the God we dare to name after the manner of Christ is still '*the* Other', the God who is Spirit, and therefore beyond all names.

Thus, the creed provides the space for *trilogue* with even those who do not call God any name, but share in the omnipresent power of the Spirit-*Shakti*.

6.2.2   *Creedal Witness to the 'Three Hands of God'*

Word and Spirit have long been regarded as the "two hands of God,"[19] revealing Godself and God's action to humankind. This definition seems dualistic and tends towards subordinationism since: (a) it seems that only the Father has the fullness of God's *nature*, the other two divine persons being 'hands', and, (b) God's *activity* is limited to 'hands' – Jesus and the Spirit – while *Abba* is an apathetic, distant 'Head' who plans and directs the action without bothering to get involved in it. Subaltern trinitarianism spatially and symbolically differs from such imagery since, in a circular *naach* of three 'persons', six hands intertwine as apparently three arms, shoulder-to-shoulder (see *naach* pictures) with feet dancing step-in-step.[20] Moreover, the three voices and words of three persons (namely, *tri-logoi*) will coalesce into one harmony just as in a trilogy. Thus, subaltern trinitarianism professes a *Tri-Une* God symbolized by 'three hands', intertwined, with each divine dancer in the steps and songs of creation/support (*Abba*), relatedness/redemption (Son) and communion/contrast (*Shakti*).

Depicting God in *naach* with 'three hands' rectifies the 'two hands' imagery because the subaltern trinitarian story tells of a creative and caring potter-*Abba* who moulds wo/man with his own hands, a subaltern-Son who dared to stretch out his hands in love and service to all his oppressed sisters and brothers till the oppressors nailed them down, outstretched, upon a cross (*kenosis*), while *Shakti*'s hands of communion and contrast countered evil and injustice by raising up Jesus (*plerosis*). While the latter two divine activities are located mainly in the 'outside the camp' privileged space of the Trinity, the *kenosis* becomes 'the condition for the possibility' of constructing *all* human communities, as follows.

While the *tri-logoi* coalesce to make up the trilogy of the Christian creed, the 'three hands of God' intertwine to demonstrate Christian *praxis*, modeled upon the divine missions (which we'll see in the last part of this chapter). While this dynamic is *explicit* in Christian creedal formulations, it is *implicit* in what could be called the 'spirituality' or 'synergy'[21] animating all *movements* that are *Other*-centered and *an-Other*-centered. Thus, this creed could also be enunciated as a '*kenotic* spirituality' (Christianity), or a '*shûnyatâ* spirituality' (Buddhism) or a '*karuna* spirituality' (Hinduism) or a 'synergy of struggle' (for oppressed groups, in general), or a 'kenotic synergy' (for postmodernists or agnostics/ atheists). In view of this universal dynamic, which is articulated differently due to the finitude of human language and knowledge, we sense *trinitarian trilogue*: [22]

> In a Trinitarian spirituality, the interconnectedness among all creatures will be deeply felt. Its transcendent God remains distinct, yet hardly aloof. The Spirit breathes, surges and groans though all things.. ..And the groanings of the creatures, whose anguish she [Spirit] assumes, reveal that the natural world still suffers, still awaits liberation. By itself, nature hardly reveals God's loving goal. The love that directs all things – though glimpsed at times in human and other natural processes – is clearly revealed only in *the astonishing self-emptying of the cross*. Only from this vantage-point can those compassionate attitudes, which form part of both 'public' and Christian discussion ... be truly perceived and enkindled.

Christocentric creeds are often considered parochial and not really generative of unity and harmony among peoples since many people – as is the case in India – do not believe in Jesus Christ as God's son and saviour of the world. But, subaltern trinitarian creed could surely be seen as *differentiating-in-oneness*. In this sense, it is *unifying-in-diversity* and does not admit of anyone being *outsider* since everyone is *insider* and offered God's salvation. This is so because subaltern trinitarianism reaffirms the sacredness of all spaces and reveals the power accessible to those who dare join hands in the eternal divine dance of *kenosis-plerosis*. While Christians do this consciously and aware of their relatedness and redemption to the historical Jesus, those of other faiths interconnect to trinitarian movements by virtue of the spirituality-and-synergism symbolized by Spirit-*Shakti* who breathes and blows way beyond what Christianity considers its 'borders'. VC II's *GS* expresses this well:[23]

> All this holds true not only for Christians, but for *all people of goodwill in whose hearts grace works in an unseen way*. For, since Christ

died for *all* and since the ultimate vocation of all human beings is in fact one, and divine, we ought to believe that *the Holy Spirit in a manner known only to God offers to every person the possibility of being associated with this paschal mystery*

Note that the Spirit's action of association is offered only as 'possibility'. This is so because, while 'making space' for all faiths and movements,[24] God works within the horizon of human freedom because God has created humans beings as intelligent, *response-able* and free.[25] Herein arises the possibility of human beings, as individuals and community, condemning themselves to being *outsiders* by refusing to enter the 'counter space' and movements of *kenosis-plerosis*. Subaltern trinitarian theology thus becomes a critique for certain types of ideologies and movements – for e.g., Indian Christian fundamentalism, Hitler's German Nazism, Modi's *Hindutva Rashtra* or former US-President George Bush's *Americanist* 'messianic nationalism'[26] – motivated not by Self-emptying but by Self-aggrandizement, subordination and violent annihilation of the Other. Here, faithfulness to the Christian trinitarian creed necessitates critiquing and challenging such forms of community.

6.3 We *'Re-Present'* God: Subaltern Trinitarian Church and Cult

We saw how the trinitarian mystery of *kenosis-plerosis* unfolded 'outside the gate' and gradually turned into a trinitarian *movement* that transformed the lives not only of Jesus' apostles and disciples, but also of all those they encountered and evangelized, as well as of those given a direct divine *darshan*,[27] and incorporated into the 'body of believers' called 'church'. This church was not understood as some 'sacred structure', but a *communion* of minds, hearts and bodies.[28] This *communion (koinonia)* was manifest in a vibrant spirit of love and service *(diakonia)*,[29] celebrated in sacrament *(leitourgia)* that empowered them for witnessing to the Trinity,[30] even unto death by martyrdom *(marturia)*. We reiterate here that the circle of *koinonia* → *diakonia* → *leitourgia* → *marturia* traces the pattern of ecclesial communion that "comes from Christ's incarnation-baptism-passion and from a *Pentecost made constantly present.*"[31] I argued that Christ's incarnation-passion were trinitarian events, from which I developed subaltern trinitarianism. These core, salvific events, which were revealed in Jesus' historical body centuries ago, must be *re-presented* to the world, today, by his mystical body, the Church.

6.3.1   *Church as Trinity's Body Re-presenting Tri-Une Naach*

The Church is called the *mystical body* and *sacrament* of Christ[32] in the sense that it historically-socially-spatially *re-presents* the crucified-risen God carrying the cosmos to final fullness. In terms of music-dance-drama, the Church tries to coordinate and connect the first movements (overture) of creation – when *Abba-Word-Shakti* spoke-intertwined-breathed outside of Godself, respectively, to bring cosmos into LIFE –[33] with the final movements (curtain call) of cosmic completion when all will *"be gathered before God,"*[34] who will be *"everything to everyone."*[35] The Church is therefore like leaven and salt for the realization of the Reign of God.

Before creation, *Abba-Son-Shakti* danced in reciprocal, *perichoretic* delight. But, God's love-life-freedom found expression in God replicating, or, one could say, *re-presenting* Godself in the 'dance of creation' (*first kenosis*). In God's Son, Jesus, becoming human, God's second dance movement (*second kenosis*), i.e., the 'naachnu of re-creation' is revealed. Symbolically, in the incarnation-birth, God neither assumes the singular grace of an Indian classical dancer nor the consummate couple-coordination of many Western dances, but God begins a communitarian, subaltern *naach outside the camp* culminating in Calvary.

Jesus' body spatially *sacramentalizes* Trinitarian nature and activity *outside the camp*.[36] But, in the *second kenosis* Jesus begins God's *'naachnu circle'* connecting despised partners (shepherds, fisherfolk, tax collectors, pagans and prostitutes),[37] dangerous *movements* (defiled dining, talking to pagan women, cleansing temples and working on Sabbaths)[38] and subversive songs ("Blessed are you, poor! I desire mercy, not sacrifice! Neither on this mountain nor in Jerusalem, … but, God is spirit, and you must worship in spirit and truth!").[39] Intertwined between his human friends, Jesus discloses the divine dancers as *Abba*-Himself/Son-*Shakti* and God's eternal plan of *re-creating* the cosmos as family called 'Kingdom of God' with 'church' as a living, dance-movement of prophets and servants. The *third kenosis* (passion-death) seems to destroy God's whole *naach*, but the *plerosis* (resurrection) not only puts Jesus' life and Kingdom-plans in perspective but launches in motion the *'naachnu of trans-creation'* that is the Church's responsibility to bring to cosmic completion, by countering anti-Kingdom and anti-God movements. This is similar to what Russian theology terms a *'kenosis of the Spirit'*.[40]

Consonant with the preceding vision, the Church is a 'derived mystery' since "the solar mystery of perichoretic communion in the

Trinity sheds light on the lunar mystery of the church."[41] Church thus becomes an 'image'[42] or 'icon'[43] that *re-presents* the Trinity. Centuries ago, Cyprian (c.200-58 A.D.) wrote: "The Church draws unity from the unity of Father, Son and Spirit."[44] Likewise, the ecclesiology of VC II envisaged the Church as "a people made one with the unity of the Father, the Son, and the Holy Spirit."[45] In subaltern trinitarianism this unity is pictured as an interconnected *naach* at many levels:[46]

> [C]hurch is both one and many, a unity in diversity and diversity in unity. The local and universal church share in the perichoresic ontology and *communio* of the Trinity and the incarnation. Just as the three persons of the one God must be understood as dancing together, ... so must the local and the universal church be understood as dancing together in joyful communion.

Here, the dance circle is 'ecumenical' since it embraces local and universal churches.[47] Ecumenical communion must always be dynamic, joyful and rooted in trinitarian love.[48] Thus, ideally, Indian local churches should retain their socio-cultural specificities without breaking the One Body (1 Cor 12), without disrupting the Tri-Une, divine-human dance. It is sad that churches in India, today, neither have any activities in common nor network in their ministries. Growing individualism and isolation is the bane of the Indian Church, today.

Subaltern trinitarian theology also makes us reflect on *Churchspace*. Many oppressed Indian Christian communities are so poor that they cannot afford to construct a 'church building' of mortar and bricks; but, their own entwined and intertwined bodies, shrunken, skeletal and broken with overwork truly *is* Church-Body.[49] Apart from this socio-physical brokenness, there is the religio-moral-spiritual brokenness of those who exploit and divide that makes the Church's 'Wounded Body' bleed. Here, the Church prays to the Spirit-*Shakti* to unify broken limbs as once it unified alien tongues.[50] The *Shakti* of communion helps churches reach some consensus in their dissent and divisions: "the consensus of a wounded body, a consensus on 'things necessary', not on everything."[51] These 'things necessary' could be held together in the *tension of trilogue*.

6.3.2 *Sacraments as Spatiotemporal Celebrations of Life*
The cosmic-human-divine *naach* invests all times and places with a sacredness. However, being finite and fallible, we are often unaware of God's presence and action in our world. Sacraments are symbolic, ritual

actions that bridge this gap and bring about this awareness. Christian sacraments must always be modeled upon the Trinity who makes us aware of our anchoring in *Abba,* and our being moved arm-in-arm, step-by-step in the circular movements of Brother-Jesus and counter movements of Sister/Mother-*Shakti.* Sacraments are prophetic, symbolic actions of the Trinity's historical-mystical body, the Church, instituted by Jesus Christ in tandem with Spirit-*Shakti*, to proclaim, celebrate and realize the life, love and liberation of the Kingdom of *Abba*-God.[52] Note that all sacraments symbolize *movement* and *passage*[53] since they are *liminal* symbolic actions,[54] as well as "basic social acts."[55] And as basic social acts or 'symbolic communitarian actions' sacraments wield great power in building or breaking community, legitimizing oppressive structures or liberating oppressed societies.[56] Furthermore, every sacrament is signed or marked with a *kenosis-plerosis* structure, movement and praxis.
.

Like the drummer dancing in the centre and providing rhythm to the *naach*, the Eucharist drums out *Eucharistic thirdspace* and invites Christians into its circle for trinitarian trilogue in all its movements that weave *kenosis-plerosis* in visible and vibrant variations.[57] Theologians have stressed the inseparable bond between Eucharist and Trinity.[58] In addition to this, subaltern trinitarianism brings *spatial trialectic* into salience, namely, Trinity → Church → World dynamically interrelate the 'three hands of God', and all three are needed for Christians to constructively commit themselves to the *Naach of Life* designed by *Abba*-Son-*Shakti.* In other words, it is the Father, *Abba*, who calls all God's children to come to, and be nourished at, the 'two tables' where The Word will be broken (lectern-pulpit) and The Bread-Cup will be shared (altar) so that, nourished at these two tables, God's children can be 'sent out' (Latin, *missa*) to nourish and be nourished at the third table, the 'table of the world'.[59] Indeed, in its liturgical-sacramental life, the Church is always called in (as community) and sent out (*com-mission-ed*) in the trinitarian dynamics to spread the good news (gospel).

One senses that, in terms of spatiality, when compared to many others, adivasi churches more powerfully proclaim, celebrate, realize Trinitarian Eucharistic presence-action since there is often no church (building) but people come in to *make church*, so to say, dancing the *naach*, arms-intertwined in communion and solidarity. Once begun, there is a lot of singing, dancing (offertory, *doxology*) and clapping of hands. Here, the *kenosis-plerosis* is not some theological *conceived space*, but *Thirdspace* where *Abba-Pahelo Vasavo-Shakti*[60] is seen communing with sunburned bodies squatting or dancing deftly upon earth. The community *lives into* the symbol of broken bread: "fruit of the earth and work of human hands" soon to become "Bread of Life."[61] After the priest's dismissive "Go, the Mass is ended!" exhortation, nourished by 'Bread of Life', the whole adivasi community sings and dances late into the night.

At night, the adivasi *naach* unfolds in the village's *lived space* at the interstices of a hard day's work and a brief night's rest,[62] *interspaced* with a consciously celebrative Mass tying up and *triloging* God-Earth-community in the *Naach of Life*. All other sacraments that Catholics celebrate can spatially be located around the Eucharist with earthy symbols of *diyas*,[63] water, oil, garland of flowers, *mangalsutra*,[64] sign of the cross, laying on of hands, etc. All these sacraments are, at heart, symbolic, prophetic acts of being consecrated and commissioned by *Abba* to interconnect with the prophetic, servant-modeled Kingdom-mission of the Son in the power of *Shakti*. However, such idealized thinking seems sterile in the face of (a) factions among the 'faith-full' and (b) power-play of pastors. Three observations are pertinent here.

First, apart from the token, annual 'Octave of Prayer for Christian Unity', little is done to foster ecumenical prayer and sacramental celebration. VC II had explicated:[65]

> As for common worship, however, it may not be regarded as a means to be used indiscriminately for the restoration of unity among Christians. Such worship depends chiefly on two principles: it should *signify the unity of the Church*; it should provide *a sharing in the means of grace*. The fact that it should signify unity generally rules out common worship. Yet the gaining of a needed grace sometimes commends it.

As 'sign of unity' intercommunion would be farcical at present because of the prevailing disunity and divisions among churches. In this case, we would be able to celebrate sacraments together only *after* restoring full unity. But, sacraments are salvific realities that *actualize grace*, too, and hence *cause* the grace of unity and reconciliation. Thus, intercommunion should be fostered, for, the grace of unity would flow from the liturgy.

Second, in the Indian context, the question of 'interfaith'[66] prayer and celebration of the Eucharist is problematic. We make a finer distinction between 'multireligious prayer' and 'interreligious prayer'[67] In the former, there is *no* public comprising of different religions *praying together* but a respectful witnessing of each other in prayer, whereas, in the latter, a whole group comes together to plan, prepare and *pray together* with each member of the group rightly claiming that the prayer is her/his own prayer to God. A *'subaltern trinitarian theology of religions'*, we have seen, enables Christians to be analysts for assembling *all* peoples for group prayers and religious rituals. However, the modalities have to be wisely worked out so that sacramental actions truly remain prophetic proclamations and symbolic celebrations of Life rather than degenerating into ritualism and legalism.[68]

Third, while priests are expected to be 'images' of Christ (*alter Christus*) who is a *God in/of movement*, they are often preoccupied with seeking property, pleasure and power for themselves. They become pawnbrokers of the 'religion of power'. Rowan Williams warns about a "corrupt politicization of faith by the religiously powerful," and adds, "The Christian church ought to carry in its language and practice a deep suspicion of the alliances between hierarchies in faith-communities and hierarchies in absolutist political administrations – Caiaphas and Pilate, and their many more recent analogues."[69] Subaltern trinitarianism is suspicious of such alliances and hierarchies. VC II's "Decree on the Bishops' Pastoral Office in the Church" (*Christus Dominus*) portrayed bishops – formerly regarded as rulers and princes – as pastors, shepherds, servants of the Church.[70]

In the Indian context, there seems to be much 'symbolic dissonance' between what Church 'shepherds-servants' (bishops/priests) wear as clerical dress, and what *outside-the-camp* shepherd castes like Gujarat's *Govaliyas* and *Bharwads* wear. Here, Church leaders require a deeper sense of service and love. Subaltern trinitarian theology envisages "a church that is more communion than hierarchy, more service than power, more circular than pyramidal, more loving embrace than bending the knee before authority."[71] This spatial imagery challenges the Church and priests to live out *kenosis*.

6.4. We *Kenosize-Plerosize* in God: Subaltern Trinitarian Conduct

Besides the *religious functions* of *creed* (beliefs) and *cult* (rituals), in the context of globalisation, religions also propose a moral *code* (ethics) that influences their involvement in the private realm of home, and the public sphere of politics, economics, and other spheres of human activity. Christianity also calls this kind of involvement as 'mission'. I believe that, in the field of morals and ethics, Indian Christianity can learn much from the basic dynamic of *kenosis-plerosis* that is at the heart of subaltern trinitarian theology. Let us now discuss how this theology can animate Indian Christian morality[72] and mission in today's world.

6.4.1 *Kenosizing Personal/Ecclesial Space: Subaltern Trinitarian Ethic*

In Christian terminology the subalterns are the 'little ones' who Jesus called *the least* (Mt 25:40,45). Indian Christianity is characterized by littleness in the sense that it is, and will always remain, a 'minority' in India. Moreover, on the one hand, as we have stressed, a large majority in this minority belongs to the underprivileged communities like Dalits and adivasis, and on the other, many Church leaders either boast about belonging to the high castes and classes, or, by virtue of their 'Fr.' or 'Rev.' prefixes seek alliances with rich and powerful communities. But, subaltern trinitarianism puts all Christians, as individuals and community, in trilogue with the triad: Self →*Kenosized Other* →Kenotic Trinity.[73]

The preceding trilogue juxtaposes Self (individual/group), the *Kenosized Other* (i.e., the *Least* in *social space*), the Kenotic Trinity symbolically in a *Naach* of Life. Concretely, this trilogue involves doing a 'hermeneutic of the cross', where the privileged space is 'outside the camp', the song is a cry of God-forsakenness, and the circular movement is broken and frustrated with the brokenness and folly of the cross. Ideally, since the Church 'images' Jesus' historical body, it must always be ready to be 'outside the camp' nailed to crosses not in passive resistance (cowardice), but, as explained earlier, as a courageous *faith option* for what it considers to be Ultimate: God-gifted Life itself. It is not by mere accident that the persecutions of Indian Christians is taking place among the 'last and the least' in remote villages, among unknown peoples like the Vasavas and Dangis of Gujarat, and the Panos and Kandhs of Orissa.[74] It is these present-day 'martyrs' who, like the great missioner and martyr Paul can say: "We are persecuted, but not forsaken; struck down, but not destroyed; always carrying *in the body* the death of Jesus, so that the life of Him may also be visible *in our bodies*" (2 Cor 4:9).

By perennially putting Church/Christians arm-in-arm with the *Kenosized Other*, quite literally "on the one hand," and the Kenotic God, on the other, Christianity is challenged to fall in line, step-by-step in God's subaltern *Naach of Life*. This involves trinitarian tension, and if one evades it, one could spatially find oneself on the "left hand of Jesus, the King" at Last Judgment (Mt 25). Thus, being hand-in-hand with *Kenosized Other-and-God* means making many movements – outside the camp, nailed to the cross, circling with the Son, countering with *Shakti*, supporting with *Abba*, crying in pain and forsakenness, etc. It involves 'making room'[75] or 'opening spaces' or 'contraction of the ego'[76] or "allowing oneself to be crushed by the other."[77] In subaltern trinitarianism this could be termed as '*kenosizing*' – defined as "*Downsizing the Self* to dance in tandem with the *Kenosized Other*-and-Kenotic Trinity." This is a basic 'kenotic' moral principle of subaltern trinitarianism.

Simple though *kenosizing* sounds, when applied to daily life, it could be very difficult and challenging. In *perceived space*, it could concretely demand downsizing of religious institutions, making elite educational institutions more accessible to the poor, downsizing church properties and ecclesiastical budgets, breaking the dividing walls of caste/class in churches and graveyards,[78] denouncing the appointment of ecclesiastical personnel on the basis of class and community,[79] etc. In *conceived space*, it would mean 'producing space' that combats society's Ego-inflation and narcissism.[80] Morality would be seen in trilogue embracing suffering humanity-Trinity-self within the framework of the ultimate symbol of power, the cross,[81] which, ironically, is "the power and the wisdom of God" (1 Cor 1:24) and the basic grammar of Christian *kerygma* (1 Cor 2:1-5). In *social space*, it could entail a total demolition of our obsolete – and we could say narcissistic and 'immoral' – way of resuscitating a former 'colonial Christendom' replete with holier-than-thou attitudes, arrogantly placing the institutional Church as 'centre' whom all must serve and to which all must submit. Rather, we must remember that the Church is always the servant, prophet, pastor of the Kingdom of God, and not vice-versa. This brings us to the question of mission.

6.4.2 *Plerosizing Planetary Space: Subaltern Trinitarian Mission*

From a subaltern trinitarian ethic we derive a subaltern trinitarian understanding of mission. While subaltern trinitarian morality enjoins Indian Christians to undergo a process of *kenosizing*, it exhorts the Church to *plerosize* our planet by *being* leaven-salt-aroma (*aniconic* representations) and *being* pastor-servant-prophet (*iconic* representatives of trilogue). *Plerosizing* could be seen as, "Upholding the *Kenosized Other* to dance in tandem with the *Kenosized Self*-and-Trinitarian *Pleroma*." While *Kenosized*

Other is the *least*, as mentioned above, Trinitarian *Pleroma* refers not only to human beings, but also to the whole cosmos *groaning* and awaiting glorification when God will be *everything to everyone* (Rom 8; 1 Cor 15). Indeed, like the sacredness of subaltern *tri-une spatiality*, nothing and no one can be left out of sacred trinitarian mission because God embraces all. Today, we're thinking of a "theology of the *noosphere*, a *noospheric* theology", which:[82]

> [It] will have the *noosphere* as its framework and centre of gravitation, beyond the short-winged visions fragmented into countries, races, cultures, religion, etc. It will not even have an anthropocentric vision or be limited only to what is human. Rather it will be open to nature, the planet, to the cosmos, to the mystery of all reality.

While the movement of morality is *inward* (introspection and opening self-space) and *upward* (gazing at the crucified Jesus), the movement of mission is *outward* (involvement and creating other-space) and *downward* (glorifying God for the *plerosis* and resurrection taking place in the *here-and-now*). Taken together, subaltern trinitarianism necessitates a *kenotic movement of introspection and conversion* (morality) and a *plerotic movement of involvement and commitment* (mission). This is so, because unless the Church/Christians convert Self, any attempts to move outward and convert Other, uphold the downtrodden or *plerosize* the cosmos will be futile, perhaps, even destructive of God's creation.

The mission of Indian Christians, then, is to form Kingdom communities based on principles of equality-difference (Son's circular movement) and support all liberative movements (*Abba*'s supportive movement). It is also vital for the Church to be boldly 'counter' the current (*Shakti*'s counter movement). This means living out *in the Body* a 'counter paradigm of power' (*kenosis-plerosis*), and, to be a 'counter-cultural' community,[83] as follows:[84]

> A counter-cultural community . has to be involved in bringing about a transformation of the present world. It does not represent an absolute or otherworldly future; it suggests an alternate way in which people can live here and now. Its witness is *rooted in history* and seeks to change its course. It will necessarily *get involved in peoples' movements*. Its favourite self-images will be *leaven or salt or light*. It does *not avoid conflict*. But its conflict will be in the perspective of community. It does not rely on political, economic or military power. Its strength is in its moral power based on truth and love.

Thus, while Christian mission is to create Kingdom-community based on truth and love, it must never avoid conflict and '*trilogal* tension' for it also demands justice, which will entail *kenosis* at every step and every movement. But in the very act of Self-giving, the Church will also experience *plerosis* not as a distant possibility but as a present reality.

Compared to this ideal *conceived space* of subaltern trinitarianism, Christian history shows that there have been conflicts in the Universal and the local churches. First, instead of facing the conflicts of sin, evil and injustice and seeing the Church as being 'sent out' on mission, the Church has been enmeshed in centuries of conflict discussing whether the Spirit proceeds from the Father, or from Father *and* Son (*filioque*).[85] Even today theologians are engaged in controversies whether trinitarian mission is first revealed through Christ or through the Spirit.[86] Subaltern trinitarian theology deems such questions irrelevant and alienating. But, it is important that Indian Christians/churches understand mission as "simply making God (for us, with us, in us) known through (their) life, the proclamation by the icon of the Icon-maker who redeems."[87] In other words, *we are trinitarian icons* who image and serve God, radiate and respond to God's Love, and thus '*re-present*' God in the world, today.

It is unfortunate that, at times, church personnel and missioners find themselves 'out-of-step' with the subaltern communities they supposedly serve. For instance, taking the context of south Gujarat, some years ago an exercise in *introspection on missionary interventions* revealed that:[88] (a) such interventions are frequently animated by Christian 'charity' that is at best, paternalistic and patronizing, and at worst, demeaning, (b) such approaches are not incarnational and result in conflicts, cultural invasion, lopsided development and unhealthy dependency, (c) there is no reference to equality, participation, democracy, accountability and integral liberation in such approaches.[89] Interestingly, as if to prove the above, it is noticeable that, when most Church personnel try to join in the adivasi *naach* circle, they often disturb the adivasi rhythm and the dance gets disrupted!

It is perhaps time to accept that the Indian Church has *not listened* sufficiently to the voices of its people and not understood the signs of the times-places-peoples, but has busily been consolidating itself in *perceived space* with more buildings, boarding-schools, chapels and hospitals. Subaltern trinitarian theology therefore: (a) calls the Church to *listen* to its songs and silences, or in the words of Lefebvre, to be a *rhythmanalyst* who, "will listen to the world, and above all to what are disdainfully called noises, which are said without meaning, and to murmurs, full of meaning – and finally listen to silences."[90] (b) to be not merely 'counter cultural' but ultimately 'counter spatial' – i.e., *re-creating* and supporting God's *Naach* in its extraordinary outreach.

6.5 Conclusion: The Divine Dance must go on

This chapter has discussed the *functional* roles and responsibilities – as regards creed, cult, conduct and mission – that Indian Christians, and the Indian Church, at large, ought to shoulder. From the subaltern perspective, I have *trilogued* with the *Self* (Indian Church), the *Kenosized Other* (disprivileged communities) and *Kenotic Trinity* (God of the poor) in the historical processes that promise to bring about *Pleroma*. By so doing, I have attempted to develop a catholic trinitarian theology that is fully catholic (universal)-*and*-fully contextual (particular). Through the many movements of this contextual approach to theology, I have highlighted 'trinitarian tension'.

Community will ever remain, in a way, with its creative conflicts, but since we are created in the image and likeness of a loving, Self-giving God, who continues to struggle with us, we also find ourselves caught up in the eternal-and-down-to-earth *Trinitarian Naach*: "the dance of giving and yielding in the endless production of a series of personal missions that makes us each distinct while uniting us."[91] Truly, we are all called to construct community and resolve conflicts arm-in-arm, step-by-step with *Tri-Une* God (*Abba*-Son-*Shakti*) who anchors, adopts, animates and activates all peoples – especially the poor and powerless, with three hands – in circular, counter and supportive movements of the Life's *Naachnu*. This Divine Dance must go on. With help from you and me.

ENDNOTES FOR CHAPTER SIX

[1] Despite allegations from fundamentalist groups that the Christian population in India is fast increasing, the percentage has never gone up more than 2.5% of the total population. In the 1991 census it was 2.35%, in 2001 the corresponding figure was 2.34%. In terms of numbers, this is roughly 23 million Christians. Of these, Dalits account for 16 million and adivasis for 2 million. Catholics account for about 1.9%.

[2] See my "Carrying in Our Body the Marks of His Passion," *VJTR* 72/11 (2009): 801-7, for my analysis and reflections on the persecutions of Christians in Orissa's Kandhamal District. A monthly *'Persecution Update'* is published by the Global Council of Indian Christians (GCIC) giving updates of the cases of violence. I feel that these persecutions will never end, and, might even be an occasion for deeper reflection of Christian mission, as well as a time to be more deeply committed to what Jesus lived and died for.

[3] See Beyer, 81-6, for details.

[4] The word 'responsible' is used since it is more suggestive of an ethical imperative rather than 'role'.

[5] The word 'tense' is intentionally used since the *Third* is the point when community is actually formed, and yet, as we saw in our development of *'trilogue'*, trinitarian thinking is always tinged with tension.

[6] Walter Kasper, *The God of Jesus Christ* (London: SCM Press Ltd, 1992), 290, writes, "The three divine persons are not only in dialogue, they *are* dialogue." Kasper claims that this has more fully been explained by Joseph Ratzinger who holds that God is a dialogical being – a Being "who lives in the Word and subsists in the Word as I and Thou and We."

[7] Welker, 323. On p.328 he holds: "God's eternity and God's temporality thus proves itself to be an important key to opening up and developing Trinitarian Theology. In differentiated ways, it can make us understand how God involves the creatures in God's actions and includes them in the divine liveliness."

[8] See the insight of Philip Rosato mentioned in endnote no. 139 in chapter 4.

[9] See "The Forgotten Trinity," *Report of the BCC Study Commission on Trinitarian Doctrine Today.*

[10] Frederick Dale Bruner and William Hordern, *The Holy Spirit: Shy Member of the Trinity* (Minneapolis: Augsburg Publishing House, 1984), 14, speak of not the shyness of self-centredness, but that of an other-centeredness, which makes it all the more easy for Christians to forget the Holy Spirit!

[11] See Hill; also, John Milbank, "History of the One God," *THJ* 40 (1999): 301-18.

[12] See Arthur H. Williams, "The Trinity and Time," *SJOT* 39/1 (1986): 65-81, who stresses that the economic doctrine to the Trinity is a theology of what God has done and is doing and will do in history.

[13] Yoder, 343. He also points out that Muslim understanding of the Trinity will be achieved largely as the truths and qualities that the doctrine represents are consistently present in the life of the Christian witness.

[14] Kaiser, 309.

[15] Clarke, 140-78, speaks of *"drumming up* representational space for subaltern religious expression."

[16] R.S. Sugirtharajah, *The Bible and the Third World: Precolonial, Colonial and Postcolonial Encounters* (U.K.: CUP, 2001), 228-39, speaks of "texts as vehicles of emancipation" for Dalits and women.

[17] See Tad Dunne, "Trinity and History," *TS* 45/1 (March 1984): 139-52, for a good discussion on the need to stress the Trinity in history as seen in the dialectic between the action of Word and Spirit.

[18] Michael Barnes, *Walking the City: Christian Discipleship in a Pluralist World* (Delhi: ISPCK, 1999), 110.

[19] The phrase "two hands of God" was first used by Ireneus (c.115-90) to speak of the Word and the Spirit.

[20] This is like the 3 hares sharing only 3 ears. This also symbolizes what we termed 'trinitarian tension'.

[21] Synergy (Greek, *synergos*), refers to a 'working together' generating energy. It is used instead of the word 'spirituality' (apt for those with 'religious faith') since the latter may be unacceptable to a person who asserts that s/he is committed to *movements* not for any 'spiritual' motive, but for the cause of humankind.

[22] Finger, 207-8; italics added.

[23] See GS, n.22; italics added. I am grateful to two of my former professors, Archbishop Luis F. Ladaria and George Gispert-Sauch for their insightful comments on this central passage dealing with the 'Other'.

[24] See George Gispert-Sauch, "A Note on GS 22," *VJTR* 59/2 (1995): 126-31, for a connection made between the paschal mystery and struggles for justice.

[25] The Catholic Church recognizes human freedom. See, for e.g., VC II's *Dignitatis Humanae* (n.2), which reads, "[T]he human person has a right to religious freedom. This freedom means that all wo/men are to be immune from coercion on the part of the individuals or of social groups and of any human power, in such wise that in matter religious no one is to be forced to act in a manner contrary to her/his beliefs .. whether privately or publicly, whether alone or in association."

[26] See Rosemary Radford Ruether, "Is There a Need for a New Barmen Declaration?" unpublished internet article, who speaks of an *Americanist Messianic Nationalism* in the context of North American invasion of Iraq and Bush's stance of pretending to pontificate as the inspired voice of Christian conscience.

[27] See, for instance, the conversion of Paul that was a direct *divine darshan* described in Acts 9:1-22.

[28] 'Church' (Latin, *ecclesia*) and its equivalents – *kirche* (German), *chiesa* (Italian), *igreza* (Portuguese), *dharmasabha* (Gujarati), etc. – are more associated with 'body' or 'assembly' rather than 'building'.

[29] See Joseph A. Bracken, "The Divine Pleroma," *Chicago Studies* 26/1 (April 1987), 34-6, who explains *koinonia* and *diakonia* in terms of these being the

ideals that must characterize any trinitarian community.

[30] This is best seen in NT descriptions of the early Christian community, for e.g., Acts 2:42-7, 4:32-7.

[31] Yves M. Congar, *The Word and the Spirit*, trans. D. Smith (London: Geoffrey Chapman and San Francisco: Harper & Row, 1986); italics added.

[32] Such ecclesiology is well developed by Heribert Mühlen, *Una Mystica Persona. La Chiesa Come il Mistero dello Spirito Santo in Cristo e nei Cristiani: Una Persona in Molte Persone* (Rome: 1968).

[33] We refer to the act of creation as explained earlier (Gen 1:1-2, 26-8; 2:7; 3:19) with earthy symbols. *Abba* speaks and moulds; Word-Son is spoken and intertwines in circular movement; *Shakti*-Spirit is breathed and blows wherever She wills. 'LIFE' (capitals) refers to all of life: divine, cosmic, human.

[34] 'Be gathered before God' is symbolic of the Last Judgment (Mt 25:32) when all will come before God.

[35] See 1 Cor 15:1-28 that provides an overview of the history of salvation.

[36] Note, for instance, how theologians like Schillebeeckx and John Robinson consider Jesus as 'Sacrament of the encounter with God,' and the 'Face of God,' respectively.

[37] See, Lk 2:8,15, 4:18-20; Jn 8:3-11, etc.

[38] See Lk 19:1-10; Jn 2:13-22, 4:5-42, and other passages.

[39] See Mt 5:3; 9:13; Lk 6:20; Jn 4:21-4, and so on.

[40] This is explained by Boris Bobrinskoy, "Models of Trinitarian Revelation," *SVTQ* 39/2 (1995): 124-6.

[41] Boff, "Trinitarian Community and Social Liberation," 307-8.

[42] Miroslav Volf, *After Our Likeness: The Church as the Image of the Trinity* (Grand Rapids: Eerdmans, 1998), discusses the ecclesiology of Zizioulas and Ratzinger, and sees the Church as image of the Trinity.

[43] See Brian Hearne, "The Church, the Icon of the Trinity," in *A New Missionary Era*, ed. P. Flanagan (New York: Orbis Books, 1982), 53-60.

[44] In his *de Oratione Domini*, 23. See PL 4/553.

[45] See *LG* 4 of VC II.

[46] Robert L. Kress, "The Church as *Communio*: Trinity and Incarnation as the Foundations of Ecclesiology," *The Jurist* 36 (1976): 157-8.

[47] Joseph Kallarangatt, "The Trinitarian Foundation of an Ecclesiology of Communion," *Christian Orient* 11/1 (March 1990): 3-16, speaks of Trinity as basis of communion with legitimate diversity. See also Boris Bobrinskoy, "A Breakthrough in Ecumenical and Trinitarian Theology," *VJTR* 60/5 (May 1996): 337-49.

[48] See, for e.g., Robert T. Sears, "Trinitarian Love As Ground of the Church," *TS* 37/4 (1976): 652-79.

[49] As pastor, I have ministered to adivasi Christian communities where members congregate under a big tree or beside a river at the end of a day's work to sing and worship and listen to God's word in Scripture.

[50] This refers to the Pentecostal Spirit that unified alien tongues to understand one *kerygma* (Acts 2:5-12).

[51] See James J. Buckley, "The Wounded Body: The Spirit's Ecumenical Work in Divisions among Christians," in *Knowing the Triune God: The Work of the Spirit in the Practices of the Church*, ed. idem and D. S. Yeago (Grand Rapids, Michigan & Cambridge, U.K.: Wm. B. Eerdmans, 2001), 230.

[52] This understanding adds to that of Michael G. Lawler, *Symbol and Sacrament: A Contemporary Sacramental Theology* (New York: Paulist Press, 1987), 51, who defines sacrament as: "Prophetic symbols modeled upon Christ, the symbol of God, in and by which the Church, proclaims, celebrates and realizes for believers who place no obstacle that presence and action of God, which is rightly called grace."

[53] See, for instance, Arnold van Gennep, *The Rites of Passage* (Chicago: UCP, 1960), who deals with this.

[54] See Victor W. Turner, *The Ritual Process* (London: Routledge & Kegan Paul, 1969), for details.

[55] See Roy A. Rappaport, *Ritual and Religion in the Making of Humanity* (Cambridge: CUP, 1990), 138.

[56] See Tom F. Driver, *The Magic of Ritual: Our Need for Liberating Rites that Transform Our Lives and Our Communities* (New York: HarperCollins Publishers, 1991), 152-65, discusses Victor Turner's concept of *comunitas* that deals with formation of community around the power of ritual.

[57] Consider, for e.g., the number of times Trinity is invoked. All prayers are trinitarian and there are also 'special moments' as *epiclesis* (Spirit), *anamnesis* (Christ), *doxology* (Father), etc.

[58] See, for instance, Anne Hunt, *The Trinity and the Paschal Mystery: A Development in Recent Catholic Theology* (Collegeville, Minnesota: The Liturgical Press, 1997) and "Psychological Analogy and Paschal Mystery in Trinitarian Theology," *TS* 59/2 (1998): 197-218; John McDade, "The Trinity and the Paschal Mystery," *THJ* 29 (1988): 175-91; also Andrew Horsman," The Shape of the Trinity: Eucharistic Worship and the Doctrine of the Trinity," *Theology* 102/805 (January-February 1999): 89-97.

[59] See my "Covenantal Celebrations at Three Tables," *VJTR* 72/10 (October 2008): 725-38, for an explanation how the Eucharistic community is always a 'covenant community' that 'comes in' and 'goes out' to live out in life what it celebrates in liturgy. The language of 'tables' – of the word, of the bread, and of the world, has been derived from VC II's *DV* 21, and also the General Assembly of the Synod of Bishops (October 2008) discussing the theme 'The Word of God in the Life and Mission of the Church'.

[60] *Pahelo Vasavo* refers to the 'First Born' of the Vasavi adivasi family who leaves his father's house to start a new home. We saw in chapter 2 that this could roughly parallel Jesus, the 'First Born' (Rom 8:29).

[61] The words in inverted commas are said by the priest, raising the bread and wine, at the Offertory

[62] See my "In India, Life Leavens Liturgy," *National Catholic Reporter* (USA) *Ministries Section*, 23 January 2004.

[63] *Diya* is an oil-lamp used in villages for Baptism instead of a candle.

[64] *Mangalsutra* is a necklace put by the bridegroom on the bride instead of a ring that is common in the West. Gujarat's adivasis use of a garland of flowers put by each spouse on the other. This shows equality.

[65] See VC II's Decree on Ecumenism *UR* 8; italics added.

[66] Note that my understanding of 'interfaith' is not synonymous with 'interreligious' and thus *includes all.*

[67] See Gavin D'Costa, *The Meeting of Religions and the Trinity*, 148-9, for details of this distinction.

[68] For instance, Michael Amaladoss, "Eucharistic Hospitality: Searching for a New Paradigm," in *Body, Bread, Blood: Eucharistic Perspectives from the Indian Church*, ed. F. Gonsalves (Delhi: Vidyajyoti & ISPCK, 2003), 3-17, argues for allowing more people to participate in the Eucharist celebrated by the Catholic Church, on the basis of their love for, and commitment to, Jesus.

[69] Rowan Williams, 9.

[70] See, for instance, VC II's *Christus Dominus*, nn. 2 and 16.

[71] Boff, "Trinitarian Community and Social Liberation," 308.

[72] Note that attempts have earlier been made to relate Trinitarian Theology to Moral Theology; see, for instance, Anthony Kelly, "A Trinitarian Moral Theology," *Studia Moralia* 39 (2001): 245-89.

[73] I use two neologisms *'kenosize'* and *'plerosize'* in the form of verbs "to kenosize" and "to plerosize" to mean "make less/smaller/empty" and "make more/bigger/fuller", respectively. I have thought of these words from the Greek words, *kenós* and *pleiron*, meaning 'empty' and 'more/greater', respectively.

[74] See Angana P. Chatterji, *Violent Gods. Hindu Nationalism in India's Present: Narratives from Orissa* (Delhi: Three Essays Collective, 2009), for details of the persecution of Orissa's Christian population.

[75] See R. Panikkar, "There is no Outer without Inner Space," 79: "Precisely because human beings are extended they exhibit a tension spreading in space. This extension allows for growth, movement and change – in Space. Space is that feature of existence, and of Being, which *makes 'room' for movement.*"

[76] See Emmanuel Levinas, *Otherwise than Being or Beyond Essence*, trans. A. Lingis (Dordrecht: Kluwer Academic Publishers, 1991), 114, who uses this term.

[77] See Levinas, *Time and the Other*, trans. R.A. Cohen (Pittsburgh: Duquesne University Press, 1987), 26.

[78] In many places in India, although people say there is no caste in Christianity, there are 'special seats' reserved in churches for the upper and lower castes, and people are even buried in separate graveyards!

[79] Note that in his letter to some bishops of Tamil Nadu (south India) on the occasion of their *ad limina* visit to Rome late-2004, Pope John Paul II mentioned his concern over the question of caste in the Church.

[80] See, for instance, Robert T. Cornelison, "Losing Oneself to Gain Oneself: Rethinking God in a Narcissistic Age," *USQR* 52/3-4 (1998): 67-84, for a trinitarian perspective that critiques narcissism.

[81] See Thomas J. Norris, "Jesus Crucified and Forsaken: The Face of God for the Modern World," *CICR* 26/4 (Winter 1999): 892-912, who develops this idea in the context of narcissistic modern society.

[82] See "Point of Departure: Toward a Pluralist, Secular, Planetary, Interreligious Theology," in *Toward a Planetary Theology: Along the Many Paths of God*, ed. J.M. Vigil (Montreal: International Theological Commission of EATWOT, 2010), 29.

[83] I borrow the term 'counter-cultural' from Michael Amaladoss, "Mission in a Post-Modern World: A Call to be Counter-Cultural," *VJTR* 60/9 (September 1996): 569-81.

[84] *Ibid.*, 579.

[85] See Christopher O'Donnell, *Ecclesia: A Theological Encyclopedia of the Church* (Collegeville, Minnesota: The Liturgical Press, 1996), s.v. "Filioque".

[86] See, for instance, Stephen B. Bevans, "God Inside Out: Toward a Missionary Theology," *IBMR* 22/3 (July 1998): 102-5, who holds that we come to know God first through the Holy Spirit and not in the order Father →Son →Spirit. Bevans's view is contested by F. Dale Bruner, who holds that Jesus is "God Inside Out." (see *ibid.*, 108). See Emilio Castro, "A Christocentric Trinitarian Understanding of Mission," *IROM* 89/355 (2000): 584-91, for a position reconciling the preceding two.

[87] William O. Gregg, "Reflections on Living Trinitarian Faith," *Modern Churchman* 34/5 (1993), 96.

[88] I was 'theological observer' for this exercise conducted with the resources, and by the personnel, of the CCD, Vadodara, Gujarat, in the years 2003-2004.

[89] See my, "Sinking Sands and Shifting Stands: Approaching Adivasi Apostolate Anew," where such observations emerged in discussion with mission personnel of the tribal belt of south Gujarat.

[90] In his *Rhythmanalysis*, 19.

[91] John R. Kevern. "The Trinity and Social Justice," *ATR* 79/1 (Winter 1997): 54.

Bibliography

WORKS CITED

Abhishiktânanda. *Saccidânanda: A Christian Approach to Advaitic Experience.* Delhi: Indian Society for Promoting Christian Knowledge, 1974.

__________. "Notes on Christology and Trinitarian Theology." *Vidyajyoti Journal of Theological Reflection* 64/8 (August 2000): 598-612.

Ahmad, Aijaz. "Globalization and Culture." In *On Communalism and Globalization: Offensives of the Far Right.* 2d ed., 93-117. New Delhi: Three Essays Collective, 2004.

Ahmad, Imtiaz. "The Right to Equality." *The Hindu,* 17 January 2001, 12.

Alam, Anwar. "Secularism in India: A Critique of the Current Discourse." In *Competing Nationalisms in South Asia,* ed. Paul R. Brass and Achin Vanaik, 85-93. New Delhi: Orient Longman, 2002.

Ali, Amir. "Case for Multiculturalism in India." *Economic and Political Weekly* 35 (July 15, 2000): 2503-5.

Aloysius, G. *Nationalism Without a Nation in India.* New Delhi: Oxford University Press, 2000.

__________. "The Study of Religion-in-Society: A View From Below." *Religion and Society* 42/1 (March 1995): 5-16.

Amaladass, Anand, and Rosario Rocha, eds. *Crossing the Borders.* Chennai: Satya Nilayam Publications, 2001.

Amaladoss, Michael, ed. *Globalisation and its Victims as Seen by its Victims.* Delhi: Vidyajyoti & Indian Society for Promoting Christian Knowledge, 1999.

__________. "Folk-Culture as Counter Culture: The Dalit Experience." *Jeevadhara* 24/139 (January 1994): 31-42.

__________. "Syncretism and Kenosis: Hermeneutical Reflections in the Indian Context." In *The Agitated Mind of God: The Theology of Kosuke Koyama,* ed. Dale T. Irvin and Akintunde E. Arkinade, 57-69. Maryknoll, New York: Orbis Books, 1996.

Amaladoss, Michael. "Mission in a Post-Modern World: A Call to be Counter-Cultural." *Vidyajyoti Journal of Theological Reflection* 60/9 (September 1996): 569-81.

__________. "From Experience to Theology: Methodological Explorations." *Vidyajyoti Journal of Theological Reflection* 61/6 (June 1997): 372-85.

__________. "Eucharistic Hospitality: Searching for a New Paradigm." In *Body, Bread, Blood: Eucharistic Perspectives from the Indian Church*, ed. Francis Gonsalves, 3-17. Delhi: Vidyajyoti & Indian Society for the Promotion of Christian Knowledge, 2003.

__________. "A Cycle Opening to Pluralism." In *The Pastoral Circle Revisited: A Critical Quest for Truth and Information*," ed. Frans Wijsen, Peter Henriot, and Rodrigo Mejia, 169-82. New York: Orbis Books, 2005.

Ambedkar, Babasaheb B.R. *Annihilation of Caste: With a Reply to 'Mahatma' Gandhi.* Bangalore: Dalit Sahitya Akademi, 1987.

__________. *Riddle of Rama and Krishna.* Bangalore: Dalit Sahitya Akademy, 1988.

Anderson, Benedict. *Imagined Communities: Reflections on the Origin and Spread of Nationalism.* New York: Verso, 1996.

Ansari, Iqbal A. "Minority Representation." *Seminar* 506 (October 2001): 37-8.

Anselm of Canterbury. *St. Anselm: Basic Writings.* Translated by S.N. Deane. Las Salle, Illinois: Open Court, 1968.

Appadurai, Arjun. "New Logics of Violence." *Seminar* 503 (July 2001): 14-8.

Appaiah, Parvathy. *Hindutva: Ideology and Politics.* New Delhi: Deep & Deep Publications, 2003.

Arbuckle, Gerald. "Communicating through Symbols." *Human Development* 8 (1987): 7-12.

Armstrong, James. *From The Underside: Evangelism From a Third World Vantage Point.* New York: Orbis Books, 1981.

Asad, Talal. "Where are the Margins of the State?" In *Anthropology in the Margins of the State*, ed. Veena Das and Deborah Poole, 279-88. New Delhi: Oxford University Press, 2004.

Augustine, P.A. "Conversion as Social Protest." *Religion and Society* 28/4 (December 1981): 51-7.

Aung, Salai Hla. "Relational Trinity and Its Conceptual Implications for Asian Community." *Asian Journal of Theology* 14/1 (April 2000): 82-92.

Aurobindo, Sri. *The Human Cycles. The Ideal of Human Unity, War and Self-Determination.* Pondicherry: Aurobindo Ashram, 1962.

Austin, Granville. *The Indian Constitution: Cornerstone of a Nation*. New Delhi: Oxford University Press, 2004.

__________. *Working a Democratic Constitution: The Indian Experience*. New Delhi: Oxford University Press, 1999.

Ayrookuzhiel, A.M. Abraham. "Religion and Culture in Dalits' Struggle for Liberation." *Religion and Society* 33/2 (June 1986): 33-44.

Bamat, T., and J-P. Wiest, eds. *Popular Catholicism in a World Church: Seven Case Studies in Inculturation*. New York: Orbis Books, 1999.

Banerjee, M. *An Historical Outline of Pre-British Chotanagpur*. Ranchi: Educational Publications, 1989.

Barbour, Ian G. *Myths, Models, and Paradigms: A Comparative Study in Science & Religion*. New York: Harper & Row Publishers, 1974.

Barnes, Michael. *Traces of the Other: Three Philosophers and Inter-faith Dialogue*. Chennai: Satya Nilayam Publications, 2000.

__________. *Walking the City: Christian Discipleship in a Pluralist World*. Delhi: Indian Society for the Promotion of Christian Knowledge, 1999.

Barrigar, Christian J. "Protecting God: The Lexical Formation of Trinitarian Language." *Modern Theology* 7 (July 1991): 299-310.

Barry, William A. *Paying Attention to God*. Notre Dame, Indiana: Ave Maria Press, 1990.

Barth, Karl. *Church Dogmatics*. *Vol. I*. Edinburgh: T & T Clark, 1936.

Barthes, Roland. *Mythologies*. Translated by Annette Lavers. London: Paladin Books, 1989.

Basham, A.L. *The Wonder That Was India*. Delhi: Rupa & Co., 1997.

Basu, Amrita, and Atul Kohli, eds. *Community Conflicts and the State in India*. New Delhi: Oxford University Press, 1998.

Batut, Jean-Pierre. "Three Pillars of Trinitarian Faith." *Communio International Catholic Review* 27/2 (Summer 2000): 300-11.

Baum, Gregory. *Theology and Society*. New York, Mahwah: Paulist Press, 1987.

__________"The Impact of Sociology on Christian Theology." In *Theology and Sociology: A Reader*, ed. Robin Gill, 130-44. London: Geoffrey Chapman, and New York/Mahwah: Paulist Press, 1987.

Bauman, Zygmunt. *Community: Seeking Safety in an Insecure World*. Cambridge: Polity Press, 2001.

Baxi, Upendra. "The Second Gujarat Catastrophe." *Economic and Political Weekly* 37 (August 24, 2002): 3519-31.

Bellah, Robert N. *Habits of the Heart: Individualism and Commitment in American Life*. New York: Harper and Row, 1985.

Berger, Peter L., and Thomas Luckmann. *The Social Construction of Reality: A Treatise in the Sociology of Knowledge.* New York: Anchor Books, 1967.

Berger, Peter L. *The Social Reality of Religion.* Norwich: Penguin University Books, 1973.

Béteille, André. *Antinomies of Society: Essays on Ideologies & Institutions.* New Delhi: Oxford University Press, 2000.

Bevans, Stephen B. "God Inside Out: Toward a Missionary Theology." *International Bulletin of Missionary Research* 22/3 (July 1998): 102-5.

Beyer, Peter. *Religion and Globalization.* London: Sage Publications, 1997.

Bhabha, Homi K. *The Location of Culture.* London and New York: Routledge, 2000.

Bhargava, Rajeev, ed. *Secularism and Its Critics.* Delhi: Oxford University Press, 1998.

________. "What is Democracy?" *Seminar* 389 (January 1992): 36-9.

________. "Religious and Secular Identities." In *Crisis and Change in Contemporary India,* ed. Upendra Baxi and Bhiku Parekh, 317-49. New Delhi: Sage Publications, 1995

________. "On the Majority-Minority Syndrome." *The Hindu,* 9 July 2002, 10.

________. "Community Sentiment and the Teaching of History." *Seminar* 522 (February 2003): 35-7.

Bharucha, Rustom. "Politics of Culturalisms in an Age of Globalisation: Discrimination, Discontent and Dialogue." *Economic and Political Weekly* 34 (February 20, 1999): 477-89

Bilimoria, Purushottama. "The Hermeneutic of Suspicion and Religion." *Journal of Dharma* 23/3 (1997): 247-74.

Black, Antony. "Communal Democracy and its History." *Political Studies* 45/1 (March 1997): 5-20.

Bloesch, Donald G. *The Battle for the Trinity: The Debate over Inclusive God-Language.* Michigan: Servant Publications, 1985.

Blumer, Herbert. *Symbolic Interactionism: Perspective and Method.* New Jersey: Prentice-Hall, Inc., 1969.

Bobrinskoy, Boris. "Models of Trinitarian Revelation." *Saint Vladimir's Theological Quarterly* 39/2 (1995): 115-26.

________. "A Breakthrough in Ecumenical and Trinitarian Theology." *Vidyajyoti Journal of Theological Reflection* 60/5 (May 1996): 337-49.

Boff, Leonardo. *Trinity and Society.* Translated by Paul Burns. New York: Orbis Books, 1988.

Boff, Leonard. *Holy Trinity, Perfect Community*. Translated by Phillip Berryman. New York: Orbis Books, 2000.

Bond, George C., and Angela Gilliam, eds. *Social Construction of the Past: Representation as Power*. London: Routledge, 1994.

Bonhoeffer, Dietrich. *The Cost of Discipleship*. London: SCM Press, 1959.

Bonino, José Míguez. *Toward a Christian Political Ethics*. Philadelphia: Fortress Press, 1983.

Boring, M. Eugene. "John 5:19-24." *Interpretation* 45/2 (April 1991): 176-81.

Bose, Pradip Kumar. "Stratification among Tribals in Gujarat." In *Social Inequality in India: Profiles of Caste, Class, Power & Social Mobility*, ed. K.L. Sharma, 411-26. Jaipur and New Delhi: Rawat Publications, 1995.

Bourdieu, Pierre. *Language and Symbolic Power*. Cambridge: Polity Press, 1991.

__________. *The Field of Cultural Production: Essays on Art and Literature*, ed. R. Johnson. Cambridge: Polity Press, 1993.

Bourke, Myles M. "The Epistle to the Hebrews." In *The Jerome Biblical Commentary*, ed. Raymond E. Brown, Joseph A. Fitzmyer, and Roland E. Murphy, 381-403. Bangalore: Theological Publications of India, 1968.

Bracken, Joseph A. *The Triune Symbol: Persons, Process and Community*. Lanham: University Press of America, 1985.

__________. "The Holy Trinity as a Community of Divine Persons – I & II." *The Heythrop Journal* 15/2&3 (April-July 1974): 166-82, 257-70.

__________. "The Divine Pleroma." *Chicago Studies* 26/1 (April 1987): 25-36.

__________. "Infinity and the Logic of Non-Dualism." *Hindu-Christian Studies Bulletin* 11 (1998): 39-44.

__________. "Trinity: Economic and Immanent." *Horizons* 25/1 (Spring 1998): 7-22.

Brague, Rémi. "On the Christian Model of Unity: the Trinity." *Communio International Catholic Review* 10 (Summer 1983): 149-66.

Breman, Jan. "Communal Upheaval as Resurgence of Social Darwinism." In *Fascism in India: Faces, Fangs and Facts*, ed. Chaitanya Krishna, 367-76. New Delhi: Manak Publications Pvt. Ltd., 2003.

British Council of Churches. *The Forgotten Trinity: Report of the BCC Study Commission on Trinitarian Doctrine Today*. London: British Council of Churches, Inter-Church House, 1989.

Brown, David. "The Trinity in Art." In *The Trinity: An Interdisciplinary Symposium*, ed. Stephen T. Davis, Daniel Kendall, and Gerald O'Collins, 329-56. New York: Oxford University Press, 1999.

Brown, David. "Trinitarian Personhood and Individuality." In *Trinity, Incarnation and Atonement*, ed. R. Feenstra and Cornelius Plantinga, Jr., 48-78. Notre Dame: Notre Dame University Press, 1988.

Bryant, M. Darrol. "Recovering the Trinitarian Foundations of Christian Experience: A Pathway to Christian Unity." *Dialogue and Alliance* 4/3 (Fall 1990): 4-20.

Buber, Martin. *Between Man and Man*. Translated by Ronald Gregor Smith. Boston: Beacon Press, 1957.

__________. *I and Thou*, 2nd ed. Translated by Ronald Gregor Smith. Edinburgh: T & T Clark, 1994.

Buckley, James J. "The Wounded Body: The Spirit's Ecumenical Work in Divisions among Christians." In *Knowing the Triune God: The Work of the Spirit in the Practices of the Church*, ed. idem and David S. Yeago, 205-30. Grand Rapids, Michigan and Cambridge, U.K.: Wm. B. Eerdmans Publishing Co., 2001.

Bujo, Bénézet. *African Theology in its Social Context*. Translated by John O'Donohue Maryknoll, New York: Orbis Books, 1992.

Buri, Fritz. "Trinity and Personality." *Iliff Review* 40 (Winter 1983): 15-24.

Burman, B.K. Roy. "The Other Side of 'Conversion'." *Mainstream* 37/8 (February 13, 1999): 7-11.

Bush, Randall B. "Trinitarian Conflict: A Re-assessment of Trinitarian Analogies in the Light of Modern Psychological and Sociological Conflict Theories." *Perspectives In Religious Studies* 19/1 (Spring 1992): 9-37.

__________. *Recent Ideas of Divine Conflict: The Influences of Psychological and Sociological Theories of Conflict upon the Trinitarian Theology of Paul Tillich and Jürgen Moltmann*. New York: The Edwin Mellen Press, 1991.

Caputo, John D. "Toward a Postmodern Theology of the Cross: Augustine, Heidegger, Derrida." In *Postmodern Philosophy and Christian Theology*, ed. Merold Westphal, 202-25. Bloomington, Indiana: Indiana University Press, 1999.

Carens, Joseph H. "Justice as Evenhandedness." *Seminar* 484 (December 1999): 46-50.

Carman, John B. *Majesty and Meekness: A Comparative Study of Contrast and Harmony in the Concept of God*. Grand Rapids, Michigan: William B. Eerdmans, 1994.

Castro, Emilio. "A Christocentric Trinitarian Understanding of Mission." *International Review of Mission* 89/355 (2000): 584-91.

Centre for Culture and Development, *Where Do We Stand?* and *Where Do We Go?* Vadodara: Centre for Culture and Development, 2003, 2004.

Chakrabarti, Debashis. "Hindutva: The Religious Incongruity." *The Hindu*, 6 February 2001, open page 1.

Chakraborty, Somen. "Gujarat: Attacks on Christians – Looking Beyond Communalism." *Economic and Political Weekly* 34 (April 17, 1999): 949-52.

Champakalakshmi, R. "Caste and Community in Pre-modern South India." *Jeevadhara* 31/181 (January 2001): 5-15.

Chandhoke, Neera. *Beyond Secularism: The Rights of Religious Minorities*. New Delhi: Oxford University Press, 1999.

________. *The Conceits of Civil Society*. New Delhi: Oxford University Press, 2003.

________. "A Nation Searching for a Narrative in Times of Globalisation." *Economic and Political Weekly* 34 (May 1, 1999): 1040-7.

________. "The Logic of Recognition?" *Seminar* 484 (December 1999): 35-9.

________. "Why Minority Rights?" *The Hindu*, 27 July 2002, 10.

________. "A Quota-driven Polity." *The Hindu*, 18 February 2003, 10.

________. "Justifying Affirmative Action." *The Hindu*, 4 June 2003, 10.

________. "Governance and the Pluralisation of the State: Implications for Democratic Citizenship." *Economic and Political Weekly* 38 (July 12, 2003): 2957-68.

________. "Crisis of Representative Democracy." *The Hindu*, 19 June 2004, 10.

________. "Reservations about Reservations." *The Hindu*, 16 August 2004, 10.

________. "'Seeing' the State in India." *Economic and Political Weekly* 40 (March 12, 2005): 1033-9.

Chandra, Bipan. *Communalism: A Primer*. New Delhi: Anamika Publishers, 2004.

Chandran, J.R. "Plurality of Religious Faith and Living in Community." *Religion and Society* 33/3 (September 1986): 73-80.

Chapman, Mark D. "The Social Doctrine of the Trinity: Some Problems." *Anglican Theological Review* 83/2 (Spring 2001): 239-54.

Chatterjee, Partha. *The Nation and Its Fragments: Colonial and Postcolonial Histories*. Delhi: Oxford University Press, 1995.

________. "Secularism and Toleration." *Economic and Political Weekly* 29 (July 9, 1994): 1768-77.

________. "Beyond the Nation or Within?" *Economic and Political Weekly* 32 (January 4, 1997): 30-4.

Chatterjee, Partha. "Secularism and Tolerance." In *Secularism and Its Critics*, ed. Rajeev Bhargava. Delhi: Oxford University Press, 1998.

________. "Community in the East," *Economic and Political Weekly* 33 (February 7, 1999): 277-82.

________. "On Civil and Political Society in Post-Colonial Democracy." In *Civil Society*, ed. Sudipta Kaviraj and S. Khilnani, 165-78. Cambridge: Cambridge University Press, 2001.

Chatterji, Angana P. *Violent Gods. Hindu Nationalism in India 's Present: Narratives from Orissa*. Delhi: Three Essays Collective, 2009.

Chaube, S.K. "The Scheduled Tribes and Christianity in India." *Economic and Political Weekly* 34 (February 27 - March 5, 1999): 524-6.

Chaudhury, Pradipta. "'The Creamy Layer': Political Economy of Reservations." *Economic and Political Weekly* 39 (May 15, 2004): 1989-91.

Chenoy, Kamal Mitra, ed. *Citizen's Commission's Report on the Incidents in Dangs District*. National Association of Women's Organizations, 1999.

Chinnappa, Archbishop A.M., and A. Philomin Raj. "Ensuring Equal Rights to all Dalits." *The Hindu*, 22 September 2005, 12.

Chomsky, Noam. *Profit Over People: Neoliberalism and Global Order*. Delhi: Madhyam Books, 1999.

Chopp, Rebecca. *The Power to Speak: Feminism, Language, God*. New York: Crossword, 1989.

Chossudovsky, Michel. *The Globalisation of Poverty: Impacts of IMF and World Bank Reforms*. Goa: The Other India Press and New Delhi Madhyam Books & Research Foundation for Science, Technology and Ecology, 1997.

Chung, Paul. "Trinity and Asian Theology of Divine *Dukkar*." *Asian Journal of Theology* 6/1 (2001): 131-47.

Clairmont, Frederic. "The Global Corporation: Road to Serfdom." *Economic and Political Weekly* 35 (January 8, 2000): 24-7.

Clark, John P.H. "Nature, Grace and the Trinity in Julian of Norwich." *The Downside Review* 100/340 (July 1982): 203-20.

Clark, Norris. "Person, Being and St. Thomas." *Communio International Catholic Review* 19 (1992): 601-18.

Clarke, Sathianathan. *Dalits and Christianity: Subaltern Religion and Liberation Theology in India*. New Delhi: Oxford University Press, 1998.

Coakley, Sarah. "Living into the Mystery of the Trinity: Trinity, Prayer, and Sexuality." *Anglican Theological Review* 80/2 (Spring 1998): 223-32.

Cody, Dom Aelred. "Hebrews." In *A New Catholic Commentary on Holy Scripture*, ed. Reginald C. Fuller, Leonard Johnston, and Conleth Kearns, 1220-39. London: Thomas Nelson and Sons Ltd., 1969.

Cohen, Anthony P. *The Management of Myths: The Politics of Legitimation in a Newfoundland Community*. Manchester: Manchester University Press, 1975.

__________. *The Symbolic Construction of Community*. Chichester: Ellis Horwood Limited and London and New York: Tavistock Publications, 1985.

Cohn, Bernard S. "Notes on the History of the Study of Indian Society and Culture." In *Structure and Change in Indian Society*, ed. idem and Milton Singer, 3-28. Jaipur and New Delhi: Rawat Publications, 1996.

Collins, Randall. *Four Sociological Traditions: Selected Readings*. New York: Oxford University Press, 1985.

Comblin, José. *Cry of the Oppressed, Cry of Jesus*. New York: Orbis Books, 1984.

Congar, Yves M. *The Word and the Spirit*. Translated by David Smith. London: Geoffrey Chapman and San Francisco: Harper & Row, 1986.

__________. "Classical Political Monotheism and the Trinity." *God as Father? Concilium* (March 1981): 31-6.

Cootsona, Greg. "Trinitarian Creation of a Complex World." *Dialog* 36/3 (Summer 1997): 175-9.

Copley, Antony, ed., *Hinduism in Public and Private: Reform, Hindutva, Gender, and Sampraday*. New Delhi: Oxford University Press, 2003.

Copley, Antony. *Religions in Conflict: Ideology, Cultural Contact and Conversion in Late Colonial India*. New Delhi: Oxford University Press, 1997.

__________. "Has Religion a Future in India?" *Religion and Society* 44/2 (June 1997): 23-52.

Coral, J.A. *Daahyaa Got: Gamit Myths and Stories. Tribal Sources – I*. Anand: Gujarat Sahitya Prakash, 2001.

__________. *The Gamit World of Meaning: Adivasi Religion and Culture. Tribal Sources – II*. Anand: Gujarat Sahitya Prakash, 2007.

Corless, Roger and Paul Knitter, eds. *Buddhist Emptiness and Christian Trinity: Essays and Explorations*. New York: Paulist Press, 1990.

Cornelison, Robert T. "Losing Oneself to Gain Oneself: Rethinking God in a Narcissistic Age." *Union Seminary Quarterly Review* 52/3-4 (1998): 67-84.

Coser, Lewis. *The Functions of Social Conflict*. Glencoe: The Free Press, 1956.

Cousins, Ewert H. "A Theology of Interpersonal Relations." *Thought* 45 (1970): 56-82.

Cousins, Ewert H. "The Trinity and World Religions." *Journal of Ecumenical Studies* 7/3 (Summer 1970): 476-98.

Craib, Ian. *Experiencing Identity*. London: Sage Publications, 1998.

Crang, Mike, and Nigel Thrift, eds. *Thinking Space*. London and New York: Routledge, 2000.

Cross, Richard. "Two Models of the Trinity?" *The Heythrop Journal* 43/3 (July 2002): 275-94.

Cunningham, David S. "Developing Alternative Trinitarian Formulas." *Anglican Theological Review* 80/1 (Winter 1998): 26-9.

D'Costa, Gavin. "Christ, the Trinity and Religious Plurality." In *Christian Uniqueness Reconsidered: The Myth of a Pluralistic Theology of Religions*, ed. Idem, 16-29. New York: Orbis Books, 1990.

__________. "The Christian Trinity: Paradigm for Pluralism?" In *Pluralism and the Religions: The Theological and Political Dimensions*, ed. John D'Arcy May, 23-7. London: Cassell, 1998.

__________. *The Meeting of Religions and the Trinity*. Edinburgh: T & T Clark Ltd., 2000.

Dale Bruner, Frederick, and William Hordern. *The Holy Spirit: Shy Member of the Trinity*. Minneapolis: Augsburg Publishing House, 1984.

Dallmayr, Fred. *Beyond Orientalism: Essays on Cross-Cultural Encounter*. Albany: State University of New York, 1996.

__________. *Alternative Visions: Paths in the Global Village*. Maryland: Rowman & Littlefield Publishers, 1998.

Dart, John. "Balancing Out the Trinity: The Genders of the Godhead." *The Christian Century* 100 (February 16-23, 1983): 147-50.

Dasgupta, Manas. "Saffronised Police Show Their Colour." *The Hindu*, 3 March 2002, 8.

Davis, Richard H. "The Iconography of Rama's Chariot." In *Making India Hindu: Religion, Community, and the Politics of Democracy in India*, ed. David Ludden, 27-54. Delhi: Oxford University Press, 1996.

De Gruchy, John W. "The Nature, Necessity and Task of Theology." In *Doing Theology in Context: South African Perspectives*, ed. idem and Charles Villa-Vicencio, 2-14. New York: Orbis Books & Johannesburg: David Philip, 1994.

De Margerie, Bertrand. *The Christian Trinity in History*. Translated by Edmund J. Fortman. Massachusetts: St Bede's Publications, 1981.

De Souza, Peter Ronald. "Whose Representative?" *Seminar* 506 (October 2001): 57-61.

Derrida, Jacques. *Margins of Philosophy*. Translated by Alan Bass. Chicago: University of Chicago Press, 1982.

________. *Writing and Difference*. Translated by Alan Bass. Chicago: University of Chicago Press, 1978.

Desai, A.R. "National Integration and Religion." In *Sociology of Religion in India*, ed. Rowena Robinson, 54-67. New Delhi: Sage Publications, 2004.

Desai, Radhika. "Hindutva's Gujarat: The Image of India's Future?" In *Slouching Towards Ayodhya*, 111-47. New Delhi: Three Essays Collective, 2003.

Deshpande, Satish. "Communalising the Nation-Space: Notes on Spatial Strategies of Hindutva." *EPW* 30 (December 16, 1995): 3220-7.

________. "Hegemonic Spatial Strategies: The Nation-Space and Hindu Communalism in Twentieth-century India." In *Community, Gender and Violence: Subaltern Studies XI*, ed. Partha Chatterjee and Pradeep Jeganathan, 167-211. Delhi: Permanent Black, 2000.

Deshpande, Satish and Nandini Sundar. "Caste and the Census: Implications for Society and the Social Sciences." *Economic and Political Weekly* 33 (August 8, 1998): 2157-9.

Deshpande, Satish and Geetika Bapna. *Dalits in the Muslim and Christian Communities. A Status Report on Current Social Scientifc Knowledge*. New Delhi: National Commission for Minorities, Goverment of India, 2010.

Devasahayam, V., ed. *Dalits and Women: Quest for Humanity*. Madras: Gurukul Lutheran Theological College and Research Institute, 1996.

Devy, Ganesh. "Tribal Voice and Violence." *Seminar* 513 (May 2002): 39-48.

Dhanagare, D.N. *Peasant Movements in India: 1920 – 1950*. Delhi: Oxford University Press, 1983.

Dhanda, Meena. "Representation for Women: Should Feminists Support Quotas?" *Economic and Political Weekly* 35 (August 12, 2002): 2969-76.

Dhavan, Rajeev. "The Minorities Case." *The Hindu*, 15 November 2002, 10.

________. "Reservation for All?" *The Hindu*, 13 June 2003, 10.

DiNoia, Joseph A. "Knowing and Naming the Triune God: The Grammar of Trinitarian Confession." In *Speaking the Christian God: The Holy Trinity and the Challenge to Feminism, ed.* Alvin F. Kimel, Jr., 162-87. Michigan: William B. Eerdmans, 1992.

Dionysius the Areopagite. *The Mystical Theology and the Celestial Hierarchies*. Surrey: The Shrine of Wisdom, 1949.

Dirks, Nicholas. *Castes of Mind: Colonialism and the Making of Modern India.* Delhi: Permanent Black and New Jersey: Princeton University Press, 2002.

Dixon, John W., Jr. "Toward a Trinitarian Anthropology." *Anglican Theological Review* 80/2 (Spring 1998): 169-85.

Downey, Michael. *Altogether Gift: A Trinitarian Spirituality.* New York: Orbis Books, 2001.

Dreze, Jean, Meera Samson, and Satyajit Singh, eds. *The Dam and the Nation: Displacement and Resettlement in the Narmada Valley.* New Delhi: Oxford University Press, 1997.

Drilling, Peter. "The Genesis of the Trinitarian Ecclesiology of Vatican II." *Science et Esprit* 45/1 (January-April 1993): 61-78.

Dumont, Louis. *Homo Hierarchicus: The Caste System and its Implications.* Delhi: Oxford University Press, 1988.

Dunn, James D.G. *Unity and Diversity in the New Testament: An Inquiry into the Character of Earliest Christianity.* London: SCM Press, 1977.

Dunne, Tad. "Trinity and History." *Theological Studies* 45/1 (March 1984): 139-52.

Dupré, Louis. *Symbols of the Sacred.* Michigan and Cambridge: William B. Eerdmans, 2000.

Dupuis, Jacques. *Toward a Christian Theology of Religious Pluralism.* Anand: Gujarat Sahitya Prakash, 2001

________. "Trinity and World Religions." *Clergy Monthly* 35 (1971): 77-81.

Durkheim, Emile. *The Division of Labour in Society.* New York: The Free Press, 1964.

Durrany, K.S. *State Measures for the Welfare of Minorities.* Bangalore: The Christian Institute for the Study of Religion and Society and Delhi: Indian Society for Promoting Christian Knowledge, 1997.

Dussel, Enrique. *Ethics and Community.* Translated by Robert R. Barr. New York: Orbis Books, 1988.

Dutt, Barkha. "The Rape of Reason." *Outlook,* 13 May 2002, 30.

Dutt, Dev. "Conversions: A Viewpoint." In *Politics of Conversion,* ed. Devendra Swarup, 35-46. New Delhi: Deendayal Research Institute, 1986.

Dutta, Nonica. "Gujarat and Majority Women." *The Hindu,* 15 June 2002, 10.

________. "Are the Sikhs Hindus?" *The Hindu,* 4 March 2003, 10.

Eck, Diana L. *Darshan: Seeing the Divine Image in India,* 2nd ed. Pennsylvania: Anima Books, 1985.

Edwards, Denis. *Jesus, the Wisdom of God: An Ecological Theology.* Homebush, N.S.W.: St. Paul's, 1995.

________. "The Discovery of Chaos and the Retrieval of the Trinity." In *Chaos and Complexity: Scientific Perspectives on Divine Action*, ed. John Russell, Nancey Murphy, and Arthur R. Peacocke, 157-75. Vatican City State: Vatican Observatory Publications and California: The Center for Theology and the Natural Sciences, 1997.

Eggen, Wiel. "Religion of a Family God?" *Studies in Interreligious Dialogue* 10/2 (2000): 175-96.

Eliade, Mircea. *Myth and Reality.* London: George Allen & Unwin Ltd, 1964.

Embree, Ainslie T. *Utopias in Conflict: Religion and Nationalism in Modern India.* Delhi: Oxford University Press, 1990.

Engineer, Asghar Ali. "Re-Emergence of Communalism in Post-Independence India." In *Secular Challenge To Communal Politics: A Reader*, ed. P.R. Ram, 58-76. Mumbai: Vikas Adhyayan Kendra, 1998.

Engineer, Asghar Ali. "Three Years After Genocide in Gujarat." *Secular Perspective* (March 1-15, 2005).

Erikson, Erik H. *Childhood and Society.* 2nd ed. New York: W.W. Norton & Co., 1963.

Fanon, Frantz. *The Wretched of the Earth.* Translated by Constance Farrington. New York: Grove Press, 1963.

Fee, Gordon D. *God's Empowering Presence: The Holy Spirit in the Letters of Paul.* Peabody, Massachusetts: Hendrickson, 1994.

________. "Paul and the Trinity: The Experience of Christ and the Spirit for Paul's Understanding of God" In *The Trinity: An Interdisciplinary Symposium on the Trinity*, ed. Stephen T. Davis, Daniel Kendall, and Gerald O'Collins, 49-72. New York: Oxford University Press, 1999.

Finger, Thomas. "Modern Alienation and Trinitarian Creation." *Evangelical Review of Theology* 17/2 (April-June 1993): 190-208.

Fortman, Edmund J. *The Triune God: A Historical Study of the Doctrine of the Trinity.* Philadelphia: Westminster Press, 1972.

Foucault, Michel. *Power/Knowledge: Selected Interviews and Other Writings – 1972-1977*, ed. Colin Gordon. New York: Pantheon Books, 1980.

________. "Space, Knowledge, and Power." In *The Foucault Reader*, ed. Paul Rainbow, 239-56. London: Penguin Books, 1984.

________. "Of Other Spaces." *Diacritics* 16 (1986): 22-7.

Frankel, Francine R. "Decline of a Social Order." In *Politics and the State in India*, ed. Zoya Hasan, 233-45. New Delhi: Sage Publications, 2000.

Friedman, Maurice S. *Martin Buber: The Life of Dialogue.* New York: Harper & Row, 1960.

Friesen, J. Glenn. "Abhishiktânandâ: Hindu Advaitic Experience and Christian Beliefs." *Hindu-Christian Studies Bulletin* 11 (1998): 31-8.

Fritsch-Oppermann, Sybille. "Trikâya and Trinity: Reflecting Some Aspects of Christian-Buddhist Dialogue." *Journal of Ecumenical Studies* 30/2 (Spring 1993): 245-61.

Frykenberg, Robert Eric, ed., *Christians and Missionaries in India: Cross-Cultural Communication since 1500.* Michigan and Cambridge: William B. Eerdmans and London: RoutledgeCurzon, 2003.

Gadamer, Hans-Georg. *Truth and Method*, 2nd ed. Translated by William Glen-Doepel. London: Sheed and Ward, 1981.

________. "The Historicity of Understanding." In *The Hermeneutics Reader: Texts of the German Tradition from the Enlightenment to the Present*, ed. K. Mueller-Vollmer, 256-92. Oxford: Basil Blackwell, 1986.

Galanter, Marc. "The Indian Constitution and Provisions for Special Treatment." In *Democracy, Difference and Social Justice*, ed. Gurpreet Mahajan, 565-77. New Delhi: Oxford University Press, 2000.

Gandhy, Rashna Imhasly. "Shadow: The Archetypal Enemy." *Seminar* 513 (May 2002): 52-5.

Gaybba, Brian. "Trinitarian Experience and Doctrine." In *Doing Theology in Context: South African Perspectives*, ed. John W. De Gruchy and Charles Villa-Vicencio, 77-88. New York: Orbis Books, 1994.

Geertz, Clifford. *The Interpretation of Cultures.* New York: Basic Books, 1973.

Geevarghese, Mar Osthathios. *Theology of a Classless Society.* Madras: The Christian Literature Society, 1980.

________. *Sharing God and a Sharing World.* Delhi: Indian Society for Promoting Christian Knowledge and Tiruvalla: Christava Sahitya Samithy, 1995.

Gellner, Ernest. *Postmodernism, Reason and Religion.* London and New York: Routledge, 2002.

Gelpi, Donald L. *The Divine Mother: A Trinitarian Theology of the Holy Spirit.* Lanham, MD: University Press of America, 1984.

________. "A Peircean Approach to Trinity as Community: A Response to Some Responses." *Horizons* 27/1 (Spring 2000): 114-30.

Ghildiyal, Subodh. "50 Years After Ambedkar, Another Conversion Wave." *The Times of India*, 21 October 2005, 1.

Ghurye, G.S. *The Scheduled Tribes*, 2d ed. Bombay: Popular Press, 1959.

Gill, Robin. *Theology and Sociology: A Reader.* London: Cassell, 1996.

Gill, Robin. "Sociology Assessing Theology." In *Theology and Sociology: A Reader*, ed. idem, 145-64. London: Geoffrey Chapman and New York/ Mahwah: Paulist Press, 1987.

Gill, S.S. "Diluting Mandal." *The Hindu*, 24 June 2003, 10.

Giri, Ananta Kumar. "Disciplinary Boundaries: Rethinking Theories and Methods." In *Frontier Violations*, ed. Felix Wilfred and Oscar Beozzo. *Concilium* 2 (1999): 54-61.

Giri, Ananta Kumar. "The Calling of a Creative Transdisciplinarity." *Futures* 34 (2000): 103-15.

________. "Promoting Multiculturalism." *The Hindu*, 3 February 2001, 12.

________. *Spiritual Cultivation For a Secular Society*: Working Paper of the Madras Institute of Developmental Studies, Chennai, n.d.

Gispert-Sauch, George. "A Note on GS 22." *Vidyajyoti Journal of Theological Reflection* 59/2 (February 1995): 126-31.

Gnanapragasam, Patrick, and Elisabeth Schüssler Fiorenza, eds. *Negotiating Borders: Theological Explorations in the Global Era. Essays in Honour of Prof. Felix Wilfred*. Delhi: ISPCK, 2008.

Golwalkar, M.S. *WE, or, Our Nationhood Defined*. Nagpur: Bharat Prakashan, 1947.

________. *Bunch of Thoughts*, 3d ed. Bangalore: Sahitya Sindhu Prakashana, 1996.

Gonsalves, Francis, ed. *Body, Bread, Blood: Eucharistic Perspectives from the Indian Church*. Delhi: Vidyajyoti & Indian Society for the Promotion of Christian Knowledge, 2003.

________. "Grisly Christmas for Christians in Gujarat." *Communalism Combat* 6/50 (January 1999): 11-4.

________. "Debating Conversions." *Indian Currents*. XI/6 (February 8-14, 1999): 35-6.

________. "Saffron Shrouds YKJ 2000 in Gujarat." *Communalism Combat* 7/ 55 (January 2000): 15-7.

________. "Gods of War and Wars of God: Religion and Violence in Contemporary Society." In *The Yearbook of Contextual Theologies*. Frankfurt: IKO – Verlag fur Interkulturelle Kommunikation (2001): 33-59.

________. "The Implications of Kenosis Christology for Contextual Christology." *Vidyajyoti Journal of Theological Reflection* 66/1 (January 2002): 7-17.

________. "Religion in Global Society: Processes and Prospects – I & II." *Vidyajyoti Journal of Theological Reflection* 66/5 & 6 (May & June 2002): 345-52, 438-50.

Gonsalves, Francis. "Making a 'Mother World' Possible." In *National Catholic Reporter Online* (USA), *Global Perspective* 1/41 (January 22, 2004).

________. "In India, Life Leavens Liturgy." In *National Catholic Reporter Online* (USA), *Ministries Section* (January 23, 2004).

________. "Sinking Sands and Shifting Stands: Approaching Adivasi Apostolate Anew." *Vidyajyoti Journal of Theological Reflection* 68/4 (May 2004): 325-37.

________. "Advani's *Yatra*." *The Hindu*, 6 April 2004, 19.

________. "Recasting Caste: A Challenge to Indian Christianity." In *National Catholic Reporter Online* (USA): *Global Perspective* 3/20 (September 27, 2005).

________. "Covenantal Celebrations at Three Tables." *Vidyajyoti Journal of Theological Reflection* 72/10 (October 2008): 725-38.

________. "Carrying in Our Body the Marks of His Passion." *Vidyajyoti Journal of Theological Reflection* 72/11 (2009): 801-7.

Gore, M. S. *Unity in Diversity: The Indian Experience in Nation-Building*. Jaipur and New Delhi: Rawat Publications, 2002.

Gottschalk, Peter. *Beyond Hindu and Muslim: Multiple Identity in Narratives from Village India*. New Delhi: Oxford University Press, 2001.

Graham, Elaine L. *Making the Difference: Gender, Personhood and Theology*. London: Mowbray, 1995.

Gramsci, Antonio. *Selections from the Prison Notebooks*. Edited and translated by Quintin Hoare and Geoffrey Nowell Smith. Madras: Orient Longman, 1996.

Gregg, William O. "Reflections on Living Trinitarian Faith." *Modern Churchman* 34/5 (1993): 93-8.

Gresham, John L., Jr., "The Social Model of the Trinity and its Critics." *Scottish Journal of Theology* 46/3 (1993): 325-43.

Griffiths, Bede. *Return to the Center*. Springfield, Illinois: Templegate, 1976.

________. "The Advaitic Experience and the Personal God in the Upanishads and the Bhagavad Gita." *Indian Theological Studies* 15/1 (March 1978): 71-86.

Grillmeier, Aloys. *Christ in Christ Tradition: From the Apostolic Age to Chalcedon (451)*, vol. I. Translated by John Bowden. Atlanta: John Knox Press, 1975.

Guha, Amalendu. "The Indian National Question: A Conceptual Framework." In *Nationalism Question in India*, 26-59. Pune: Training for Development Scholarship Society, 1987.

Guha, Ramachandra, "Savaging the Civilized: Verrier Elwin and the Tribal Question in Late Colonial India." *Economic and Political Weekly* 31/35-7 (September 1996): 2375-89.

Guha, Ranajit, ed. *Subaltern Studies: Writings on South Asian History and Society*, vol. I. Delhi: Oxford University Press, 1991.

__________. "Discipline and Mobilize." In *Subaltern Studies VII: Writings on South Asian History and Society*, ed. Partha Chatterjee and Gyanendra Pandey, 69-120. Delhi: Oxford University Press, 1992.

__________. "On Some Aspects of the Historiography of Colonial India." In *Subaltern Studies I: Writings on South Asian History and Society*, ed. Idem, 1-7. Delhi: Oxford University Press, 1991.

Gunton, Colin E. *The One, The Three and The Many: God, Creation and the Culture of Modernity*, vols. I & II. Cambridge: Cambridge University Press, 1993.

Gupta, Dipankar. "Ethnicity and Politics." In *Politics in India*, ed. Sudipta Kaviraj. Delhi: Oxford University Press, 2000.

__________. "Recasting Reservations in the Language of Rights." In *Democracy, Difference and Social Justice*, ed. Gurpreet Mahajan, 509-26. New Delhi: Oxford University Press, 2000.

__________. "Survivors or Survivals: Reconciling Citizenship and Cultural Particularisms." *Economic and Political Weekly* 34 (August 14, 1999): 2313-23.

Gustafson, James M. "Possibilities and Problems for the Study of Ethics in Religiously Pluralistic Societies." In *Culture, Religion and Society*, ed. Saral K. Chatterji and Hunter P. Mabry, 240-59. Delhi: Indian Society for Promoting Christian Knowledge, 1996.

Gutierrez, Gustavo. *The God of Life*. New York: Orbis Books, 1981.

__________. *The Power of the Poor in History*. New York: Orbis Books, 1983.

__________. *The Poor and the Church in Latin America*. London: Catholic Institute, 1987.

Hall, Stuart. "The Problem of Ideology: Marxism without Guarantees." In *Stuart Hall: Critical Dialogues in Cultural Studies*, ed. David Morley and Kuan-Hsing Chen. London: Routledge, 1996.

Hansen, Thomas Blom. *The Saffron Wave: Democracy and Hindu Nationalism in Modern India*. Delhi: Oxford University Press, 2001.

Hardiman, David. *The Coming of the Devi: Adivasi Assertion in Western India*. Delhi: Oxford University Press, 1987.

__________. "Adivasi Assertion in South Gujarat: the Devi Movement of 1922-3." In *Subaltern Studies – III: Writings on South Asian History and*

Society, ed. Ranajit Guha, 196-230. Delhi: Oxford University Press, 1992.

Häring, Hermann. "Christian Belief in the Threefold God." In *The Many Faces of the Divine*, ed. Hermann Häring and Johann Baptist Metz. *Concilium* 2 (1995): 39-51.

Hariss, John. "Political Participation, Representation and the Urban Poor." *Economic and Political Weekly* 40 (March 12, 2005): 1041-54.

Harris, Harriet A. "Should We Say that Personhood is Relational?" *Scottish Journal of Theology* 51/1 (1998): 214-35.

Hart, Kevin. "The Kingdom and the Trinity." *The Australian Catholic Record* 73/3 (July 2001): 321-39.

Hart, Trevor "Person & Prerogative in Perichoretic Perspective: An Ongoing Dispute in Trinitarian Ontology Observed." *Irish Theological Quarterly* 58/1 (1992): 46-57

Harvey, A.E. *Jesus and the Constraints of History*. London: Gerald Duckworth & Co., 1982.

Harvey, David. *The Condition of Postmodernity: An Enquiry into the Origins of Cultural Change*. Oxford: Basil Blackwell, 1989.

Hasan, Mushirul. "Myths of Appeasement." *The New Indian Express*, 7 February 2001, 8.

Hasker, William. "Tri-unity" *Journal of Religion* 50/1 (1974): 1-32.

Hearne, Brian. "The Church, the Icon of the Trinity." In *A New Missionary Era*, ed. Padraig Flanagan, 53-60. New York: Orbis Books, 1982.

Heidegger, Martin. *Being and Time*. Translated by John Macquarrie and Edward Robinson. New York: Harper & Row, 1962.

Heim, S. Mark. *The Depth of the Riches: A Trinitarian Theology of Religious Ends*. Grand Rapids, Michigan/Cambridge, U.K.: William B. Eerdmans Publishing Company, 2001.

Henry, Martin. "God in Postmodernity." *Irish Theological Journal* 63/1 (1998): 3-21.

Heredia, Rudolf C. *Changing Gods: Rethinking Conversion in India*. New Delhi: Penguin Books, 2007.

Hertz, Rosanna, ed., *Reflexivity & Voice*. California: Sage Publications, 1997.

Hill, William. "Does the World Make a Difference to God?" *The Thomist* 38/1 (January 1974): 146-64.

Hindu Vivek Kendra, *Religious Conversions: Frequently Asked Questions*. Mumbai: Hindu Vivek Kendra, 1999.

Hingle, G.S. *Hindutva Reawakened*. Delhi: Vikas Publishing, 1999.

Hodgson, Leonard. *The Doctrine of the Trinity*. London: Nisbet & Co., 1944.

Hollenbach, David. *Claims in Conflict: Retrieving and Renewing the Catholic Human Rights Tradition*. New York: Paulist Press, 1979.

_________. *The Common Good and Christian Ethics*. Cambridge: Cambridge University Press, 2003.

Horton and Hunt, *Sociology*. New York: McGraw Hill, 1968.

Hoskote, Ranjit. "For a Casteless Society." *The Hindu*, Magazine Section, 13 November 2005, 1.

Hunt, Anne. *The Trinity and the Paschal Mystery: A Development in Recent Catholic Theology*. Collegeville, Minnesota: The Liturgical Press, 1997.

_________. "Psychological Analogy and Paschal Mystery in Trinitarian Theology." *Theological Studies* 59/2 (1998): 197-218.

_________. *What Are They Saying About the Trinity?* New York: Paulist Press, 1998.

Huntington, Samuel P. *The Clash of Civilizations and the Remaking of World Order*. New Delhi: Viking & Penguin Books India (P) Ltd. 1996.

Ilaiah, Kancha. *Why I Am Not a Hindu: A Sudra Critique of Hindutva Philosophy, Culture and Political Economy*. Calcutta: Samya, 1996.

_________. *Buffalo Nationalism: A Critique of Spiritual Fascism*. Kolkata: Samya, 2004.

_________."Needed, a Transformation." *The Hindu*, 23 April 2002, 10.

_________. "Trishuls, Lathis and Books." *The Hindu*, 16 May 2003, 10.

_________. "Demanding a Share." *The Week* 22/36, 8 August 2004, 36-7.

Jaffrelot, Christophe. *The Hindu Nationalist Movement in India 1925 to the 1990s: Strategies of Identity-Building, Implantation and Mobilisation*. New Delhi: Viking Penguin, 1996.

Jain, L.C. "Securing their Future." *Seminar* 523 (March 2003): 63-7.

Jaki, S.L. *The Road of Science and the Ways to God*. Edinburgh: Scottish Academic Press, 1978.

Jayaraj, D., and S. Subramanian, "Abusing Demography." *Economic and Political Weekly* 39 (March 20, 2004): 1227-36.

Jayaram, N., and Satish Saberwal, eds. *Social Conflict*. New Delhi: Oxford University Press, 1995.

Jeanrond, Werner. *Theological Hermeneutics: Development and Significance*. London: SCM Press Ltd, 1994.

Jensen, Michael P. "Is There Anything in What We Say? A Trinitarian Response to the Challenge of Postmodernism." *The Reformed Theological Review* 60/1 (April 2001): 18-29.

Jenson, Robert W. *The Triune Identity: God According to the Gospel*. Philadelphia: Fortress, 1982.

Jha, Shefali. "Representation and Its Epiphanies: A Reading of Constituent Assembly Debates." *Economic and Political Weekly* 39 (September 25, 2004): 4357-60.

Jinkins, Michael, and Stephen Breck Reid. "God's Forsakenness: The Cry of Dereliction as an Utterance within the Trinity." *Horizons in Biblical Theology* 19/1 (June 1997): 33-57.

John Paul II. "Trinity is Mysteriously Present in Creation." *L'Osservatore Romano*. 2 February 2000, 11.

John, T.K., ed. *One Volume Dalit Bible Commentary: New Testament*. New Delhi: Centre for Dalit/Subaltern Studies, 2010.

Johnson, Elizabeth A. *She Who Is: The Mystery of God in Feminist Theological Discourse*. New York: Crossroad, 1992.

________. "The Incomprehensibility of God and the Image of God Male and Female." *Theological Studies* 45/3 (September 1984): 441-65.

Johnson, Paul. *A History of Christianity*. London: Penguin Books, 1978.

Joncas, Jan Michael. "Tasting the Kingdom of God: The Meal Ministry of Jesus and its Implications for Contemporary Worship and Life." *Worship* 74/4 (July 2000): 329-65.

Joseph, Jojo. "Trinitarian Experience of a Christian and Advaitic Experience of a Hindu," *Journal of Dharma* 27/2 (April-June 2002): 207-31.

Joseph, Sarah. "Politics of Contemporary Indian Communitarianism," *Economic and Political Weekly* 32 (October 4, 1997): 2517-23.

________. "Of Minorities and Majorities." *Seminar* 484 (December 1999): 30-4.

________. "Society vs State? Civil Society, Political Society and Non-Party Political Process in India." *Economic and Political Weekly* 37 (January 26, 2002): 299-305.

Joshi, A.P., M.D. Srinivas, and J.K. Bajaj, *Religious Demography of India*. Chennai: Centre for Policy Studies, 2003.

Joshi, Satyakam. "Tribals, Missionaries and Sadhus: Understanding Violence in the Dangs." *Economic and Political Weekly* 34 (September 11, 1999): 2667-75.

Juel, Donald H. "The Trinity and the New Testament." *Theology Today* 54 (1997): 312-24.

Juergensmeyer, Mark. *Religious Nationalism Confronts the Secular State*. Delhi: Oxford University Press, 1993.

Juergensmeyer, Mark. *Terror in the Mind of God: The Global Rise of Religious Violence*. New Delhi: Oxford University Press, 2001.

Jüngel, Eberhard. "The Relationship between Economic and Immanent Trinity." *Theology Digest* 24 (1976): 179-84.

Kaiser, Christopher. "The Ontological Trinity in the Context of Historical Religion." *Scottish Journal of Theology* 29/4 (1976): 301-10.

Kakar, Sudhir. *The Inner World: A Psychoanalytic Study of Childhood and Society in India*. New Delhi: Oxford University Press, 1982.

________. *The Colours of Violence*. New Delhi: Viking and Penguin, 1995.

________. "Some Unconscious Aspects of Ethnic Violence in India." In *Mirrors of Violence: Communities, Riots & Survivors in South Asia*, ed. Veena Das, 135-45. Delhi: Oxford University Press, 1990.

Kallarangatt, Joseph. "The Trinitarian Foundation of an Ecclesiology of Communion." *Christian Orient* 11/1 (March 1990): 3-16.

Kallistos of Diokleia, "The Human Person as an Icon of the Trinity." *Sobornost* 8/2 (1986): 6-23.

Kaniyamparampil, Emmanuel. *The Spirit of Life: A Study of the Holy Spirit in the Early Syriac Tradition*. Kottayam, Vadavathoor: Paurastya Vidyapeetham, 2003

Kannabiran, Kalpana. "Adivasis and the Genocide." *The Hindu*, 24 April 2002, 10.

Kanungo, Pralay. *RSS's Tryst with Politics: From Hedgewar to Sudarshan*. Delhi: Manohar Publications, 2002.

Kärkkäinen, Veli-Matti. "How to Speak of the Spirit Among Religions: Trinitarian "Rules" for a Pneumatological Theology of Religions." *International Bulletin of Missionary Research* 30/3 (July 2006): 12-6.

Kasper, Walter. *The God of Jesus Christ*. London: SCM Press Ltd, 1992.

Katju, Manjari. *Vishva Hindu Parishad and Indian Politics*. New Delhi: Orient Longman, 2003.

Kaufman, Gordon D. *The Theological Imagination: Constructing the Concept of God*. Philadelphia: The Westminster Press, 1981.

Kaviraj, Sudipta, ed. *Politics in India*. New Delhi: Oxford University Press, 2000.

Kaviraj, Sudipta. "The Imaginary Institution of India." In *Subaltern Studies VII: Writings on South Asian History and Society*, ed. Partha Chatterjee and Gyanendra Pandey, 1-39. Delhi: Oxford University Press, 1992.

Keenan, John P. *The Meaning of Christ: A Mahâyâna Theology*. New York: Orbis Books, 1989.

Kelly, Anthony. *The Trinity of Love: A Theology of the Christian God*. Wilmington, Delaware: Michael Glazier, 1989.

________. "A Trinitarian Moral Theology." *Studia Moralia* 39 (2001): 245-89.

Kelly, J.N.D. *Early Christian Doctrines*. San Francisco: Harper & Row, 1978.

Kevern, John R. "The Trinity and Social Justice." *Anglican Theological Review* 79/1 (Winter 1997): 45-54.

Khare, Harish. "After Gujarat." *Seminar* 521 (January 2003): 30-3.

Kilby, Karen. "Perichoresis and Projection: Problems with Social Doctrines of the Trinity." *New Blackfriars* 81/956 (October 2000): 432-45.

Kim, Sebastian C.H. *In Search of Identity: Debates on Religious Conversion in India*. New Delhi: Oxford University Press, 2003.

Kimel, Alvin F. Jr., "The God Who Likes His Name: Holy Trinity, Feminism, and the Language of Faith." In *Speaking the Christian God: The Holy Trinity and the Challenge to Feminism*, ed. idem, 188-208. Michigan: William B. Eerdmans Publishing Co., 1992.

Kishwar, Madhu. "Politics of Majoritarianism vs. Minoritarianism." In *Minority Identities and the Nation-State*, ed. D.L. Sheth and Gurpreet Mahajan, 138-68. New Delhi: Oxford University Press, 1999.

Kitamori, Kazoh. *Theology of the Pain of God*. London: SCM Press, 1966.

Klostermaier, Klaus K. "The Hermeneutic Center." *Journal of Ecumenical Studies* 34/2 (Spring 1997): 159-70.

Klyuev, Boris. *Religion in Indian Society: The Dimensions of 'Unity in Diversity'*. New Delhi: Sterling Publishers, 1989.

Kochuthara, Thomas. "The Biblical Tradition of the Trinitarian Mystery." *Jnanatirtha* 6/2 (July – December 2006): 137-56.

Kohli, Atul. *Democracy and Discontent: India's Growing Crisis of Governability*. Cambridge: Cambridge University Press, 1991.

Komonchak, John, Mary Collins, and Dermot A. Lane, eds. *The New Dictionary of Theology*. Bangalore: Theological Publications in India. 1993.

Koonathan, Varghese Palatty. *The Religion of the Oraons: A Comparative Study of the Concept of God in the Sarna Religion of the Oraons and the Christian Conception of God*. Shillong: Don Bosco Centre For Indigenous Cultures, 1999.

Kosambi, D.D. *The Culture and Civilization of Ancient India in Historical Outline*. New Delhi: Vikas Publishing House, 1981.

Kothari, Rajni. "From Religions to Religiosity." *Jeevadhara* 20/115 (January 1990): 72-88.

Kramrisch, Stella. *The Art of India: Traditions of Indian Sculpture, Painting and Architecture*. London: The Phaidon Press, 1955.

Kress, Robert L. "The Church as *Communio*: Trinity and Incarnation as the Foundations of Ecclesiology." *The Jurist* 36 (1976): 127-58.

________. "Unity in Diversity and Diversity in Unity: Toward an Ecumenical Perichoresic Kenotic Trinitarian Ontology." *Dialogue and Alliance* 4/3 (Fall 1990): 66-70.

Kujur, Sudhir Kumar. "Tribal Concept of the Divine: A Trinitarian Perspective." *Sevartham* 21 (1996): 115-31.

Kullu, Paulus. "Tribal Religion and Culture." *Jeevadhara* 24/140 (1994): 89-109.

Kumar, Pradeep. "Reservations within Reservations: Real Dalit-Bahujans." *Economic and Political Weekly* 36 (Sept. 15, 2001): 3505-7.

Küng, Hans, and Helmut Schmidt, eds. *A Global Ethic and Global Responsibilities: Two Declarations*. London: SCM Press Ltd, 1998.

Kurien, C.T. *Global Capitalism and the Indian Economy*. New Delhi: Orient Longman Limited, 1994.

La Due, William J. *The Trinity Guide to the Trinity*. Harrisburg, Pennsylvania: Trinity Press International, 2003.

Laclau, Ernesto. *Emancipation(s)*. London and New York: Verso, 1996.

LaCugna, Catherine Mowry. *God For Us: The Trinity and Christian Life*. New York: HarperCollins, 1991.

________. "The Baptismal Formula, Feminist Objections, and Trinitarian Theology." *Journal of Ecumenical Studies* 26/2 (Spring 1989): 235-50.

Lahker, Abinash, and Uma Dhanushkodi, *Troubled Times: Communal Fascism Arrives*. Bangalore: Bhoomika, 2002.

Langer, Susanne K. *Philosophy in a New Key: A Study in the Symbolism of Reason, Rite, and Art*. New York: New American Library, 1951.

Lannoy, Richard. *The Speaking Tree: A Study of Indian Culture and Society*. New Delhi: Oxford University Press, 1971.

Larson, Duane. *Times of the Trinity: A Proposal for Theistic Cosmology*. New York: Peter Lang, 1995.

Lash, Nicholas. *Believing Three Ways in One God: A Reading of the Apostles' Creed*. Notre Dame, Indiana: Notre Dame University Press, 1992.

Lee, Jung Young. *The Theology of Change*. New York: Orbis Books, 1979.

Lee, Jung Young. *The Trinity in Asian Perspective*. Nashville: Abingdon Press, 1996.

Lefebvre, Henri. *La Présence et l'absence*. Paris: Casterman, 1980.

________. *The Production of Space*. Translated by Donald Nicholson-Smith. Oxford UK & Cambridge USA: Blackwell Publishers, 1991.

Lefebvre, Henri. *Rhythmanalysis: Space, Time and Everyday Life*. Translated by Stuart Elden and Gerald Moore. London & New York: Continuum, 2004.

Leftow, Brian. "Anti Social Trinitarianism." In *The Trinity: An Interdisciplinary Symposium on the Trinity*, ed. Stephen T. Davis, Daniel Kendall, and Gerald O'Collins, 203-49. New York: Oxford University Press, 1999.

Lele, Jayant K. *Hindutva: The Emergence of the Right*. Madras: Earthworm Books, 1995.

Levinas, Emmanuel. *Totality and Infinity*. Translated by Alphonso Lingis. Pittsburgh: Duquesne University Press, 1969.

Levinas, Emmanuel. *Time and the Other*. Translated by Richard A. Cohen. Pittsburgh: Duquesne University Press, 1987.

_________. *Otherwise than Being or Beyond Essence*. Translated by Alphonso Lingis. Dordrecht: Kluwer Academic Publishers, 1991.

Lévi-Strauss, Claude. *Myth and Meaning*. London & Henley: Routledge & Kegan Paul, 1978.

Lewis, Alan E., ed., *The Motherhood of God*. Edinburgh: The Saint Andrew Press, 1984.

Lienhard, Joseph T. "*Ousia* and *Hypostasis*: The Cappadocian Settlement and the Theology of 'One *Hypostasis*'." In *The Trinity: An Interdisciplinary Symposium on the Trinity*, ed. Stephen T. Davis, Daniel Kendall, and Gerald O'Collins, 99-121. New York: Oxford University Press, 1999.

Lindbeck, George A. "Reflections on Trinitarian Language." *Pro Ecclesia* 4 (Summer 1995): 261-4.

Lipner, Julius. *Brahmabandhab Upadhyay: The Life and Thought of a Revolutionary*. Delhi: Oxford University Press, 1999.

Lipner, Julius, and George Gispert-Sauch, eds. *The Writings of Brahmabandhab Upadhyay*, vol. I, Bangalore: The United Theological College, 1991.

Lobo, Lancy. *Globalisation, Hindu Nationalism and Christians in India*. Jaipur: Rawat Publications, 2002.

_________. "We Belong to Bharat, not Hindustan," *Communalism Combat* 8/75-6 (January - February 2002): 40-2.

_________, and Biswaroop Das, *Geography of Gujarat Riots, 2002: Causatives and Spatial Spread Patterns of Related Factors*. Vadodara: Centre for Culture and Development, 2004

Lonergan, Bernard. *Method in Theology*. London: Darton, Longman & Todd, 1975.

Longchar, A. Wati, and Larry E. Davis, eds. *Doing Theology with Tribal Resources*. Jorhat, Assam: Tribal Study Centre, Eastern Theological College, 1999.

Lotman, Yuri. *Universe of the Mind: A Semiotic Theory of Culture.* Translated by Ann Shukman. Bloomington: Indiana University Press, 1990.

Luntley, Michael. *Reason, Truth and Self: The Postmodern Reconditioned.* London & New York: Routledge, 1995.

Lyotard, Jean-François. *The Postmodern Condition: A Report on Knowledge.* Translated by Geoff Bennington and Brian Massumi. Minneapolis: University of Minnesota Press, 1984.

Maciver, R.M. *Community: A Sociological Study.* London: Macmillan and Co., 1928.

Mackey James P. "Are there Christian Alternatives to Trinitarian Thinking?" In *The Christian Understanding of God Today*, ed. J. Byrne, 66-75. Dublin: Columbia, 1993.

Madan, T.N. *Modern Myths, Locked Minds: Secularism and Fundamentalism in India.* Delhi: Oxford University Press, 1998.

Madan, T.N "Secularism in its Place." In *Politics in India*, ed. Sudipta Kaviraj, 342-8. New Delhi: Oxford University Press, 2000.

Mahadevia, Darshini. "Communal Space Over Life Space." In *Fascism in India: Faces, Fangs and Fact*, ed. Chaitanya Krishna, 377-403. New Delhi: Manak Publications Pvt. Ltd., 2003.

Mahajan, Gurpreet, *Identities and Rights: Aspects of Liberal Democracy in India.* New Delhi: Oxford University Press, 2001.

__________. *The Multicultural Path: Issues of Diversity and Discrimination in Democracy.* New Delhi: Sage Publications, 2002.

__________, ed. *Democracy, Difference and Social Justice.* New Delhi: Oxford University Press, 2000.

__________. "Civil Society and Its Avatars: What Happened to Freedom and Democracy?" *Economic and Political Weekly* 34 (May 15, 1999): 1188-96.

Malacky, Belonick, Deborah. "Revelation and Metaphors: The Significance of the Trinitarian Names, Father, Son and Holy Spirit." *Union Seminary Quarterly Review* 40/3 (1985): 31-41.

Marriott, McKim, ed. *Village India: Studies in the Little Community.* Chicago: University of Chicago Press, 1955.

Marty, Martin E., and R. Scott Appleby, eds. *Fundamentalisms and the State: Remaking Polities, Economies, and Militance.* Chicago & London: University of Chicago Press, 1993.

Marx, Karl. *Selected Writings in Sociology and Social Philosophy*, ed. T. B. Bottomore and M. Rubel. Harmondsworth: Penguin Books, 1963.

Mascall, E.L. *The Triune God: An Ecumenical Study*. Sussex: Churchman Publishing Ltd., 1986.

Massey, James. *Roots: A Concise History of Dalits* (2nd) ed. Delhi: Indian Society for Promoting Christian Knowledge, 1994.

Mathew, P.T. *We Dare the Waters: The World & the Worldview of the Mukkuvar*. Chennai: University of Madras, 2001.

Mathothu, Kurian. *The Development of the Concept of Trimurti in Hinduism*. Bangalore: St. Paul's Press, 1974.

Mattam, Joseph. *Land of the Trinity: A Study of Modern Christian Approaches to Hinduism*. Bangalore: Theological Publications in India, 1975.

__________ and Sebastian Kim, eds., *Mission and Conversion: A Reappraisal*. Mumbai: St. Pauls, 1996.

McCann, Dennis P. "Option for the Poor: Rethinking a Catholic Tradition." In *The Preferential Option for the Poor*, ed. Richard J. Neuhaus, 35-52. Grand Rapids, Michigan: William B. Eerdmans, 1988.

McDade, John. "The Trinity and the Paschal Mystery." *The Heythrop Journal* 29 (1988): 175-91.

McFadyen, Alistair I. *The Call to Personhood: A Christian Theory of the Individual in Social Relationships*. Cambridge: Cambridge University Press, 1990.

__________. "The Trinity and Human Individuality: The Conditions for Relevance." *Theology* 95/763 (1992): 10-8.

McFague, Sallie. *Metaphorical Theology*. Philadelphia: Fortress Press, 1982.

__________. *Models of God*. Philadelphia: Fortress Press, 1987.

McFague, Sallie. *The Body of God: An Ecological Theology*. Minneapolis: Fortress Press, 1993.

McLuhan, Marshall, and Bruce R. Powers. *Transformations in World Life in the 21st Century*. New York: Oxford University Press, 1989.

McMurray, John. *Persons in Relation*. London: Faber and Faber, 1961.

Mead, George Herbert. *The Social Psychology of George Herbert Mead*, ed. Anselm Strauss. Chicago: University of Chicago Press, 1956.

Mehta, Pratap Bhanu. "Minority Institutions and the State." *The Hindu*, 10 August 2002, 10.

Menon, Meena. "Narmada: They Have Little to Cheer About." *The Hindu*, 29 November 2005, 15.

Merrifield, Andy. "Henri Lefebvre: A Socialist in Space." In *Thinking Space*, ed. Mike Crang and Nigel Thrift, 167-82. London and New York: Routledge, 2000.

Metz, Johannes Baptist. *Faith in History and Society: Toward a Practical Fundamental Theology*. Translated by David Smith. London: Burns & Oates, 1980.

Migliore, Daniel L. "The Trinity and Human Liberty." *Theology Today* 36 (January 1980): 488-97.

Milbank, John. "History of the One God." *Heythrop Journal* 40 (1999): 301-18.

Miller, David, ed. *Blackwell Encyclopaedia of Political Thought*. Oxford: Blackwell, 1987.

__________. *Principles of Social Justice*. Cambridge and London: Harvard University Press, 1999.

Minz, Albert. "Dalits and Tribals: A Search For Solidarity." In *Frontiers of Dalit Theology*, ed. V. Devasahayam, 130-58. Delhi: Indian Society for Promoting Christian Knowledge and Madras: Gurukul Lutheran Theological College and Research Institute, 1997.

Minz, Nirmal. "Dalit-Tribal: A Search for Common Ideology." In *Towards A Common Dalit Ideology*, ed. Arvind P. Nirmal, 97-107. Madras: Gurukul Lutheran Theological College and Research Institute, and The Department of Dalit Theology, n.d.

Minz, Nirmal. "Religion and Culture as Power in the Context of Tribal Aspirations in India." In *Pearls of Wisdom: Selected Essays from Lifetime Contributions by Bishop Dr. Nirmal Minz, An Adivasi Intellectual*, ed. Joseph Marianus Kujur and Sonajharia Minz, 143-54. New Delhi: Indian Social Institute and Bangalore: Christian Institute for the Study of Religion and Society, 2007.

Mitchell, Donald W. *Spirituality and Emptiness: The Dynamics of Spiritual Life in Buddhism and Christianity*. New York: Paulist Press, 1991.

Moddie, A.D. "Understanding the Demonization Process." *Seminar* 484 (December 1999): 62-5.

Moltmann, Jürgen. *The Crucified God: The Cross of Christ as the Foundation and Criticism of Christian Theology*. London: SCM Press, 1974.

__________. *History and the Triune God*. Translated by John Bowden. New York: Crossroad, 1992.

__________. *The Trinity and the Kingdom: The Doctrine of God*. Translated by Margaret Kohl. Minneapolis: Fortress Press, 1993.

__________. "Knowing and Community." In *On Community*, ed. Leroy S. Rouner, 162-7. Notre Dame: Notre Dame University Press, 1991.

Moltmann, Jürgen. "The Motherly Father. Is Trinitarian Patripassianism Replacing Theological Patriarchalism?" In *God as Father? Concilium* (March 1981): 51-6.

Momin, Sajeda. "In The Ghetto: Gujaratis Live In A Segregated Society." *The Statesman*, 4 April 2002, 4.

Monachanin, Jules, and H. le Saux. *Ermites du Saccidânanda: Un Essai d'Intégration Chrétienne de laTradition Monastique de l'Inde*. Paris: Casterman, 1957.

__________. *A Benedictine Ashram*, rev. ed. Douglas: Times Press, 1964.

Moore, Sebastian. *The Crucified Jesus is No Stranger*. New York: Paulist Press, 1977.

Mukherjee, Nivedita. "Playing With The Future." *The Week* 22/36 (August 8, 2004): 32-40.

Muller, Earl. "Real Relations and the Divine: Issues in Thomas's Understanding of God's Relation to the World." *Theological Studies* 56 (1995): 673-95.

Munda, Ram Dayal. *Adi-Dharam: Religious Beliefs of the Adivasis of India*. Coimbatore: Sarini & Jharkhand: BIRSA, n.d.

Mundu, John B. *The Ho Christian Community: Towards a New Self-Understanding as Communion*. Delhi: Media House, 2003.

Nadkarni, M.V. "Ethics and Relevance of Conversions: A Critical Assessment of Religious and Social Dimensions in a Gandhian Perspective." *Economic and Political Weekly* 38 (January 18, 2003): 227-35.

Nakamura, Hajime. *Ways of Thinking of Eastern Peoples: India-China-Tibet-Japan*. Honolulu: University of Hawaii Press, 1985.

Namishray, Mohandas. "The Violence in Gujarat and the Dalits." In *Gujarat: The Making of a Tragedy*, ed. Siddharth Varadarajan, 267-70. New Delhi: Penguin Books, 2002.

Nandy, Ashis. "A Critique of Modernist Secularism." In *Politics in India*, ed. Sudipta Kaviraj, 329-41. New Delhi: Oxford University Press, 2000.

__________. "Obituary of a Culture." *Seminar* 513 (May 2002): 15-8.

Neuner, J. and J. Dupuis. *The Christian Faith in the Doctrinal Documents of the Catholic Church*, 6 ed. New York: Alba House, 1996.

Nicholls, David. "Trinity and Conflict." *Theology* 96 (1993): 19-27.

Nirmal, Arvind P. "Towards a Dalit Christian Theology." In *A Reader in Dalit Theology*, ed. idem, 53-70. Madras: Gurukul Lutheran Theological College & Research Institute, n.d.

Norris, Thomas J. "Jesus Crucified and Forsaken: The Face of God for the Modern World." *Communio International Catholic Review* 26/4 (Winter 1999): 892-912.

Nyamiti, Charles. "Divine Immanent Responsibility: An African Approach to the Mystery of the Trinity." *African Christian Studies* (1998): 1-46.

__________. "The Trinity as Source and Soul of African Family Ecclesiology." *African Christian Studies* (1999): 34-92.

O'Collins, Gerald. *The Tripersonal God: Understanding and Interpreting the Trinity*. Mahwah, New Jersey: Paulist Press, 1999

__________. and Edward G. Farrugia, *A Concise Dictionary of Theology*. London: HarperCollins, 1991.

.O'Donnell, Christopher. *Ecclesia: A Theological Encylcopedia of the Church*. Collegeville: The Liturgical Press, 1996, s.v. "Filioque."

O'Donnell, John J. *The Mystery of the Triune God*. New York/Mahwah: Paulist Press, 1989.

__________. "The Trinity As Divine Community: A Critical Reflection Upon Recent Theological Developments." *Gregorianum* 69/1 (1988): 5-34.

O'Hanlon, Gerry. "The Trinitarian God: Towards a New Ireland." *The Irish Theological Quarterly* 55/2 (1989): 99-113.

O'Murchu, Diarmuid. *Quantum Theology*. New York: Crossroad, 1998.

Omvedt, Gail. *Dalits and the Democratic Revolution: Dr. Ambedkar and the Dalit Movement in Colonial India*. New Delhi: Sage Publications, 1994.

Omvedt, Gail. "Buddhism, Bhakti and the VHP – I." *The Hindu*, 23 December 2002, 10.

__________. "Buddhism, Bhakti and the VHP – II." *The Hindu*, 24 December 2002, 10.

Oommen, George. "Historiography of Indian Christianity and Challenges to Subaltern Methodology." *Journal of Dharma* 28/2 (April–June 2003): 212-31.

Oommen, T.K. *Protest and Change: Studies in Social Movements*. New Delhi: Sage Publications, 1990.

__________. *State and Society in India: Studies in Nation-Building*. New Delhi: Sage Publications, 1990.

Ormerod, Neil "The Psychological Analogy for the Trinity: At Odds with Modernity," *Pacifica* 4/3 (October 2001): 281-94.

Oxford-Carpenter, Rebecca. "Gender and the Trinity." *Theology Today* 41/1 (April 1984): 7-25.

Painter, Joe. "Pierre Bourdieu." In *Thinking Space*, ed. Mike Crang and Nigel Thrift, 239-59. London and New York: Routledge, 2000.

Pandey, Gyanendra. *The Construction of Communalism in Colonial North India*. Delhi: Oxford University Press, 1990.

Pandey, Gyanendra. "Community and Violence: Recalling Partition." *Economic and Political Weekly* 32 (August 9, 1997): 2037-45.

Panicker, Lalita. "Saffron Sisterhood: An Illusory Promise of Power." *The Times of India*, 25 March 2002, 10.

Panikkar, K.N., *Communal Threat Secular Challenge*. Madras: Earthworm Books, 1997.

_________, ed. *The Concerned Indian's Guide to Communalism*. New Delhi: Viking, 1999.

_________. "Alternative Historiographies: Changing Paradigm of Power." In *The Struggle for the Past: Historiography Today*, ed. Felix Wilfred and Jose D. Maliekal, 11-20. Chennai: University of Madras, 2002.

Panikkar, Raimundo. *The Trinity and World Religions: Icon-Person-Mystery*. Bangalore: The Christian Institute for the Study of Religion and Society, 1970.

_________. *The Intrareligious Dialogue*. Bangalore: Asian Trading Corporation, 1984.

_________. *The Cosmotheandric Experience: Emerging Religious Consciousness*. Delhi: Motilal Banarsidass Publishers Private Limited, 1993.

_________. "Toward an Ecumenical Theandric Spirituality." *Journal of Ecumenical Studies* 5/3 (Summer 1968): 507-34.

Panikkar, Raimundo. "The Ultimate Experience." *Theology Digest* 20 (1972): 219-26.

_________. "Indian Theology: A Theological Mutation." In *Theologizing in India*, ed. M. Amaladoss, T. K. John, and G. Gispert-Sauch, 23-42. Bangalore: Theological Publications in India, 1981.

_________. "The Cosmotheandric Intuition." *Jeevadhara* 14/79 (January 1984): 27-35.

_________. "There is No Outer without Inner Space." *Cross Currents* 43/1 (Spring 1993): 60-81.

Pape, W. Roy. "Keshub Chunder Sen's Doctrine of Christ and the Trinity: a Rehabilitation." *The Indian Journal of Theology* 25/1 (January – March 1976): 55-71.

Parappally, Jacob. "Jesus Christ, the Word of God Revealing a Trinitarian God; Christian Faith in Dialogue with Islamic Faith." *Vidyajyoti Journal of Theological Reflection* 69/11 (November 2005): 832-43.

Parekh Bhiku. *Rethinking Multiculturalism: Cultural Diversity and Political Theory*. New York: Palgrave, 2000.

_________. "What is Multiculturalism?" *Seminar* 484 (December 1999): 14-7.

Parekh Bhiku. "A Case for Positive Discrimination." In *Democracy, Difference and Social Justice*, ed. Gurpreet Mahajan, 380-8. New Delhi: Oxford University Press, 2000.

__________. "Making Sense of Gujarat." *Seminar* 513 (May 2002): 26-31.

__________. "Some Reflections on the Hindu Theory of Tolerance." *Seminar* 521 (January 2003). 48-53.

Parish, Steven M. *Hierarchy and its Discontents: Culture and the Politics of Consciousness in Caste Society*. Delhi: Oxford University Press, 1997.

Parker, Thomas D. "The Political Meaning of the Doctrine of the Trinity: Some Theses." *Journal of Religion* 60/2 (April 1980): 165-84.

Peters, Ted. *God – The World's Future: Systematic Theology for a Postmodern Era*. Minneapolis: Fortress, Press, 1992.

__________. *God as Trinity. Relationality and Temporality in Divine Life*. Louisville, Kentucky: John Knox Press, 1993.

__________. "The Battle Over Trinitarian Language." *Dialog* 30 (Winter 1991): 44-9.

Philip, A.J. "Hindutva, the Lexical Way: Delegitimising the Adivasi." *The Indian Express*, 8 March 1999.

Pichalakkatt, Binoy. "Dialoguing With Symbols: Exploring Zero, *Sunyata* and Trinity for a Holistic Reality." *Omega – Indian Journal of Science and Religion* 5/2 (December 2006): 25-41.

Pieris, Aloysius. *An Asian Theology of Liberation*. New York: Orbis Books, 1988.

Plantinga, Cornelius, Jr., "Social Trinity and Tritheism." In *Trinity, Incarnation and Atonement*, ed. idem and R. Feenstra. Notre Dame, Indiana: Notre Dame University Press, 1989.

Plantinga, Cornelius, Jr., "The Threeness/Onesss Problem of the Trinity." *Calvin Theological Journal* 23 (April 1989): 37-53.

Ponnaiah, James. "Spirituality of the Subalterns." *Vaiharai* 9/3 (September 2004): 32-58.

Porteous, J. Douglas. *Landscapes of the Mind: Worlds of Sense and Metaphor*. Toronto: University of Toronto Press, 1990.

Porter, Lawrence B. "On Keeping 'Persons' in the Trinity: a Linguistic Approach to Trinitarian Thought." *Theological Studies* 41/3 (September 1980): 530-48.

Prabhakar, M.E. "Christology in Dalit Perspective." In. *Frontiers of Dalit Theology*, ed. V. Devasahayam, 402-32. Madras: Gurukul Lutheran Theological College and Research Institute, and Delhi: Indian Society for Promoting Christian Knowledge, 1997.

Prabhakar, M.E. "The Search for a Dalit Theology." In *A Reader in Dalit Theology*, ed. Arvind P. Nirmal, 41-52. Madras: The Department of Dalit Theology, Gurukul Lutheran Theological College & Research Institute, n.d.

Prades, Javier. "From the Economic to the Immanent Trinity: Remarks on a Principle of Renewal in Trinitarian Theology – I & II." *Communio International Catholic Review* 27/2 & 3 (Summer & Fall 2000): 240-61, 562-93.

Purcell, Michael. "Leashing God with Levinas: Tracing a Trinity with Levinas." *Heythrop Journal* 40/3 (July 1999): 301-18.

Putti, Joseph. *Theology as Hermeneutics: Paul Ricoeur's Theory of Text Interpretation and Method in Theology*. Bangalore: Kristu Jyoti Publications, 1991.

Quinn, Philip L., and Kevin Meeker, eds. *The Philosophical Challenge of Religious Diversity*. New York: Oxford University Press, 2000.

Radford Ruether, Rosemary. *Sexism and God-Talk: Towards a Feminist Theology*. Boston: Beacon Press, 1983.

————. "Is There a Need for a New Barmen Declaration?" Unpublished Internet article.

Radhakrishnan, P. "Sensitising Officials on Dalits and Reservations." *Economic and Political Weekly* 37 (February 16, 2002): 653-9.

Raguin, Yves. *The Depth of God*. Translated by Kathleen England. Hertfordshire: Anthony Clarke, 1979.

Rahner, Karl, and Herbert Vorgrimler. *Concise Theological Dictionary*, 2nd. ed. London: Burns & Oates, 1983.

————. *The Trinity*. Translated by Joseph Donceel. London: Burns & Oates, 1986.

Raj, Ebe Sunder. *The Confusion Called Conversion*. Chennai: Bharat Jyoti, 1998.

Ram, P.R. "Crime and (No) Punishment: Communal Violence, Inquiry Commissions and Deliverance of Justice." In *Secular Challenge to Communal Politics*, ed. idem, 120-32. Mumbai: Vikas Adhyayan Kendra, 1998.

————. "Hindutva Offensive: Social Roots and Characterisation." In *Secular Challenge to Communal Politics*, ed. idem, 90-117. Mumbai: Vikas Adhyayan Kendra, 1998.

————. *In the Name of Religion: Truth Behind Conversions and Acts of Violence*. Mumbai: EKTA, 1999.

Ramsey, Ian T. *Religious Language*. London: SCM Press, 1957.

Rao, M.N. "Religious Freedom – Legal Restrictions on Conversions." *The Hindu*, 8 July 2003, 16.

Rao, Nandini. "Interpreting Silences: Symbol and History in the Case of Ram Janmabhoomi/Babri Masjid." In *Social Construction of the Past: Representation as Power*, ed. George C. Bond and Angela Gilliam, 154-64. London: Routledge, 1994.

Rao, Ramesh N. *Secular 'Gods' Blame Hindu 'Demons': The Sangh Parivar Though the Mirror of Distortion*. New Delhi: Har-Anand Publications, 2001.

Rappaport, Roy A. *Ritual and Religion in the Making of Humanity*. Cambridge: Cambridge University Press, 1990.

Rawls, John. *A Theory of Justice*. Oxford: Oxford University Press, 1972.

__________. *Political Liberalism*. New York: Oxford University Press, 1993.

Reddy, C. Rammanohar. "Facts on 'Appeasement'." *The Hindu*, 14 September 2002, 10.

__________. "Statistics and Demography." *The Hindu*, 30 March 2004, 10.

Redfield, Robert. *The Little Community and Peasant Society and Culture*. Chicago: The University of Chicago Press, 1971.

Rege, Sharmila. "Histories from the Borderlands." *Seminar* 495 (November 2000): 55-61.

Richard, Lucien J. *A Kenotic Christology: In the Humanity of Jesus The Christ, The Compassion of Our God*. Washington, D.C.: University Press of America, Inc., 1982.

Richman, Paula, ed. *Many Rāmāyanas: The Diversity of a Narrative Tradition in South Asia*. Delhi: Oxford University Press, 1994.

Ricoeur, Paul. *The Philosophy of Paul Ricoeur*, ed. L.E. Hahn. Chicago and La Salle, Illinois: Open Court, 1996.

Ritzer, George. *The McDonaldization of Society: An Investigation into the Changing Character of Contemporary Social Life*. California: Pine Forge Press, 1993.

Robert T. Sears. "Trinitarian Love As Ground of the Church." *Theological Studies* 37/4 (1976): 652-79.

Roberts, Richard. "Globalized Religion?" In *Theology and Sociology*, ed. Robin Gill, 471-85. London: Cassell, 1996.

Robinson, John A. *Thou Who Art: The Concept of the Personality of God*. New York and London: Continuum, 2006. (reviewed in *The Journal of Theological Studies* 58/1 (April 2007), p. 371.

Rocca, Gregory. "The Trinity and Feminism." *Theology Today* 57/3 (July 1993): 509-20.

Rogers, Eugene F., Jr. *After the Spirit: A Constructive Pneumatology from Resources outside the Modern West*. Grand Rapids, Michigan/Cambridge, U.K.: William B. Eerdmans Publishing Company, 2005.

Rourke, Thomas R. "Contemporary Globalization: An Ethical and Anthropological Evaluation." *Communio International Catholic Review* 27/3 (Fall 2003): 490-510.

Roy, Anupama. "Community, Women Citizens and a Women's Politics." *Economic and Political Weekly* 36 (April 28, 2001): 1441-7.

Russell, John, Nancey Murphy, and Arthur R. Peacocke, eds. *Chaos and Complexity: Scientific Perspectives on Divine Action.* Vatican City: Vatican Observatory Publications and California: The Center for Theology and the Natural Sciences, 1997.

Saberwal, Satish. *Roots of Crisis: Interpreting Contemporary Indian Society.* New Delhi: Sage Publications, 1996.

————. "On Crossing Boundaries." *Seminar* 495 (November 2000): 29-32.

Sahi, Jyoti. *The Child and the Serpent: Reflections on Popular Indian Symbols.* London: Routledge & Kegan Paul Ltd., 1980.

Saberwal, Satish. *Stepping Stones: Reflections on the Theology of Indian Christian Culture.* Bangalore: Asian Trading Corporation, 1986.

Sahni, Ajai. "Gujarat: Communal Ghetto or Global Enterprises?" In *The Black Book of Gujarat,* ed. M.L. Sondhi and Apratim Mukarji, 53-68. New Delhi: Manak Publications Pvt. Ltd., 2002.

Said, Edward. *Orientalism: Western Conceptions of the Orient.* New Delhi: Penguin Books, 2001

Sainath, P. "When Farmers Die." *The Hindu,* 22 June 2004, 10.

————. "Seeds of Suicide – I & II." *The Hindu,* 20 & 21 July 2004, 10.

Sarkar, Sumeet. "The Fascism of the Sangh Parivar." In *Secular Challenge To Communal Politics: A Reader,* ed. P.R. Ram, 77-89. Mumbai: Vikas Adhyayan Kendra, 1998.

Sartre, Jean Paul. *No Exit and Three Other Plays.* New York: Random House, 1955.

Sarukkai, Sundar. "The 'Other' in Anthropology and Philosophy." *Economic and Political Weekly* 32 (June 14, 1997): 1406-9.

Sarup, Madan. *An Introductory Guide to Post-Structuralism and Postmodernism.* Athens: The University of Georgia Press, 1993.

Sassen, Saskia. *Globalization and its Discontents: Essays on the New Mobility of People and Money.* New York: The New Press, 1998.

————. "The Global City: Strategic Site/New Frontier." *Seminar* 503 (July 2001): 29-39

Sathe, Vasant. "Reform Hindu Society to Stop Conversion." *The Times of India.* 22 January 1999.

Sathyamurthy, T.V. "Nationalism in the Era of Globalisation." *Economic and Political Weekly* 33 (August 15, 1998): 2247-52.

Savarkar, V.D. *Hindutva*. Bombay: Veer Savarkar Prakashan, 1969.

Sawant, P.B. "The Constitution and Reservations." *The Hindu,* 2 July 2003, 10.

Say Pa, Anna May. "The Feminine Image of God." *In God's Image* 19/2 (June 2000): 2-9.

Sayers, Dorothy L. *The Mind of The Maker*. London: Methuen, 1941.

Schillebeeckx, Edward and B. Iersel, eds., "A Personal God?" *Concilium* (1977).

Schindler, David L. "Trinity, Creation, and the Order of Intelligence in the Modern Academy." *Communio International Catholic Review* (Fall 2001): 406-28.

Schnackenburg, Rudolf. *God's Rule and Kingdom,* (2nd) ed. New York: Herder & Herder, and London: Burns & Oates, 1968.

Schneiders, Sandra M. "The Foot Washing (John 13:1-20): An Experiment in Hermeneutics." *Catholic Biblical Quarterly* 43/1 (January 1981): 76-92.

Schoffeleers, Matthew. "Religion and Power: Introduction." *Social Compass* 32/1 (1985): 5-13.

Schoonenberg, P.J.A.M. "Trinity – The Consummated Covenant: Theses on the Doctrine of the Trinitarian God." *Studies in Religion* 5/2 (1975-6): 111-6.

Schreiter, Robert J. *Constructing Local Theologies*. London: SCM Press Ltd., 1985.

__________. *The New Catholicity: Theology between the Global and the Local*. New York: Orbis Books, 2000.

Scott, David C., ed. *Keshub Chunder Sen: A Selection*. Madras: The Christian Literature Society and Bangalore: United Theological College, 1979.

Scott, James C. *Weapons of the Weak: Everyday Forms of Peasant Resistance*. Delhi: Oxford University Press, 1990.

Scruton, David L. *Sociophobics: The Anthropology of Fear*. Boulder & London: Westview Press, 1986.

Sebastian, C.D. "Trikaya, Trimurti and Trinity: Three Facets of the Holy in Buddhism, Hinduism and Christianity." *Jnanatirtha* 6/2 (July – December 2006): 118-36.

Segundo, Juan Luis. *Our Idea of God*. New York: Orbis Books, 1974.

__________. *Signs of the Times: Theological Reflections*. Translated by Robert R. Barr. New York: Orbis Books, 1993.

Segundo, Juan Luis. "The Hermeneutic Circle." In *Third World Liberation Theologies: A Reader*, ed. DeaneWilliam Ferm, 64-92. New York: Orbis Books, 1986.

Sen, Amartya. "Capability and Well-Being." In *The Quality of Life*, ed. idem and Martha C. Nussbaum, 30-53. Oxford: Clarendon Press, 1995.

__________. *On Economic Inequality*. New Delhi: Oxford University Press, 1999.

Sengupta, Chandan, Anil Kumar, and Katy Y. Gandevia. *Communal Riots in Gujarat, 2002: A Study of Contextual Factors*. Mumbai: Tata Institute of Social Sciences, 2003.

Sengupta, Roshni. "Communal Violence in India: Perspectives on Causative Factors." *Economic and Political Weekly* 40 (May 15, 2005): 2046-50.

Shah, A.M. "The 'Dalit;' Category and its Differentiation." *Economic and Political Weekly* 37 (April 6, 2002): 1317-8.

__________. "The Tribes – So-called – of Gujarat: In the Perspective of Time." *Economic and Political Weekly* 38 (January 11, 2003), 95-7.

Shah, Ghanshyam. *Social Movements in India: A Review of the Literature*. New Delhi: Sage Publications, 1990.

__________. "Conversion, Reconversion and the State: Recent Events in the Dangs." *Economic and Political Weekly* 34 (February 6, 1999): 312-8.

__________. "Caste, Hindutva and Hideousness." *Economic and Political Weekly* 35 (April 13, 2000): 1391-3.

__________. "Contestation and Negotiations: Hindutva Sentiments and Temporal Interests in Gujarat Elections." *Economic and Political Weekly* 37 (November 30, 2002): 4838-43.

__________. "The 1969 Communal Riots in Ahmedabad: A Case Study." In *Communal Riots in Post-Independence India*, ed. Asghar Ali Engineer. Mumbai: 1991.

__________. "Unrest Among the Adivasis and their Struggles." In *The Other Gujarat: Social Transformations Among Weaker Sections*, ed. Takashi Shinoda. Mumbai: Popular Prakashan, 2002.

Shah, Mihir. "Governance Reform for India's Forests." *The Hindu*, 20 May 2005, 10.

Sharma, Arvind, ed. *Hinduism and Secularism After Ayodhya*. Hampshire and New York: Palgrave Publishers, 2001.

Sharma, Ram Nath. *Gujarat Holocaust: Communalism in the Land of Gandhi*. Delhi: Shubhi Publications, 2002.

Sheridan, Daniel P. "Grounded in the Trinity: Suggestions for a Theology of Relationship to Other Religions." *The Thomist* 50/2 (1986): 260-78.

Shimray, Shimreingam, and Limatula Longkumer. *Tribal Theology On The Move*. Jorhat, Assam: Tribal/Women Study Centres, 2006.

Shinoda, Takashi, ed. *The Other Gujarat: Social Transformations Among Weaker Sections*. Mumbai: Popular Prakashan, 2002.

Shourie, Arun. *Harvesting Our Souls: Missionaries, their Design, their Claims*. New Delhi: ASA Publications, 2000.

Singer, Milton. *When a Great Tradition Modernizes: An Anthropological Approach to Indian Civilization*. Delhi: Vikas Publishing House, 1972.

Singh, Amrik. "After the Minority Rights Verdict." *The Hindu*, 30 May 2003, 10.

Singh, Niranjan S. "Shakti." In *Gems from India*, ed. George Gispert-Sauch. Delhi: ISPCK & VIEWS, 2006.

Smith, John E. "The Individual, the Collective, and the Community." In *The Philosophy of Gabriel Marcel. The Library of Living Philosophers*, vol. 17, ed. Paul Arthur Schilpp and Lewis Edwin Hahn, 337-49. Carbondale: Southern Illinois University, 1984.

Soares-Prabhu, George. "The Kingdom of God: Jesus' Vision of a New Society." In *The Indian Church in the Struggle for a New Society*, ed. D.S. Amalorpavadass, 579-608. Bangalore: NBCLC, 1981.

__________. "Anti-greed and Anti-pride." *Jeevadhara* 24/140 (1994): 130-50.

Sobrino, Jon. *Spirituality of Liberation: Toward Political Holiness*. Translated by Robert R. Barr. New York: Orbis Books, 1988.

__________, and Felix Wilfred, eds. "Globalization and its Victims." *Concilium* 5 (2001).

__________. "Faith, Justice, and Injustice." In *The Pastoral Circle Revisited: A Critical Quest for Truth and Information,*" ed. Frans Wijsen, Peter Henriot, and Rodrigo Mejßa, ix-xvii. New York: Orbis Books, 2005.

Sölle, Dorothee. "God's Pain and Our Pain." In *The Future of Liberation Theology: Essays in Honor of Gustavo Gutiérrez*, ed. Marc H. Ellis and Otto Maduro, 326-33. New York: Orbis Books, 1989.

Sondhi, M.L., and Apratim Mukarji, eds. *The Black Book of Gujarat*. New Delhi: Manak Publications, 2002.

Soni, Vikram. "Tribal People and Preserving Prime Forests." *The Hindu*, 29 November 2005, 14.

Soskice, Janet M. *Metaphor and Religious Language*. Oxford: Clarendon Press, 1985.

__________. "Trinity and 'the Feminine Other.'" *New Blackfriars* 75/878 (1994): 2-17.

Spivak, Gayatri. "Can the Subaltern Speak?" In *Marxism and the Interpretation of Culture*, ed. C. Nelson and L. Grossberg, 271-313. Urbana: University of Illinois Press, 1988.

Srinivas, M.N. *The Dominant Caste and Other Essays*. Delhi: Oxford University Press, 1987.

__________. "Mobility in the Caste System," In *Structure and Change in Indian Society*, ed. Milton Singer and Bernard S. Cohn, 189-200. New Delhi: Rawat Publications, 1996.

Stiglitz, Joseph. *Globalization and Its Discontents*. London: Penguin Press, 2002.

Strenski, Ivan. "Mircea Eliade: Some Theoretical Problems." In *The Theory of Myth: Six Studies*, ed. Adrian Cunningham, 40-78. London: Sheed & Ward, 1973.

Stumpf, Samuel Enoch. *Socrates to Sartre: A History of Philosophy*. New York: Mc-Graw-Hill Book Company, 1975.

Sugirtharajah, R. S. *The Bible and the Third World: Precolonial, Colonial and Postcolonial Encounters*. United Kingdom: Cambridge University Press, 2001.

Swaminathan, Padmini. "Some Issues Confronting 'Women's Movement' in India." In *Dalits and Women: Quest for Humanity*, ed. V. Devasahayam, 179-89. Madras: Gurukul Lutheran Theological College and Research Institute, 1996.

Tam, Eckman P.C. "The Trinity and World Religions Reconsidered." *Studies in Interreligious Dialogue* 8/2 (1998): 52-66.

Taylor, Charles. *Sources of the Self: The Making of the Modern Identity*. Cambridge, Massachusetts: Harvard University Press, 1989.

__________. "The Politics of Recognition." In *Multiculturalism: Examining the Politics of Recognition*, ed. Amy Gutmann, 25-73. Princeton: Princeton University Press, 1994.

Tennent, Timothy C. "Trinity and Saccidananda in the Writings of Brahmabandhav Upadhyay." *Dharma Deepika* 7/1 (January – June 2003): 61-75.

TeSelle, Eugene. *Augustine the Theologian*. New York: Herder, 1970.

Thanzauva, K. *Theology of Community: Tribal Theology in the Making*. Aizawl: Mizo Theological Conference, 1997.

Thapar, Romila. *History and Beyond*. New Delhi: Oxford University Press, 2000.

__________. "Communalism and the Historical Legacy: Some Facets." In *Secular Challenge to Communal Politics: A Reader*, ed. P.R. Ram, 6-24. Mumbai: Vikas Adhyayan Kendra, 1998.

Thapar, Romila. "The Ramayana Syndrome." *Seminar* 353 (January 1989): 71-5.

__________. "The Tyranny of Labels." In *The Concerned Indian's Guide to Communalism*, ed. K.N. Panikkar, 1-31. New Delhi: Viking, 1999.

Thengadi, Dattopant. *Nationalist Pursuit*. Bangalore: Sahitya Sindhu Prakashana, 1992.

Thistlethwaite, Susan Brooks. "On the Trinity." *Interpretation* 45/2 (April 1991): 159-71.

Thistleton, Anthony C. *Interpreting God & the Postmodern Self: On Meaning, Manipulation & Promise*. Edinburgh: T & T Clark, 1995.

Thompson, John. *Modern Trinitarian Perspectives*. New York: Oxford University Press, 1994.

Thurmer, John H. *A Detection of the Trinity*. Exeter: The Paternoster Press, 1984.

__________. "The Analogy of the Trinity." *Scottish Journal of Theology* 34/6 (1981): 509-15.

Tilley, Terrence W. *Talking of God: An Introduction to Philosophical Analysis of Religious Language*. New York: Paulist Press, 1978.

Tilliette, Xavier. "Trinity and Creation." Communio International Catholic Review (Summer 2001): 296-310.

Tom F. Driver. *The Magic of Ritual: Our Need for Liberating Rites that Transform Our Lives and Our Communities*. HarperCollins Publishers, New York, 1991.

Tönnies, Ferdinand. *Community and Association*. Translated by Charles P. Loomis. London: Routledge & Kegan Paul, 1974.

Torrance, Alan J. *Persons in Communion: Trinitarian Description and Human Participation*. Edinburgh: T & T Clark, 1996.

Torrance, James B. *Worship, Community, and the Triune God of Grace*. Carlisle, U.K.: Paternoster Press, 1996.

Torrance, Thomas F. *The Christian Doctrine of God: One Being Three Persons*. Edinburgh: T & T Clark, 1988.

__________. "The Christian Apprehension of God the Father." In *Speaking the Christian God: The Holy Trinity and the Challenge to Feminism*, ed. Alvin F. Kimel, Jr., 120-43. Michigan: William B. Eerdmans, 1992.

Tracy, David. "Kenosis, Sunyata, and Trinity: A Dialogue with Masao Abe." In *The Emptying God: A Buddhist–Jewish–Christian Conversation*, ed. John B. Cobb, Jr., and Christopher Ives, 135-54. New York: Orbis Books, 1990.

__________. "The Paradox of the Many Faces of God in Monotheism." In *The Many Faces of the Divine: Concilium* 2 (1995): 30-8.

Tracy, David. "Trinitarian Speculation and the Forms of Divine Disclosure." In *The Trinity: An Interdisciplinary Symposium on the Trinity*, ed. Stephen T. Davis, Daniel Kendall, and Gerald O'Collins, 273-93. New York: Oxford University Press, 1999.

Turner, Jonathan H. *The Structure of Sociological Theory*, 4th ed. Jaipur: Rawat Publications, 1987.

Turner, Victor W. *The Ritual Process*. London: Routledge & Kegan Paul, 1969.

Uberoi, J.P.S. *The European Modernity: Science, Truth and Method*. Delhi: Oxford University Press, 2002.

Vähakängas, Mika. "African Approaches to the Trinity." *African Theological Journal* 23/2 (2000): 33-50.

Van Beeck, Frans Jozef. "Trinitarian Theology as Participation." In *The Trinity: An Interdisciplinary Symposium on the Trinity*, ed. Stephen T. Davis, Daniel Kendall, and Gerald O'Collins, 295-325. New York: Oxford University Press, 1999.

Van der Veer, Peter. *Religious Nationalism: Hindus and Muslims in India* New Delhi: Oxford University Press, 1998.

________."Riots and Rituals: The Construction of Violence and Public Space in Hindu Nationalism." In *Riots and Pogroms*, ed. Paul R. Brass, 154-76. Macmillan Press, 1996.

Van Exem, A. *The Religious System of the Munda Tribe: An Essay in Religious Anthropology*. St. Augustin: Haus Völker und Kulturen, and Ranchi: Catholic Press, 1982.

Van Gennep, Arnold. *The Rites of Passage*. Chicago: The University of Chicago Press, 1960.

Van Rheenen, Gailyn. *Communicating Christ in Animistic Contexts*. Grand Rapids, Michigan: Baker Book House, 1991.

Van Roo, William A. *Man the Symbolizer*. Rome: Gregorian University Press, 1981.

Vandana, Sr. "Indian Theologizing: The Role of Experience." In *Theologizing in India,* ed. M. Amaladoss, T. K. John, and G. Gispert-Sauch, 81-115. Bangalore: Theological Publications in India, 1981.

Vanstone, W.H. *The Stature of Waiting*. London: Darton, Longman & Todd, 1982.

Varadarajan, Siddharth, ed. *Gujarat: The Making of a Tragedy*. New Delhi: Penguin, 2002.

Varshney, Ashutosh. *Ethnic Conflict and Civic Life: Hindus and Muslims in India*. New Delhi: Oxford University Press, 2002.

Vattimo, Gianni. *Belief*. Translated by Luca D'Isanto and David Webb. Cambridge: Polity Press, 1999.

Veliath, Dominic. "The Trinity in Indian Theology." *Kristu Jyoti* 8/2 (June 1992): 1-24.

Vickers, Jason E. *Invocation and Assent: The Making and Remaking of Trinitarian Theology*. Michigan/Cambridge, U.K.: William B. Eerdmans Publishing Co., 2008.

Vidyarthi, L.P. and Binay Kumar Rai. *The Tribal Culture of India*. 2nd ed. New Delhi: Concept Publishing Company, 1985.

Vigil, José M. "The Option for the Poor is an Option for Justice, and not Preferential: A New Theological-Systematic Framework for the Option for the Poor." *Vidyajyoti Journal of Theological Reflection* 68/7 (July 2004): 509-20.

__________, ed. in *Toward a Planetary Theology: Along the Many Paths of God*. Montreal: International Theological Commission of EATWOT, 2010.

Viswanathan, Gauri. *Outside the Fold: Conversion, Modernity, and Belief*. New Delhi: Oxford University Press, 2001.

Voloshinov, Valentin N. *Marxism and the Philosophy of Language*. Translated by L. Matejka and I.R. Titunik. New York: Seminar Press, 1973.

Von Balthasar, Hans Urs. *Mysterium Paschale: The Mystery of Easter*. Michigan: William B. Eerdmans Publishing Co., 1990.

__________. *Theo-Drama: The Action*, vol. IV. San Francisco: Ignatius Press, 1994.

__________. "Creation and Trinity." *Communio International Catholic Review* 15/3 (Fall 1988): 285-93.

Von Brück, Michael. *The Unity of Reality: God, God-Experience and Meditation in the Hindu-Christian Dialogue*. New York: Paulist Press, 1991.

__________. "*Advaita* and Trinity: Reflections on the Vedantic and Christian Experience of God with Reference to Buddhist Non-Dualism." *Indian Theological Studies* 20/1 (March 1983): 37-60.

__________. "Buddhist Shûnyatâ and the Christian Trinity: The Emerging Holistic Paradigm." In *Buddhist Emptiness and Christian Trinity: Essays and Explorations, ed.* Roger Corless and Paul Knitter, 44-66. New York: Paulist Press, 1990.

__________. "Trinitarian Theology: Hegelian vis-à-vis *Advaitic*." *Journal of Dharma* 8/3 (July–September 1983): 283-95.

Vroom, Hendrik M. "Religious Hermeneutics, Culture and Narratives." *Studies in Interreligious Dialogue* 4/2 (1994): 189-213.

__________. *No Other Gods: Christian Belief in Dialogue with Buddhism, Hinduism, and Islam*. Translated by Lucy Jansen. Michigan & Cambridge: William B. Eerdmans Publishing Company, 1996.

Wadley, Susan Snow. *Shakti: Power in the Conceptual Structure of Karimpur Religion*. New Delhi: Munshiram Manoharlal Publishers Pvt. Ltd., 1985.

__________, ed. *Powers of Tamil Women*. New Delhi: Manohar Publications, 1991.

Wainwright, Geoffrey. "The Doctrine of the Trinity: Where the Church Stands or Falls" *Interpretation* 45/2 (April 1991): 117-32,

__________. "Trinitarian Worship." In *Speaking the Christian God: The Holy Trinity and the Challenge to Feminism*, ed. Alvin F. Kimel, Jr., 209-21. Michigan: William B. Eerdmans Publishing Co., 1992.

Walters, Albert Sundararaj. *We Believe in One God? Reflections on the Trinity in the Malaysian Context*. Delhi: Indian Society for Promoting Christian Knowledge: 2002.

Walzer, Michael. *Spheres of Justice: A Defense of Pluralism and Equality*. New York: Basic Books, 1983.

__________. *Towards a Global Civil Society*. Providence: Berghahn Books, 1998.

Ward, Graham, ed., *The Postmodern God: A Theological Reader*. Oxford: Blackwell Publishers, 1997.

Ward, Keith. *God, Faith and the New Millennium: Christian Belief in an Age of Science*. Oxford: Oneworld Publications, 2002.

Weber, Max. *The Theory of Social and Economic Organization*. Translated by A.M. Henderson and Talcott Parsons. New York: The Free Press, 1964.

__________. *The Protestant Ethic and The Spirit of Capitalism*. Translated by Talcott Parsons. New York: Charles Scribner's Sons, 1976.

__________. "Class, Status, Party." In *Social Stratification*, ed. Dipankar Gupta, 455-70. Delhi: Oxford University Press, 1991.

Welch, Claude. *In This Name: The Doctrine of the Trinity in Contemporary Theology*. London: SCM Press, 1953.

Welker, Michael. "God's Eternity, God's Temporality & Trinitarian Theology." *Theology Today* 55/3 (October 1998): 317-28.

Wells, Harold G. "Trinitarian Feminism: Elizabeth Johnson's Wisdom Christology." *Theology Today* 52/3 (October 1995): 330-43

Westermann, Claus. *Genesis 1-11: A Commentary*. Translated by John J. Scullion. Minneapolis: Augsburg Publishing House, 1984.

Wilfred, Felix. *On the Banks of Ganges: Doing Contextual Theology*. Delhi: Indian Society for Promoting Christian Knowledge, 2002

__________. *Asian Dreams and Christian Hope: At the Dawn of the Millennium*. 2nd ed. Delhi: Indian Society for Promoting Christian Knowledge, 2003.

Wilfred, Felix. *The Sling of Utopia.* Delhi: Indian Society for Promoting Christian Knowledge, 2005.

__________. "Towards a Subaltern Hermeneutics: Beyond the Contemporary Polarities in the Interpretation of Religious Traditions." In *Voices from the Third World, Ecumenical Association of the Third World Theologians* 19/2 (1996).

__________. "Towards an Inter-Religious Asian Public Theology." *Vidyajyoti Journal of Theological Reflection* 74/2 (February 2010): 103-16.

__________, and Jose D. Maliekal, eds. *The Struggle for the Past: Historiography Today.* Chennai: University of Madras, 2002.

Wilkinson, Steven I. "Putting Gujarat in Perspective." *Economic and Political Weekly* 37 (April 27, 2002): 1579-83.

Williams, Arthur H. "The Trinity and Time." *Scottish Journal of Theology* 39/1 (1986): 65-81.

Williams, David T. "Trinitarian Ecology." *Scottish Bulletin of Evangelical Theology* 18/2 (Autumn 2000): 142-59.

Williams, Rowan. "Trinity and Pluralism." In *Christian Uniqueness Reconsidered,* ed. Gavin D'Costa, 3-15. New York: Orbis Books, 1990.

Williams, Stephen. "The Trinity and 'Other Religions'." In *The Trinity in a Pluralistic Age: Theological Essays on Culture and Religion,* ed. Kevin J. Vanhoozer, 26-40. Grand Rapids, Michigan/Cambridge, U.K.: William B. Eerdmans Publishing Company, 1997.

Wilson, Michael P. "St John, the Trinity, and the Language of the Spirit." *Scottish Journal of Theology* 41/4 (1988): 471-83.

Witherington, Ben and Laura M. Ice, *The Shadow of the Almighty: Father, Son, and Spirit in Biblical Perspective.* Grand Rapids, Michigan & Cambridge, U.K.: William B. Eerdmans, 2002.

Yagnik, Achyut, and Suchitra Sheth. "Whither Gujarat? Violence and After." *Economic and Political Weekly* 37 (March 16, 2002): 1009-11.

__________. "Search for Dalit Self-Identity in Gujarat." In *The Other Gujarat: Social Transformations Among Weaker Sections,* ed. Takashi Shinoda. Mumbai: Popular Prakashan, 2002.

__________. "The Pathology of Gujarat." *Seminar* 513 (May 2002): 19-25.

Yewangoe, A. A. "The Trinity in the Context of Tribal Religion." *Studies in Interreligious Dialogue* 13/1 (2003): 86-105.

Yinger, J. Milton. *The Scientific Study of Religion.* New York: Macmillan, 1970.

Yoder, Jason J. "The Trinity and Christian Witness to Muslims." *Missiology* 22/3 (July 1994): 339-46.

Yung, Hwa. *Mangoes or Bananas? The Quest for an Authentic Asian Christian Theology*. Oxford: Regnum and Paternoster Publishing, 1997.

Zakaria, Rafiq. *The Widening Divide: An Insight Into Hindu-Muslim Relations*. Delhi: Viking-Penguin, 1995.

________. *Communal Rage in Secular India*. Mumbai: Popular Prakashan, 2002

Zaner, Richard M., and H. Tristram Engelhardt, Jr., *The Structures of the Life-World*. Evanston: Northwestern University Press, 1973.

Zavos, John. *The Emergence of Hindu Nationalism in India*. New Delhi: Oxford University Press, 2000.

________. "Searching for Hindu Nationalism in Modern Indian History: Analysis of Some Early Ideological Developments." *Economic and Political Weekly* 34 (August 7, 1999): 2269-76.

Zizioulas, John, D. *Being as Communion: Studies in Personhood and the Church*. London: Darton, Longman and Todd, 1985.

SPECIAL ISSUES ON TRINITRIAN THEOLOGY

Communio International Catholic Review 27/2 (Summer 2000) is on the "Trinity and Eucharist."

Concilium: A Personal God? Ed. Edward Schillebeeckx and Bas van Iersel. New York: The Seabury Press, 1977.

Concilium: God as Father? Edited by Johannes-Baptist Metz and Edward Schillebeeckx. Edinburgh: T & T Clark Ltd. And New York: The Seabury Press, 1981.

Concilium: The Many Faces of the Divine, ed. Hermann Häring and Johann Baptist Metz. London: SCM Press and Maryknoll: Orbis Books, 1995, no. 2.

Dialogue & Alliance (Fall 1990) has special articles on Trinity.

Interpretation 45/2 (April 1991) is on the Doctrine of the Trinity.

Modern Theology 2/3 (April 1986) is a Special Issue on the Trinity.

SPECIAL ISSUES OF PERIODICALS, REPORTS & OTHER DOCUMENTS

"Gujarat Genocide 2002," *Communalism Combat* (March – April, 2002).... Special issue

"Society Under Siege," *Seminar* 513 (May 2002). .... Special issue.

"Crime Against Humanity" 2-part report on the Gujarat Carnage carried out by the "Concerned Citizens Tribunal", 2002.

"Primary Census Abstract" from the *Census of India Data, 2001*. New Delhi: Office of the Registrar General of India.

The Gujarat Pogrom: Indian Democracy in Danger. New Delhi: Indian Social Institute, 2002.

"Myths About the Adivasis," in *Facts Against Myths*. Mumbai: Vikas Adhyayan Kendra (June 1995).

"An Enumerative Tool or a Communal Implement? The Myths behind Census Data 2001," in *Facts Against Myths*. Mumbai: Vikas Adhyayan Kendra (August-September 2004).

"We Have No Orders To Save You: State Participation and Complicity in Communal Violence in Gujarat," *Human Rights' Watch* 14/3c (April 2002).

"Compounding Injustice: The Government's Failure to Redress Massacres in Gujarat," *Human Rights Watch* 15/4c (July 2003);

"The Gujarat Carnage 2002: A Report to the Nation,"

At the Receiving End: Women's Experiences of Violence in Vadodara People's Union for Civil Liberties and Vadodara Shanti Abhiyan (May 31, 2002); 19-24.

"How Has the Gujarat Massacre Affected Minority Women? The Survivors Speak," Fact-Finding by a Women Panel sponsored by Citizen's Initiative (Ahmedabad, 2002).

"Communalism as a Political Strategy, " in *Human Rights Watch* 15/4 (July 2003): 51-64.

CHURCH DOCUMENTS

The Documents of Vatican Council II.

Encyclical Letter *Sollicitudo Rei Socialis* of Pope John Paul, II on Social Concern (December 1987).

The Compendium of the Church's Social Teachings (October 2004).

Let Justice be done to all Dalits! CBCI Commission for SC/ST/BC (2009).

STATEMENTS OF THE INDIAN THEOLOGICAL ASSOCIATION

"Towards an Indian Christian Theology of Religious Pluralism: Our Ongoing Search." Statement of the Indian Theological Association's 13th Annual Meeting from December 28-31, 1989. In *Jeevadhara* 20/116 (March 1990): 151-64.

"Political Theology in the Indian Context." In *Theologizing in Context: Statements of the Indian Theological Association*, ed. Jacob Parappally. Bangalore: Dharmaram Publications, 2002.

"Dalits' Concerns and an Indian Theological Response," Statement of the Indian Theological Association's 28th Annual Meeting from April 24 – 28, 2005. In *Vidyajyoti Journal of Theology* 69/11 (November 2005): 855-69.

DOCUMENTARY FILMS

Suma Josson, *Gujarat: A Laboratory*

__________. *I Want My Father Back.*

Rakesh Sharma, *The Final Solution* – Parts I & II

WEBSITES CITED

ZENIT Internet News, Vatican City, Italy.

National Catholic Reporter, U.S.A

www.ingramcontent.com/pod-product-compliance
Lightning Source LLC
LaVergne TN
LVHW040430180726
843492LV00014B/17